Systems of Care for Children's Mental Health

Series Editors:
Beth A. Stroul, M.Ed.
Robert M. Friedman, Ph.D.

Promoting Cultural Competence in Children's Mental Health Services

Other Volumes in This Series

Promoting Cultural Competence in Children's Mental Health Services

Edited by

Mario Hernandez, Ph.D.
Louis de la Parte Florida Mental Health Institute
University of South Florida
Tampa, Florida

and

Mareasa R. Isaacs, Ph.D.
The Annie E. Casey Foundation
Baltimore, Maryland

·P A U L·H·
BROOKES
PUBLISHING CO.

Baltimore • London • Toronto • Sydney

Paul H. Brookes Publishing Co.
Post Office Box 10624
Baltimore, Maryland 21285-0624

www.pbrookes.com

Typeset by A.W. Bennett, Inc., Hartland, Vermont.
Manufactured in the United States of America by
Versa Press, East Peoria, Illinois.

The case studies in Chapters 11 and 13 are based on actual people and actual circumstances, but names and other identifying information have been changed to protect individuals' identities.

Library of Congress Cataloging-in-Publication Data
Promoting cultural competence in children's mental health services /
    edited by Mario Hernandez and Mareasa R. Isaacs.
        p.   cm. — (Systems of care for children's mental health)
    Includes bibliographical references and index.
    ISBN 1-55766-287-8
    1. Child mental health services—United States—Cross-cultural
studies.   2. Children of minorities—United States—Mental health.
I. Hernandez, Mario, Ph.D.   II. Isaacs, Mareasa R.   III. Series.
RJ501.A2P76   1998
362.2'083'0973–dc21   98-8149
                                                                                CIP

British Library Cataloguing in Publication data are available from the British
Library.

Contents

Series Preface

In 1982, Knitzer's seminal study, *Unclaimed Children*, was published by the Children's Defense Fund. At that time, the field of children's mental health was characterized by a lack of federal or state leadership, few community-based services, little collaboration among child-serving systems, negligible parent involvement, and little or no advocacy on behalf of youngsters with emotional disorders. Since that time, substantial gains have been realized in both the conceptualization and the implementation of comprehensive, community-based systems of care for children and adolescents with serious emotional disorders and their families.

A vast amount of information has emanated from the system-building experiences of states and communities and from research and technical assistance efforts. Many of the trends and philosophies emerging in recent years have now become widely accepted as the "state of the art" for conceptualizing and providing services to youngsters with emotional disorders and their families. There is now broad agreement surrounding the need to create community-based systems of care throughout the United States for children and their families, and the development of these systems has become a national goal. Such systems of care are based on the premises of providing services in the most normative environments, creating effective interagency relationships among the key child-serving systems, involving families in all phases of the planning and delivery of services, and creating service systems that are designed to respond to the needs of culturally diverse populations.

A major need is to incorporate these concepts and trends into the published literature. This need stems from the critical shortage of staff who are appropriately trained to serve youngsters in community-based systems of care, with new philosophies and new service delivery approaches. Of utmost importance is the need to provide state-of-the-art information to institutions of higher education for use in the preservice education of professionals across disciplines, including the social work, counseling, psychology, and psychiatry fields. Similarly, there is an equally vital need for resources for the in-service training of staff in mental health, child welfare, education, health, and juvenile justice agencies to assist the staff in working more effectively with youngsters with emotional disorders and their families.

This book series, *Systems of Care for Children's Mental Health,* is designed to fulfill these needs by addressing current trends in children's mental health service delivery. The series has several broad goals:

- To increase awareness of the system-of-care concept and philosophy among current and future mental health professionals who will be providing services to children, adolescents, and their families
- To broaden the mental health field's understanding of treatment and service delivery beyond traditional approaches to include innovative, state-of-the-art approaches
- To provide practical information that will assist the mental health field to implement and apply the philosophy, services, and approaches embodied in the system-of-care concept

Each volume in this continuing series addresses a major issue or topic related to the development of systems of care. The books contain information useful to planners, program managers, policy makers, practitioners, parents, teachers, researchers, and others who are interested and involved in improving systems of care for children with emotional disorders and their families. As the series editors, it is our goal for the series to provide an ongoing vehicle and forum for exploring critical aspects of systems of care as they continue to evolve.

REFERENCE

Knitzer, J. (1982). *Unclaimed children: The failure of public responsibility to children and adolescents in need of mental health services.* Washington, DC: Children's Defense Fund.

Editorial Advisory Board

Contributors

Alfredo Aguirre, M.S.W., L.C.S.W.
Deputy Director
Child and Youth System of Care
San Mateo County Mental Health
Services Division
225 West 37th Avenue
San Mateo, California 94403

William Arroyo, M.D.
Clinical Assistant Professor of
Psychiatry and Behavioral Sciences
University of Southern California
School of Medicine
LAC and USC Medical Center
Graduate Hall
1937 Hospital Place
Los Angeles, California 90033

Marva P. Benjamin, M.S.W.
Director, Cultural Competence
Initiative
National Technical Assistance Center
for Children's Mental Health
Child Development Center
Georgetown University
3307 M Street, NW
Suite 401
Washington, D.C. 20007

José A. Bernard, M.P.A.
Cultural Competence Manager
Department of Behavioral Health
Services
County of Ventura
300 Hillmont Avenue
Ventura, California 93001

Debora Burns
Graduate Research Assistant
Department of Child and Family
Studies
Louis de la Parte Florida Mental
Health Institute
University of South Florida
13301 Bruce B. Downs Boulevard
Tampa, Florida 33612

Amando Cablas, Ph.D.
Director of Mental Health Research
Services
County of Santa Clara, Mental Health
Research
650 South Bascom Avenue
San Jose, California 95128

Ana Mari Cauce, Ph.D.
Professor
Department of American Ethnic
Studies
University of Washington
Padelford Building
Campus Box 354380
Seattle, Washington 98195

H. Westley Clark, M.D., J.D., M.P.H.
Associate Clinical Professor of
Psychiatry
University of California at San
Francisco
San Francisco Veterans
Administration Medical Center
4150 Clement Street (116E)
Building 8, Room 124
San Francisco, California 94121

Ricardo Contreras-Neira, M.A.
Graduate Research Assistant
Department of Child and Family
    Studies
Louis de la Parte Florida Mental
    Health Institute
University of South Florida
13301 Bruce B. Downs Boulevard
Tampa, Florida 33612

Nora Coronado, M.S.W.
Graduate Student
School of Social Welfare
University of Washington
Seattle, Washington 98195

Linda N. Freeman, M.D.
Assistant Professor of Clinical
    Psychiatry
Columbia University
722 West 168th Street, Box 78
New York, New York 10032

Saundra H. Glover, M.B.A., Ph.D.
Assistant Professor
Department of Health
    Administration
School of Public Health
University of South Carolina
116F Health Science Building
Sumter and Green Streets
Columbia, South Carolina 29208

Susan D. Greenbaum, Ph.D.
Associate Professor
Department of Anthropology
University of South Florida
4202 East Fowler Avenue
Tampa, Florida 33620

Marcela Gutiérrez-Mayka, Ph.D.
Assistant Professor in Research
Department of Child and Family
    Studies
Louis de la Parte Florida Mental
    Health Institute
University of South Florida
13301 Bruce B. Downs Boulevard
Tampa, Florida 33612

Jerome H. Hanley, Ph.D.
Director
Division of Children, Adolescents,
    and Their Families
South Carolina Department of
    Mental Health
2414 Bull Street
Suite 304
Columbia, South Carolina 29201

Mario Hernandez, Ph.D.
Associate Professor
Department of Child and Family
    Studies
Louis de la Parte Florida Mental
    Health Institute
University of South Florida
13301 Bruce B. Downs Boulevard
Tampa, Florida 33612

Mareasa R. Isaacs, Ph.D.
Coordinator of the Urban Mental
    Health Initiative
The Annie E. Casey Foundation
701 Saint Paul Street
Baltimore, Maryland 21202

Daniel D. Jordan, Ph.D.
Director
Center for Health Outcomes
    Research and Evaluation
Ventura County Health Care Agency
300 Hillmont Avenue
Ventura, California 93003

Tami V. Leonhardt, Ph.D.
Licensed Clinical Psychologist
Research and Clinical Assistant
    Professor
Department of Neuropsychiatry and
    Behavioral Science
University of South Carolina
Clinical Education Building
3555 Harden Street Extension
Columbia, South Carolina 29203

Terry Michael McClanahan, M.A.
Public Policy Analyst
University of California at San
    Francisco
Veterans Administration Medical
    Center
4150 Clement Street (116W)
Building 8, Room 124
San Francisco, California 94121

Teresa Nesman, M.A.
Research Assistant
Louis de la Parte Florida Mental
    Health Institute
University of South Florida
13301 Bruce B. Downs Boulevard
Tampa, Florida 33612

Andres J. Pumariega, M.D.
Professor and Chair
Department of Psychiatry and
    Behavioral Sciences
East Tennessee State University
107 Hillrise Hall
Post Office Box 70567
Johnson City, Tennessee 37614

Karen Lea Sees, D.O.
Assistant Clinical Professor
Department of Psychiatry
University of California at San
    Francisco
Veterans Administration Medical
    Center
4150 Clement Street (116W)
San Francisco, California 94121

Velva Taylor Spriggs, M.S.W.
Technical Advisor
Family Advocacy and Support
    Association, Inc.
3600 10th Street, NW
Washington, D.C. 20010

Mary Telesford
Casey Site Advisor
Federation of Families for Children's
    Mental Health
1021 Prince Street
Alexandria, Virginia 22314

**Josie Torralba-Romero, M.S.W.,
L.C.S.W.**
Professor
San Jose State University
One Washington Square
San Jose, California 95138

Jennifer Watson
Graduate Student
Department of Psychology
University of Washington
Seattle, Washington 98195

Harry H. Wright, M.D., M.B.A.
Professor
Department of Neuropsychiatry
University of South Carolina School
    of Medicine
3555 Harden Street Extension
Suite 104A
Columbia, South Carolina 29203

Foreword

In the 1960s, discussions of culture and its relevance to intergroup relationships centered on concepts such as sensitivity and awareness. The idea that professionals, scholars, and everyday citizens needed to become culturally competent had not yet found its way into our consciousness, not to mention into our training. At that time, it was widely believed that what needed changing were people's attitudes and feelings. These early ideas failed to take into account the key role of cognitive understanding and the critical importance of language, religion, cultural traditions, and values on human development. Because of these circumstances, our understanding of the impact that these matters had on how people interacted with helping professionals left much to be desired. Specifically, the failure to consider the skill of the professional in dealing with people from other cultures often led to unsatisfactory intervention outcomes.

Still, the goal of increasing the sensitivity and awareness of members of the wider society represented a move forward from the nation's comfort and commitment to theories supporting the "melting pot" and "colorblindness." For their time, these two notions represented progressive thought and served to advance the American ideal of democracy. They did not, however, adequately address the growing ethnic pride and the quest for dignity—private feelings about which members of so-called ethnic minority groups now make public demands.

The dramatic events occurring on the social and political scene from the mid-1950s through the 1960s have had a profound and lasting effect on views about race, ethnicity, and culture in the United States. These events have affected not only how people think about race and ethnicity but also how the wider society deals with members of minority groups.

A brief summary of some of the more salient of these events places the importance of cultural competence in perspective. The Civil Rights movement precipitated by African Americans began to achieve some key victories. Legal segregation in the public schools was struck down by the Supreme Court's *Brown v. Board of Education* (1954) decision. The gains made by people participating in the freedom rides and later the marches led by Dr. Martin Luther King, Jr., propelled the United States to a greater consciousness of racial oppression. As important as these events were in bringing about a national confrontation with attitudes toward people of other cultures, they did not succeed in providing the conceptual tools to move beyond awareness and sensitivity.

The authors of this book have undertaken the task of correcting this situation. By articulating the nature of cultural competence, they have given it conceptual substance. They have also made possible meaningful discourse and debate on a most important subject that is part of the intellectual property of all relevant disciplines. Having accomplished this, the authors point us in the direction of processes and methods by which the subject matter of cultural competence can be taught and learned.

Cultural competence, as the authors suggest, has both intellectual and practical dimensions. In calling attention to culture, the book articulates the substance of an idea that is real in the minds of those who dwell outside the dominant American culture. The validity of this idea, however, is frequently denied by those who subscribe to the idea of colorblindness or by those whose belief in the melting pot persists. The concept of *competence*, however, asserts the action component of the idea. The thesis of this book is that professionals working in cross-cultural situations not only must possess the knowledge and skill requisite to their professions but also must add to those competencies an understanding, an appreciation and knowledge, of how people whose cultures differ from their own view the world.

The concept of cultural competence is valuable for at least four reasons. First, it calls attention to the important role of culture in the lives of all people, an importance that cannot be dismissed with clichés such as "We're all the same under the skin." Any persuasive power that that cliché ever had has been lost in the more powerful light of cultural competence. Second, the concept assumes that all people may be in need of becoming culturally competent, dismissing the belief that one is born with cultural competence or that one derives it from one's race or ethnicity. Third, the concept assumes that people of all races and cultures are capable of becoming culturally competent. This is important because, for many years, it was believed by many people that proficiency in cultural competence was the sole province of ethnic minorities. Finally, the concept of cultural competence as discussed in this book is valuable because it is presented in an apolitical manner. The concept is offered as a means of addressing human needs and problems in ways that strengthen the individuals being served, respect their dignity, and have the potential for increasing the effectiveness of children's mental health services.

Leon W. Chestang, Ph.D.
Wayne State University
Detroit, Michigan

REFERENCE

Brown v. Board of Education, 347 U.S. 483 (1954).

Introduction

It has been almost a decade since the Child and Adolescent Service System Program (CASSP) National Technical Assistance Center at the Georgetown University Child Development Center published the seminal work on cultural competence, *Towards a Culturally Competent System of Care* (Cross, Bazron, Dennis, & Isaacs, 1989), by members of the center's Minority Initiative Resource Committee. In that monograph, the authors articulated what has become known as the *cultural competence model*, delineating definitions, core components, sustaining principles, and underlying values.

In the late 1980s, few could have foreseen the enormous impact and crucial relevance that the concept of *cultural competence* would have on children's mental health services, as well as on so many public child and family service systems in American society. In the late 1990s, almost all federal grants and initiatives require grantees to address and apply cultural competence strategies in their applications. The public systems with these requirements include not only mental health but also education, maternal and child health, substance abuse, child welfare, and juvenile justice. Many states also require attention to these issues to gain access to state grants and funds. In addition, state agencies have developed plans, conducted training, and established mechanisms to begin to address cultural competence issues more systematically (Isaacs, 1998). Human services agencies and family-focused organizations have struggled with how to incorporate cultural competence into their daily operations and services to be offered to clients and consumers. Even academicians have found merit in cultural competence concepts, and many university and college courses use monographs and articles on cultural competence to train future practitioners and scholars.

Thus, cultural competence is rapidly emerging as a field of study with research opportunities. Like most emerging fields of study, people do not always totally agree about the definitions, terminology, and overall approaches and principles. Reflecting some of the diverging perspectives on definitions and terminology, the contributing authors of this book may use terms to refer to various ethnic groups that are inconsistent across chapters or that some readers may believe are not "politically correct." Just the fact that there is debate and controversy speaks to a recognition of the importance and endurance of cultural competence concepts.

This interest in the further development of cultural competence—its conceptual framework and applications—is occurring because of several major factors that are having an impact on public service systems and will continue to have an impact through the turn of the 21st century. First, children of color—that is, children of African American, Latino and Hispanic, Asian American and Pacific Islander, and Native American and Alaska Native descent—are the fastest-growing population group in the United States. According to the Children's Defense Fund (1991), these children comprised 30% of the population younger than the age of 19 years in 1990 and will comprise 33% by 2000. This trend is expected to continue so that, by 2020, children of color will constitute approximately 40% of the child population in the United States. These changing demographics portend tremendous reliance on these youth for the United States' continued growth and prosperity in the 21st century (Isaacs-Shockley, Cross, Bazron, Dennis, & Benjamin, 1996).

This growth of diversity within American society also compels institutions that serve families to deal with race and discrimination (Chang, Leong, & Salazar, 1994). In the late 1990s, many institutions and systems within American society adversely affect children and families of color. These children are disproportionately represented in special education classes, out-of-home child welfare placements, and juvenile detention and training centers. These children continue to be underserved in community-based mental health systems. Furthermore, these groups are increasingly overrepresented in U.S. prison populations. These trends need to be reversed in order for the United States to maintain a productive and competitive society.

Another factor fueling greater interest in cultural competence is the emphasis on government efficiency, effectiveness, and accountability. There is increasing focus on measurable goals, outcomes, and cost-effectiveness in U.S. human services and education systems. There is a growing realization that better outcomes for children and families of color are intrinsically related to understanding, acknowledging, and adapting services to reflect cultural norms (Isaacs & Benjamin, 1991).

Finally, there is growing tension and isolation among ethnic groups and the dominant culture in the United States. The isolation of the poor, who are disproportionately members of minority groups, in inner cities and other harsh environments has also tended to increase stereotypes and fears of people who are culturally different. This is exacerbated by a growing reliance on the media for knowledge about cultural groups—often negative images—that increases intolerance and stereotyping as well as by an alarming increase in white hate groups and militias. The President's Commission on Race was established to address this lack of understanding and dialogue among the different ethnic groups within the United States.

Despite acceptance of the concepts and principles of cultural competence, the continuance of these factors points to the need for further development and application of cultural competence concepts to policies and practices within American societal institutions. With an emphasis on children's mental health, this book highlights strategies and approaches that can be used to deepen understanding and use of cultural competence skills to create more responsive organizations for children and families from diverse cultural backgrounds.

OVERVIEW OF THE BOOK

This book addresses the implications and applications of cultural competence to key areas that have been identified as critical to its further development. Thus, it begins with an introductory chapter and is organized into four sections. The introductory chapter sets the tone and addresses the need to consider culture in mental health systems of care. The authors also reiterate the definitions and elements of cultural competence.

Section I focuses on the need to develop organizational infrastructures that support and further cultural competence. Over the years, most of the focus on cultural competence has centered on individual responses rather than on institutional ones (Isaacs, 1998). The need to incorporate cultural competence into organizational structures within mental health services has emerged as an important component in institutionalizing cultural competence. Chapter 2 addresses the development of cultural competence plans as a critical process for organizations to undertake. The author of Chapter 2 provides a framework for the development of cultural competence plans that has been effective in several counties in California. Again emphasizing planning as a critical component of organizational cultural competence development, Chapter 3 explores methods for incorporating cultural competence into systems of care planning models. The chapter includes critical planning issues that should be included in this process. Chapter 4 discusses an example of how one state mental health system was able to incorporate cultural competence principles within its state public mental health system. The chapter highlights the importance of leadership, commitment, an inclusive assessment and planning process, and specific implementation targets and strategies. One of the most important aspects of culturally competent organizations is the recruitment, retention, training, and supervision of staff. Chapter 5 suggests approaches and strategies that can ensure that recruitment and retention of culturally diverse staff are achieved as well as emphasizes the importance of ongoing training and supervision as critical to the incorporation of cultural competence into the structure of an organization. Given the major shift in financing mental health services and the dramatic development of behavioral health managed care entities, Chapter 6 examines how these organizational structures and approaches can include cultural competence. The chapter outlines 10 key issues in promoting and sustaining cultural competence in managed care environments and organizations.

Just as managed care has significantly changed the way mental health services are financed, so, too, has the locus of mental health service development changed. There is increasing development of mental health systems of care at the local community level and even at neighborhood levels. This shift toward locally based systems of care has major ramifications for cultural competence. Section II of this book reviews methods for incorporating cultural competence principles in these efforts. Chapter 7 discusses the role of ethnographic approaches, common in anthropology, to understanding and developing systems of care in communities of color. Utilizing work conducted within the Annie E. Casey Foundation's urban mental health sites, the author of Chapter 7 reviews what ethnographic approaches can offer to the understanding and development of knowledge of these culturally diverse communities. Chapter 8 furthers this understanding by focusing on the importance of including community residents in system reform. The authors of Chapter 8 outline a culturally receptive approach that they consider critical to ensuring community participation in evaluation and research related to such efforts. Chapter 9 discusses the importance of involving families of color in determining the services that their children need. Furthermore, the chapter focuses on how to involve these families more effectively in existing family organizations that tend to be predominantly white and focused on issues that may not be as pertinent to families of color. Suggestions for how to develop common agendas and strategies within these organizations are included.

Section III is focused on special issues related to serving culturally diverse populations. The first part of Section III delves into issues that adversely and disproportionately affect children and families of color. Chapters 10 and 11 address the impact of violence on children and families of color. Chapter 10 addresses this impact from a more systemic approach; Chapter 11 discusses the issue from a clinical assessment and treatment approach. Both chapters use examples to increase the understanding of the impact of violence on children. Chapter 12 addresses the importance of recognizing the impact of substance abuse on families of color and discusses ways to link substance abuse issues with other aspects of systems of care development.

The second part of Section III recognizes that there are special populations within culturally diverse groups that deserve and need specialized focus and attention. Chapter 13 addresses the need to ensure that there are culturally competent service approaches developed for infants, toddlers, and preschoolers. The chapter describes one such approach developed at a prominent medical school. Chapter 14 focuses on the specialized and critical needs of immigrant children and their families. The lives of these children and families are significantly affected by policies created by the larger society as well as by their struggles to acculturate and acclimate to a new country.

Section IV highlights the need to continue to research and evaluate the development of culturally competent services and systems. Cultural competence in systems of care is an emerging field of study, so there is a great need to develop tools and methodologies that can measure and enumerate the effectiveness of approaches to developing culturally competent systems and services. The chapters in Section IV reflect approaches to these issues that may be helpful to many others. In Chapter 15, the authors discuss the need for children's mental health epidemiological research to include and encompass culturally diverse populations. This inclusion needs to ensure that these populations are sufficiently represented so that appropriate and adequate analyses can be developed on each specific ethnic or cultural group. Chapter 16 explores the conceptual, methodological, and statistical issues inherent in conducting culturally competent research. Using concrete examples, this chapter outlines the areas that need refinement and development. Chapter 17 discusses culturally competent methods based on evaluation and research, with an emphasis on how to use research results to further cultural competence in systems of care.

This book will stimulate thought and discussion about the implications and applications of cultural competence for organizations, community-based services, and research and evaluation efforts. The book also provides mental health administrators and service providers with assessment tools, troubleshooting suggestions, and tips for developing culturally competent staff and incorporating these principles into behavioral health managed care environments. Finally, the book acknowledges that cultural competence is a concept and an approach that will have increasing importance as the United States enters the 21st century. It adds to the knowledge needed to prepare service providers positively for the first decade of the 21st century.

REFERENCES

Chang, H.C., Leong, C., & Salazar, D. (1994). *Drawing strength from diversity: Effective services for children, youth and families.* San Francisco: California Tomorrow Publications.
Children's Defense Fund. (1991). *The state of America's children.* Washington, DC: Author.

Cross, T., Bazron, B.J., Dennis, K., & Isaacs, M.R. (1989). *Towards a culturally competent system of care: Vol. I. A monograph on effective services for minority children who are severely emotionally disturbed.* Washington, DC: Georgetown University Child Development Center, National Technical Assistance Center for Children's Mental Health.

Isaacs, M.R. (1998). *The state-of-the-states: Responses to cultural competence and diversity.* Washington, DC: Georgetown University Child Development Center, National Technical Assistance Center for Children's Mental Health.

Isaacs, M., & Benjamin, M.P. (1991). *Towards a culturally competent system of care: Vol. II. Programs which utilize culturally competent principles.* Washington, DC: Georgetown University Child Development Center, National Technical Assistance Center for Children's Mental Health.

Isaacs-Shockley, M., Cross, T., Bazron, B.J., Dennis, K., & Benjamin, M.P. (1996). Framework for a culturally competent system of care. In B.A. Stroul (Ed.), *Children's mental health: Creating systems of care in a changing society* (pp. 23–39). Baltimore: Paul H. Brookes Publishing Co.

Promoting
Cultural Competence
in Children's
Mental Health Services

CHAPTER 1

Perspectives on Culturally Competent Systems of Care

Mario Hernandez,
Mareasa R. Isaacs, Teresa Nesman, and Debora Burns

Culture influences most, if not all, aspects of human social interactions. Culture's effects can be found in people's food preferences, clothing, family structure, and beliefs about an afterlife. The term *culture* refers to the way of life of a people and includes the tools or methods by which they extract a livelihood from their environment (Corsini, 1987). Culture influences people over the entire course of their lives. Although culture is omnipresent, it is frequently invisible, especially to those enmeshed within a particular culture. This potential lack of visibility with regard to culture often leads people to develop ethnocentric opinions, poor intercultural communication, and racist notions. This chapter explains why culture is an important consideration when planning and providing human services; describes challenges in the planning and delivery of services that require attention to culture; defines the concept of cultural competence and its implications; and discusses special issues such as acculturation, engaging communities of color, and evaluation.

According to Cross (1995/1996), some argue that all people are the same on the inside, and therefore no accommodation to or understanding of their culture is required. To some degree, this position is accurate in the sense that all people share basic needs such as shelter, food, and spirituality. However, culture determines the various approaches that people adopt in meeting these needs. For example, culture influences a group's definitions of illness and its beliefs about the causes of illness as well as its beliefs and practices with regard to remediating problems. Often culture is viewed synonymously with race, ethnicity, or socioeconomic status; but these factors alone do not truly describe the scope and breadth of culture, even though they may play a role in helping to shape it and determining how it will be manifested. To clarify this distinction, *culture* can be defined as ways of living or people's approaches to living

1

and interpreting their environment. Because of the dimensions of culture's influence on people, understanding various cultures can be a great resource for human services providers in meeting the needs of families of color as well as in capitalizing on their strengths (Cross, 1995/1996).

The powerful personal meaning that culture carries for individuals is evident when a people face the loss of their culture and identity, which can occur for new immigrants and resident minorities who experience discrimination (Gibbs & Huang, 1989). For example, among the Yup'ik of Alaska, the loss of their culture has had devastating effects on entire Yup'ik generations (Davidson, 1993). Yup'ik children attend schools in which Western culture is dominant. As a result, education leaves the Yup'ik children torn between their traditional world and the modern Western world and unprepared to live in either. For example, Davidson stated that whereas among the Yup'ik

> Native teaching always encouraged children to share and serve their families and community, Western education tells them to compete, promote themselves, beat the other guy. When children return [to their communities] educated, they no longer are the same children that parents and community members saw leave for school. Some of the children become strangers to their own people and strangers to themselves. (1993, p. 17)

The clash of Yup'ik values with those of the dominant culture has created pain, confusion, and alienation among Yup'ik people. Fetal alcohol syndrome, which results from maternal consumption of alcohol during pregnancy, has become prevalent among Yup'ik children. In addition, the suicide rate among Yup'ik people has increased dramatically, with a rate for native Alaskan men that is 10 times that for other American men. As a further illustration of the problem, during a 16-month period, one village of 550 Yup'ik people experienced eight suicides, dozens of other suicide attempts, two murders, and four drownings (Davidson, 1993). These social ills can be attributed to the Yup'iks' loss of their traditional culture and personal identities and illustrate the need for cultural awareness and sensitivity in planning and implementing social policies and services.

The contemporary world provides rapid forms of communication and travel that facilitate cultural exchanges and interactions between people who have significantly different views and definitions of reality. Every day this exchange and interaction between cultures is effecting gradual changes in the various cultures themselves, either through elimination of cultures or through cultural adaptations and accommodations. Often members of various populations and their subgroups bring into their interactions historical experiences that include past differences with each other (Rosado & Elias, 1993). This history often influences the type and quality of interactions that individuals have with people from different cultures.

Social interaction is at the heart of human services and defines the primary method of service delivery. It is this singular fact that points to how human services can be most effective in the context of a multicultural world. Effective interaction that is sensitive to culture is particularly important in the delivery of mental health services, where rapport among a provider, a child, and the child's family is essential. In fact, mental health providers' indifference to culture can often cause clients to turn away from treatment even after they have crossed cultural barriers in order to find help for themselves or their families (Woodward, Dwinell, & Arons, 1992).

Given the powerful influence of culture, it is essential that organizations and individual professionals develop an appreciation for and understanding of how culture mediates human behavior. Individual professionals need to learn about their own cultures of origin, the cultural orientation of their organization, and the professions that shape their behavior and attitudes toward the people whom they serve. Without this understanding, it becomes increasingly difficult for professionals to be effective in their cross-cultural helping relationships. For example, routinely applying traditional psychotherapy techniques that have been successful with middle-class Caucasian Americans to people who are from different cultures, are from urban environments, and have low incomes is often contraindicated (Rosado & Elias, 1993). Moreover, researchers have found that culturally relevant treatment targeted for use with ethnic populations is linked to improved mental health among clients receiving such treatment (Hall, 1988; O'Sullivan, Peterson, Cox, & Kirkeby, 1989).

THE NEED TO CONSIDER CULTURE IN SYSTEMS OF CARE

Young people in the United States are becoming increasingly ethnically diverse. Estimates indicate that by 2005, children and adolescents of color will make up as much as 40% of the U.S. youth population ("Embracing the Dynamics of Difference," 1997). It has been estimated that the Latino community will become the largest ethnic group in American society (*Household and Family Characteristics*, 1990; U.S. Commission on Civil Rights, 1982) and that 12% of Latinos are adolescents (Hoberman, 1992). Asians and Pacific Islanders make up the second-fastest-growing minority; of that group, 50% are new immigrants, and about one third are younger than age 17. Asian and Pacific Islander immigrants to the United States are projected to increase by 39% by 2005 (Uba & Sue, 1991). In this same time period, the proportion of African Americans in the U.S. population is expected to increase to 12%, with 50% of those individuals being under age 17. The Native American population is expected to increase to 6%, 25% of whom will be adolescents (Hoberman, 1992). Concurrently, the population of Caucasian children in the United States is expected to decrease by about 3% (Kids Count, 1997).

Historically, children, adolescents, and families of color have been unserved, underserved, or inappropriately served by most public and private sector human services systems within the United States ("Embracing the Dynamics of Difference," 1997). When programs that support personal growth and development fail to serve children and adolescents of color, the result is a self-perpetuating cycle of relying on programs that are based on social control; that is, such programs use punishment, incarceration, and removal of children from their families. In most juvenile justice systems around the United States, youth of color are overrepresented and are not being served appropriately by mental health professionals either because of lack of services or because services have been designed based on the majority culture's perspective (Courtney et al., 1996). Hoberman (1992) cited higher rates of identification of behavior disorders and delinquency among African American male adolescents, who also accounted for 23% of juvenile arrests and 26% of juveniles in residential facilities. In addition, Hoberman found that there were four times more African American than Caucasian adolescent males in correctional institutions.

A 1994 five-state analysis (Goerge, Wulczyn, & Harden, 1994) showed overrepresentation of African American children in the child welfare system. The study found 3–10 times more involvement with the child welfare system among African American children than among Caucasian children. Courtney and colleagues (1996) found that, once children of color were within the child welfare system, they consistently received fewer services than Caucasian children, even when they were assessed as having an equivalent degree of need. With the child welfare services provided, fewer children of color and their families than Caucasian children and their families experienced positive results, leading them to experience lengthier out-of-home placements and higher return rates to foster care and other out-of-home placements than Caucasian children experienced.

The education system also fails to adequately assess the needs of children of color (Coulter, 1996). Coulter found children of color to be overrepresented in special education programs. He found that enrollment in special education classes in Louisiana was substantially racially imbalanced. In addition to this overrepresentation in special education programs, children of color have an increasing high school dropout rate. In 1995, the Caucasian high school dropout rate was 17%; for African Americans, it was 26%; and for Hispanics, it was 46% (U.S. Bureau of the Census, 1995).

There are increasing numbers of youth of color who are identified with mental health problems but who are receiving inappropriate treatment ("Embracing the Dynamics of Difference," 1997). In 1982, Knitzer found that children of color with mental health problems often were not identified and went without appropriate treatment. In 1993, McGarrell reported that children of color were less likely than Caucasian children to receive a variety of forms of treatment and were particularly likely to be served in correctional facilities. In the McGarrell study of 17 states, there was a 10% decrease in Caucasian youth placed in detention from 1985 to 1989, whereas non-Caucasian placements increased by 65%. In addition, other researchers have demonstrated that the delivery of mental health services has been insufficient for economically distressed urban clients of color (Abad, Ramos, & Boyce, 1974; Sue & Zane, 1987).

Failure to adapt service delivery to various sociocultural perspectives also results in underuse of services and consequently in unmet needs. Asian Americans and Pacific Islander Americans have been found to significantly underuse formal mental health services, which is attributed to a mismatch of cultural perspectives and language barriers (Yamashiro & Matsuoka, 1997). There is an extensive body of research demonstrating that mental health service delivery systems do not adequately address culturally based perceptions and behaviors such as value orientation, ethnic identity, indigenous supports, bilingualism and biculturalism, socioecological conditions, religious beliefs, acculturation forces, and family structure (Gibbs & Huang, 1989; Rosado & Elias, 1993). Probably as a result, there is a substantial amount of unmet mental health services need in communities of color (Deserly & Cross, 1996; Drachman, 1996).

The increasing magnitude and severity of poverty, family disintegration, community disorganization, violence, substance abuse, illiteracy, and teen pregnancy have profound effects on the unmet service needs of people of color (Kids Count, 1997). The impact of these conditions, together with economic distress, is additive and generates increasing levels of stress in children and families (Canino & Canino, 1980; Montijo, 1985; Rosado, 1980). Service providers and policy makers need to recognize that many children and adolescents of color are adversely affected by societal conditions such as poverty, poor nutrition, lack of health care, geographic isolation, and institutionalized discrimination.

These conditions affect the emotional and psychological well-being of minority children and adolescents and should be acknowledged in the delivery of appropriate social services ("Embracing the Dynamics of Difference," 1997).

Immigrants and refugees entering the United States represent a large percentage of people of color living in poverty. The International Labor Office estimated that more than 350,000 illegal immigrant women worked as low-paid domestics in the U.S. market in 1993 (Stalker, 1994). According to the U.S. Department of Labor (1994), women composed approximately two thirds of all part-time and three fifths of all temporary workers in the United States in 1993, and a majority of these women were women of color and/or immigrants to the United States. At the same time, the number of women living in poverty in the United States increased dramatically, which indicates that many working women were earning low wages (U.S. Department of Labor, Women's Bureau, 1994). Hondagneu-Sotelo (1994) found that more than 350,000 illegal immigrants in the United States are employed as domestics, with some earning as little as $90–$140 per week in exclusive California residential suburbs. Although many immigrant women work, the benefits that they receive can be minimal because of their undocumented status. In 1993, 5% of people who received Aid to Families with Dependent Children (a program since renamed Temporary Assistance for Needy Families) were foreign born (National Council for Research on Women, 1995b) and people who were foreign born received less than 1% of the money spent by the largest assistance programs for immigrants and refugees (National Council for Research on Women, 1995a). Taken together with federal and state welfare reform policies that reduce available assistance to families, these funding priorities tend to perpetuate conditions of poverty for immigrant women and their children.

In spite of present and future challenges for systems of care posed by emerging population changes in the United States and the economic and social conditions that immigrant and minority populations in the United States face, there appear to be few examples of systems that have altered the amount and variety of their services to address the needs of children of color. Issues of culture have made limited progress as a guide for service delivery in the 1990s, and mental health services agencies need to move from viewing attention to culture as optional to recognizing it as being integral to effective service provision ("Embracing the Dynamics of Difference," 1997). In spite of the cultural awareness requirement for service delivery stated in the American Psychological Association's (APA's) code of ethics, the APA recognizes that a serious lack of culturally focused training programs continues to exist (Sue, Arrendondo, & McDavis, 1992). Others in the field have asserted that ethical and professional standards are violated when there is a failure to formulate service delivery policies for the presenting problems of people of color within their sociocultural perspectives; as a result, these policies fail to consider treatment that may be compatible with cultural realities that differ from those of the professionals employed by the agency (De La Cancela, 1985; Inclan, 1985; Juarez, 1985; Montijo, 1985).

The inadequate state of culturally anchored services challenges state and local governments as well as private sector providers to develop concepts and processes to increase the probability that interactions between children of color and service systems will be productive. Attending to issues of culture in service delivery and policy development provides the opportunity for practitioners, agencies, and systems to respond appropriately to the unique needs of populations whose cultures differ from the dominant culture ("Embracing the Dynamics of Difference," 1997). It is important to devote explicit attention to cultural differences and how to appropriately respond to them because of the pervasiveness of policies based on implicit assumptions of cultural similarity and assimilation (Zambrana, 1995).

DEFINITION OF *CULTURAL COMPETENCE*

Cultural competence is defined as "a set of congruent behaviors, attitudes, and policies that come together in a system, agency or among professionals and enables that system, agency or those professionals to work effectively in cross cultural situations" (Cross, Bazron, Dennis, & Isaacs, 1989, p. 13). The terms *cultural* and *competence* were chosen for specific reasons. *Cultural* was selected to direct attention to the role that culture plays in shaping human behavior (Cross et al., 1989). Within the cultural competence concept, *culture* is defined as "the integrated pattern of human behavior that includes thoughts, communication styles, actions, customs, beliefs, values, and institutions of a racial, ethnic, religious or social group" (Cross et al., 1989, p. 13).

Action is implied by the use of the term *competence*. Cultural competence is an action-oriented concept. This term was selected to indicate that the skills necessary to interact in cross-cultural situations can be acquired. The implication is that all human services providers, regardless of their ethnicity or socioeconomic status, are capable of becoming culturally competent. This notion is especially important because most human services providers are not people of color. In many cases, the few available service staff members of color are inappropriately relied on to represent the views of entire communities (Bernard, Cablas, Hanley, Hernandez, & Romero, 1996). People of color who find themselves in this position often report that they feel put on the spot by their co-workers and supervisors and that this results in the agency's failure as an organization to own the issue of providing culturally competent services (Bernard et al., 1996). The burden that this places on service providers of color is overwhelming. Moreover, many service providers of color feel that their organizations view them as single-issue employees. Using the term *competence* places the burden on all employees of an organization and challenges all to become a part of a process of providing culturally competent services.

Organizations that are culturally competent incorporate five essential elements at all levels of functioning. These elements are

1. Valuing diversity
2. Cultural self-assessment
3. Cross-cultural dynamics
4. Institutionalization of cultural knowledge
5. Adaptation to diversity (Cross et al., 1989)

Valuing diversity means understanding and accepting that other cultures might have a higher regard for certain actions, values, and ways of interrelating than the dominant culture does. Assessing their own cultural perspectives and how they interact with those of other cultures enables organizations to choose policies and practices that minimize cross-cultural barriers. An awareness of the dynamics of cross-cultural interactions and the potential for misjudgment based on a service provider's past experiences can decrease the frustration felt by both helper and client. Recognition of differences in communication styles, etiquette, and problem-solving methods can help to circumvent misunderstandings on both sides and can lessen distrust when there are power differentials. Institutionalization of cultural knowledge includes the development of mechanisms for determining what is culturally appropriate for the specific populations that an organization serves and for providing cross-cultural training and supervision for all staff. It may include research, demonstration projects, and establishing networks of communication with community leaders and groups. Adapting to diversity includes the institutionalization of cultural interventions as a legitimate helping approach, such that programs and services address not only individuals' needs but also cultural group needs that affect the well-being of children of color. It may include activities or policies designed to counteract negative stereotypes and prejudices encountered in the media or in school. The five elements of cultural competence can be incorporated throughout an organization that is motivated by its commitment to providing quality services for all groups served, but they also require an awareness that considering cultural differences must be part of that commitment.

Becoming culturally competent can be conceptualized as part of a developmental process that evolves over time. The concept of cultural competence allows organizations and individuals to assess and set goals for themselves as they provide more effective services to the diverse array of individuals who may seek their services. The essential goal of the model is for systems, agencies, and practitioners to develop the capacity to respond to the unique needs of populations whose cultures differ from what might be called the dominant or mainstream American culture. The cultural competence model emphasizes understanding the importance of culture and building service systems that recognize, incorporate, and value cultural diversity.

The Cultural Competence Continuum

The definition of *cultural competence* exists within a continuum from low to high in the achievement of competence. The continuum enhances the definition of *cultural competence* and is both action oriented and developmental. It allows for self-assessment and goal setting. The continuum ranges from cultural destructiveness at one end to advanced cultural competence at the other. Cross and colleagues (1989) described six points along the cultural competence continuum and the characteristics that an agency or an individual might exhibit at each level of the continuum. It is unfortunate that though numerous examples of actions that can be classified as culturally destructive can be provided, few examples of advanced cultural competence can be identified.

Cultural Destructiveness The most negative end of the continuum is represented by attitudes, policies, and practices that are destructive to cultures and to the individuals within those cultures. Examples of this orientation can be found in programs and policies that promote cultural genocide (i.e., the purposeful destruction of a culture). Historically, some U.S. human services agencies have been actively involved in services that have denied people of color access to their natural helpers, removed children of color from their families for adoption into majority-culture homes, or purposely risked the well-being of minority individuals in social or medical experiments without their knowledge or consent. A system that practices such cultural destructiveness assumes that one race or culture is superior and should eradicate or control "lesser" races because of their perceived inferior position. Bigotry coupled with power differentials allows dominant groups to disenfranchise, control, exploit, or systematically destroy less powerful populations.

Cultural Incapacity In the position of cultural incapacity on the continuum, the system, the agency, or the individual does not intentionally or consciously seek to be culturally destructive. Instead, the capacity to help people and communities of color is missing. Nevertheless, at this position along the cultural competence continuum, the agency or individual remains extremely biased, believes in the racial superiority of the dominant group, and assumes a paternalistic posture toward the perceived lesser races and cultures. These agencies and individuals may disproportionately apply resources and discriminate against people of color. Such agencies and individuals may support segregation as a desirable policy or may act as agents of oppression by enforcing racist policies that reflect racial stereotypes. Such agencies are characterized by ignorance and an unrealistic fear of people of color. Other characteristics of cultural incapacity include discriminatory hiring practices, subtle messages to people of color that they are not valued or welcome, and generally lower expectations for clients from minority groups.

Cultural Blindness At the midpoint along the cultural competence continuum, a system and its agencies or an individual has expressed the belief of being unbiased as an organization or as an individual. The philosophy that ethnicity, race, or culture makes no difference and that all people are the same characterizes cultural blindness. Therefore, culturally blind agencies and individuals are characterized by service approaches traditionally used by the dominant culture because those approaches are believed to be universally applicable. This ethnocentric view reflects a well-intended liberal philosophy, and its driving force is not racism. However, the consequences of such a belief are services that are ethnocentric and potentially useless to all but the most assimilated people of color.

Culturally blind agencies may participate in special projects for minority populations when grant dollars are available. These projects typically operate with the intent of rescuing people of color rather than of working collaboratively with them (Kretzman & McKnight, 1993). As a result, such projects are often conducted without community guidance. They are also the first casualties when funds run short and programs must be cut.

Culturally blind agencies suffer from a lack of information and often are not aware of the avenues through which they can obtain needed information. Although these agencies often view themselves as unbiased and responsive to minority needs, their ethnocentrism is reflected in attitudes, policies, and practices.

Cultural Precompetence As agencies or individuals move toward the positive end of the continuum, they reach a position referred to as *cultural precompetence*. The precompetent agency realizes that it has weaknesses in serving people of color and attempts to improve some aspects of its services to specific populations. Such agencies try innovations in service approaches, hire diverse staff, explore how to reach out to people and communities of color, initiate culturally relevant training for their workers, and recruit minority individuals for their boards and advisory committees. Precompetent agencies are characterized by the desire to deliver high-quality, culturally relevant services.

A danger at this point along the continuum is either a false sense of accomplishment or failure with regard to a service approach that prevents the agency from moving forward along the continuum. These agencies may believe that the accomplishment of one culturally competent goal or activity fulfills their obligation to minority communities or that an initial failure means that the whole approach is not practical.

Another cautionary note at the precompetence level is that agencies sometimes hire one or more professionals of color and thus believe that they are thereby equipped to meet the needs of people of color. Although hiring staff of color is important to achieving cultural competence, it is no guarantee that services will be improved, because the training of professionals itself is a process of assimilation into the majority culture. Professionals of color are frequently trained in the dominant culture's frame of reference and may be only slightly more competent in cross-cultural practice than other co-workers. These professionals of color, like all professionals, need training in the function of culture and its impact on clients.

Basic Cultural Competence Culturally competent agencies and individuals are characterized by acceptance of and respect for difference, continuing self-assessment regarding culture, careful attention to the dynamics of difference, continuous expansion of cultural knowledge and resources, and adaptation of their service models in order to better meet the needs of communities of color. The culturally competent agency works to hire unbiased employees, seeks advice and consultation from these communities, and actively decides what it is capable of providing to clients of color. Often there is ongoing dialogue and input from communities of color with the culturally competent agency at all levels of the organization and an external network with other formal and informal supports from the communities that they serve.

Advanced Cultural Competence At the most positive end of the continuum is advanced cultural competence. Agencies and individuals at this point along the continuum hold cultures in high esteem. The advanced culturally competent agency seeks to add to the knowledge base of culturally competent practice by developing new therapeutic approaches that adapt to cultural differences, evaluating and disseminating the results of demonstration projects for examination and feedback from stakeholders, and experimenting with changes in its organizational structures that support the cultural values and beliefs of the people whom they serve. These agencies hire staff who are specialists in culturally competent practice and advocate for cultural competence throughout their systems and the systems of others.

Summary

In sum, the degree of cultural competence that an agency achieves is not dependent on any one factor. Attitudes, policies, and practices are three major areas in which development can and must occur if an agency is to move toward cultural competence. Attitudes must change to become less ethnocentric and less biased. Policies must change to become more flexible and culturally sensitive. Practices must become more congruent with the culture of the client from initial contact through termination of services.

Ongoing commitment is required if cultural competence is to become an integral part of service delivery and policy development. This can happen only if individuals of all cultures who are policy makers, administrators, clients, service providers, and advocates accept responsibility for becoming culturally competent ("Embracing the Dynamics of Difference," 1997).

HISTORY AND DEVELOPMENT OF CULTURAL COMPETENCE

In the 1990s, the concept of cultural competence in service delivery systems has become a major component of most federal and state system reform initiatives focused on children and families. There have been a plethora of activities and tasks undertaken by states and localities to address the inclusion of cultural competence in their system development activities on many levels and across a variety of systems ("Embracing the Dynamics of Difference," 1997). For example, cultural competence has been viewed as a core principle of mental health system of care development under the Child and Adolescent Service System Program (CASSP), a child mental health initiative funded by the National Institute of Mental Health, since 1983. In 1989, cultural competence was incorporated as a major system of care component, along with the core components of interagency collaboration, meaningful family involvement, community-based service, and individualization of service. After 1989, each existing and future CASSP grantee was required to develop specific strategies for ensuring that cultural competence had been addressed by the state in which it was located.

Despite the infusion of cultural competence as a concept into state policies, planning activities, and service delivery practices, implementation of service modifications has proved to be difficult and slow moving ("Embracing the Dynamics of Difference," 1997). For example, in a review of achievements in mental health system of care development, Stroul (1993) found that cultural competence was absent as a major goal of system development and that it was not mentioned as an achievement or outcome of any of the identified community-based systems of care reviewed.

CONTRAST BETWEEN CULTURAL
COMPETENCE AND OTHER CONCEPTS

There are many different terms used to describe the process of becoming conscious of and attuned to cultural differences. Two of the most commonly used terms are *cultural awareness* and *cultural sensitivity*. *Cultural awareness* suggests that it may be sufficient for one just to read and gain knowledge about other cultures in order to meet their needs. *Cultural sensitivity* connotes the ability to empathize and identify with emotional expressions and with the problems, struggles, and joys of someone from a different cultural group. Cultural awareness and sensitivity, although limited in their impact on systems and individuals, are necessary elements of cultural competence. However, these approaches are not enough in and of themselves to significantly alter the practices and perceptions of many of those people working with children and families of color. Awareness and sensitivity are different because they represent attitudes but do not necessarily carry through to policies and practices.

Another term often used is *cultural diversity*. *Cultural diversity* in its broadest definition refers to differences in race, ethnicity, language, nationality, or religion among various groups within a community, organization, or nation (Orlandi, 1992). *Diversity* describes demographic characteristics of a population. *Competence* refers to the professional's capacity to understand how culture mediates human behavior. Although there is much debate about whether *diversity* encompasses *competence* or vice versa, it seems fair to say that cultural diversity has almost always been used in the context of work force issues. In comparison, cultural competence goes beyond understanding and valuing cultural differences in the work force by focusing on fundamental shifts in organizational structures, policies, attitudes, and practices (Cross et al., 1989).

Acculturation and Cultural Competence

Although culture is often described in static terms, understanding it as an everchanging variable is important to providing culturally competent services. For example, one major task that immigrants to the United

States and their offspring must face is how to adapt to a new cultural environment and how to function within it (Rosenthal & Feldman, 1990). The culture of these people of color is often changed as a result of their immigration; they must learn to adjust their behavior to accommodate the rules and expectations of another culture while retaining aspects of their culture of origin.

Acculturation is the term used to describe this basic process of cultural change and encompasses a range of adaptations that may include a blending of cultures or complete assimilation and virtual loss of the original culture. Although defined in various ways in the literature, there is general agreement that acculturation is a learning process through which at least some of the cultural patterns of the host country are adopted by an individual (Celano & Tyler, 1990). In this definition, acculturation involves the psychosocial adaptation of individuals from their culture of origin to a new or host cultural environment (Wells, Golding, & Hough, 1989). Corsini (1987) added to this definition the idea of acculturation as a process of learning about rules of behavior.

At its simplest level, acculturation can be described within the context of the length of time that an individual has been exposed to a new culture by residing in it (Gordon, 1964). Szapocznik, Scopetta, Kurtines, and Aranalde (1978) included a description of two independent processes in acculturation rather than a simple linear progression: accommodation to the host culture and either retention or relinquishment of the culture of origin. This view of acculturation recognizes the possibility that an immigrant may become acculturated without giving up his or her own traditional customs or identity (Celano & Tyler, 1990). Similarly, Berry's (cited in Celano & Tyler, 1990) definition of *acculturation* encompasses the contributions of both the acculturating group and those of the host culture. In this manner, acculturation can be seen as an interactional process between the culture of the immigrant and the host culture's response to the immigrant's culture.

Investigators have used terms such as *culture stress, culture shock, culture fatigue, role shock*, and *language shock* to describe the stress associated with the acculturation process (Byrnes, 1966; Oberg, 1960; Padilla, Olmedo, & Loya, 1982; Smalley, 1963). Reactions to this stress can range from mild irritability to panic and crisis (Adler, 1975), which can be fostered by misunderstanding new experiences and the individual's emotional reactions to new cultural stimuli that have no personal meaning for him or her. Because information that is relevant to self-identity is typically obtained from the social network to which individuals belong (Padilla, 1980; Smart & Smart, 1995), the loss of this source of information can create anxiety and uncertainty about oneself and one's role in the community. This lack of information can result in feelings of helplessness and irritability and fears of being cheated, contaminated, injured, or disregarded (Adler, 1975) and thus can affect decision making and judgment (Smart & Smart, 1995).

Often mothers, fathers, and other adult relatives in a family acculturate at different rates from their children (Aronowitz, 1984; Sung, 1985). The differences that emerge between generations in cultural identification, social skills, attitudes, values, and norms create the conditions for both intrafamilial conflict and a youth's poor community adjustment (Vega, Gil, Warheit, Zimmerman, & Apospori, 1993). Delinquency has been associated with the different rates of acculturation between children and their parents (Santisteban, Szapocznik, Kurtines, & Rio, 1994). The converse of this is that, when acculturation issues within a family are successfully navigated, adolescents experience more success within the host culture (Spencer & Dornbusch, 1990). Other studies have found better youth adjustment occurring when parents value their own culture while not devaluing the host culture, which substantially influences the lives of their children (Sam, 1995).

In the case of Native American society, negative impacts of forced acculturation of its members through the removal of children to boarding schools has been documented for some time (Deserly & Cross, 1996). These impacts include school dropout, negative self-image, low achievement, suicides and suicide attempts, and academic failure. Deserly and Cross offered an example of generational stress that was the result of forced acculturation:

> Children began to change in ways that their parents and grandparents could not understand. Often they returned home for vacations expressing serious identity confusion. Some children became ashamed of being Indian and bitterly disowned the values and lifestyle of their families. Others became rebellious, distrustful, and withdrawn or depressed. (1996, p. 3)

These children could identify neither with their native heritage nor with the non–Native American culture of the dominant society (Deserly & Cross, 1996).

Acculturation processes present families of color with a variety of other challenges and dilemmas that must be understood by professionals if they are to be helpful and useful to families (Cross, 1995/1996). Immigration and acculturation experiences have consistently been linked to substance abuse and mental health problems (Arensberg & Niehoff, 1964; Beauvais & La Boueff, 1985; Delgado, 1989; Schinke, Moncher, Palleja, Zayas, & Schilling, 1988). Contact with a new culture is believed to influence substance abuse by exposing immigrants to competing cultural values concerning substance use and by increasing the degree of psychosocial stress (Schinke et al., 1988). For example, acculturation stress has been linked to increasing levels of substance abuse among Asian refugees in the United States (Kitano, 1989) and among Native Americans migrating from rural to urban areas within the United States (Guyette, 1982).

The various acculturation experiences of different immigrant groups challenge mental health professionals to pay attention to issues such as accurate assessment of stress, unique language needs, needs for social support and social skills building, use of a loss-and-adaptation model, and familiarity with immigration law (Smart & Smart, 1995). Consideration of these issues for immigrants can add depth and breadth to the types and quality of services provided.

Evaluation and Cultural Competence

In a special issue of the *American Journal of Community Psychology*, Seidman stated,

> Community psychologists and other social scientists have argued cogently that research methodology must be attuned to the unique aspects of culture in both basic and action research. In practice, however, research on non-mainstream cultures continues to be dominated by the use of traditional methodology at each phase of the research enterprise. (1993, p. 683)

Part of the reason for this lack of culturally competent research and evaluation is the belief that research and evaluation should be objective. This belief in objectivity results in approaches to evaluation that are culturally blind. As a result, investigators often fail to examine the underlying values and perspectives guiding their work.

Ignoring culture as a variable in research evaluation involving human services is impossible. It can be assumed that culture influences the ways and methods used. In effect, research and evaluation are culturally bound in their attempt to portray reality. Regardless of that fact, few evaluators and researchers acknowledge or consider culture in the selection of their tools and methodologies. Unexamined assumptions in research with nonmainstream cultures create ethnocentric biases at every stage of research (Hughes, Seidman, & Williams, 1993; Sasao & Sue, 1993). Looking at the various aspects of evaluation can help to focus attention on what should be improved in the practice of culturally competent evaluation practice.

The manner in which evaluators describe the issue under study or the population being addressed is the first step toward becoming culturally competent. The description of the client population can be approached from the point of view of weaknesses or from the point of view of strengths. Similar to describing communities of color in negative terms, descriptions of clients can have the effect of stereotyping people of color and reinforcing the negative perceptions of the larger society.

In addition, an understanding of diversity within populations is important if an accurate description of a group of people is to occur. Cross (1995/1996) suggested that one barrier to understanding cultures is the diversity among and within various groups. Cross stated that professionals often describe individuals from populations of color as if they were all the same. Varying levels of acculturation as well as the variety of cultures that exist within a large group contribute to within-group diversity. For example, African Americans are often discussed in research findings as if they were from one homogeneous group, even though, for example, some are influenced by their experiences with living in the various regions of the United States. Other differences include living in rural or urban settings, amount of exposure to crime and violence, and variation in socioeconomic levels.

In addition, information that describes the context within which a population lives is important. Simple sociodemographics are not sufficient if an evaluator is to describe the cultural context fully. Hines (1993) and Maton (1993) suggested combining qualitative and quantitative methods to derive such a description. Unfortunately, little research involving culturally diverse groups has joined the two approaches (Hines, 1993; Maton, 1993), and, when both types are used, often there is an overreliance on quantitative methods. The value of qualitative methods such as ethnography in research is in their effective description of cultural contexts, which include values, customs, beliefs, and other characteristics of a particular population or community (Seidman, 1993). The methodology that supports ethnographic work can involve field observations, interviews, and participation with community residents in their special events. The results could yield information that may not have been anticipated by the evaluator and thus a fuller understanding of the cultural dynamics of a particular population could be gained. These dynamics include beliefs about physical and mental health, family relationships, and the histories that community residents have with government services.

Evaluation efforts can also become culturally competent in their description of interventions under study. First, it is important to know whether the intended intervention occurred as expected and whether or how local cultural factors influenced the actual application of the intervention. This knowledge can assist in the culturally competent interpretation of both negative and positive findings and may provide a crucial explanation of the success or failure of an intervention for particular groups of people served. For example, an intervention stressing service coordination involving African American families may have been effective because of the ability of the workers to form family-like relationships with the families served. This may be in conflict with the intended model of service delivery that encourages staff to keep a professional distance from clients. If the actual method of engagement used by staff is not discovered, the evaluation will erroneously attribute results to an intervention that never occurred. Evaluation efforts need to use methods that collect information about the actual implementation of an intervention in order to later articulate what occurred. This information allows the evaluator to increase the chances that the cause-and-effect relationships between interventions and outcomes that are being established are accurate.

Finally, cultural competence is crucial to the appropriate selection of outcomes. It is important to ensure that selected evaluation outcomes are congruent with the expectations and desires of the people being served. According to Hines (1993), research on diverse communities should include an awareness of cultural issues, a knowledge of the problems and concerns of these communities, and methods that elicit relevant and accurate information that affects service interventions and the lives of people seeking help. If a project is attempting to evaluate a teen pregnancy program by measuring the rates of teen pregnancy, it is important to determine whether this outcome is desired by the community within which the targeted teenagers reside. Community residents may believe that positive outcomes for a teen pregnancy prevention program should not be limited to a decrease in the number of teen pregnancies but should also include better prenatal care and hence an increase in healthy births as an additional positive outcome. The latter outcome may be more important to a community than reducing the total number of births among teenage parents.

As an example of how families view outcomes differently from service systems, Harry (1992) studied Puerto Rican families whose children were identified by the schools as having significant learning disabilities. In one of her case studies, she described a mother's reacting with confusion to a school psychologist's report that pointed out her daughter's inability to read and that recommended that her daughter attend special education classes. The expected outcome of the psychologist was that the child would be able to read. The mother stated that there was nothing wrong with her daughter and compared her daughter with her husband, who, the mother believed, did well at his job even though he had never been able to read. The mother did not value the outcome of reading ability to the same degree as school officials. This example illustrates the importance of selecting outcomes that are congruent with the values of the people who will actually receive a particular intervention.

Engaging Communities as a Path to Becoming Culturally Competent

It is important for systems to look at the larger community context from which families of color emerge (Kretzman & McKnight, 1993). To be culturally competent in the design and implementation of services, systems of care need to move beyond a focus on individual children and their families and consider the cultural contexts and communities within which they live. To focus systems on communities and neighborhoods, it is critical for formal systems to engage communities in working partnerships. System of care professionals with culturally blind beliefs who do not consider community characteristics in service design and implementation can generate culturally inappropriate services for families of color. Professionals who hold negative stereotypes about communities of color add to a system's inability to develop culturally competent services.

Focusing on communities is important; however, the approach to service delivery resulting from this focus on the community determines whether service delivery is culturally competent. Many service system strategies that attempt to engage communities of color fall short of being culturally competent because of their isolated attention to the problems in these communities. According to Kretzman and McKnight (1993), this engagement strategy can be characterized as a needs-driven approach and leads to the stereotyping of communities through the creation of negative images of violence, drugs, gangs, and poverty. Furthermore, the result of these images is the stereotyping of residents of these communities as needy and problematic. Kretzman and McKnight contended that the needs-driven approach to planning and delivering services determines how problems are addressed and hence how people from the affected community view themselves. In the most extreme cases, these residents can come to believe that their well-being depends on being a client of human services. Kretzman and McKnight suggested other consequences of the culturally incompetent, deficiency-driven approach to service delivery design. These consequences included the following:

- Viewing the community as having a nearly endless list of problems and needs denies the community's wisdom
- Targeting resources based on needs directs funding to service providers, not to residents
- Providing resources on the basis of what is lacking in the community underlies the perception that only outside experts can provide real help
- Relying on needs as a planning guide ensures that there is a deepening dependence on outside support and funding (Kretzman & McKnight, 1993, p. 4)

Effective neighborhood leaders recognize the drawbacks of a problem-oriented approach to working with communities and focus on a community's strengths in their efforts (Kretzman & McKnight, 1993). Fair, president and chief executive officer of the Greater Miami Urban League, has built a reputation for working collaboratively with neighborhoods and is an example of this strength-based approach to leadership (Maxwell, 1997). In response to a question about the pathologies of the inner city, Fair responded,

> Pathologies be damned. We keep making up all these excuses. Some of our greatest black scholars came from terrible economic circumstances. What has happened is that we have placed value on the wrong things and have allowed the pathologies to become real. If you define them as real, they become real. If you believe that black children who live in a certain neighborhood, who come from certain kinds of families, cannot learn, then you will give them a school where they cannot learn and provide them with teachers who don't teach them. (Maxwell, 1997, p. 5D)

Fair further stated that

> One reason that we have not solved some of the problems in Liberty City [i.e., an inner-city neighborhood in Dade County, Florida] is that we don't understand the culture of this community. (Maxwell, 1997, p. 5D)

Culturally competent community engagement takes place when residents from a community are themselves interested in participating (Kretzman & McKnight, 1993). Systems of care that approach communities of color from a paternalistic perspective often fail to recognize whether the community wants their help. Respecting the desires and perceptions of residents and community leaders is a primary prerequisite to becoming culturally competent and successful in service delivery.

CONCLUSIONS

Cultural competence is a concept that can drive changes in the way system of care services can be designed and delivered. To accomplish this goal, systems need to become aware of the cultural values and beliefs that determine the services that they provide and incorporate this knowledge into their structures, policies, and priorities. In addition, it is important for systems of care to acknowledge the cultural influences on their employees from the professions within which they have been trained. Together, the underlying factors influencing systems and the staff who provide services and the perspectives of the individuals whom these systems are trying to serve must be understood.

The role of culture as a major determinant in the ways in which different groups of people approach and use mental health and other human services must be understood. What may be seen as a supportive service in one culture may be seen as disrespectful in another. Discovering these differences and then modifying the ways in which services are defined and delivered is the ultimate goal for systems of care in becoming culturally competent.

Acculturation is a powerful force that affects many people of color in the United States. The process of adapting to another culture, even under good circumstances, is a stressful process. Parents see their children becoming less like them and more like the strangers from the host culture. This loss of cultural identity can lead to problems with delinquency, substance abuse, and other mental health problems.

Evaluation endeavors sometimes define what systems of care value by identifying and measuring service systems for people in need of mental health services. Because evaluation practice is itself determined by the majority culture, their findings can perpetuate stereotypes about people of color. Acknowledging the role of culture in the ways in which methods are selected and in the variables under study is the first step in making evaluation culturally competent. Mixing methods from quantitative and qualitative approaches can ensure that evaluation is more culturally competent. It is important also to reflect the diversity that exists within seemingly similar populations of color in the United States.

Cultural competence, by definition, implies action and the ability to learn and become more knowledgeable regarding the dynamics of difference when different cultures interact. Cultural competence is everyone's responsibility, not just the responsibility of professionals of color. Developing action plans for systems of care that articulate the roles and responsibilities of all staff in the accomplishment of cultural competence is central to reforming the ways in which systems of care are planned and implemented. Ultimately, cultural competence should become a requirement for professionals in the practice of truly individualized service delivery. Professionals should contribute to the improvement of services for all participants in the process, including both the recipients and the providers of services and regardless of whether they are members of minority cultures or the mainstream culture.

Although much has been said about cultural competence in the 1990s, little systemic change has occurred in terms of the ways in which systems of care provide services. It is important to go beyond rhetoric and find ways to make culturally competent services a reality. Developing the tools and the strategies for accomplishing this goal is the challenge for the 21st century.

REFERENCES

Abad, W., Ramos, J., & Boyce, E. (1974). A model for the delivery of mental health services to Spanish-speaking minorities. *American Journal of Orthopsychiatry, 44,* 585–595.

Adler, P.S. (1975). Transitional experience: An alternative view of culture shock. *Journal of Humanistic Psychology, 15,* 13–23.

Arensberg, C., & Niehoff, A. (1964). *Introducing social change.* Hawthorne, NY: Aldine de Gruyter.

Aronowitz, M. (1984). The social and emotional adjustment of immigrant children: A review of the literature. *International Migration Review, 18,* 237–257.

Beauvais, F., & La Boueff, S. (1985). Drug and alcohol abuse intervention in American Indian communities. *International Journal of the Addictions, 20,* 139–171.

Bernard, J.A., Cablas, A., Hanley, J., Hernandez, M., & Romero, J.T. (1996, June). *Operationalizing cultural competence.* Paper presented at Child and Adolescent Service System Program's Institute on Developing Local Systems of Care, Training Institutes, Traverse City, MI.

Berry, J.W. (1981, June 18). *Acculturation: A comparative analysis of alternate forms.* Paper presented at Florida International University, Miami.

Byrnes, F.C. (1966). Role shock: An occupational hazard of American technical assistants abroad. *Annals of the American Academy of Political and Social Sciences, 368,* 95–108.

Canino, I.A., & Canino, G. (1980). Impact of stress on the Puerto Rican family: Treatment considerations. *American Journal of Orthopsychiatry, 50,* 535–541.

Celano, M.P., & Tyler, F.B. (1990). Behavioral acculturation among Vietnamese refugees in the United States. *Journal of Social Psychology, 131,* 373–385.

Corsini, R.J. (1987). *Concise encyclopedia of psychology.* New York: John Wiley & Sons.

Coulter, W.A. (1996, April). *Alarming or disarming? The status of ethnic difference within exceptionalities.* Paper presented at the annual convention of the Council for Exceptional Children, Orlando, FL.

Courtney, M.E., Barth, R.P., Berrick, J.D., Brooks, D., Needell, B., & Park, L. (1996). Race and child welfare services: Past research and future directions. *Child Welfare, 75,* 99–137.

Cross, P. (1995/1996, Fall/Winter). Developing a knowledge base to support cultural competence. *Culture and Family-Centered Practice: Family Resource Coalition Report, 14*(3-4), 2–7.

Cross, T.L., Bazron, B.J., Dennis, K.W., & Isaacs, M.R. (Eds.). (1989). *Towards a culturally competent system of care: Vol. I. A monograph on effective services for minority children who are severely emotionally disturbed.* Washington, DC: Georgetown University, Child Development Center, Child and Adolescent Service System Program, Technical Assistance Center.

Davidson, A. (1993). *Endangered peoples.* San Francisco: Sierra Club Books.

De La Cancela, V. (1985). Toward a sociocultural therapy for low-income ethnic minority. *Psychotherapy, 22,* 427–435.

Delgado, M. (1989). Treatment and prevention of Hispanic alcoholism. In T.D. Watts & R. Wright (Eds.), *Alcoholism in minority populations* (pp. 77–92). Springfield, IL: Charles C Thomas.

Deserly, K.J., & Cross, T.L. (1996). *American Indian children's mental health services: An assessment of tribal access to children's mental health funding.* Portland, OR: National Indian Child Welfare Association.

Drachman, D. (1996). Immigration status and their influences in service provision, access, and use. In P.L. Ewalt, E.M. Freeman, S.A. Kirk, & D.L. Poole (Eds.), *Multicultural issues in social work* (pp. 117–133). Washington, DC: National Association of Social Workers Press.

Embracing the dynamics of difference: Cultural competence in children's mental health. (1997, Spring). *Networks: National Technical Assistance Center Newsletter.*

Gibbs, J.T., & Huang, L.N. (1989). *Children of color: Psychological interventions with minority youth.* San Francisco: Jossey-Bass.

Goerge, R.M., Wulczyn, F.H., & Harden, A. (1994). *Foster care dynamics: California, Illinois, Michigan, New York, and Texas: A first-year report from the multi-state care data archive.* Chicago: University of Chicago, Chapin Hall Center for Children.

Gordon, M.M. (1964). *Assimilation in American life: The role of race, religion, and national origin.* New York: Oxford University Press.

Guyette, S. (1982). Selected characteristics of American Indian substance abusers. *International Journal of the Addictions, 17,* 1001–1014.

Hall, L.K. (1988). Cultural diversity relevant mental health services for Central American immigrants. *Hospital and Community Psychiatry, 39,* 1139–1144.

Harry, B. (1992). *Cultural diversity, families and special education system: Communication and empowerment.* New York: Teachers College Press.

Hines, A.M. (1993). Linking qualitative and quantitative methods in cross-cultural survey research: Techniques from cognitive science. *American Journal of Community Psychology, 21,* 729–746.

Hoberman, H.M. (1992). Ethnic minority status and adolescent mental health services utilization. *Journal of Mental Health Administration, 19*(3), 246–267.

Hondagneu-Sotelo, P. (1994). Latina immigrant women and paid domestic work: Upgrading the occupation. *Clinical Sociology Review, 12,* 268–269.

Household and family characteristics (Series P-20, No. 477). (1990, March). Washington, DC: U.S. Government Printing Office.

Hughes, D., Seidman, E., & Williams, N. (1993). Cultural phenomena and the research enterprise: Toward a culturally anchored methodology. *American Journal of Community Psychology, 21,* 687–703.

Inclan, J. (1985). Variations in value orientations in mental health work with Puerto Ricans. *Psychotherapy, 22,* 324–334.

Juarez, R. (1985). Core issues in psychotherapy with the Hispanic child. *Psychotherapy, 22,* 444–448.

Kids Count. (1997). *Kids count data book.* Baltimore: The Annie E. Casey Foundation.

Kitano, H.H.L. (1989). Alcohol and the Asian American. In T.D. Watts & R. Wright (Eds.), *Alcoholism in minority populations* (pp. 143–156). Springfield, IL: Charles C Thomas.

Knitzer, J. (1982). *Unclaimed children: The failure of public responsibility to children and adolescents in need of mental health services.* Washington, DC: Children's Defense Fund.

Kretzman, J.P., & McKnight, J.L. (1993). *Building communities from the inside out: A path toward finding and mobilizing a community's assets.* Evanston, IL: Northwestern University, Center for Urban Affairs and Policy Research, Neighborhood Innovations Network.

Maton, K.I. (1993). A bridge between cultures: Linked ethnographic-empirical methodology for culture anchored research. *American Journal of Community Psychology, 21,* 747–773.

Maxwell, B. (1997, September 28). The fair way. *St. Petersburg Times*, D1, D5.

McGarrell, E.F. (1993). Trends in racial disproportionality in juvenile court processing: 1985–1989. *Crime and Delinquency, 39*, 29–48.

Montijo, J.A. (1985). Therapeutic relationship with the poor: A Puerto Rican perspective. *Psychotherapy, 22*, 436–440.

National Council for Research on Women. (1995a). Building a fund for new citizens. *Issues Quarterly, 1*(3), 20–21.

National Council for Research on Women. (1995b). IQ eye openers. *Issues Quarterly, 1*(3), 6.

Oberg, K. (1960). Cultural shock: Adjustment to new cultural environments. *Practical Anthropology, 7*, 177–182.

Orlandi, M.A. (1992). Defining cultural competence: An organizing framework. In M.A. Orlandi, R. Weston, & L.G. Epstein (Eds.), *Cultural competence for evaluators: A guide for alcohol and other drug abuse prevention practitioners working with ethnic/racial communities* (pp. 293–299) [Monograph]. Washington, DC: U.S. Department of Health and Human Services.

O'Sullivan, M.J., Peterson, P.D., Cox, G.B., & Kirkeby, J. (1989). Ethnic populations: Community mental health services ten years later. *American Journal of Community Psychology, 17*, 17–30.

Padilla, A.M. (1980). The role of cultural awareness and ethnic loyalty in acculturation. In A.M. Padilla (Ed.), *Acculturation: Theory, models and some new findings* (pp. 47–84). Boulder, CO: Westview Press.

Padilla, E.R., Olmedo, E., & Loya, F. (1982). Acculturation and the MMPI performance of Chicano and Anglo college students. *Hispanic Journal of Behavioral Sciences, 4*, 451–466.

Rosado, J.W. (1980). Important psychocultural factors in the delivery of mental health to lower-class Puerto Rican clients: A review of the literature. *Journal of Community Psychology, 8*, 215–226.

Rosado, J.W., & Elias, N.J. (1993). Ecological and psychocultural mediators in the delivery of services for urban, culturally diverse Hispanic clients. *Professional Psychology: Research and Practice, 24*, 450–459.

Rosenthal, D.A., & Feldman, S.S. (1990). The acculturation of Chinese immigrants: Perceived effects on family functioning of length of residence in two cultural contexts. *Journal of Genetic Psychology, 15*, 495–513.

Sam, D.L. (1995). Acculturation attitudes among young immigrants as a function of perceived parental attitudes toward cultural change. *Journal of Early Adolescence, 15*, 238–258.

Santisteban, D.A., Szapocznik, J., Kurtines, W.M., & Rio, A.T. (1994). Behavior problems among Hispanic youth: The family as moderator of adjustment. In J. Szapocznik & H. Munos (Eds.), *An Hispanic family approach to substance abuse prevention* (pp. 19–39). Washington, DC: U.S. Government Printing Office.

Sasao, T., & Sue, S. (1993). Toward a culturally anchored ecological framework of research in ethnic-cultural communities. *American Journal of Community Psychology, 21*, 705–727.

Schinke, S.P., Moncher, M.S., Palleja, J., Zayas, L.H., & Schilling, R.F. (1988). Hispanic youth, substance abuse, and stress: Implications for prevention research. *International Journal of the Addictions, 23*, 809–826.

Seidman, E. (1993). Culturally anchored methodology: An introduction to the special issue. *American Journal of Community Psychology, 21*, 683–685.

Smalley, W. (1963). Culture shock, language shock, and the shock of self-discovery. *Practical Anthropology, 10*, 49–56.

Smart, J.F., & Smart, D.W. (1995). Acculturative stress of Hispanics: Loss and challenge. *Journal of Counseling and Development, 73,* 390–396.

Spencer, M.B., & Dornbusch, S.M. (1990). Minority youth in America. In S.S. Feldman & G.R. Elliot (Eds.), *At the threshold: The developing adolescent* (pp. 123–146). Cambridge, MA: Harvard University Press.

Stalker, P. (1994). *The work of strangers: A survey of international labour migration.* Geneva: International Labour Office.

Stroul, B. (1993). *Systems of care for children and adolescents with severe emotional disturbances: What are the results?* Washington, DC: Georgetown University, Child Development Center, Child and Adolescent Service System Program, Technical Assistance Center, Center for Child Health and Mental Health Policy.

Sue, D.W., Arrendondo, P., & McDavis, R.J. (1992). Multicultural counseling competencies and standards: A call to the profession. *Journal of Multicultural Counseling, 20,* 64–88.

Sue, S., & Zane, N. (1987). The role of culture and cultural techniques in psychotherapy: A critical reformulation. *American Psychologist, 42,* 37–45.

Sung, B.L. (1985). Bicultural conflicts in Chinese immigrant children. *Journal of Comparative Family Studies, 26,* 255–269.

Szapocznik, J., Scopetta, M.A., Kurtines, W., & Aranalde, M.A. (1978). Theory and measurement of acculturation. *Inter-American Journal of Psychology, 12,* 113–130.

Uba, L., & Sue, S. (1991). Nature and scope of services for Asian and Pacific Islander Americans. In N. Mokuau (Ed.), *Handbook of social services for Asians and Pacific Islanders* (pp. 3–19). Westport, CT: Greenwood Publishing Group.

U.S. Bureau of the Census. (1995). *Statistical abstract of the United States* (115th ed.). Austin, TX: Reference Press.

U.S. Commission on Civil Rights. (1982). *Unemployment and underemployment among blacks, Hispanics, and women.* Washington, DC: U.S. Government Printing Office.

U.S. Department of Labor, Women's Bureau. (1994). *1993 handbook on women workers: Trends and issues.* Washington, DC: U.S. Department of Labor.

Vega, W., Gil, A.G., Warheit, G.J., Zimmerman, R.S., & Apospori, E. (1993). Acculturation and delinquent behavior among Cuban American adolescents: Toward an empirical model. *American Journal of Community Psychology, 21,* 113–125.

Wells, K.B., Golding, J.M., & Hough, R.L. (1989). Acculturation and the probability of use of health services by Mexican Americans. *Health Services Research, 24,* 237–257.

Woodward, A.M., Dwinell, A.D., & Arons, D.S. (1992). Barriers to mental health care for Hispanic Americans: A literature review and discussion. *Journal of Mental Health Administration, 19,* 224–236.

Yamashiro, G., & Matsuoka, J.K. (1997). Help-seeking among Asian and Pacific Americans: A multiperspective analysis. *Social Work, 42,* 176–186.

Zambrana, R.E. (Ed.). (1995). *Understanding Latino families: Scholarship, policy and practice.* Thousand Oaks, CA: Sage Publications.

Organizational Infrastructure Development

Cultural Competence Plans

A Strategy for the Creation of a Culturally Competent System of Care

José A. Bernard

If you don't care where you're going, any road will get you there.

Source unknown

Since the publication of *Towards a Culturally Competent System of Care: A Monograph on Effective Services for Minority Children Who Are Severely Emotionally Disturbed* (Cross, Bazron, Dennis, & Isaacs, 1989), dozens of books and training materials on cultural competence and its sister field in the private sector, managing diversity, have been published. Yet, despite the consistent call for commitment to a long-term developmental process, organizations too often maintain the simplistic view, if they express any view at all, that recruitment of bilingual and bicultural service providers and training in culturally related topics alone will lead to a culturally competent organization. Token, sporadic, poorly thought-out efforts that are purported to address cultural competence issues are a waste of valuable agency resources and lead to diminished credibility with clients and their families and polarization and conflict among agency staff[1] (Quigley, 1993).

The "if you don't care where you're going, any road will get you there" way of doing business is incongruent with organizational effectiveness and cultural competence and is simply an unacceptable way for a human services organization to operate. Developing a sound plan that facilitates the development of a culturally competent system of care is a formidable task but an achievable goal for most organizations. This chapter presents a simple, common-sense approach to developing a plan of substance that will assist any organization in developing a culturally competent system of care.

---

[1]The ideas in this chapter are applicable to agencies, organizations, and departments; therefore, these three terms are used interchangeably throughout this chapter.

PLANNING COMPONENTS

There are a number of ways to develop a culturally competent system of care, but all require a plan of some type. The six key planning components described in this section will enhance significantly the successful development and implementation of a cultural competence plan for any mental health services agency. The details described in each subsection should be viewed as basic guidelines. An agency may occasionally be able to bypass a number of the particular guidelines because its level of development may permit it without compromising the essential elements of planning involved in the developmental process. Service organizations that choose to invest in the development of a culturally competent system of care, however, should be conscious of and clear about the distinct differences between engaging in a challenging developmental process and skipping vital steps in applying a quick-fix solution. Simply stated, ill-conceived ideas and shortcuts are likely to result in token efforts; yield confusion and increase resistance, uncertainty, and frustration; and ultimately result in failure.

An organization concerned with serving culturally diverse clients effectively—whether the motive is socially or business driven—must take into account a wide range of policy, administrative, and service issues that ultimately affect client and family outcomes. From a broad organizational perspective, six interdependent areas are absolutely essential to address in the development of a cultural competence plan. These are

1. Leadership
2. Establishing a common understanding of cultural competence
3. Assessment of organizational culture
4. Training
5. Plan development
6. Management of the plan

The process of developing a quality plan that has a good chance of being implemented begins at the moment a key person in the organization is given the directive to begin exploring the steps necessary to develop a culturally competent organization. The key components of the process mentioned in the preceding paragraphs are interdependent and begin with the critical nature of leadership in the change process.

Leadership

Effective leadership is a prerequisite to success in the reform of any social services delivery system. A number of primary factors are required within the leadership of an organization if it is to utilize its resources successfully to develop a culturally competent system of care. Effective leaders are systematic, outcome oriented, proactive, and determined to realize their vision for the organization. Effective leaders have managerial styles that are inclusive, flexible, and goal oriented and that place strong emphasis on the accountability of key players. A leader of an organization interested in developing a culturally competent system of care must have a basic understanding of cultural competence and a clear vision of how it benefits the organization. The leader's vision and ability to effectively communicate is especially critical to any reform process because it is "the most fundamental statement of a corporation's values, aspirations, and goals" (Quigley, 1993, p. 5). In mental health services agencies in particular, the leader's vision is "an appeal to its members' hearts and minds" (Quigley, 1993, p. 5).

The leader's vision of the future must also be communicated effectively and consistently throughout the organization so that "people see clearly in their mind's eye where the change will take them and why it matters" (Katzenbach, 1995, p. 66). If a leader has a good vision for the organization but is unable or unwilling to communicate it as a goal, then he or she at least must have the wisdom to surround him- or herself with a competent manager or managers who are committed to focusing the organization's resources to implement it. Effective leaders are able to determine fairly accurately the depth and scope of resistance to change, what the agency's assets are, and which directions the agency must take in order to overcome barriers to change. In short, effective leadership in any organization requires "a distinctive combination of tough, balanced performance standards and a fresh sense of how to motivate and mobilize" (Katzenbach, 1995, p. 8) its human resources.

Leaders who define and establish clear objectives for other managers and supervisors may establish the expectation that supervisors are also change agents. If leaders hold these key players accountable, they may pass on a sense of responsibility to promote cultural competence within their respective units and actively encourage the recruitment of change agents at all levels. At a fundamental level, however, good leadership ensures that people holding management and supervisory positions in fact have the managerial skills and knowledge to conceptualize, plan, implement, and evaluate their programs and to recruit, train, supervise, mentor, and retain the best possible staff to implement the department's vision (Thomas, 1991). Effective leaders also promote cultural competence outside their agencies because it enhances interagency collaboration and cooperation based on a mutual understanding of community, client, and family issues. Finally, as a core value, good leadership and cultural competence are conceptually synonymous. They complement each other in that they maintain that "the customer always comes first" (Quigley, 1993, p. 12).

Establishing a Common Understanding of Cultural Competence

The term *cultural competence* is often misinterpreted. Left open to anyone's interpretation, the term can be intimidating to some; embraced or dismissed by others; and, more important with regard to resistance, viewed as just another initiative to benefit minorities at the expense of whites.[2] An unfortunate outcome of this misperception is that cultural competence becomes yet another divisive issue that prevents people of color and whites from engaging in a constructive dialogue about culture and how it relates to client services. Adding to the potential for conflict are the organizational issues related to change, which often create considerable ongoing resistance. Often it seems that just about any type of change, including those changes agreed on by members of an organization, causes turmoil and conflict. Thus, it is critical to establish a common language and a common understanding of what cultural competence is and is not.

Defining *cultural competence* in simple, easy-to-remember, inclusive phrases such as "working effectively in cross-cultural situations" (Cross et al., 1989, p. 13) provides a common reference point, a foundation for a leveled playing field for everyone across gender, ethnicity, and job classifications to understand. The simple definition of *cultural competence* should be amplified to address initial apprehension and resentment that may arise from the word *competence*, which many staff interpret to imply that they are incompetent. The specific objective at this point is to communicate cultural competence as an inclusive framework and in terms that will be appealing or have a message or "hook" to obtain as broad an audience as possible. Thus, the characteristics and merits that distinguish cultural competence from past cultural or minority-related initiatives (e.g., cultural awareness, cultural sensitivity) also need to be emphasized and established early in the developmental process. The following are among the distinguishing factors that should be emphasized early in the process:

- Cultural competence is for everyone and is inclusive. Cultural competence enables the organization to serve all clients better; thus, consumers, providers, the minority community, the organization, the funding agency, and the taxpayer all benefit (Lee, 1991).
- Cultural competence is a long-term developmental process, not a quick fix.

---

[2]The term *white* is used to refer to people of European descent generally.

- Cultural competence calls for true, fundamental institutional change, not token efforts.
- Cultural competence helps reduce agency risk, liability, and the cost of service delivery.
- Cultural competence can be learned.

A basic strategy for making meaningful changes aimed at achieving cultural competence should include the requirement that all aspects of the organization be examined, modified, and changed accordingly. This strategy includes a review of all of the basic organizational areas: policies and administrative practices, human resources, client and family services, and evaluation. In this review process, the specific needs within each area can be addressed in a more relevant and meaningful way.

Too often the most obvious but most powerful unifying need that all people have in common, regardless of socioeconomic status or cultural heritage, is overlooked or taken for granted: the need to be treated with dignity, respect, and understanding. The treatment of clients and their families should be discussed, and methods that support dignity, respect, and understanding should be elaborated; openly promoted; and defined as explicit, fundamental organizational values.

Finally, in the absence of accurate definitions or opportunities for rebuttal, the status quo—misconceptions, misguided beliefs, stereotypes, and misinformation—defines cultural issues in an organization. To counteract this tendency, everyone must understand and work to promote the idea that working effectively in cross-cultural situations is a win-win form of doing business.

Assessment of Organizational Culture

The third area to consider in the development of a cultural competence plan is the organization's past and present cultures. Knowing and understanding the organization's history, development, current values, and operational climate—as well as the levels of cultural awareness of top management, supervisors, and line staff—all are important to the development of an effective strategy. Simply defined, *organizational culture* comprises "the basic assumptions driving life in a given organization" (Thomas, 1991, p. 13). In addition, *organizational culture* is "a pattern of assumptions and beliefs deeply held in common by members of an organization" (Nolan, Goodstein, & Pfeifer, 1993, p. 34). In essence, commonly held views, beliefs, and values ultimately determine "the way business is done" within an organization, regardless of whether the business is done well. For example, beliefs that service organizations commonly hold are that their services are accessible to all people and that their resources are equitably distributed among their service population. Of course, many clients who receive those services view these conceptions of equal access and equitable services as myths rather than as realities. The differences in perception of the scope and quality of services that often exist between agencies and clients are the reason why an assessment of the organization's culture is so important.

Careful consideration needs to be given to the organization's history and development to determine whether the current environment will support and contribute to the development and implementation of culturally competent practices. An understanding of the dynamics of potential culture clashes in organizations is also useful at this stage because of their implications for any form of change. *Culture clash* involves "the conflict over basic values that occurs between groups of people with different core identities and . . . occurs when the values, attitudes and behaviors of the dominant group are questioned by others and in turn, create a disturbance within the organization" (Loden & Rosener, 1991, p. 121).

The introduction of cultural competence as a way of doing business is likely to clash with an organization's existing culture. An organizational culture that is resistant to change detracts from and undermines the development and implementation of cultural competence initiatives. In such cases, a strategy unique to the organization's history of reactions to new initiatives and changes is required to successfully blend or refine the existing organizational culture with the explicit values of cultural competence. Following are some sample questions that should be addressed as part of the preparation for initial training in cultural competence:

1. What experience does the organization or its components have with change or reform?
2. How will reform or any type of change be received by governing boards, staff, and the community?
3. Does the agency have a mission statement, and is the statement consistent with the values that drive the agency?
4. What is the fiscal state of the agency, and how do financial issues affect its operational climate and program priorities?
5. What are the history and prevailing attitudes toward affirmative action and other equity-related initiatives? What, if anything, do the agency's affirmative action and retention of minority staff records say about the agency?
6. Is the ethnic composition of the community reflected
    a. On the governing board of the agency?

    b.   In the agency's personnel across job classifications?

    c.   In the makeup of the client population?

7.   What are the agency's historical relationship and standing with regard to diversity, especially with traditionally underrepresented groups? Have dialogues taken place? Have alliances been established? Have partnerships been formed? Is there trust or distrust between the agency and the ethnic minority community?

These questions and others like them may constitute an informal early assessment that provides a starting point, the beginning of a strategy for developing a cultural competence plan built around the unique characteristics of the particular agency. The preceding list of questions should also make it clear that the answers will likely raise a number of thorny issues, dichotomies, and problems associated with the history of the agency and society's inadequacies in dealing with its "isms" (e.g., racism, sexism, ageism) that need to be confronted with honesty and commitment if the problems are to be addressed at their roots.

Organizational assessment also requires one to ask and obtain answers to fundamental questions such as the following:

1.   Do managers have levels of managerial skills and knowledge that are up to the task of implementing true institutional change? Do they know how to recruit and interview effectively, or do they consistently hire and promote within their self-images and professional disciplines? Are they autocratic or democratic managers? As individuals and as a group, can these top managers and supervisors manage and supervise effectively?

2.   What is management's understanding of leadership as it relates to their roles as key potential change agents? Does top management understand the difference between leadership and management? To what extent is the leadership of the agency capable of assuming a positive role model posture that demonstrates a priority on cultural competence and promotes it effectively? Is the prevailing attitude among top managers that staff need to be trained but top managers do not? Do they know how to supervise and mentor staff?

3.   Where and how are business decisions *really* made, and who makes them? What does the network of the informal organization look like?

4.   What is the agency's history and experience in dealing with organizational change? To what extent is the agency able to make a genuine commitment to making fundamental institutional change and investing in a long-term developmental process?

5. What are the organization's prevailing attitudes toward training? Are the resources that are available, for instance, adequate to begin addressing the ongoing cultural competence training needs of the agency? Is there a structured method of assessing staff training needs and a developmental plan consistent with the agency's goals and needs? When staff receive training, how does the work environment reinforce or discourage the use of new knowledge, understanding, and skills from the workshops or training seminars?

6. What are the organization's resources for evaluating programs?

Some thought may also be given at this point to the subject of evaluation and the organization's orientation and capacity to evaluate programs. By thinking about evaluation at this stage, the leadership of the agency takes several small but important steps:

1. Leaders acknowledge early in the process the importance of having a baseline for the measurement of progress and set an expectation of accountability.

2. Leaders establish a precedent for including evaluation at the front end of any cultural competence–related initiative.

3. Leaders may begin to identify a problem with regard to the agency's capacity and need to conduct evaluations.

Regardless of the route to evaluation that the organization takes, evaluation must be kept as simple as possible. The data generated must be easy to understand and useful to staff at all levels, and reports must be produced consistently.

Finally, a facilitator should be identified and included early in the planning process for the initial training. The agency needs a competent facilitator whose knowledge and style match the organization's needs. Facilitator competence means that in the eyes of the organization, the facilitator's credentials and credibility with regard to the scope and depth of their knowledge and understanding of cultural issues in the service field itself are impeccable. Careful consideration needs to be given to the facilitator's cultural values and attitudes about other cultural groups, commitment, and past experiences in developing and implementing culturally inclusive and effective service programs. Clearly, a facilitator who promotes participation and inclusion enhances the chances of success in the development and implementation of any cultural competence plan that is developed.

Ignoring organizational needs, underestimating the strength of the organization's culture to resist change, ignoring the subtle and persistent levels of denial of the needs of people other than those from the dominant culture, and ignoring issues related to a good organizational match with a consultant all lead to the alternate course of limited success and downright failure. Failure in these areas effectively gives administrators and line staff alike license to adopt the too-often-assumed posture of "We've tried that; we've been there—that cultural competence stuff doesn't work."

Training

Careful attention to preparation, planning, and implementation of initial training is also critical for the plan's successful development. Meeting times and resources need to be identified and committed; a training consultant or facilitator must be identified and secured; a cross-section of key personnel from all of the organization's divisions, job classifications, ethnicity, and gender categories must be identified; and common expectations must be defined. The following is a checklist of some issues to be addressed in preparing for the training itself; in some ways, the checklist represents a wish list that must be balanced with an organization's resources:

1. Obtain a commitment to conduct cultural competence training at a site that is away from the pressure of the day's routine and free of interruptions for all players, particularly those in top management positions. The degree and level of participation of managers convey a clear message about how serious cultural competence is to the organization.
2. Make certain that all key players, including policy makers and clients as appropriate, are committed to attending the training.
3. Secure a commitment from management that participants shall devote adequate time to achieve the objectives of the training.
4. Make certain that the facilitator develops a list of materials and needed equipment.
5. Establish clear objectives for the training session. To keep expectations realistic and consistent, consult and guide key agency personnel and the facilitator in the development of the objectives. At least three objectives are fundamental to any effort involving the development of a cultural competence plan:
   a. Develop a common understanding of cultural competence as a win-win way of doing business.
   b. Identify agency strengths and weaknesses based on the cultural competence model.
   c. Based on the agency's assets and weaknesses, identify objectives and develop a cultural competence master plan.

The primary goal of the training is twofold: to become familiar with the cultural competence model and to construct a plan that is developed collaboratively by and thus is embraced by members of the organization. The key to this goal is to set and maintain a positive tone around the subject of cultural competence by defining it as a win-win way of delivering services. Early in the training, a common understanding—a common *expectation*—should be established by stressing the positive, tangible attributes of cultural competence. The point must be made that cultural competence reduces misperceptions and resistance among the organization's personnel as the group of beneficiaries, for instance, is expanded to include clients and service providers, the mental health services agency, the funding source, and the taxpayer. Apprehensions are reduced as participants begin to understand that cultural competence is a constructive, unifying, proactive approach to addressing cultural differences; that it is inclusive and transcends the attributes of race, age, and gender; and that it can be learned. By the end of the first half of the training, it should be clear to participants that, in order for cultural competence to be successful, staff participation and support are required at all levels of the organization and that everyone within the organization, not just the usual handful of interested and invested individuals concerned with underserved populations, must assume responsibility for cultural competence.

Although cultural competence is a positive and constructive approach to working in cross-cultural situations, the historical and continuing experience of discrimination against, for example, women, ethnic minority groups, and people with disabilities in American society should be neither denied nor understated. Ideally, some room should be made in this initial training to acknowledge the inherent dichotomies and contradictions of America's promises and the exclusionary realities experienced by people of color, women, older adults, and people with disabilities, among others. This is not to say that the training should be allowed to digress into a dispute over the merits or shortcomings of the U.S. government; rather, it is important from the beginning of this process to be honest, forthcoming, open, and realistic about white privilege (McIntosh, 1988) and about the less flattering view of the barriers that prevent agency and client resources from being fully used. The point is fundamentally important: The agency's willingness to face and confront honestly the more challenging and sensitive issues related to cultural competence sends a clear message to everyone involved that management is serious, unafraid, and committed to eliminating the barriers that prevent the agency from meeting its potential and full responsibility to its community.

Plan Development

Once the meaning, scope, and depth of cultural competence are defined and established, an organization can progress to developing the plan within the context of the cultural competence model. Again, in the spirit of maintaining a positive tone, the facilitator may direct the participants to identify and review some of the agency's strengths and accomplishments. Programs that target and serve a particular ethnic minority group well may be reviewed and acknowledged. If a supervisor has done an excellent job of cultivating, mentoring, and promoting staff by affording them flexible schedules so that they may enter and complete education programs and degrees, then acknowledge and celebrate their initiative. If a policy or advisory group reflects the ethnic makeup of the community, take credit for this circumstance as a reflection of the agency's commitment. This recognition helps participants realize a collective sense of organizational, programmatic, interpersonal, and individual accomplishment; acknowledges and gives credit where it is due; and helps set a more complete foundation for the agency's plan.

The next step (using the cultural competence model as a guide) is to identify barriers and agency issues that prevent the agency from developing a culturally competent system of care. Issues may be sorted according to whether they involve policies and procedures, human resources (including recruitment and retention practices and staff training and development), client and family services, and evaluation. As an initial informal assessment of the organization's current status, an agency may use as simple a process as the cultural competence continuum or a more structured and in-depth tool such as the one set forth in *Journey Towards Cultural Competency: Lessons Learned* (Texas Department of Health, Maternal and Child Health Bureau, Center on Cultural Competency, 1996). Whatever the major categories of barriers selected, organizations must make certain that the action plan outline is comprehensive and that its potential impact is agency- and systemwide.

There are some general categories of objectives that apply to most organizations. For example, policy-making bodies should generally reflect the makeup of the community that they serve. The agency should also commit to offering a cultural competence curriculum and require personnel across job classifications to attend a series of clearly related cultural competence classes or workshops that, when viewed as a whole, comprise a clear foundation of cultural knowledge, skills, and abilities relevant to the agency's day-to-day work. Some fundamental workshops include an introductory cultural competence class, a cultural self-assessment class that is interactive and directed at prejudice awareness and reduction, and ethnicity-specific workshops.

Whenever possible, objectives should be stated in measurable terms. For instance, if an agency can realistically commit to increasing its Asian American clinicians by 25% in its first year and 50% in its second year, then it is much better off than it would be if it developed a process objective such as "To develop a recruitment and retention plan to increase Asian American clinicians." Depending on the organization's situation, either type of objective may be appropriate; however, measurable objectives are preferable to process objectives because their successful attainment can be evaluated more easily.

Other objectives are specific to the particular organization. For example, if an agency is strongly driven by its mission statement, it needs to review and perhaps revise its mission statement to include cultural competence language that is explicit about services that are inclusive of the entire community. If the agency, for instance, has a history of losing clinicians of African American descent and has no idea why they leave, it may establish recruitment and retention of a specific number of African American clinicians within a given time period as a human resources objective. As the group progresses through the process of identifying objectives, the activities, resources needed, time lines, and evaluation criteria should also be discussed and decided on. All objectives should identify staff, either individually or in committees, who are to be responsible for ensuring that each objective is met, to whom staff are to report, and the target completion dates for meeting the objectives. Although the plan should be as specific as possible, it should also be viewed as a "living document" that remains relevant by being flexible and open to change.

It is unlikely that an agency will finish a plan by the end of the initial training session; but at that stage it should have a good draft of short- and long-term objectives organized by major categories that, taken together, make up the comprehensive service delivery system of the organization. How the plan is to be completed, by whom, and when all are issues that need to be resolved before the initial group disperses. The makeup of the team that will manage and monitor the plan's implementation and the scope and depth of their duties will need to be defined at this stage as well. Any individual assigned to be a member of the implementation team must have good communication skills at the organizational and interpersonal levels. The implementation team should also be composed of managers (who contribute conceptual skills and decision-making authority) and line staff (who bring their knowledge of clients' needs and systemic barriers) (Nolan et al., 1993). A system of communication and accountability within the group also needs to be established to ensure that the group and agency staff are informed and kept apprised of the plan's progress.

Management of the Plan

Plans are only as good as the commitment that people make to ensure their implementation. In essence, the agency's making a commitment means that it is willing to "walk the talk." If the initial training is planned and implemented well, participants will leave with a sense of accomplishment, confident of their plan and their ability to implement it. A team that will implement the plan should be in place to coordinate, evaluate, and fine-tune the plan as progress is made. If the organization is large, participants in the initial cultural competence workshop should be placed on the agendas of their division's or program's first meeting and should communicate the results of the training and the roles that staff can anticipate that they will play in the future. It is important to remind people again and again that cultural competence is an inclusive and developmental process.

Implementation of several of the following steps capitalizes on the initial momentum that is developed in the first training session:

- Complete the final plan as quickly as possible.
- Sort and identify the more challenging objectives from the easier ones; do the easier ones first to help establish a sense of expectation and accomplishment.
- Set periodic (e.g., quarterly) and annual review dates, and include key investors and stakeholders.
- For the first year's follow-up session, it is preferable to use the same facilitator who worked with the group in the initial training.
- If at all possible, set a schedule for providing introductory cultural competence workshops to the balance of staff and agencies with which the organization has interagency or contract agreements. At the workshops, present and review the cultural competence plan as a work in progress. This encourages and promotes the sense of ownership for the plan by seeking and integrating additional ideas that staff may have to enhance development of a culturally competent system of care.
- Identify and make known staff who were participants in the initial training, and present them as prospective resource people for other staff members.
- Integrate the plan as part of the continuous quality improvement process of the agency.
- Promote the merits of the agency's cultural competence plan by sharing plan outcomes and benefits with, for example, related government agencies or departments and funding sources.
- Establish a reinforcement process whereby the leadership of the organization recognizes, celebrates, and rewards innovation and superior performance. Accomplishments that reflect integration of cultural factors and practices in the agency's day-to-day operations and revenue enhancement opportunities and benefits need to be communicated regularly through department meetings or newsletters.

As a note of caution, throughout this initial change process, whoever is selected to lead the implementation team must be sensitive and astute. Moreover, this individual must be able to accurately interpret for the organization the subtle levels of miscommunication and misunderstanding between organizations run by the dominant values of American society and the different values of the diverse cultural communities that the agency serves. Members of the service organization must also be willing to refrain from the too common tendency to engage in denial in its various manifestations and levels. The following passage, in which the Executive Director of the Rio Grande Foundation in Santa Fe, New Mexico, describes his long and sometimes painful learning process with the American Indian population, offers an illustration of this tendency:

> I have had to learn to be honest, particularly with the words I use. The opposite of honesty is often not outright deception but an artifice so elaborate as to disguise the dishonesty it embodies. Confronting Indian peoples, we have always been dishonest in this way, by structuring the world in language so as to deny the reality of Indian conceptions and ultimately deny wrongdoing on our part for eliminating these "pagan," or "savage," or "uncivilized," or "useless," or "primitive institutions" and peoples. (Williams, 1979, p. 14)

Even under the best of circumstances, organizational cultures are resistant to change in part because staff at all levels are reluctant to admit, and are uncomfortable with the idea, that there are issues present within their professions and organizations that they are ill equipped to address. The leadership and the task group assigned to implement the plan must anticipate and address this reluctance effectively. In assigning someone to lead an organization's cultural competence efforts, the lead person's insight, knowledge, and experience must be considered primary. An organization must not cater to the ignorance or to the comfort level of people who want to continue to conduct business as they have in the past. If the lead person is delegated the responsibility of developing cultural competence within the organization and is actually supported to implement the objectives of the plan, the organization will go far in bridging the gap between agencies and people in the community who are outside the mainstream culture.

Progress toward the implementation of a culturally competent system of care is made evident by the presence of some of the following circumstances:

- The organization maximizes its use of resources with staff, clients and their families, contract organizations, and interagencies.

- Clients actually experience equal access, receive equitable services, and achieve equitable outcomes.[3]
- There is an improvement in client satisfaction with services.
- The department enjoys clients' support and a trusting working relationship with the minority community and advocacy groups. Clear avenues for policy input are set, and the interested groups are consulted in a timely manner about new agency initiatives and projects.
- Other service agencies are active partners in cultural competence initiatives.
- Policies and practices are always subject to a cultural competence review.
- All staff assume and share responsibility for cultural competence initiatives and tasks in proportion to their authority and job duties.
- Other agencies such as state, county, and city departments and local nonprofit organizations take notice of the agency's improved working atmosphere and success with its cultural competence initiatives.
- The agency makes a complete paradigm shift, making cultural factors an integral part of its day-to-day business.
- The organization is constantly learning, exploring, and experimenting with new ideas to better serve its public (Cross et al., 1989; Finefrock, 1995).

The preceding list describes but a few of the guidelines and factors that an agency needs to consider. The organization's resources and environment determine which management and implementation strategy will be most effective. In the end, commitment, tenacity, persistence, and time—and a sound strategy grounded in leading and managing organizational change (Kotter, 1996)—determine the level and degree of success that the organization's plan enjoys. An organization may claim success in developing a culturally competent system of care when cultural competence principles are the "norms of behavior" of the organization (Kotter, 1996). Plan on this organizational process taking 5–10 years.

CONCLUSIONS

This chapter has provided some useful information that will enable agency staff to take on the task of developing a fundamentally sound cultural competence plan. The plan development process requires little more than the exercise of common sense and the practice of basic, pru-

---

[3]These are conceptual terms developed by Daniel D. Jordan of the Ventura County Department of Behavioral Health Services, Ventura, California.

dent management principles; commitment; and effective leadership. If agency staff rely on the plan alone to develop cultural competence in an organization, however, that plan will likely fail.

People who continually raise cultural issues and advocate for needed organizational changes experience tremendous resistance and frustration even under the best of circumstances. In the face of continuous adversity, some may continue to advocate for institutional change; but too many either give up on the system or risk burning out altogether. Who can blame them? Much of their cultural knowledge, experience, and program ideas are ignored, and their experiences teach them that their cultural assets are of little or no value to the organization. For them, agencies that regularly subscribe to the "any road will get you there" mode of operation with regard to cultural issues is a source of perpetual resentment and, unfortunately, a bitter reality with which they learn to live.

Finally, the development of a cultural competence plan is simply an exercise of the head. This intellectual process is certainly an important step in the right direction, but only one part of the required process of developing a culturally competent system of care. To make cultural competence a reality also requires a commitment of the heart and a willingness to confront and get beyond cultural baggage. Bias, prejudice, stereotypes, and outright racism and bigotry, as well as attitudes and feelings of shame, guilt, hate, and anger about cultural and class differences, are formidable barriers to cultural competence. Awareness and reduction of employees' cultural baggage enables the organization to collectively evolve into understanding, respect, and appreciation for cultural differences and thus be open to discovering the tremendous assets and resources that are inherent in all cultures. These issues involving attitudes and feelings are better addressed through empathy, which comes from the heart.

REFERENCES

Cross, T.L., Bazron, B.J., Dennis, K.W., & Isaacs, M.R. (Eds.). (1989). *Towards a culturally competent system of care: Vol. I. A monograph on effective services for minority children who are severely emotionally disturbed.* Washington, DC: Georgetown University, Child Development Center, Child and Adolescent Service System Program, Technical Assistance Center.

Finefrock, M. (1995, April/May). Developing an organizational change plan in diversity. *Community Action,* 4–7.

Katzenbach, J.R. (1995). *Real change leaders: How you can create growth and high performance at your company.* New York: Random House.

Kotter, J.P. (1996). *Leading change: Why transformation efforts fail.* Boston: Harvard Business School Press.

Lee, E. (1991, January). *Cultural competence training handbook.* Ventura, CA: County of Ventura Health Care Agency, Mental Health Services.

Loden, M., & Rosener, J.B. (1991). *Workforce America: Managing employee diversity as a vital resource.* Homewood, IL: Business One Irwin.

McIntosh, P. (1988). *White privilege and male privilege* (Working Paper No. 189). Wellesley, MA: Wellesley College, Center for Research on Women.

Nolan, T., Goodstein, L., & Pfeifer, W.J. (1993). *Plan or die: Ten keys to organizational success.* San Diego: Pfeifer & Co.

Quigley, V.J. (1993). *Vision: How leaders develop it, share it, and sustain it.* New York: McGraw-Hill.

Texas Department of Health, Maternal and Child Health Bureau, Center on Cultural Competency. (1996). *Journey towards cultural competency: Lessons learned* [Handout]. Austin: Author.

Thomas, R.R. (1991). *Beyond race and gender: Unleashing the power of your total work force by managing diversity.* New York: AMACOM Books.

Williams, J.F. (1979, March/April). On being non-Indian. *Foundation News.*

Cultural Competence and the Systems of Care Planning Model
Consolidation of Two Planning Strategies

Daniel D. Jordan

As people from differing cultural backgrounds come into more frequent contact with each other, cultural competence is becoming an increasingly important issue for human services systems of care. Cultural competence is fundamental to providing cost-effective services that reduce risk, avoid liability, and maintain high-quality outcomes. A variety of approaches have been proposed for implementing cultural competence plans, but they have neither required nor been incorporated into a larger human services system planning framework. Cultural competence models tend to be stand-alone systems that are added to existing frameworks. This work is an effort to merge two models—one of which focuses on cultural issues and the other of which concentrates on a general systems-planning framework—into a single planning strategy that is based on open systems theory. The combined model offers a more complete structure for planning and evaluating human services systems than either model offers alone.

The sentiment with regard to racism and discrimination in many quarters of American society as the United States begins the 21st century is that "enough is enough." The United States has progressed far enough and enough has been done in its efforts to create an equal society that it can stop compensating for historical social inequities. Affirmative action programs have taken a beating and are being rolled back, and their eventual elimination is being discussed. Regardless of the flaws in the concept of affirmative action, no new strategies are being proposed; all that is being discussed is the elimination of one of the few public efforts to reverse discrimination.

United Nations statistics reveal a flaw in the arguments in favor of rolling back affirmative action programs. The United Nations Development Program (1993) created an Index of Human Development designed to assess countries in terms of not just limited economic development but also a number of other measures, including civil rights and housing and employment opportunities. Japan was ranked first according to this index, followed by four Scandinavian countries. All of the top five countries are small and culturally fairly uniform. The United States was ranked sixth, which might be considered impressive, considering that the United States is a large, heterogeneous country.

The United Nations Development Program also analyzed human development according to major ethnic categories within countries. In this disaggregated picture, the results were different. Caucasians in the United States were ranked first in terms of human development, ahead of all other ethnic categories, including Japanese Asians. African Americans were ranked thirty-first, and Hispanic Americans were ranked thirty-fourth, behind Afghanis. Clearly, the actual status of cross-cultural relations in American society does not match the rather glib rhetoric that seems to be driving public policy to reverse efforts to improve the social and economic equity among ethnic and cultural groups.

WHY CULTURAL COMPETENCE IS IMPORTANT

The scenario described in the preceding section calls for practical planning to increase cultural competence in the face of public policy that seems intent on reducing cultural equity for members of ethnic minority groups. Implementing strategies that support diversity and acknowledge the value of cultural variation and richness may be one way to help dominant cultures understand the benefits of cultural diversity. It is as important to maintain cultural diversity within a social system as it is to maintain diversity within a gene pool. In terms of the long-range survival of a society, engaging in cultural chauvinism or, to put it another way, deciding that there is one best way to understand the nature of reality is just as dangerous as deciding that there is one best set of genes, which would lead to inbreeding and thus the decline of the species.

The word *culture* "seems to refer to learned or acquired behaviors or traits attributable to the socialization experiences resulting from membership in particular systems or institutions within a society" (Helms, 1992, p. 1091). Any organization working in a community comprising people of diverse cultural backgrounds needs to understand the varieties of learned or acquired behaviors, beliefs, attitudes, and assumptions within the various cultural groups within its area of influence. An organization must also recognize that the concept of culture or ethnicity may be useful at some level, that cultural identity is a heterogeneous concept, and that people's identification with a particular culture may not lend much information in the way of predictive validity to service providers working with those people (Phinney, 1996). These concepts demand that the organization examine its level of cultural competence. States whose demographic changes reflect significant increases in the numbers of people from ethnic minority groups or of new immigrants experience increasing challenges to their service delivery systems. Cultural competence is not a specialty relevant only to certain people. It is a fundamental component of providing services to all people, regardless of their ethnicity, cultural background, age, or sex (Ogawa, 1990; Pedersen, 1991). Cultural competence is just as important for Caucasian middle-class males as it is for recent immigrants from different cultures. Speight, Myers, Cox, and Highlen stated that "all counseling is cross-cultural or multicultural" (1991, p. 29).

Cultural competence is a win-win situation because it benefits everyone in the following ways:

- *Providers* are empowered to work more effectively and efficiently with the increasingly diverse communities that they serve.
- *Clients* receive services that are in tune with their cultural beliefs and consistent with their needs.
- The *system of care* is better used and equitably distributes resources, develops higher staff morale, and works in harmony with the ethnic minority community that it serves.
- *Minority communities* are able to express their views and let their needs be articulated and included as an integral part of an ongoing agency assessment and service delivery process.
- *Funding agencies* can demonstrate to legislators the effective use of taxpayer dollars.
- *Taxpayers* can see that their tax dollars are more efficiently used and are not being wasted.

In the long run, cultural competence also increases the richness of the fabric of a society.

THE APPROACH

Efforts to improve the competence of individuals must be developed within the framework of efforts to increase the overall competence of systems. The cultural competence model is a nationally recognized approach sponsored by the National Institute of Mental Health (Cross, Bazron, Dennis, & Isaacs, 1989). Cross and colleagues defined *cultural competence* as "the capacity to work within the context of culturally integrated patterns of human behavior as defined by the group" (1989, p. 3). Cultural competence is a set of congruent behaviors, attitudes, and policies that come together in a system or agency or among individuals that enables them to work effectively in cross-cultural situations.

Cross and colleagues' (1989) cultural competence model offers a continuum of levels of cultural competence, from destructiveness to advanced cultural competence. For the purposes of analyzing the existing status of an organization, this concept is useful. It allows an analyst to scale an organization's cultural competence status in a way that can help point to improvements that can be made. The continuum itself, however, has no links to how to understand the components of an organization. To understand an organization's components requires an organizational model such as the open systems theory–based approach that Senge (1990) developed, which breaks down an organization into its component processes and work and information flows.

Figure 1 offers a blank template that allows planners to conduct a self-assessment of their organizations' levels of cultural competence. An organization can be rated according to its level of cultural competence, and it can begin to develop plans for increasing its ability to provide more culturally competent services. Planners can use this tool to review their own systems of care and to note their organizations' levels of competence. Using this tool can be a productive exercise through which to take policy makers and planners. The tool offers insights into the present status of a system of care and what may need to be done to improve the system's levels of competence.

Figure 1 can also be adapted to contain any type of organizational components across the top of the matrix. For example, a planner may want to evaluate the status of the human resources division of an organization. Functions such as recruitment practices, retention activities and incentives, advertising distribution, policies for advancement, and complaint procedures all may be inserted as column headings in the matrix. Each function can then be rated for its level of cultural competence.

An Applied Example

The cultural competence continuum can be applied to the internal operations of an agency (e.g., personnel procedures) or to the manner in which services are actually delivered. The systems of care model (Jordan, 1997; Jordan & Hernandez, 1989) provides a way to organize the components of a service system.

The six characteristics of the systems of care planning model outlined in the list that follows provide a conceptual framework for implementing systemwide changes. The goal is to develop an improved service delivery system and a marketing strategy to promote the system with the taxpayer, politicians, and policy makers. Briefly, the planning components in this approach follow the following six steps:

Cultural competence continuum	Systems of care model categories				
Levels of cultural functioning	Risk pools and targeted populations	System goals	Partnerships	Services	Evaluation
Advanced cultural competence Standards					
Competence					
Precompetence					
Cultural blindness					
Incapacity					
Destructiveness					
Covert destructiveness via exclusion					
Overt destructiveness via maltreatment					

Figure 1. Cultural competence and systems of care matrix.

51

1. *Risk pools:* Identify the populations from which targeted clients are to be drawn. For example, the state of California has established residents who are eligible for Medi-Cal as the primary risk pool from which county mental health departments are to draw their clients.
2. *Targeted populations:* Targeted populations in the mental health field are those citizens with severe mental illnesses for whom public sector agencies have joint responsibility and are incurring expenses. These clients are drawn from the established risk pools, defined in this case by public policy as residents who are eligible for Medi-Cal.
3. *Goals:* The goals, broadly stated, are to increase independent living skills and opportunities (e.g., the abilities of children to stay with their families, function in school, stay out of correctional facilities). Central to these goals is offsetting costs by reducing the need for and use of public sector services such as group homes, state hospitals, and jails.
4. *Partnerships:* At all levels of the system, create partnerships among public agencies, private service providers and funding sources, and even the families and clients themselves. Discover what resources actually exist in the community. Identify the current flow of clients through each public agency and where agencies interact. Both of these elements may change; therefore, create "before" and "after" sets of flow diagrams.
5. *Services:* Based on the outcomes of the four preceding steps, integrate services across relevant agencies. Consider which structural characteristics need to be modified to provide collaborative services. Every service should be conceptualized as an alternative to a more expensive program. The point is to figure out which services the targeted populations need, what the system of care is designed to achieve, and with whom agencies can and should work and then design services on the basis of that information. Following this approach will lead to the design of different systems of care across communities. They may focus on different groups and be structured in unique ways.
6. *Evaluation:* Identify the system's critical success factors. These are the indicators that, if the trends go in the right direction, will lead policy makers and planners to agree that the system has succeeded; thus, such indicators can be used to garner support for continued funding for the system of care. Also, implement evaluation methods that provide internal feedback loops to enable managers and staff to adjust their course as time goes on. In the current policy climate, it is critical to focus on measures that provide fiscal account-

ability. External costs, not just costs within a component of the system of care, must be included in the evaluation.

Combining the continuum of levels of cultural competence with the systems of care planning model allows for a more detailed understanding of an organization's status regarding its ability to serve a diverse population. A schema of the combined models is presented in Figure 2. The systems of care planning model's six planning categories are listed across the top of the table, and the cultural competence continuum is displayed down the left-hand column. The table lists identifying features that would be seen if, for example, a system identified risk pools and targeted its intervention populations in a culturally proficient manner (see the cell in the upper-left-hand corner).

A NEW DEFINITION OF ADVANCED CULTURAL COMPETENCE

Once an analysis of an organization is conducted, the goal is to develop a plan that will help the organization's managers and planners improve the organization's competence level. With this goal, a further definition of the concept of *advanced cultural competence* is needed. Cross and colleagues' (1989) definition is rhetorically useful but is not easily operationalized as presented. A system engaged in advanced cultural competence is made up of three components:

1. Equal access
2. Appropriate services
3. Equitable outcomes

Equal Access

The equal access component of advanced cultural competence proposes that a system of care must ensure that all members of a community have equal access to services, regardless of differences in language, cultural background, social status, or any other demographic variable that differentiates one group from another. The equal access component has three interacting features. The first addresses the question of comparing the pool of served clients with the underlying census of likely potential clients. This issue goes to the question of outreach. The second feature addresses whether potential clients who request services are admitted or rejected at similar rates across relevant ethnic and cultural groups. Questions related to admissions criteria, policies, structures, and methods are addressed in this feature. Third, once clients are admitted into the system of care, the equal access component addresses into which pathways clients are routed to receive services. "Managed care systems

Cultural competence continuum	Systems of care model categories				
Levels of cultural functioning	Risk pools and targeted populations	System goals	Partnerships	Services	Evaluation
Advanced cultural competence Standards	Agency is vigilant about and has policies and procedures to respond to new ethnic groups in client pool. Outreach is extended to all ethnic groups in the demographic pool. Target population members who receive services are drawn equitably from all local cultural and ethnic groups. Individual groups are identified and valued.	Provision of culturally relevant services Provision of equitable and culturally relevant services to all cultural groups Proactive plans to learn about the culture and history of new ethnic groups Mutual education about the dominant and ethnic minority cultures Agency continuously learns about cultural groups and improves its competencies.	Proactive involvement with institutions in contact with new groups Conduct cultural competence advocacy and training with other agencies Form partnerships with culture-specific agencies Federal, state, and local elected officials coordinate efforts with local public and private agencies consistent with values of the various cultural groups.	Multicultural and multilingual staff Provided in each client's dominant language Service providers understand and utilize the strengths of a culture in service delivery. System and cultural groups work in harmony with each other. Cultural groups and agencies are educated (by the agency, if necessary) about the operations of the system. Service delivery staff engage in empathic experiencing. Services are designed to improve the cultural relations not just between staff and clients but also among all clients and the community.	Includes ethnicity as a variable in critical areas Evaluates differences in outcomes across cultural groups and provides feedback with plans for improvement Evaluates distribution of clients compared with demographic pool Evaluates involvement with other agencies, including training, participation, and distribution of clients from those agencies

Figure 2.   Sample filled-in cultural competence and systems of care matrix.

(continued)

Advanced cultural competence Standards—*continued*					
Examples	The client mix reflects the demographic distribution of ethnic groups. Services are designed to meet the particular needs of each cultural group.	To improve the relationship, on a cultural level, between staff and clients. To help other agencies become more culturally proficient. To help clients improve their relationships with members of other cultural groups. Goals are consistent with cultural values of each group. The system provides services designed to enhance and improve relationships among members of differing ethnicities.	Inform public and community groups of available services and how to utilize the system to meet needs of target population. Partnerships are formed with cultural and community groups to improve communications bewen the system and the community.	Cultural proficiency assessment tools and processes are utilized for the agency. Staff have language skills matching local language groups. The decor of program sites reflects the unit's cultural distribution.	The evaluation includes outcome breakdowns by ethnic categories. Ethnicity-specific measures are included where appropriate. Ethnic groups help inform the design of the evaluation system.

(continued)

Figure 2. (continued)

Cultural competence continuum	Systems of care model categories				
Levels of cultural functioning	Risk pools and targeted populations	System goals	Partnerships	Services	Evaluation
Competence	Client distribution matches demographic base. The target population comprises a variety of minority, ethnic, and cultural groups, and those groups are identified.	Goals allow for differences across ethnic groups. To expand cultural knowledge and resources. Commitment to and support for policies that enhance services to clients from diverse backgrounds	Seeks advice from the various minority communities	Continuous self-assessment. Service models and practices are adapted to the needs of individual minority groups.	Compares client ethnicity distributions with population distributions. Compares each client ethnic group against other groups for resource allocation and outcomes
Precompetence	Distribution of clients by ethnicity is understood to be an issue, but nothing is done to change policies and procedures to make it happen.	To deliver quality services. Commitment to civil rights. To help. To improve recognized systemic weaknesses. Basic goals are set to fulfill the obligation to minorities, but no more.	Partnerships with cultural agencies are allowed but are not sought.	Staff may lack information about the possibilities of how to provide culturally proficient services. Staff explore how to serve their clients more proficiently. Token hiring practices	Compares each client ethnic group against other groups but makes no comparisons against population distributions

(continued)

| Cultural blindness | Clients are selected for treatment without regard to ethnic or cultural background. Only those target population members who are willing to assimilate are accepted for service. | Goals are set without regard to cultural issues. Goals do not build on and incorporate strengths of minority cultures. | No efforts are made to connect with cultural groups or agencies. | Clients are assigned to staff without regard for matching skills and interests with a client's cultural issues. Services are designed according to one standard template for all groups. Clients are socialized to accept what is offered; those who do not are isolated or ejected from service as noncompliant. Services reject strengths of a culture and attempt to impose the dominant culture's strengths and values. Services focus on how minority members have created their own problems, thus blaming the victim. | No evaluation of ethnic distribution of resources, outcomes, or other measures are conducted. Ethnicity is not included as an evaluation variable. |

(continued)

Figure 2. *(continued)*

Cultural competence continuum	Systems of care model categories				
Levels of cultural functioning	Risk pools and targeted populations	System goals	Partnerships	Services	Evaluation
Incapacity	Clients are segregated by ethnicity.	To help keep people of differing ethnicities "in their place"	Discriminatory policies of other agencies are reinforced and supported.	No efforts are made to serve minority clients in the community. No multilingual services are available. Services are "separate but equal." Services are disproportionately provided to the dominant cultural group.	Evaluation is slanted to show that what minority groups receive is really the best for them.
Destructiveness Covert destructiveness via exclusion	Ethnic minority clients who meet target population criteria are excluded from services.	Minimal expectations of excluded groups	Federal, state, and local elected officials coordinate efforts with local public and private agencies to exclude cultural groups.	"Separate but equal" treatment	Evaluation describes how excluded groups should be content with their lot.
Overt destructiveness via maltreatment	Ethnic minority target population members are mistreated, "punished" for needing services. Specific groups are selected for maltreatment.	"Keep people in their place" "Elimination" of the group from society	Federal, state, and local elected officials coordinate efforts with local public and private agencies to oppress cultural groups.	Services designed to keep people in their places	Evaluation points out how minorities get too much, uses negative events and cases to stereotype entire groups.

today largely ignore issues of quality of care and *access to care* [emphasis added]" (Van den Bos, 1993, p. 288). Kiesler (1992) also made the point that health and mental health policies have been driven mainly by funding issues and by controlling costs for those who receive Medicare or Medicaid while they have ignored the implications of what happens to those who are not allowed access to services. Public policies with regard to so-called access questions have focused mostly on whether people who have an identified diagnosis actually have access to services that are appropriate to that diagnosis or need. For example, does someone who is identified as having an appendix that is about to rupture get appropriate medical care? Those who have a problem or an illness but are not identified are ignored in typical discussions about access.

Evaluating access, appropriateness, and outcomes requires different types of information and strategies. Equal access involves comparing population, risk pool, and current client base demographic characteristics. Such data are typically reasonably straightforward, if often labor intensive, to collate. For example, local census data should be relatively easy to find but may require a fair amount of labor to tabulate into geographic units of analysis useful to program planners. A program's geographic boundaries may not fit neatly within ZIP codes or census tracts. As noted, in California, people eligible to receive Medi-Cal have been identified as public mental health agencies' primary risk pool. Having identified this risk pool, all three levels of data, general census, risk pools (i.e., Medi-Cal recipients), and actual clients served can be compared. In the case of one county, the three sets of numbers yielded unexpected results. In brief summary, about two thirds of the general population of the county are Caucasian, one quarter are Hispanic, and the rest are African American and other. This demographic pattern matches the county mental health department's client distribution to within a few percentage points. Thus, at first glance, it appears that the agency has done a good job of offering equal access to all residents. The issue of access, however, is more complex than that. Because the officially recognized risk pool for provision of public mental health services is people who are eligible to receive Medi-Cal, the client group must be compared with that group; but people who receive Medi-Cal have a different ethnic distribution. Roughly two thirds of people eligible to receive Medi-Cal are Hispanic, one quarter are Caucasian, and the rest are African American and other. This distribution essentially reverses the population demographics of the two largest ethnic groups in the county. Comparing the client pool with the makeup of the general population yields apparently reasonably balanced results; however, comparing clients with the identified risk pool does not. This contradiction suggests that the department needs to be more proactive in its outreach efforts to the Hispanic population.

Members of various cultural groups may not respond to public service agencies in the same ways. Even when these agencies employ aggressive outreach strategies, members of a particular cultural group may simply choose to use services at higher or lower rates than individuals from other cultural groups. Whether the client demographic distribution patterns exactly match either population or risk pool demographic distribution patterns is thus not an outcome issue per se. That is the difference in this approach from affirmative action, which calls for (or at least is argued to call for) numeric parity based on some criteria. Equal access provides a marker that offers suggestions about outreach needs.

If such outreach is actually and sincerely conducted and different cultural groups continue to respond at different rates, then the effects of culture may be playing an important role in determining whether and how people choose to utilize services. An external verification might be to work with representatives of the cultural group who could provide insights into why a group may tend to underutilize available resources. Consulting with knowledgeable representatives may provide useful insights into the design of outreach strategies and tactics. Relevant questions may include, for example, the following:

- Are needs assessments conducted to determine the distribution of linguistic and cultural groups in the communities served?
- Does the distribution of clients by ethnicity resemble the distribution of ethnicities in the community? Note that because the number of clients may be small, yielding little statistical power, assessing the distribution of ethnicity among a system's clients may not be possible on a strictly statistical basis.
- Do all clients have equal access to the various categories of service in a system?
- Are the ethnic and cultural groups represented in the client population equally distributed among the various classes of services?
- Are ethnicity-specific services available (e.g., Spanish-speaking therapists and service coordinators, therapy groups conducted in Spanish)?

One simple method for increasing staff's awareness of cultural factors is to include their assessments in client intakes. Mental health intake procedures typically include diagnostics, family or social supports, presenting symptoms, and the like. Adding "Cultural Factors Affecting the Client" as an intake variable category for clinicians to assess is a simple matter. Although including this category will not make staff instantly competent in their interactions with clients of color, it will get them to attend to the impact of culture on the client who is being assessed.

Appropriate Services

As noted previously, Medicaid policy originally defined *access to services* essentially as whether people received appropriate services after being admitted to a system of care. For example, did someone who needed to have his or her appendix removed actually get it done, or did the medical team mistakenly take out his or her tonsils instead? Access questions were asked only with regard to those people who had gotten inside the door. In this model, the question of access focuses on who receives services relative to the risk pool. Once all targeted population members have an equal chance of gaining access to services, the services actually provided must be tailored to the specific needs of each cultural group. It is not enough to lure people in but then provide "cookie cutter," "one size fits all" services.

Systems of care and program planners should not try to export or import model programs. The details of a situation that make a program successful in one location may not be relevant in another situation. This point is especially important when addressing cultural factors. A program or service design that is effective for one cultural group may not be applicable to another group. The systems of care model's emphasis on the need to tailor services becomes doubly important when the need to design services for culturally diverse populations is confronted.

Service systems may adopt different strategies for providing equal access ranging along a continuum from complete integration within every program and site to separate programs tailored to the needs of each relevant cultural group. Both of these extremes have built-in weaknesses and strengths. Fully integrating all services and forcing all clients into the same program may tend to homogenize resources and force ethnic minority groups into a larger unified approach to services. Conversely, separating services by cultural groups leads to complaints leveled against so-called separate but equal types of programming. In the end, keeping programs equal in terms of quality and quantity of care will be a problem. The best strategy may be a blending of these two types of approaches: having some services designed so that anyone can take advantage of them and others tailored to meet specific needs.

Ethnicity-specific services may be relevant in some settings. Professionals have debated whether ethnicity-specific services can be culturally competent or represent a form of reverse discrimination. The solution to this question is to address cultural competence at the system of care level. The relevant issue is whether appropriate services are available in the system to all cultural groups. Any one program may be tailored to a specific cultural group (including even programs tailored to Caucasian males), whereas other services may be fairly generic and available to all clients (e.g., socialization centers). The issue is whether those who need services can find appropriate services. Such strategies require ongoing needs assessments and careful attention to changing needs among and within cultural groups.

A major implication of such thinking is that systems of care and their staff members must be amenable to change. The days of implementing a program that remains static for the entire careers of its staff members are gone (if they ever really were legitimate). Staff must be socialized to accept change and the idea that everything that they know or to which they are accustomed may be changed to accommodate some new service design. Staff adaptability is a paramount need. Cultural competence requires not that every staff member have an intimate knowledge of every culture but that they have an attitude about being open to understanding new cultures and interpreting new events with that same kind of openness to trying to see circumstances through another person's eyes.

Whether services are appropriate for meeting the needs of each individual is a complicated issue. The problem is in trying to identify what are appropriate services across cultural groups. Clearly, the traditional 50-minute hour does not work for everyone (including many dominant-culture Caucasians). Relatively basic issues include making efforts to hire staff who speak the languages represented in the potential client pool and staff who share the ethnic background of the clients that the system serves. In addressing these issues, system of care administrators need to ask themselves questions such as the following:

- Do all clients have access to a range of services?
- Are services provided in the languages of the communities served?
- Have staff been trained in the principles of cultural competence, and are they familiar with the ethnic groups in their service area?
- Are program facilities decorated in such a way as to help anyone who enters feel comfortable in his or her surroundings? For example, magazines may be made available for people in waiting rooms or drop-in centers. They should include ethnicity-specific magazines and/or magazines written in the clients' primary languages.
- Are staff trained to understand the idea that, for example, just because a client says something like "Demons are invading my body" does not mean that the client is necessarily psychotic. The client may simply be describing a pain using his or her only known cultural metaphor as a framework.

An example may help to illustrate the last item in the preceding list. An older monolingual Spanish-speaking Mexican woman visiting her family in the United States was brought to a hospital emergency room. She was complaining of demons invading her body and causing pain. In her culture, the types of symptoms she was experiencing were attributed to these demons. The emergency room physician immediately tried to send her to the hospital's psychiatric unit. A mental health worker who understood the woman's culture was able to interpret not just the woman's description of demons but her meaning. She was able to turn descriptions of demons into the language of modern medicine and get the physician to assess the underlying symptoms themselves. The physician was then able to make an accurate diagnosis of spinal meningitis, resulting in delivery of a proper intervention and perhaps saving the woman's life. Had she been sent to the psychiatric unit under the assumption that she was displaying psychotic symptoms, she likely would have been mistreated and may even have died.

Equitable Outcomes

The results of cultural competence efforts in systems of care must be assessed. Systems of care may provide equal access and even tailor services to specific groups but may fail in achieving positive outcomes with a particular group. The adjective *equitable*, not *equal*, is used to describe outcomes of mental health services with clients from differing ethnic backgrounds. Different groups may have different needs and want different outcomes within a category of need. Services must be tailored to clients' needs, and outcomes must be assessed with the same level of cultural specificity.

An overall systems goal may be improving clients' living situations. This goal could be valid for all clients served. To understand the impact of their efforts, service providers must understand how each cultural group served defines a good living situation. For example, as a broad generalization, Hispanic cultures tend to have stronger and more extensive family supports than Caucasians. It is more common and acceptable for Hispanics to live in extended-family settings. Although one goal of a mental health system may be to help its clients find and stay in decent housing, that may mean different things based on the clients' cultural contexts. Care must be taken to understand how the goal of decent housing is understood in different cultural contexts and incorporate these distinctions into evaluation strategies.

Analysis of equitable outcomes requires measuring those areas relevant to both the service system and the individuals and cultural groups served. Cultural competence outcomes can apply to internal procedural issues, organizational structures, and the actual results of service delivery. The fact that some outcomes may not apply or that they apply differently to some groups must be balanced against the danger that allowing for different outcomes could result in some groups' receiving lower-quality services. For example, for a Caucasian male from a nuclear family background, finding an apartment and living independently (i.e., alone) may be a very positive outcome. For someone from a culture in which continuing to live in an extended-family environment throughout adulthood is common and valued (both by the culture and, more important, by the identified client), being able to remain stably with the extended family may be considered an equally good outcome. Attempting to direct that person into a single-room apartment may be highly inappropriate and may even cause harm. Allowing for such differences while maintaining high standards for each client is a delicate balance.

Equitable outcomes are evident when levels of satisfaction with services and functional outcomes are similar across cultural groups. Equity in outcomes can be measured by levels of satisfaction across cultural groups. For example, are Hispanics and Caucasians equally satisfied with the outcomes of their interventions related to improvements in their living situations? Their actual situations may be different; but if the groups are equally satisfied, then there is equity in their outcomes. Relevant questions may include the following:

- Are clients from served cultural groups equally satisfied with services and with the outcomes of those services?
- Are clients from different ethnic groups as likely to report improvements in their lives in the various categories measured?
- Do clients achieve improvements in the areas considered relevant by program managers and evaluators?
- Do all clients report improvements in their lives? Allowing clients to establish those areas relevant to their own situations is necessary, and clustering the patterns across ethnic groups is required.

PLANNING FOR INDIVIDUAL MANAGERS AND STAFF MEMBERS

Each staff member in the system of care organization can make an individual action plan for improving his or her personal cultural competence as well as the organization's competence. This planning can be begun by the staff member's asking him- or herself two questions:

1. What additional knowledge, new skills, and changes in attitude do I need to help me promote and provide equal access, appropriate services, and equitable outcomes?

2. What do I need to do to improve my knowledge, skills, and attitudes to promote and provide equal access, appropriate services, and equitable outcomes?

Each staff member should establish a list of activities in which to engage and a time line for pursuing them. Whatever his or her role in the organization, each staff member should examine his or her responsibilities and establish how far along the hierarchy of competence each activity is. Then the staff member should ask him- or herself what he or she can do to improve his or her status in terms of clients' access to services, the services themselves, and outcomes of intervention. Then staff can begin the process of making those changes and monitoring how well their efforts are working. Perhaps most important, staff must work with others in the organization to coordinate efforts into a unified organizational strategy for change.

REFERENCES

Cross, T.L., Bazron, B.J., Dennis, K.W., & Isaacs, M.R. (1989). *Towards a culturally competent system of care: Vol. I. Monograph on effective services for minority children who are seriously emotionally disturbed.* Washington, DC: Georgetown University, Child and Adolescent Service System Program, Technical Assistance Center.

Helms, J.E. (1992). Why is there no study of cultural equivalence in standardized cognitive ability testing? *American Psychologist, 47,* 1083–1101.

Jordan, D.D. (1997). The Ventura Planning Model: Lessons in reforming a system. In M.C. Roberts (Ed.), *Model programs in child and family mental health* (pp. 373–390). Mahwah, NJ: Lawrence Erlbaum Associates.

Jordan, D.D., & Hernandez, M. (1989). The Ventura Planning Model: A proposal for mental health reform. *Journal of Mental Health Administration, 17,* 26–47.

Kiesler, C.A. (1992). U.S. mental health policy: Doomed to fail. *American Psychologist, 47,* 349–360.

Ogawa, B. (1990). *Color of justice.* Sacramento: State of California, Office of Criminal Justice Planning.

Pedersen, P.B. (1991). Multiculturalism as a generic approach to counseling. *Journal of Counseling and Development, 70,* 6–12.

Phinney, J.S. (1996). When we talk about American ethnic groups, what do we mean? *American Psychologist, 51,* 918–925.

Senge, P.M. (1990). *The fifth discipline: The art and practice of the learning organization.* New York: Doubleday.

Speight, S.L., Myers, L.J., Cox, C.I., & Highlen, P.S. (1991). A redefinition of multicultural counseling. *Journal of Counseling and Development, 70,* 29–36.

United Nations Human Development Program. (1993). *Human development report 1993: People's participation.* New York: Oxford University Press.

Van den Bos, G.R. (1993). U.S. mental health policy: Proactive evolution in the midst of health care reform. *American Psychologist, 48,* 283–290.

Applying Cultural Competence Principles within a State Mental Health System

Commitment, Planning, and Implementation

Jerome H. Hanley

With the inception of the national Child and Adolescent Service System Program (CASSP) in 1984, the concept of cultural competence received its initial national exposure (Day & Roberts, 1991). Through the widely accepted work of Cross, Bazron, Dennis, and Isaacs (1989) on cultural competence, the struggle to disseminate the concepts underlying cultural competence and foster their application has been the mission of the Georgetown Cultural Competence Committee (formerly the CASSP Minority Initiative Committee). The committee, composed of children's mental health professionals and parents from the four major ethnic groups in the United States (African Americans, Latinos, Native Americans, and Asian Americans), was formed in 1988 and has served as the "cultural competence conscience" of CASSP. Although cultural competence is most frequently viewed in terms of clinical services (Gibbs & Haring, 1989; Pinderhughes, 1989), application of cultural competence concepts in large organizations and systems of care has always been of paramount importance (Isaacs & Benjamin, 1991).

The author thanks the South Carolina Department of Mental Health Division of Children, Adolescents, and Their Families team members for their unwavering support of and commitment to South Carolina's children and adolescents and their families and for being a super group of professionals: Kathy B. Bryant, Beth V. Freeman, and Louise K. Johnson. The author also extends a special thank-you to Veronica W. Gates for her devoted preparation of this manuscript of this chapter. May the Creator continue to watch over each of you. The author also wishes to thank Delores Macy, Director of the South Carolina Department of Mental Health Cultural Action Program, and the department-wide cultural competence committee for their perseverance and commitment to the principles of cultural competence.

This chapter conveys the efforts and activities involved in planning and implementing a broad-based cultural competence initiative within a statewide public mental health system of care. What follows is an effort to present not a blueprint for all cultural competence initiatives but rather an account of how the South Carolina Department of Mental Health (SCDMH) developed its cultural competence program, the Cultural Action Program (CAP), in the hope that one state's cultural competence development process may serve as a model for other states to follow.

HISTORICAL AND CONTEXTUAL
BASES FOR ADDRESSING DIVERSITY ISSUES

No issue has been more divisive in the United States than that of color, beginning with the exclusionary decisions of America's founders regarding race (Higginbotham, 1978). Division of people along color and cultural lines benefits few and harms many (Conniff & Davis, 1994; Franklin, 1993; National Spiritual Assembly of the Baha'is of the United States, 1991; Turner & Cabbell, 1985; West, 1996). Notwithstanding rhetoric to the contrary in the 1990s, racism—at both the individual and institutional levels—continues to flourish (Hacker, 1992; Kozol, 1991). The concept of cultural competence was always intended to acknowledge the existence and dangers of racism (Hanley, 1994). It is therefore disturbing when cultural competence is confused with affirmative action, bilingualism, and quotas and particularly so when it is referred to as a return to segregation (Egan, 1993; Steele, 1991).

STATE OVERVIEW AND PRECURSOR TO
SOUTH CAROLINA'S CULTURAL COMPETENCE INITIATIVE

The movement from the initial stages of an idea to the formulation of the proposal to the launching of a systemwide initiative is complex and requires good timing and spiritual intervention. To appreciate the barriers that were overcome and the planning and implementation strategies that were selected for South Carolina's cultural competence initiative, one needs to understand the historical and cultural contexts of both South Carolina and SCDMH, especially in terms of previous attempts to address issues of racial and cultural diversity.

South Carolina, like the other southeastern states, has a long history of racial diversity (see Table 1). The primary racial groups of the state's population have been African Americans and Caucasians. This demographic pattern remains in the 1990s, even though the representation of other racial and ethnic groups in the state's population is growing (Pender & Gibson, 1995). In *Towards a Culturally Competent System of*

Table 1. South Carolina's diverse population, 1990

Race	N	Percentage of statewide population
White	2,406,974	68.8716
African American	1,039,884	29.7546
Latino	30,551	.8742
Native American	8,246	.2359
Other	9,217	.2637
Total	3,494,872	

Source: Pender and Gibson (1995).
N, total population broken down by ethnicity

Care: Programs Which Utilize Culturally Competent Principles (Isaacs & Benjamin, 1991), 10 programs that were chosen from more than 100 that had been nominated from across the United States were used to highlight various cultural competence principles. Few program nominations were received from the southeastern states, and, upon review, not one was identified as embodying the core principles and warranting an extensive site visit. To find an explanation for what appeared to be a lack of commitment to cultural competence in South Carolina, the author of this chapter conducted an informal survey of Caucasian employees older than the age of 50 in the SCDMH. The informally derived finding was a perception that, in focusing on cultural differences, the call for cultural competence was in conflict with the goals of the civil rights movement, which sought "to foster all people being treated the same" (Hanley, 1991, quoted in Isaacs & Benjamin, 1991, p. 4). Ironically, some consider the attempt to challenge racism by recognizing and reinforcing cultural diversity a return to segregation.

In 1990, the SCDMH employed 6,057 people, a figure that had increased only slightly by 1995 to 6,174. As the South Carolina public mental health authority, SCDMH operates 17 community mental health centers and 8 hospitals. In 1990, African Americans comprised 52.7% of the department's work force, primarily in support and unskilled positions. Asian Americans, Latinos, and Native Americans comprised only .012% of the total SCDMH work force in 1995.

In 1990, none of the community mental health center directors and hospital directors employed by SCDMH were African Americans, Asian Americans, Native Americans, or Latinos. Two African Americans served on the department's management team: the deputy commissioner for clinical services (a psychiatrist) and the department's affirmative action officer. During the same period, the department served 79,991 clients (duplicated count [i.e., same client may have been served more than once]), of which 63.4% were Caucasians and 35.7% were African Americans; the combined total of Latinos, Asian Americans, Native Americans, and all others amounted to less than 1% of the clients whom the department served (SCDMH, 1996).

FIRST DEPARTMENTAL ATTEMPT TO ADDRESS DIVERSITY

In 1978, a group of SCDMH employees, most of whom were African Americans, joined forces to create the Cross-Cultural Action Council for Mental Health. The primary purpose of this group was to raise the consciousness of the agency toward African American employees and clinical issues through cross-cultural discussions and an annual 3-day conference. Each February, the group holds a conference that targets mental health and related human services issues. The conference is supported philosophically and financially by the SCDMH. Unfortunately, few Caucasians have attended the conference over the years. Prior to 1991, the conference was the sole cross-cultural diversity-training effort within the department. The Cross-Cultural Council, an independent, multiracial organization, eventually became a not-for-profit organization, broadening its membership to include professionals from the state's other health and human services agencies that are concerned with cross-cultural issues. The conference continues to exist and grow and has expanded its focus to include discussion of gay and lesbian issues as well as issues of Caucasian subcultural groups such as the residents of Appalachia.

SECOND DEPARTMENTAL ATTEMPT TO ADDRESS DIVERSITY

The Rural and African American Task Force was established within the SCDMH in 1991 through the office of the deputy commissioner for clinical services—the third-ranking position in the department, which at the time was held by an African American. The SCDMH Affirmative Action Officer was appointed chair of the task force, and the task force was composed of department, university, medical, community, and law enforcement representatives. In hindsight, this effort probably was doomed from its inception. Several of the more salient reasons for that conclusion included the following:

- The effort was viewed by many as not having the support of the SCDMH director.
- The effort lacked the personal involvement of the deputy director for clinical services.
- Over time, the participants' energy and commitment waned as indicated by declining and sporadic attendance because few concrete results were being realized.

Nonetheless, a report that highlighted the development of a mission statement, guiding principles, value statement, and administrative and organizational issues was completed. To no task force member's surprise, this effort and its resultant documentation had no impact on the department's operations or policies, and none of its recommendations were formally adopted or implemented.

SETTING THE STAGE FOR CULTURAL COMPETENCE

The collapse of the SCDMH task force's effort was dramatic evidence of the need for a systemwide, broad-based cultural competence effort; a need to enhance the value of the Cross-Cultural Council and its conference; and the desirability of demonstrating the benefits of the specific cultural competence initiative in the Division of Children, Adolescents, and Their Families (CAF) of the SCDMH. When these developments were occurring in 1993, the political climate in South Carolina appeared favorable for such an initiative.

Systems change does not occur in a vacuum. Identifying opportunities and framing change strategies in the context of those opportunities are critical to their acceptance. Members of the Black Caucus of the South Carolina state legislature had been meeting with the SCDMH agency director to express their concerns over the dearth of people of color in management and other positions carrying a high degree of responsibility and the large number of grievances being initiated by African American employees in low-status jobs (e.g., mental health specialist, housekeeping classifications). Meanwhile, in addition to the state legislature's concerns, the Cross-Cultural Council had raised several issues that had contributed to the creation of the African American Rural Task Force.

Under those circumstances, CAF initiated a major effort to diversify its work force racially as the first step in a broader cultural competence effort in the department's 17 community mental health centers. The driving change in policy was that staff and management of any service offered to children and their families should reflect the racial and ethnic distribution of the community's population. When communities see mental health services and programs offered, they must see representatives of their communities in responsible professional and clinical positions. The implementation of the CAF policy did not mean then, nor does it mean in 1998, that Caucasian staff should serve only Caucasian clients and that African American staff should serve only African American clients.

At the same time as the CAF policy was being developed, the cultural competence issue was being discussed with the community mental health centers' directors and CAF service providers at their monthly meetings, with training in cultural competence being provided at some centers. As new services and programs were developed (e.g., family preservation, school-based day treatment, child welfare), a strong emphasis was placed on staff diversity and cultural competence. The most tangible result was an increase in CAF staff of color from 18% in 1990 to 27% in 1995. Although these efforts were confined to children's services, they were indicative of a possibility that a broader agency effort could likewise be successful.

EARLY FACTORS IN CONCEPTUALIZING
AN AGENCYWIDE CULTURAL COMPETENCE INITIATIVE

The conception of the agencywide cultural competence initiative rested with a small group of people, allowing for strategic planning and constituency building. The initial goal was to ensure that intragroup divisiveness did not weaken the effort. Because the Cross-Cultural Council was so well established and had served as the voice of employees of color, gaining their support was imperative.

The visionary of the cultural competence initiative called a meeting with the executive committee of the Cross-Cultural Council. He explained that the efforts of the council had been to address specific issues as they arose and to provide training to individuals on a voluntary basis. However, the intent of the proposed cultural competence initiative was to effect agencywide changes in all aspects of the SCDMH. The cultural competence initiative was intended not to replace the council or to indicate any failure on the part of the council but rather to build on its work. The Cross-Cultural Council's annual conference was to continue to train individual practitioners, clients, and administrators while becoming a broader cultural competence teaching vehicle. The conference's function would continue to be to improve the knowledge and skill levels of those individuals who attended. With the support of the cross-cultural executive committee and the success of CAF, the author of this chapter believed that the time was right to meet with the agency director to present the proposal and solicit his philosophical and fiscal support.

KEY ELEMENTS OF THE SOUTH CAROLINA DEPARTMENT
OF MENTAL HEALTH CULTURAL COMPETENCE INITIATIVE

The proposal for the SCDMH cultural competence initiative had to be simple while pointing out the specific problems that the initiative would address positively, in addition to describing implementation procedures; the resources required to support the initiative; and political considerations, including the potential risks—primarily political and regarding staff morale—to the director and the SCDMH itself. The following points constituted the basis of the proposal presented:

1. The SCDMH work force, including both service providers and management, lacked ethnic diversity. Most employees of color were clustered in lower-grade positions, a situation that had been challenged by the South Carolina legislature's Black Caucus.

2. A large percentage of the SCDMH's current and potential clients at the time that the proposal was developed were African Americans, and there were increasing numbers of Latino and Native American clients. Case outcomes among members of these populations were unsatisfactory.

3. CAF had achieved notable successes in its cultural competence pilot program.

4. Political and organizational risks existed that were exacerbated by the reluctance of South Carolina's general population and its legislature to deal with issues of race.

5. The South Carolina Department of Health and Environmental Control (DHEC) had established the Office of Minority Health, but that office had received only limited resources to support the cultural competence initiative.

6. Other states' public mental health authorities had embarked on similar initiatives and were available to provide consultation.

7. The current cultural competence status of the SCDMH could be measured and its progress could be assessed along the dimensions of staff knowledge of communities, personal involvement, resources, and linkages, as well as with regard to organizational policies and procedures, staffing, and outreach to communities of color.

8. Considered in light of the anticipated return on the investment for the initiative, the initial and long-term costs were minimal (e.g., initial consultation, salary of staff member to lead initiative).

9. The Cross-Cultural Council supported the initiative, as did key advocacy groups and the SCDMH human resources development director.

10. The employee initiating and presenting the proposal had a solid track record on issues of diversity, both within the agency and nationally.

11. The SCDMH had embarked on a significant Total Quality Management initiative, and development of cultural competence was a natural component of that effort (Weiss, 1991).

12. The initiative was clearly the right thing to do, and the timing for its implementation was right.

The strategy, presented to and accepted by Joseph J. Bevilacqua, agency director, was to utilize the consultative services of James Mason of Portland State University to assess the SCDMH's level of cultural competence, develop and hold a workshop for key staff, and consult with the departmental cultural competence committee. Bevilacqua publicized this initiative through the agency's two publications and authorized the cultural competence committee to develop an agencywide cultural competence plan for implementation. The CAP director answered directly to the SCDMH director.

ASSESSMENT, ACCEPTANCE, AND INITIAL IMPLEMENTATION OF THE PLAN

Bevilacqua acted with vision, courage, and commitment in supporting and personally implementing CAP. Unlike comparable state mental health directors, the SCDMH director is employed by and answers to a seven-member commission appointed by the governor of South Carolina. The commission oversees the SCDMH's policies. Early in the development of CAP, the author of this chapter decided that if CAP was to be truly successful agencywide, the commission would have to endorse and support Bevilacqua's decisions. Mason's work was central to selling the proposal to initiate the project and assess the organization for cultural competence. In the late 1980s, Mason had developed and field tested the only known instrument to assess an organization's level of cultural competence (Mason, 1993). His experience and credibility decreased the SCDMH director's residual anxiety about embarking on such an emotionally intense journey. Mason also conducted an initial workshop for 105 managers, including program directors, SCDMH management team members, center directors, hospital directors, medical directors, and other key SCDMH personnel.

The consultant's assessment instrument was distributed to the managers with the promise of their anonymity. No identifying information (e.g., name, department) was solicited on the instrument. Even with this safeguard, the assessment raised the anxiety levels of some managers who were concerned that their responses would be used against them and that a lack of knowledge would reflect negatively on them. The 76% return rate reflected the sensitive nature of the issue as well as participants' assumptions that, for example, "this too shall pass" because they had seen other priorities come and go. The surveys were collected and forwarded to the consultant for analysis and for the preparation of a report. Simultaneously, the SCDMH created a cultural competence committee chaired by an African American, with three of the four major groups of color represented on the committee (African American, Latino, and Native American). The committee's membership also represented a cross-section of clinical, administrative, program, central office, mental health center, and hospital personnel.

The first major decision that the committee made was to adhere to the model set out in *Towards a Culturally Competent System of Care: A Monograph on Effective Services for Minority Children Who Are Severely Emotionally Disturbed* (Cross et al., 1989) and initially to focus only on the major four groups of color (African Americans, Latinos, Native Americans, and Asian Americans). Significantly, this position was endorsed and supported by the Caucasian members of the committee. Upon completion of his analysis, Mason conducted a full-day workshop at which he presented the survey results and spoke about potential future directions and activities. The findings of Mason's survey were as follows:

- *Knowledge of communities:* This subscale concerns awareness of the respective groups of color and other ethnic minority populations encountered. With respect to the people of color whom the agency served, at least one third of those responded that they barely knew or did not know the life expectancies, infant mortality rates, income differentials, cultural strengths, clients' definitions of mental health and mental illness, and culturally inappropriate practices with regard to those ethnic minority groups.
- *Personal involvement:* This subscale concerns the degree to which professionals and agencies demonstrate reciprocity, establish ongoing linkages, and generally create better relationships with communities of color. Of those responding, 61% reported that they seldom attended or did not attend cultural group ceremonies; 54% did not pursue leisure or recreational activities in communities of color; 90% did interact with people of color in providing mental health services; and 68% purchased goods or services in communities of color.
- *Resources and linkages:* This subscale is an indication of the system's ability to acknowledge and use both formal and informal networks of support. Of the respondents surveyed, 54% replied that they seldom had linkages with such resources; 46% replied that they relied on such organizations seldom to often; and 86% replied that they had taken few or no ethnic studies courses.
- *Staffing:* This subscale addresses the recruitment and retention of staff from diverse cultural backgrounds; preparation of new staff;

and training of existing staff in cultural competence, maintaining a work force from diverse cultural backgrounds, and issues associated with providing culturally competent mental health services. Given the SCDMH staff's talent and experience, the report concluded that they might yield a high number of untapped contacts and resources from communities of diverse cultural backgrounds. Staff preparation was also a concern. New staff should be supported by curricula highlighting cultural competence concerns. The hiring of aides and natural support helpers is an untapped resource.

- *Organizational policies and procedures:* This subscale concerns the various practices and procedures that reflect cultural competence principles but are yet to be mandated by policy. There are many good practices being conducted by agency staff, contract agency personnel, and many of the respondents. Few of the good practices are reflective of specific agency policies.
- *Reaching out to communities:* This subscale suggests methods of empowering clients and communities of color by working in collaboration with natural supports, leaders, and networks. Areas in which considerable strength existed were places of worship and formal, traditional state and local agencies. Another asset is that there was considerable agreement that the various communities were aware of agency services and programs.

The workshop effectively marked the beginning of CAP. The agency hired an African American Director for the Cultural Action Program, under the direct supervision of the agency head. CAP contracted with an African American psychiatrist to aid the CAP director with clinical matters, and an Asian American member was added to the committee. The committee was given permanent status. The committee developed a cultural competence plan for the agency. After the final plan was developed and distributed, training was conducted at mental health centers and hospitals, a support staff member for the committee was hired, and cultural competence committees at the mental health centers and hospitals were established. The committee began planning for statewide Latino and Native American conferences and voiced its continuing support of the annual African American Male Conference. Finally, a federal grant to CAF underwrote agency collaboration with Benedict College in South Carolina, a historically African American institution, for student training and placement and faculty support.

UTILIZING THE EXPERIENCES OF OTHER STATES: NO ONE SUCCEEDS ALONE

From the beginning of the initiative, articles were published in the SCDMH's two publications, *Focus* and *Images*, that highlighted the initiative and the SCDMH director's commitment to it. *Focus* is a quarterly eight-page magazine that presents in each issue an in-depth report on a given program or initiative of the SCDMH. The January/February 1995 issue (Craft, 1995) presented the history of the SCDMH cultural competence initiative, the status of the departmentwide cultural competence committee, activities that had taken place up to that point, and a summary of the SCDMH's cultural competence plan. *Images* began publishing a series of articles on various aspects of the cultural competence initiative in 1993 (Bevilacqua, 1993) that were accompanied by photographs of activities, committee members, consultants, and the annual Cross-Cultural Conference and other training. The director's column was used to reinforce the importance of and the director's support of the initiative (Bevilacqua, 1993, 1994; Byrd, 1994; Donnelly, 1994; McEachern, 1994, 1995).

South Carolina was not the first state to develop a cultural competence plan. A decision was made early in the planning stages to draw from the experiences of other states. Plans from California (Ventura County [*Ethnic Populations Mental Health Service*, 1988; Ventura County Mental Health Department, 1991], Ohio [Minority Concerns Committee, 1992], and Washington State [Balderrama, 1991], as well as the City and County of San Francisco [*General Principles for Desigining and Developing*, 1993]), were reviewed. The significance of the South Carolina experience was that it required strategic sensitivity to both internal and external racial politics. It demonstrates the impact of a few committed people who were in a position to assess the system's environment and develop coalitions that enhanced and broadened the base of support for a single vision.

STATUS OF INITIATIVE

CAP continues to gain momentum and converts. Most mental health centers and all hospitals have their own cultural competence committees. In addition, the cultural competence division has one additional full-time staff member, a Latina nurse. The management team has worked with members of the cultural competence committee to conduct 24 focus groups with nonsupervisory center, hospital, and central office employees. The information gathered is being used to determine how far the cultural competence initiative has penetrated the organization and to inform future training efforts. In addition, as of 1998, 2 of the 17 community mental health center directors were African Americans, two of the seven members of the board of commissioners were African Americans (appointed by the governor), and the CAP director holds a seat on the SCDMH's central management team.

CONCLUSIONS

It is imperative to believe that a small group can bring about changes in large systems of care through commitment, planning, and strategic implementation. These efforts to effect change require realistic assessments of risks and barriers as well as of opportunities. Ongoing active support from the organization's chief executive officer is essential.

In this kind of work, no one succeeds alone; and, drawing upon the knowledge, failures, successes, and lessons learned in other states, organizations and systems should be given priority. The initial evaluation period should include discovery of opportunities; identification of leverage points; and finding, solidifying, and using existing supports.

According to an Ashanti proverb, "He who cannot dance blames the drum." The client can no longer be blamed for mental health system of care service providers' lack of cultural knowledge. *Cultural competence* must be more than a politically current phrase used in reports. Instead, it should be implemented in the provision of services to people of all cultural backgrounds.

REFERENCES

Balderrama, C.H. (1991). *Washington State Department of Social and Health Services Mental Program Plan for Ethnic Minority Services.* Olympia, WA: Department of Social and Health Services.

Bevilacqua, J.J. (1993, September/October). Director's update. *Images, 2.*

Bevilacqua, J.J. (1994, May/June). Commission approves new mission statement. *Images, 2.*

Byrd, K.S. (1994, January/February). Cultural competence committee present plan. *Images, 2.*

Conniff, M.L., & Davis, T.J. (1994). *Africans in the Americas: A history of the black diaspora.* New York: St. Martin's Press.

Craft, S.F. (1995, January/February). Cultural competence: A priority that makes good sense. *Focus,* 1–6.

Cross, T.L., Bazron, B.J., Dennis, K.W., & Isaacs, M.R. (1989). *Towards a culturally competent system of care: Vol. I. A monograph on effective services for minority children who are severely emotionally disturbed.* Washington, DC: Georgetown University, Child Development Center, Child and Adolescent Service System Program, Technical Assistance Center.

Day, C., & Roberts, M.C. (1991). Activities of the Child and Adolescent Service System Program for improving mental health services for children and families. *Journal of Clinical Psychology, 20,* 340–350.

Donnelly, M. (1994, March/April). Cross-cultural conference examines diversity in the workplace. *Images, 4.*

Egan, T. (1993, October 11). Diversity training too much "shock therapy" for some. *The State,* reprinted from the *Washington Post,* A7.

Ethnic populations mental health service in Santa Clara County: A long-term solution to community distress. (1988). Sacramento, CA: Ethnic Population Services Planning Task Force.

Franklin, J.H. (1993). *The color line: Legacy for the twenty-first century.* Columbia: University of Missouri Press.

General principles for designing and developing culturally competent programs. (1993). San Francisco: City and County of San Francisco Committee for Culturally Competent Systems of Care.

Gibbs, J.T., & Haring, L.N. (Eds.). (1989). *Children of color: Psychological interventions with minority youth.* San Francisco: Jossey-Bass.

Hacker, A. (1992). *Two nations: Black and white, separate, hostile, unequal.* New York: Scribner.

Hanley, J.H. (1991). *Cultural competence: Considerations for implementation in southern states.* Unpublished manuscript, State of South Carolina, Department of Mental Health, Division of Children, Adolescents, and Their Families, Columbia.

Hanley, J.H. (1994, Summer). Terry Cross: A person behind the concept. *Newsletter: A Quarterly Publication of the National Association for Family-Based Services, 2,* 13–14.

Higginbotham, A.L., Jr. (1978). *In the matter of color: Race and the American legal process: The colonial period.* New York: Oxford University Press.

Isaacs, M.R., & Benjamin, M.P. (1991). *Towards a culturally competent system of care: Volume II. Programs which utilize culturally competent principles.* Washington, DC: Georgetown University, Center for Child Health and Mental Health Policy, Child Development Center, Child and Adolescent Service System Program, Technical Assistance Center.

Kozol, J. (1991). *Savage inequalities: Children in America's schools.* New York: Crown.

Mason, J.L. (1993). *Cultural Competence Self-Assessment Questionnaire.* Portland, OR: Portland State University, Multicultural Initiative Project.

McEachern, A. (1994, September/October). DMH implements cultural competence plan. *Images, 2.*

McEachern, A. (1995, January/February). Annual cross-cultural conference set for Greenville. *Images, 2.*

Minority Concerns Committee. (1992). *Use of public mental health services by minorities in Ohio* (Report by the Minority Concerns Committee to the Ohio Department of Mental Health). Columbus: Ohio Department of Mental Health.

National Spiritual Assembly of the Baha'is of the United States. (1991). *The vision of race unity: America's most challenging issue.* Wilmette, IL: Baha'i Publishing.

Pender, A., & Gibson, G. (Eds.). (1995). *South Carolina statistical abstract.* Columbia: South Carolina State Budget and Control Board, Office of Research and Statistics.

Pinderhughes, E. (1989). *Understanding race, ethnicity, and power.* New York: Free Press.

South Carolina Department of Mental Health (SCDMH). (1996). *Management information system.* Unpublished raw data.

Steele, S. (1991). *The content of our character.* New York: HarperPerennial.

Turner, W.H., & Cabbell, E.J. (Eds.). (1985). *Blacks in Appalachia.* Lexington: University Press of Kentucky.

Ventura County Mental Health Department. (1991). *Cultural competence master plan.* San Mateo, CA: Author.

Weiss, C.I. (1991, May). *Quality improvement and cultural competence: Two paradigms in search of a linkage.* Paper presented at the 14th annual conference of the Eastern Evaluation Research Society, Princeton Junction, NJ.

West, C. (1996, February 2). Untitled speech delivered at Benedict College, Columbia, SC.

Recruitment, Retention, Training, and Supervision of Mental Health Services Staff

Josie Torralba-Romero

Mental health systems of care face many challenges as they enter a managed care environment. One factor contributing to this challenge is the changing demographics of the targeted Medicaid population and its implications for services. Another is the staff competencies needed to position organizations to compete in a marketplace in which cultural competencies are key. In the behavioral health field, providers must pay attention to ineffective services and an increasing number of costly malpractice suits. These are often brought about by the lack of well-defined cultural competency skills necessary to communicate and serve clients with limited English and/or monolingual clients.

The Latino, Asian American, and African American populations are increasing in many states; in some states, these minority groups as an aggregate already form a demographic majority. Those people who are eligible for Medicaid are largely the poor and the older adult population, a large percentage of whom are Latino, African American, and Asian American. Comparing the Medicaid population profiles with the changing characteristics of the work force reveals that approximately 60% of Medicaid clients are women and children, and they are predominantly members of ethnic minority groups. The U.S. work force demographic composition is not keeping pace with the changing demographics of Medicaid clients. The available work force in the mental health professions does not reflect the ethnic characteristics of the population eligible for Medicaid, who often use mental health services. There is a disparity between those needing and seeking mental health services and those providing those services.

These changing characteristics require that mental health systems of care retrain their staff to ensure that staff have the capacity to meet the needs of an increasingly culturally diverse client base. Managed care requires that services be provided in the most cost-effective manner possible, that services meet the industry's standards for quality (Western Interstate Commission on Higher Education, 1997), and that they produce desirable outcomes for the client. To ensure effective services and outcomes, agencies and clinicians must first be able to attract clients to their services and then engage and retain clients during interventions. Clinicians and agencies must be prepared to tailor their services in a way that makes cultural sense and so that services are easily accessible by clients. Culturally competent skills and knowledge are required to provide effective services.

RECRUITMENT AND RETENTION OF
CULTURALLY DIVERSE STAFF AS AN ISSUE OF POLICY

How does one go about recruiting, retaining, training, and supervising a culturally diverse staff that is clinically competent? Targeted recruitment and development of culturally competent staff do not just happen. Agency administrators, managers, and supervisors need to have in place a strategic plan that will achieve these results. First, agencies need to know who their current and future clients are or will be. Demographic profiles must include ethnicity, primary languages, region, and socioeconomic and educational levels. This information is fundamental to embarking on a plan to recruit staff. Matching staff resources—culturally and linguistically as well as geographically and, at times, socioeconomically—is critical to success in gaining access to, engaging, and retaining a client base.

Research reveals that clients who are matched ethnically and linguistically to their clinicians, therapists, and service coordinators are engaged in and complete their interventions more often than those who are not. Such matching reduces the premature termination of interventions, which is common in many clinics serving ethnic minority populations and the poor. Language and cultural matching provide clients with the ability to express emotions and feelings without having to explain themselves. Clients' ability to use their primary language in therapy provides them with control of their internal cognitive processes, which is the source of emotions. Thus, clients' emotions are not subject to "translation" by way of the effects of linguistic translation, which can include intonation patterns, voice volume, and gestures. In times of stress, bilingual clients most often revert to their primary language, in which their emotions can achieve fullest expression. Clinicians who are not fluent in their client's primary language and do not understand their client's cultural dynamics are not able to assess their client's emotions and thus do not understand and cannot assess the totality of the information that their client has provided. The clinician's ability to decipher the client's verbal and nonverbal communication patterns is critical to a comprehensive and accurate assessment of the client (Romero, 1996).

In the behavioral health professions as in the medical profession, most practitioners have become tolerant of providing second-class interventions, which can be described as interventions provided by health care providers or organizations and professional staff with limited second-language skills and/or with the aid of untrained interpreters who speak the client's primary language and attempt to do their best, though they have not been trained in mental health care issues. In such cases, there are multiple victims: the client, whose health and life are possibly at stake, as well as the professional and the interpreter, who are asked to do a job at risk of legal liability to their agency or organization and/or harm to themselves and that compromises their professional ethics and standards. In such circumstances, one is led to ask the following: What is the agency's policy? What are its professional ethics? Would a member of an ethnic minority group who received Medicaid want to subscribe to a managed care plan that did not provide that client with services by staff with whom he or she could communicate and by staff who were capable of providing quality services? As with any other administrative assignment, practitioners must start by assessing the extent of the client's need, what services are already in place, and what steps need to be taken. The following steps are commonly overlooked:

- Determine whether ethnic minority populations are represented in the agency's caseload to the degree of need determined to exist in the community among these populations. If not, why not?
- Review current job descriptions at the agency. Do they reflect the abilities and attributes of staff who can serve the targeted demographics in the community?

Many mental health providers have not taken the time to reevaluate existing job descriptions that no longer are applicable to the demand for a model of service delivery that is required for effective competition in a managed care environment. Many job descriptions are written in such a way that they actually reflect the opposite of what one wants to achieve in those positions. For example, a job description is selling its organization short if it places great importance only on professional credentials, licensing, and experience in psychotherapeutic processes and does not emphasize equally important knowledge of culturally diverse, community-based, family-focused systems of care experience and bilingual skills. A combination of both types of professional expertise is essential for effective service delivery to culturally diverse clients. In addition, such a job description rules out many potential culturally diverse aides and other beginning professionals who have experience and have achieved success in the latter qualifications area. Adding a combination of professional and aide staff allows for the beginning of a culturally diverse staffing pattern. Population-based planning helps the agency familiarize staff with the client population in the region and gives the agency an idea of the skills that it will require of staff to provide quality, culturally competent services. Training staff in clinical care management skills is easier than training them in a second language and providing them with in-depth cultural understanding. This statement does not imply that staff cannot learn a second language and cannot be taught cross-cultural dynamics and cultural competency skills; however, teaching professionally trained and credentialed staff who have bicultural experience and bilingual skills the techniques of particular clinical interventions and care management skills appropriate to their credentials and/or work experience is an easier and more effective approach to staff development.

Cultural competence is a developmental process in which skills are refined and improved by consistent practice. The more experience the clinician has, the better the outcomes that he or she is likely to produce. The key is not to separate clinical competencies from cultural competencies; they must be integrated for best results. As one performs an intervention, the intervention must pass the cultural screens of the client. Learning a second language as an adult takes time, commitment, and interest. One who develops fluency in a second language also increases one's knowledge of that particular culture. An emphasis on staff's acquiring fluency does not imply that staff must be from the same culture as the client; instead, staff's attitude, skills, knowledge, and experience are an important consideration when agency administrators are matching staff with clients.

How does one "select in," as opposed to "weed out," certain types of staff? Job descriptions must be inviting and must emphasize the values important to the organization. How does one appeal to and attract staff who are likely to contribute to quality services for a culturally diverse client base? The following are a few suggestions:

- Identify the specifically targeted populations for which the agency needs staff who have experience and competency, and include in the position description phrases such as *cultural skills highly desirable.*
- Write a job description that is current and applicable to the skills needed in the job today and that specifically requires staff with flu-

ency in the primary language of the agency's target client populations.

- If staff positions allow for opportunities to start at an aide level with the potential of moving up as the staff member's educational credentials increase, that information must be noted in the agency's fliers and recruitment materials to attract staff who are willing to start at the bottom and so that potential applicants do not fear bumping into a "glass ceiling" if hired.

- Those who do the agency's hiring must be familiar with the agency's mission, vision, and values to "screen in" staff with compatible backgrounds and profiles. Agency personnel who hire new staff must share the agency's interests and commitment to developing a culturally diverse work force and must be the best representatives of the agency in order to "sell" the agency to potential new hires.

- Review the convenience of the application process, including aspects such as opportunities for potential applicants to fax and mail in applications and to receive application packages by mail. Also pay attention to the waiting period that applicants must endure between their initial application and their first interview. Remember that other organizations—locally, statewide, and nationally—are competing for staff with the same sets of skills; therefore, excessive delays in interviewing and hiring qualified applicants may diminish an agency's ability to hire people with the best qualifications.

- If the agency has a recruiting or personnel staff, they must know what the agency wants and needs in new staff members. If they do not, they must receive enough guidance and information so that they will not impose undesirable barriers in the recruitment process. Instead of setting up personnel procedures to keep certain types of applicants out of the hiring process, recruiters should seek out and act as a gateway to the agency for qualified, culturally diverse applicants.

- Once the agency's personnel department's readiness to support the recruitment plan is established, determine whether the personnel department will be recruiting off-site or only at the agency's offices and only according to the agency's standard hiring process. Proactive recruitment off-site is often an effective means of finding and attracting qualified applicants. Such recruiting can be done at universities, conferences, and professional forums (e.g., ethnicity-specific conferences and seminars, professional association gatherings).

- Successful recruitment plans often include an individual who has been identified and assigned the duties of recruitment and outreach to potential sources where bilingual and bicultural staff can be found. This person becomes known as the gateway to hiring qualified staff to the system of care and ultimately as a mentor in providing culturally diverse staff to the divisions that need them. This person needs to be assigned and given time to develop and enhance his or her existing network for recruitment purposes, and he or she must have the support of the agency's administration.

- The agency's administration must be willing to embark on an ongoing, long-term recruitment process, which is necessary to maintain a list of currently available, qualified applicants for positions as professionals and aides.

- In geographic areas in which bilingual and bicultural professionals are not in the available pool from which to draw, agency administrators must trust their skills enough to train on the job for those technical skills needed in return for capitalizing on the contributions and strengths of culturally diverse staff. Flexibility and on-the-job training increase an agency's competitive edge and reduce its potential exposure to malpractice lawsuits. Agencies that capitalize on their staff's strengths can create a win-win situation for potential new staff and for the agency and its clientele. At times, administrators and supervisors need to make a decision to hire a person with less clinical skills but with strong cultural and linguistic skills. When confronted with this dilemma, they need to trust that they can do on-the-job training of clinical skills much faster than they can train for cultural and linguistic competency skills. These choices allow the agency to respond to the needs of a culturally diverse community in a more timely manner and thus to create a win-win situation for staff, the agency, clients, and the community. When hiring is based on skills needed to respond to a client population, one is not compromising quality standards, because these should be set based on clients' needs and not only in traditional clinical practice. Challenging traditional clinical practices is not easy for supervisors. Supervisors must look to balance those standards by including a multicultural perspective that is reflective of the client population.

The next step is to plan a recruitment strategy. The reality of today's available pool of bilingual and bicultural mental health services agency applicants is dismal. Private and public universities have been unable to meet the demand of the mental health services market. Therefore, universities are not necessarily the best sources of potential staff. Some of the most successful recruitment and retention plans have been those that have developed a "grow your own" philosophy by looking at community and in-house resources. The identification of potential staff who can be trained, whose skills and experience can be developed, and whose higher education can be subsidized is important. Staff who live nearby and work in related fields may be good candidates for agency employment. There are likely some ideal aides located near every mental health services agency among whom the agency can identify potential bilingual staff, including the following:

- Social services staff doing eligibility-related work
- Local community mental health agency staff (e.g., health aides, outreach workers, school liaisons, teacher's aides)
- Local residential care facility staff
- Aides working in nursing homes
- Church group leaders
- Hospital language interpreters
- Courthouse language interpreters
- Local elementary, junior high school, and high school outreach staff (Aides in schools represent a local pool of people who not only are committed to serving populations at risk for requiring mental health services and families of diverse cultural backgrounds but also would welcome the opportunity for professional careers. With this group, a well-defined staff development plan is needed to ensure that the minimum skill requirements are taught. A partnership could be developed with local junior colleges and universities for issuing certified credentials.)
- Meet with staff at local junior colleges and universities at which workplace reentry programs designed for women as well as continuing education programs are available. This resource allows agencies to explore the work force availability characteristic of the area that they serve.
- The local state employment office may have existing profiles of qualified unemployed people in the area.
- Meet with the local welfare department's retraining program director, which may be able to provide leads to potential applicants of diverse cultural backgrounds.
- Establish good working relationships with nearby universities that have programs in psychology, social work, marriage and family counseling, nursing, and substance abuse counseling and rehabilitation. Establish a memorandum of understanding with the university that the agency will provide interns with field placement experience, and specify the benefits of placing students from diverse cultural backgrounds, particularly those with bilingual skills.

One of the most effective ways to "grow your own" culturally competent work force is by establishing a paid internship program with state colleges and universities, which can

- Provide, at no cost to the agency, a local pool of potential applicants and future professionals who are familiar with the agency and its services and procedures
- Increase the available ethnic minority applicant pool because interns chosen to work at the agency can be from ethnic minority groups, which will increase the staff's diversity and cultural competence skills
- Allow the agency to select the most competent individuals and those who meet the agency's requirements and share the agency's mission, vision, and values
- Allow long-term recruitment through the annual process of selecting new interns
- Expose staff without credentials to role models who can encourage others, such as clerical staff and service coordinators, to return to school for training
- Allow development of an on-site curriculum established for interns, thus challenging existing staff to continue their own professional development

Following are suggestions for establishing an effective internship program:

- Specifically request students with cultural and linguistic competencies; ask the university to recruit students of diverse cultural backgrounds in order to meet the agency's market demand.
- Assign a student intern as coordinator of the internship program, and have him or her develop a training curriculum for interns and intern supervisors to encourage the university to continue to use the agency for intern placements.

To increase success in recruiting bilingual and bicultural staff, offer a stipend as an incentive. This stipend in essence is reimbursable by the agency's collection of fees for the services that students provide under the supervision of a licensed professional. The stipend represents a worthwhile long-term investment in the professional recruitment process; when an agency invests its time and resources to "grow its own" staff, it increases the success of attracting both aides and professional staff.

RETENTION OF STAFF

Retaining staff, including qualified, competent bicultural and bilingual staff, is a challenge. Staff have four basic needs that, if met, tend to keep them with the agency longer. One of the biggest challenges for an agency trying to retain staff of diverse cultural backgrounds begins with the agency's ability to develop its own culturally competent supervisors in order to enable them to understand how the four universal needs apply uniquely to staff from specific cultures.

Agencies increase their success in retaining diverse staff when they reach a "critical mass" of three or more staff from a particular ethnic group. The existence of such a group of professionals at the agency increases the opportunity of development of a learning environment as well as opportunities for program development and within-group support. This group also diffuses the stress that often is experienced by a staff member who is the only representative of a particular ethnic group and who is therefore expected to be "everything to everybody" with regard to that ethnic group. Token hiring of staff from particular ethnic groups is demeaning to professionals from those ethnic backgrounds. It is not cost effective and does not promote staff retention and professional growth or add value to the agency. Increasing the retention of qualified staff with cultural competence skills also requires that managers assess and manage the work environment. For example, it is important to ensure the following:

- The workplace must not allow a racially hostile environment. Ensure that the workplace does not foster covert or overt racism. Establish a zero-tolerance policy that is actively enforced.
- Staff must feel respected and valued by agency supervisors.
- Staff must be given the flexibility and the opportunity to advance and provided with professional support and competent supervision.
- Staff must be given the challenges and tools that allow them to thrive in their jobs and do their best.
- Staff must receive competitive salaries.
- Agency administrators and staff must develop a team philosophy in which cultural diversity is respected and valued by all. After recruitment, the challenge to develop and supervise a culturally diverse team begins. Be aware that the dynamics of a culturally diverse team are different from those of a culturally homogeneous team. Being able to manage a culturally diverse team is a skill requirement for managers.

Not all mental health agency supervisors have been trained in supervision. Most of them have been promoted from within the staff. This situation presents a challenge because supervision requires an understanding of the basic principles of interpersonal communication and organizational behavior in addition to the adult learning theories and the technical skills related to the agency's work. Many supervisors have only the latter skills. Therefore, training supervisors to be coaches and consultants is important.

SUPERVISION OF A CULTURALLY DIVERSE WORK FORCE

Culturally competent supervision has its own set of principles in addition to the typical principles of supervision, which include the importance of having clear boundaries between staff and managers, respecting and protecting the dignity of the individual, and setting clear performance expectations. When supervising cross-culturally, the supervisor must take time to get to know staff members as people and to understand their cultural experiences. Listening to and discussing these experiences give supervisors and staff members an opportunity to get to know each other in a more in-depth way. It also allows for the development and earning of each other's trust and respect. As with all cultures, there are differences among individuals; what works with one member of the group does not necessarily work with all other members of the group. The following are some other ways to increase cultural competence in supervision:

- Identify the unique strengths and weaknesses of each staff member. Not all staff have the same needs; therefore, equal treatment of all staff is ineffective. Some staff members need more of the supervisor's time and direction, and some need less. Being able to discern these variations among staff is essential with regard to staff retention and development.
- Develop and foster harmonious working relationships among a team from diverse cultural backgrounds or in a culturally diverse work environment. A culturally competent supervisor is also a good coach and a good mentor. He or she uses *fair* (not *equal*) judgment.
- Enable and model team support and allow for unique experiences to be shared among peers from similar cultural groups.
- Do not tolerate racist or sexist remarks, and do not allow them to go unchallenged.

Following are some suggestions for supervisors who want to become culturally competent:

- Allow oneself to be taught what is unique to the staff's culture and be a patient listener.
- Listen to staff to learn about what it takes to deliver culturally appropriate services and provide them with the necessary support.
- Provide encouragement and support in difficult situations; be available but not intrusive.

- Be flexible when situations and/or services need to be provided in a manner that is unfamiliar.
- Acknowledge staff members' contributions, no matter how small.

STAFF TRAINING: SELECTION OF TYPES, WHICH STAFF MEMBERS TO TRAIN, AND WHEN TO PROVIDE TRAINING

When an agency is beginning to develop culturally competent services and programming, one of the most essential elements of achieving its goals is a comprehensive and inclusive training plan that provides the same information to all staff members, from administrators to clerical staff. The next step is to operationalize the training plan's meaning as it applies to each staff level. Training plans that fail to include clerical and administrative staff in addition to clinicians are unsuccessful. The delivery of culturally competent services is everyone's business, not just the business of the clinicians from diverse cultural backgrounds. Therefore, the training plan must start with the basics for all. It must be a systemwide effort because changing an organization's culture is not easy.

Developing cultural knowledge within an institution must be given top priority. It is important for an agency and its staff to be familiar with the community profile of its residents and clients, including its culturally diverse community. The agency should conduct a self-assessment to measure its level of cultural knowledge. There are many self-assessment tools available. Agencies should invest in training that is practical, useful, and necessary to perform the services that they deliver. The training must contribute to the implementation of the agency's vision, mission, values, and standards of care. The training curriculum should be developed for different levels of staff knowledge and should be appropriate for different staff members' responsibilities.

Focus on teamwork as a value. A high level of skills, knowledge, and competency—from the receptionist to top-level administrative staff—is critical to the agency's success. Specify that all training provided to staff must address the implications for culturally diverse clients. It must include topics such as

- Outreach techniques
- Interagency collaborations
- A system of care approach
- Interdisciplinary culturally diverse teamwork
- Family-focused and client-based services
- Engaging and partnering with families
- Service coordination
- Short-term interventions

- Strength-based and culturally specific functional assessments
- Cross-cultural clinical interventions

Beware of and avoid "cookbook" presentations, which are susceptible to using stereotypes. Do not engage in any training that promotes stereotypes with regard to gender and cultural groups. Beware of a style of training that does not take into account the fundamental within-group differences (e.g., differences among group members in levels of acculturation, socioeconomic status, education) within any culture; however, this is not to say that there are no common generalities within cultural groups and that this knowledge is not helpful. It can be helpful, but it must be put in context so that staff are not misled. Focus on training that begins with basic cultural competence principles and frameworks so that staff can learn to apply them to individuals based on an individual's culture, language, acculturation and assimilation levels, and the individual's family's length of residence in the United States. Develop a training program that promotes skills in assessing the uniqueness of cultural strengths within each client and family and in using these skills in interventions.

Cultural competence training must not be segregated in the agency's budget, because it will invariably receive only a small percentage of the budget. Staff are more likely to select training in topics that are more familiar to them and therefore are easier for them to process and integrate into their work. It is important to place equal value on all training; therefore, presenters must be able to address the application of cultural competence skills across cultures. An agency is more successful in building a culturally competent work force when it infuses cultural competency skills into all of its training programs. When it does so, the agency inoculates its staff from the common attitude among some staff of "I already know that; I don't need to learn it." Staff members who have that attitude have a mental block against cultural competence training but are the ones most in need of reeducation. It also prevents the "preaching to the choir" syndrome.

Clearly, cultural competence skills training is a developmental process, not a one-time-only program. It is not unusual to see that those who attend cultural competence training are those staff members who are open to receiving this specialized training. To avoid this occurrence, make sure that training sessions are attended by all staff. The purpose of a well-balanced training plan is to take into consideration the cultural competence skills required and systematically infuse them into the organization in order to meet the agency's vision, mission, and values and to produce positive outcomes for all clients. This is one way in which an agency keeps a competitive edge in a managed care environment.

CONCLUSIONS

This chapter describes fundamental steps for successful recruitment, retention, supervision, and training of a work force that will take an organization to a higher level of cultural competence and competitiveness in a managed care environment. The steps outlined require careful and strategic planning. An agency's results will depend on the commitment, future-driven vision, mission, and goals of its staff. Achievement of an agency's cultural competence goals takes, on average, 2–6 years; therefore, the sooner an agency starts its cultural competence training programs, the better. Recruitment and retention of culturally competent staff is not an easy task; however, it is doable and essential to establish a cost-effective and competitive environment that provides quality care.

The agency's cultural competence plan must be multidimensional. It must emphasize developing cultural competence among its own existing staff. Partnering with local universities, junior colleges, and high schools is critical. Addressing retention as a value and as a cost-effective program goal is critical and requires that agency managers, supervisors, and administrators be held accountable for achieving it. New supervision skills are required in the managed care era. Supervisors must be able to develop self-directed teams and facilitate culturally diverse team development. They must also be effective in mitigating cultural and racial conflicts that may arise as staff learn to work together and value each other's strengths and contributions. Training is key to reeducating staff and operationalizing cultural competence in systems of care. Training must be strategically planned and must be client based. The inclusion of clients and family members as trainers is one way to achieve this goal. Training must be dynamic and practical. It must be targeted at skills and services that the agency wants to enhance. All clients are entitled to quality care, so standards of care should not be compromised. Professionals and staff in general want to do the best job possible; therefore, provide them with the tools that exemplify recommended practices in cultural competence, which will create a win-win situation for all: clients, staff, and the entire system of care. *¡Sí, se puede!* Yes, it can be done!

REFERENCES

Romero, J.T. (1996, June). *Operationalizing cultural competency: Recruitment, retention and training of culturally diverse mental health staff.* Paper presented at the Child and Adolescent Service System Program Conference. Traverse City, MI.

Western Interstate Commission on Higher Education. (1997, October). *Cultural competence standards in managed care: Mental health services for four underserved/underrepresented racial/ethnic groups* (Grant funded by SAMHSA). Washington, DC: Author.

CHAPTER 6

Community Mental Health Services in a Managed Care Environment

10 Key Issues in Promoting Cultural Competence

Alfredo Aguirre

Both county-operated and privately operated nonprofit community mental health systems are beginning to integrate the organizational, fiscal, and service delivery components of managed care. As these changes occur, the evolution of culturally competent systems of care for children and adults will involve new opportunities, challenges, and potential pitfalls. This chapter presents 10 key issues in the development of culturally competent community mental health services in a managed care environment. Throughout this chapter, the San Mateo County Mental Health Services Division is used as an example of an organization that is implementing a managed care system that is confronting these key issues of cultural competence. As defined by the California State Department of Mental Health, *managed care* is a planned, comprehensive approach to the provision of health care that combines clinical services and administrative procedures within an integrated, coordinated system that is carefully constructed to provide timely access to care in a cost-effective manner.

BACKGROUND

San Mateo County covers a 450-square-mile area just south of San Francisco and has a total population of 691,500. It is one of the most diverse

The author acknowledges the many contributions of the following colleagues and associates: Beverly Abbott, Robert Cabaj, Mark Constantz, Janet Crist-Whitzel, Marty Giffin, Rachel Guerrero, Mario Hernandez, Carol S. Hood, Mareasa R. Isaacs, Patricia Jordan, Nancy Mills, Abram Rosenblatt, Deborah Torres, and Herbert Z. Wong. The views expressed in this chapter are those of the author only.

counties in California in terms of having rural and urban areas and an increasingly rich mix of ethnicities among its population (State of California, Department of Finance, 1995). Ethnic minorities represent 39.5% of the county's total population. The breakdown of specific ethnic group populations is shown in Table 1.

Prior to implementing its managed care plan, the San Mateo County Medicaid Mental Health Managed Care Plan (hereinafter referred to as the Mental Health Plan), the San Mateo County Mental Health Division served 7,000 clients, had a budget of $40 million, and operated as part of the San Mateo County Health Services Agency. Its budget included all inpatient, outpatient, service coordination, rehabilitation, and long-term care services (San Mateo County Mental Health Services, 1995).

San Mateo County was one of two counties in California to develop its own health insurance organization for Medicaid (Medi-Cal in California) recipients. In 1984, a federal waiver was obtained for freedom of choice, and the county organized the Health Plan of San Mateo. The waiver allowed the county to offer individuals who are eligible for Medicaid a single plan using a county-organized health system model. No other required provisions under Medicaid were waived. This insurance plan covered all Medi-Cal services except long-term care. With regard to mental health services, the plan included those services previously provided through fee-for-service Medi-Cal on both an inpatient and an outpatient basis. It did not include eligible Medi-Cal services provided by the county mental health system (San Mateo County Mental Health Services, 1995).

In 1993, as part of its statewide plan for Medicaid managed care, the state of California made the decision to carve out mental health services coverage from health services coverage. A phased-in insurance plan was developed that included consolidation of fee-for-service Medi-Cal inpatient services with county programs beginning on January 1, 1995, and consolidation of outpatient services as of July 1, 1997. In addition, state legislation was passed to allow a field test of the system in counties that had organized health systems. San Mateo County was the only California county included in the Medicaid waiver application submitted to the federal government, and the waiver was approved for startup of the Mental Health Plan on April 1, 1995 (San Mateo County Mental Health Services, 1995).

San Mateo County developed a system of care for children and youth and their families through two major state grants. In 1988, the Child and Youth Services program of the San Mateo County Mental Health Division received a 3-year state demonstration grant to implement an integrated system of care for children and youth (San Mateo County Mental Health Services, 1987). This funding helped San Mateo County evolve a system of care that featured the following six major elements:

Table 1. Ethnic group representation in the general population of San Mateo County, California, 1995

Ethnic group	Representation (%)
African Americans	5
Asian Americans/Pacific Islanders	16
Caucasians	60.5
Latinos	18
Native Americans	0.5

Source: State of California, Department of Finance (1995).

1. A clearly defined target population
2. Clear and measurable goals and objectives
3. An interagency coalition governing local system of care policies and directions
4. Integrated, collaborative service delivery
5. Culturally competent individualized care that demonstrates a partnership among parents, caregivers, and family members
6. Evaluation

In 1994, San Mateo County received a federal grant from the Center for Mental Health Services, a division of the Substance Abuse and Mental Health Services Administration of the U.S. Department of Health and Human Services, that helped advance the county's system of care and specifically addressed wraparound or flexible funding and service planning, cultural competence, family–professional partnership development, and managed care related-services development (e.g., early intervention, new access points, screening and assessment) (State of California, Department of Mental Health, 1993).

The subsequent sections in this chapter discuss the following 10 key issues in promoting cultural competence in community mental health services in a managed care environment:

1. The system of care must drive managed care.
2. Fiscal and administrative reform must be organized, clear, and efficient.
3. Services must be culturally competent, must enhance clients' access to those services, and must encourage clients' input.
4. Systems of care principles and approaches must be incorporated into early intervention services.
5. Mental health services should be integrated with primary health care services.
6. The professional service provider pool and service modalities should encourage cultural competence.
7. Inpatient service providers need to adhere to principles of systems of care.

8. Collaborative relationships must be reinforced with other children's services agencies.
9. Customer relations and grievance procedures must be culturally competent.
10. Evaluations must be responsive to populations of diverse ethnicities.

THE SYSTEM OF CARE MUST DRIVE MANAGED CARE

The major elements of a system of care must drive managed care in community mental health systems. For example, systems of care elements such as culturally competent individualized care and inclusion of families as full partners at all levels of the system must endure as fiscal and organizational principles of managed care are adopted. Furthermore, natural support systems provided by family–professional partnerships and cultural competence are essential allies in avoiding more complex, more costly services (Valle & Vega, 1982).

A community mental health services system that is developing a well-organized, efficient, and responsive system of care is positioned to present high standards of quality and cost-effective care. These standards cannot be compromised as the organization integrates managed care in a highly visible public environment. Because these system of care elements have historically set community mental health systems apart from private behavioral health care companies, a community mental health system that compromises these elements forfeits portions or all of its integrity and competitive edge as a service provider (San Mateo County Mental Health Services, 1995).

Systems of care typically feature an interagency council that provides direction, review, and overview for the system. This interagency group should include but should not be limited to juvenile probation, child welfare, education, and clients (e.g., parents, family members, youth services recipients). This council is charged with upholding systems of care principles and values. The council must ensure that risks are shared and managed by all agencies represented. A healthy collaboration also embraces a holistic approach to serving children and youth at high risk, thus avoiding tendencies to "dump" the most problematic youth in the lap of one agency. In San Mateo County, the Child and Youth System of Care relies on the Child and Youth System of Care Advisory Committee (CYSOC) to initiate systems of care policy and program development activities. CYSOC directs its cultural competence planning and evaluation through the Child and Youth Cultural Competence Task Force. As an example of systems of care driving managed care, this interagency task force responds to managed care challenges in a systems of care planning structure. The task force ensures that cultural competence is applied to managed care strategic planning, covering areas such as access to care, early intervention and prevention, contracting, outcomes-driven evaluation, and fiscal and administrative operations.

FISCAL AND ADMINISTRATIVE REFORM
MUST BE ORGANIZED, CLEAR, AND EFFICIENT

Claiming that a community-based system of care is in the best position to serve the mental health needs of a particular population because "it knows how" is too narrow an argument. A county-operated organization with a combined county-funded and privately funded provider network such as the one in San Mateo County must demonstrate fiscal viability and administrative capacity to convince policymakers and funding sources that it can compete in a competitive behavioral health care environment.

Mental health services agencies that plan to enhance cultural competence in systems of care must weigh additional costs and the ability to reallocate resources to achieve their objectives. These additional costs can include additional training for staff (e.g., loss of revenue for redirecting staff from reimbursable activities), establishing appropriate per diem staffing in inpatient facilities to provide services in other languages, developing and implementing an interpreter program, ensuring that oral interviewing boards are composed of staff of diverse ethnicities (redirecting bilingual staff from reimbursable activities), providing materials and forms in the various primary languages spoken by the populations within the community that the agencies serve, and accommodating contracting agencies' needs to hire professionals at rates higher than the agencies' salary structures so that they can compete with other organizations.

Budgeting for activities previously described in this chapter can potentially yield important savings. Savings can be achieved by avoiding costs in the following areas: discrimination-in-hiring lawsuits, patients' grievances and/or fair hearing actions, and long acute care stays that are due to the organization's inability to accurately assess clients with linguistic and/or cultural characteristics that differ from those of the medical or intervention staff. In addition, staffing with appropriate language capacity and cultural skills in screening or access service teams can often avoid more costly and complex levels of intervention or costly repeat visits to these front-line services teams.

A system of care that prides itself on its ability to individualize care in a culturally competent manner can also run the risk of handling smaller caseloads and incurring higher costs per case. Such circumstances are often the result of expanding the intervention and/or service coordination function to meet the needs of a client from a particular cultural and socioeconomic background. To ensure that mental health workers do not spread themselves too thin, to the point that quality and efficiency of service provision are compromised, it is imperative that interagency agreements are made, reinforced, or changed to define the roles of providers from different agencies in such a way that they are complementary. The appropriate use of clients, volunteers, and aides in a system of care may also pay substantial dividends in enhancing the quality of care provided while maintaining costs at an appropriate and competitive level.

SERVICES MUST BE CULTURALLY COMPETENT, MUST ENHANCE CLIENTS' ACCESS TO THOSE SERVICES, AND MUST ENCOURAGE CLIENTS' INPUT

Publicly operated community mental health systems, particularly in communities with established systems of care for children and youth with serious mental disorders and those at risk of being in need of mental health services, should be in a position to provide accessible, culturally relevant, higher-quality services for people who receive Medicaid. Community mental health agencies, in varying degrees, have worked with schools, juvenile justice agencies, health and social services agencies, and institutions such as psychiatric inpatient and residential intervention facilities as well as group homes to serve children and youth with serious emotional disabilities. Generally, in California, slightly more than 60% of children and youth with serious emotional disabilities are eligible for Medicaid (State of California, Department of Mental Health, 1994).

Most counties in California have increased their percentage of representation of bicultural and bilingual staff, particularly with regard to Spanish-speaking service providers. In addition, many county-contracted, community-based organizations have developed impressive credentials in serving ethnic minority populations. Agencies such as Centro de Salud Mental in Los Angeles, Instituto Familiar de la Raza in San Francisco, Bayview Hunters Point Mental Health in San Francisco (an organization that serves predominantly African Americans), Richmond Maxi Center in San Francisco (an organization that serves predominantly Asian Americans), and Casa del Sol in Oakland have pioneered culturally relevant programs, particularly in the areas of early intervention with children, social and peer group support programs for adults and older adults, and dual (e.g., mental health issues including substance abuse) and triple diagnosis (e.g., mental health issues including substance abuse and acquired immunodeficiency syndrome [AIDS]) programs (Bayview Hunters Point Foundation for Community Improvement, Inc., 1996; Romero, 1982; Wong, 1982).

In San Mateo County, the Mental Health Plan has demonstrated access and culturally competent features not previously offered to those Medicaid recipients, including

1. Employment of Spanish-speaking staff with clinical capacity at the screening level (The county has deployed to the ACCESS team one Spanish-speaking staff member to work with children and youth and one Spanish-speaking staff member to work with adults and older adults. This staffing decision has ensured equitable and appropriate screening services for Spanish-speaking clients.)
2. A pool of professional service providers from an expanded range of disciplines and a number of different community-based organizations offers more staff diversity and the possibility of fluency in a greater number of languages, such as Spanish and Tagalog
3. A continuum of care from early intervention to inpatient care that has available Spanish-speaking service providers to ensure clients' assignments into an appropriate level of care, clinical diagnosis, and appropriate inpatient discharges (This ability of agency staff to communicate with Spanish-speaking clients advances equity and cultural competence in their work with the Spanish-speaking population throughout the system of care.)
4. A bicultural and bilingual lead child psychiatrist who oversees psychiatric services for all children and youth who are eligible to receive Medicaid (This position has demonstrated leadership that promotes cultural competence in the medical and general clinical intervention domains in San Mateo's system of care.)
5. Bicultural and bilingual capacity to address clients' concerns

Because of their accountability to the community at large, publicly operated managed care systems are expected to meet the diverse needs of the Medicaid population and be equitable in serving indigent and underinsured children and youth. The public mental health agency's multiple responsibilities to administer a mental health plan for its clients who are eligible for Medicaid and serve clients with a range of mental health problems as well as clients with serious mental disorders who may or may not be insured are the greatest challenges for public systems of care.

Unlike private behavioral health managed care companies, public mental health care agencies cannot easily shield themselves with limited benefits packages or defined services criteria, largely because county systems are the risk holders for youth who require hospitalization, juvenile justice institutionalization, or foster care. Because ethnic minority youth, particularly African American and Latino youth, are disproportionately represented in institutional facilities, such as hospitals and juvenile justice facilities, and in foster care, cultural competence in assessment of and intervention planning for this population is essential. The factors that set publicly operated programs apart from their competitors are the ability to provide access to care; clear and consistent standards that determine the levels of service needed; measurable outcomes for children and youth; and effective partnerships with schools, agencies, and community groups.

SYSTEMS OF CARE PRINCIPLES AND APPROACHES MUST BE INCORPORATED INTO EARLY INTERVENTION SERVICES

Historically, early intervention programs such as Head Start (Institute for Human and Social Development, Inc., 1996) and California's Healthy Start (SRI International, 1996) have targeted ethnic minority children. These children and their families are disproportionately eligible for Medicaid benefits in comparison with the general population (State of California, Department of Health Services, 1994). Any initiative designed to provide mental health managed care services to Medicaid recipients must incorporate an early intervention strategy to avoid more involved and more costly interventions with children. Early intervention features such as screening instruments, psychoeducation programs, consultation with child care providers, and use of school aides and community workers to help parents handle difficult children must be culturally competent at the planning, intervention, and evaluation levels.

San Mateo County, through a community-based contract provider agency, has initiated an early intervention program for a number of federally subsidized child development centers. In at least two of these centers that had enrolled a high percentage of African American children, it became quite apparent that, before introducing centerwide screening activities, the clients' trust in the centers would need to be developed. Without a clear understanding of a particular screening tool, center staff and the families served may perceive screening as an intrusion or as outsiders assuming that there is a high prevalence of behavior problems in a classroom (Peninsula Children's Center/Zonta, 1996).

Although many of the components (e.g., the Pediatric Symptom Checklist [Pagano et al., 1996] screening tool) have been tested with Latino children in San Mateo County, caution must be exercised in using instruments and modalities with other emerging ethnic minority populations. In San Mateo County and the San Francisco Bay area, ethnic minority children whom agencies serve include Pacific Islander Americans, Russian Americans, and Southeast Asian Americans. The field test of the Pediatric Symptom Checklist with Head Start program participants in Ventura County, California, is an example of cultural competence in administering that instrument. That field test demonstrated that, for the monolingual, Spanish-speaking, predominantly Mexican American immigrant population, the oral administrations or interpreter-assisted administrations of the checklist resulted in a consistently higher incidence of true positive scores than those that were self-administered by the children's parents (Murphy et al., 1996). Community members and, if possible, human services providers representing the ethnic groups served by the agency must be woven into the planning and evaluation process to ensure appropriate administration of an instrument or service protocol. Also, because public mental health systems cannot discriminate, in terms of services provided, children who are from indigent families or are uninsured from children whose families receive Medicaid, it is critical to maximize group, classroom, and community forum interventions to reduce the costs of services provided. In the example previously described, the contract provider dedicated private fund-raising efforts to subsidize early intervention services for children whose families did not receive Medicaid.

MENTAL HEALTH SERVICES SHOULD BE INTEGRATED WITH PRIMARY HEALTH CARE SERVICES

A key component of a prevention and early intervention subsystem under managed care is primary care–based services. In many ethnic minority communities, particularly those of Latinos and Asian Americans, primary care providers or clinics serve the health, social services, and mental health care needs of individuals and families (Attkisson, Hohmann, & Miranda, 1994; Bernal, Munoz, Perez-Stable, & Ying, 1995; Broadhead, 1994; Castillo, Escobar, & Waitzkin, 1994; Dobrof, Rocha, Silverton, & Umpierre, 1990). The range of services provided in these environments may include screening, consultation with primary care providers, service coordination, brief counseling and therapy, health education and psychoeducation, multidisciplinary case planning, and providing information and referrals to resources such as substance abuse intervention services.

As with other early intervention services, it is essential that agencies field-test primary care screening tools and other prevention or early intervention instruments sufficiently before embarking on their widespread use. For example, San Mateo County field-tested the Pediatric Symptom Checklist in a predominantly Spanish-speaking primary care clinic. Adjustments were made to the Spanish version of that instrument to accommodate specific Spanish dialects, and the number of items on the checklist was reduced to ensure a greater degree of participation among the families served. Initial results of using the instrument showed a trend of lower positive scores compared with the perceived need for the agency's services in the community (Pagano et al., 1996). In communities where clients perceive a lower incidence of psychosocial problems than that perceived by primary care providers, behavior change in individuals and families may be accomplished through primary health care services rather than through more traditional counseling or mental health centers (Pagano et al., 1996).

A well-designed, culturally competent mental health consultation service model can provide the necessary support and assistance to avoid more involved and expensive mental health interventions and/or physical health care for many individuals and families. In addition, effective primary care–based mental health services increase the capacity of primary health care providers to screen for mental health problems and better use mental health services (San Mateo County Mental Health Services, 1995). San Mateo County has begun to field-test this concept by assigning mental health staff to two primary care clinics serving predominantly ethnic minority adults and children. In addition, the county has stationed nurse practitioners in mental health clinics to ensure that the primary health care needs of people with serious mental illnesses are more easily and more conveniently met.

Serving individuals who are uninsured or indigent in Medicaid mental health managed care environments is also an issue in primary care clinics. Fiscal strategies that are able to pool all available health and human services care resources are essential to ensuring that prevention and early intervention do not discriminate against those clients who are ineligible for Medicaid. In San Mateo County, public agencies and nonprofit private agencies working together have attracted federal, state, local, and private foundation funds to develop a relatively strong community-based psychosocial service network to augment the primary health care system. This network has the potential to manage risk related to avoiding not solely more costly and more complex medical care but also costly child welfare, special education, juvenile and criminal justice, and substance abuse intervention programs. The network does not necessarily have to locate services in primary care environments but must be accessible to primary care clinics for referral, liaison, and collaborative intervention planning.

THE PROFESSIONAL SERVICE PROVIDER POOL AND SERVICE MODALITIES SHOULD ENCOURAGE CULTURAL COMPETENCE

Culturally competent standards should help publicly operated community mental health systems that are accountable to the communities that they serve in delivering services equitably to all clients. This position is in direct contrast to fee-for-service private sector provider Medicaid systems that serve people who receive Medicaid, who often have lower expectations with regard to the services provided to them. Their low expectation levels are primarily due to the fact that historically many health care providers have opted not to serve people who receive Medicaid.

Publicly operated community mental health systems are in a unique position to serve people of diverse ethnicities who receive Medicaid by broadening their provider pools. Provider pools can include community-based private nonprofit agencies, individual private practitioners, and private practice groups. Through a well-organized process of requesting proposals and ideas, a range of service modalities in prevention, early intervention, assessment, and intervention areas can be developed. A mental health managed care system is in a position to establish cultural competence standards with regard to, for example, language capability, cross-cultural program requirements, and service capacity for people with disabilities (e.g., people with hearing impairments) for its provider network. As another example, the managed care system can purchase slots in existing community-based group intervention services designed for a particular ethnic group.

San Mateo County requires all of its Medicaid outpatient provider agencies to employ staff with Spanish-speaking ability. This requirement is based on the county's demographics, which include a Spanish-speaking community widely dispersed throughout the county. San Mateo County cases involving Medicaid recipients who speak a primary language other than Spanish or English are handled on a case-by-case basis in conjunction with an independent contractor or another contracting agency. If significant clusters of speakers of a particular language emerge in the county, the division will seek an agency or a group outpatient provider to serve that group.

INPATIENT SERVICE PROVIDERS NEED TO ADHERE TO PRINCIPLES OF SYSTEMS OF CARE

Once a system of care assumes control over inpatient care, the principles of the system of care extend across the continuum from early intervention to acute care. These principles include individualized care, interagency collaboration, clear outcomes and accountable systems, family-centered care, and cultural competence. Consistent with the concepts presented in this chapter, the following points focus on the principles of cultural competence and family-centered care. Historically, in varying degrees, Medicaid recipients and their mental health care providers have been sealed off from inpatient intervention discharge planning; however, in California, this should no longer be the case because inpatient care has been consolidated within its counties.

Culturally competent inpatient programs comprise policies, human resources development plans, and services that respond to the multicultural needs of their clients. These programs are also thorough in their demonstration of valuing diversity in the workplace, from the design and decor of their offices to the promotion of diversity among their staffs. Standards that are set for culturally competent services must go beyond the multilingual skills of staff to include the knowledge base required to understand the cultural issues affecting clinical diagnosis and functioning. These standards do not necessarily require the inpatient program to show an ideal mix of multicultural staff for a given region, but they do require that the program have the ability to expand its intervention team beyond the program's staff to include family members, outpatient and service coordination staff, other human services staff, and consultants in the community. Managed care systems can ensure adherence to culturally competent standards in inpatient programs in the contracting process with their inpatient providers. San Mateo County clearly delineates its Spanish-speaking requirements for its inpatient providers. The county must continue to work with service providers to improve their linguistic capacities in languages other than English and Spanish and needs to elaborate more fully the nonlanguage cross-cultural program features that service agencies need to have in place.

Inpatient practice and commitment to family–professional partnership principles is vital to a well-developed system of care and specifically to a culturally competent system of care. The concept of involving parents and caregivers as partners in intervention planning is often foreign and threatening to inpatient systems. At times, parents are blamed for their children's conditions or are thought of patronizingly as victims who have lost the capacity or the will to take care of their children. This type of attitude in interventions can lead to hastily made discharge recommendations for out-of-home placements. Including parents and family members in intervention planning and service delivery allows the intervention team to draw from familial and cultural strengths to help stabilize a child who is in psychiatric crisis. For ethnic minority families, particularly for African American and Latino families, encouraging the participation of extended family, close neighbors, or other trusted community members (e.g., clergy) in intervention and discharge planning can be a powerful tool in helping youth to return to the community and move toward healthier participation in school and the community and at home. In a managed care environment, inpatient stays are often short; there is not always time for families to become more involved and make a difference. For this reason, it is essential that outpatient service coordinators and others who support the family work in concert with inpatient service providers to facilitate parents' and caregivers' involvement.

In San Mateo County, parents of children and youth who are hospitalized with serious emotional disabilities feel alienated from, mistrustful of, or intimidated by the inpatient environment. Alienation among families from ethnic minority groups and with low incomes can be magnified by racism, economic dependency, immigration, or other cultural factors (e.g., their deference to authority, their belief that doctors know best) (Garnaccia, Parra, Deschamps, & Millstein, 1992). Often inpatient staff perceive families from ethnic minority groups as uninvolved in their children's care. These kinds of attitudes contribute to families' feeling distant from inpatient service providers. San Mateo County has inpatient contract requirements for family and professional involvement. Close monitoring must be ensured to shift contract commitments from rhetoric to action. Parent outreach specialists who are paid by the San Mateo County system of care are beginning to have their presence felt in inpatient arenas by helping parents and caregivers play more active roles in service planning. One of these specialists in the San Mateo County system of care is a Latino male. In addition, one of the previous specialists, an African American male, still works with the system on occasional special assignments. These staff members are invaluable in helping to bridge the gap between families from ethnic minority groups and inpatient units.

Historically, inpatient assessments and discharge planning have been guided by the premise that there is something wrong with the family or that the family cannot provide what the child needs. Typically, family strengths or the resources that a family needs are not considered in assessment, intervention, and discharge planning. For an increasing number of families of children and youth with serious emotional disorders in San Mateo County, parent outreach specialists ask parents the question "What would it take to keep your child home after he or she returns from the hospital?" and discuss with parents intervention options that can avoid placements that would be more costly in both human and fiscal terms.

COLLABORATIVE RELATIONSHIPS MUST BE REINFORCED WITH OTHER CHILDREN'S SERVICES AGENCIES

Although some argue that a system of care is in the best position to manage care for children and youth whose families are eligible to receive Medicaid, particularly for those who are involved in multiple agencies, the system of care also faces an assortment of challenges best illustrated by the child welfare and foster care systems. A system of care that is managing care for children in foster care whose families are eligible for Medicaid has a unique opportunity to consolidate resources to offer a rich continuum of mental health services. This system of care should be consistent in assessing needed levels of care based on the severity of the children's mental health conditions or problems. Historically, children in foster care have been subjected to a fragmented mental health services system characterized by the following features:

- Inconsistency in assessments
- Rigid and dogmatic programs that require children to fit in
- Excessive service provider turnover, leading to ineffective bonding between children and therapists
- Lack of service options because a designated provider has been assigned to the foster care facility or because of the lack of an available psychiatrist or psychologist in the fee-for-service provider pool
- Lack of access to bilingual and/or bicultural service providers

Through the consolidation of resources and providers, a system of care is in an excellent position to remedy the problematic features just listed. Specifically, in the area of cultural competence, the system should insist on appropriate assessment of cultural variables in intervention planning, cross-cultural consultation with the foster care providers, and accessibility of bilingual and/or culturally competent service providers for clients. Often children are placed in communities that are far away and different from their own and in which bilingual and culturally competent staff are scarce. Thus, the placement-planning process becomes even more crucial in securing providers who can address more appropriately children's cultural and social needs.

A well-developed program of services within a system of care should have the advantage of individualizing care that meets the cultural needs of children and their families. For example, intensive in-home services, respite care, and therapeutic foster care can practice cultural competence by providing access to a diverse and trained service provider population that can be matched with individual clients' needs.

Under its consolidated mental health services managed care plan, San Mateo County is working with its Human Services Agency (which includes child welfare services) to develop a more cohesive, more consistent, and more accessible mental health services system. The child welfare system in San Mateo County has relied on specialized contracts with independent providers to assess and to provide treatment for children from ethnic minority groups, particularly African American children. The mental health system of care plan must find a way to merge these providers' services into the provider network pool while remaining consistent in reimbursing providers within the established rate structure.

To achieve interagency cohesion and improved access to system of care services for children and youth who are in foster care, the San Mateo County Mental Health Services Division, in conjunction with the county's Human Services Agency, must establish a protocol to implement a number of important activities. These activities include

- Maintaining an inventory of all foster care children, their mental health needs, and the levels of care that they receive
- Establishing a referral process for service authorization
- Implementing a utilization review protocol
- Maintaining a database of information such as ethnicity and language or cultural capacity of the provider network for the area where the child is placed

CUSTOMER RELATIONS AND GRIEVANCE PROCEDURES MUST BE CULTURALLY COMPETENT

Managed care programs' client relations and complaint and grievance procedures must ensure equitable participation of and system of care response to all communities. Historically, children's services institutions and agencies have developed sophisticated client relations and complaint and grievance policies and procedures with the intent of resolving problems between clients and their providers at the earliest and least complicated stage. A good example in California is the process by which parents redress their complaints and disagreements and/or file grievances with regard to special education programs. Unfortunately, the history of clients' relationships with systems of care is one of mixed results for ethnic minority communities that have participated in and benefited from customer relations and grievance processes.

A child and youth system of care that values a family–professional partnership has no choice but to develop processes that nurture trust and encourage pragmatic problem solving among family members and service providers from all major partner agencies, mental health services programs, and designated grievance coordinators. Service providers in these systems need to understand systemic as well as their own personal weaknesses and strengths relating to cultural competence. A strong client service philosophy and complaint and grievance protocol 1) works with both the individual service provider and the system at large so that service providers do not become defensive and 2) honors the life experiences and perceptions of the individuals presenting complaints.

In San Mateo County, administrators of the Mental Health Plan have designated the coordinator of the family partnership team as the individual who handles clients' complaints and informal grievances as part of the customer service and grievance protocol. The coordinator brings strong assets to this function, including highly developed skills and experience in developing culturally competent programs and activities. The family partnership team is culturally diverse, including African American and Latino and Spanish-speaking family outreach workers who can be enlisted to help resolve clients' complaints early in the grievance process. The family partnership team coordinator and the outreach workers are steadily building trust and strong collaborative working relationships with both mental health services providers and other partner agency personnel. These positive working relationships are absolutely necessary to resolve client–provider problems and to avoid more costly formal grievance and fair hearing activities.

San Mateo County is just beginning to test different customer service–oriented practices such as point-in-time "How was your service today?" questionnaires, bulletin board quizzes for clients related to their mental health care knowledge, and psychoeducation presentations at clinics covering topics such as awareness regarding various medications and understanding particular mental illnesses. It is critical for any system engaged in such initiatives to build culturally and linguistically relevant material into its client services procedures.

EVALUATIONS MUST BE RESPONSIVE
TO POPULATIONS OF DIVERSE ETHNICITIES

In order for a public mental health services managed care plan to compete and succeed in managing insurance plans for Medicaid recipients and people who are indigent and/or uninsured, it must demonstrate both cost effectiveness and the ability to effect positive change in clients' overall functioning. Evaluations of such a plan should focus on two primary areas: 1) the relative success of system and client functioning outcomes measures when the outcomes achieved with ethnic minority clients are compared and 2) system-related objectives as outlined in cultural competence plans.

Evaluation of systems of care for children and youth has a rich history of achieving positive overall systemic or aggregate outcomes, such as reductions in out-of-home placements, increased school achievement, and lower levels of juvenile delinquency recidivism (Abbott, Jordan, & Murtaza, 1995; Attkisson et al., 1997; Rosenblatt, Attkisson, & Fernandez, 1992). However, systems of care have not shown consistent outcome success among specific ethnic minority populations, primarily because data gathered for ethnic minorities have been limited or because the data are often not organized by ethnicity (Attkisson, Dresser, & Rosenblatt, 1995). As managed systems of care begin to address issues such as whether the service works or clients are getting what they want, it is critical that evaluation programs be able to present data for specific ethnic minority communities and compare these results with those of the dominant culture community. It is important to consider that ethnic groups served over a period of time may experience change for reasons other than the intervention. Reasons for change among members of ethnic minority groups in the community may include acculturation, generational changes, and specific events in the life of a community (Szapoznik, Scopetta, & King, 1978).

Systems of care have advanced the concept and framework for cultural competence (Cross, Bazron, Dennis, & Isaacs, 1989). The framework lays out a continuum of competence that can be applied to the assessment of policy, programs and services, and human resources development. In the area of programs and services, it is important to evaluate how the program philosophy matches up with the cultural values of the target population, including areas such as spirituality and family orientation (Pumariega, 1996). Cultural competence plans must be adopted as part of managed care plans at all levels of the system of care in order to track an organization's progress in moving along this continuum. Cultural competence plans need to illustrate clients' access to all resources and benefits available within a particular plan. Evaluation of clients' access would address how particular ethnic communities gain access to care and the barriers that they face (Pumariega, 1996). A cultural competence plan must be consistent in the system of care's assessment and delivery of care for all beneficiaries. Although systems of care value individualized care and the availability of flexible funds and services, caution must be shown in not rallying for providing services tailored for one community at the expense of others.

Organizations that have excellent cultural competence plans with clear standards for cultural competence and that have solid track records of human resources development may still be plagued by blind spots that can impede their progress along the cultural competence continuum. These blind spots may include tendencies among staff to make faulty assumptions about ethnic minority groups that influence their practice or an organization's overconfidence that its services are culturally competent based solely on the number of bilingual staff available. The latter blind spot may divert attention from developing the bicultural capacity of staff or from increasing the cultural competence skills of Caucasian staff. Mental health services organizations and their staffs must be assessed not only for cultural competence in the broader policy, services, and human resources development dimensions but also in specific areas that help shed light on these blind spots. Helpful evaluation instruments include

- Questionnaires and surveys that ask clients whether their culture is respected and valued
- Questionnaires and surveys that ask partner agency staff whether mental health staff are sensitive to their clients' cultures
- Comprehensive systemwide studies that contact a sample of service providers, clients, partner agency staff, and advocates to probe their impressions of the system's level of cultural competence (Macro International Inc., 1996)
- Interviews and focus groups (e.g., cultural audits) (Shusta, Harris, Levine, & Wong, 1995) that assess staff perceptions of the organization's ability to value and manage diversity

The validity and reliability of these instruments are enhanced by culturally sophisticated evaluation teams. These teams may include individuals indigenous to the community being evaluated, mental health services providers, interagency representatives, and clients (Hayes-Roizner, 1996).

A well-developed system of care can bring together interagency partners and clients in a process to evaluate cultural competence plans. In San Mateo County, an interagency task force under the CYSOC completed an updated cultural competence plan (San Mateo County Mental Health Services, 1996). The plan specified clear objectives, who is responsible for carrying out activities, and success indicators. Although managed care consolidation and its ramifications were reflected in the plan, the plan required modifications to include more managed care–focused objectives such as inpatient care use and early intervention.

CONCLUSIONS

This chapter establishes a framework for further analysis of cultural competence in a managed care environment. Systems of care for children and youth should be in a strong position to advance cultural competence as these systems begin to integrate with managed care. A system of care's mastery of the 10 issues discussed in this chapter can produce a system that demonstrates cost effectiveness, successful outcomes for the clients whom it serves, and clients' satisfaction. These key results valued by systems of care in a managed care environment can be achieved by taking the following steps:

- Achieve both positive systemwide and positive individual functioning outcomes.
- Establish clear standards of culturally competent care.
- Increase access to services among all populations in the community.
- Develop the ability to draw strengths from the various cultures represented by those served.
- Operate according to a strong client service philosophy to ensure clients' satisfaction across all communities.
- Value diversity in the workplace.
- Institute a high degree of family-centered care and family–professional partnerships.
- Provide a rich continuum of services that are well integrated with those of other human services agencies and that are individualized to meet the unique needs of the individual, family, culture, and community.
- Present high standards of quality and cost-effective care.
- Demonstrate fiscal viability, administrative competence, and system accountability.
- Avoid costly intervention options in multiple areas, including high-end institutional services, more complex outpatient services (e.g., early intervention, primary care–based services), service involvement in other areas of health and human services, formal grievances and fair hearings, discrimination actions, and controlling staff turnover.
- Practice strong interagency collaboration and partnerships, and share risks.

In order for cultural competence to prevail in a managed care environment, the values, principles, and elements of systems of care must drive managed care rather than be driven by managed care.

REFERENCES

Abbott, B., Jordan, P., & Murtaza, N. (1995). Interagency collaboration for children's mental health services: The San Mateo County model for managed care. *Administration and Policy in Mental Health, 22*(3), 301–313.

Attkisson, C.C., Dresser, K., & Rosenblatt, A. (1995). Service systems for youth with severe emotional disorder: System-of-care research in California. In L. Bickman & D. Rog (Eds.), *Children's mental health service systems: Policy, services, and evaluation* (pp. 236–280). Thousand Oaks, CA: Sage Publications.

Attkisson, C.C., Hohmann, A.A., & Miranda, J. (1994). Epidemiology of mental disorders in primary care. In J. Miranda, A.A. Hohmann, C.C. Attkisson, &

D.B. Larson (Eds.), *Mental disorders in primary care* (pp. 3–15). San Francisco: Jossey-Bass.

Attkisson, C.C., Rosenblatt, A.B., Dresser, K.L., Baize, H.R., Clausen, J.M., & Lind, S.L. (1997). Effectiveness of the California system of care model for children and youth with severe emotional disorder. In C.T. Nixon & D. Northrup (Eds.), *Evaluating mental health services: How do programs for children "work" in the real world?* (pp. 146–208). Thousand Oaks, CA: Sage Publications.

Bayview Hunters Point Foundation for Community Improvement, Inc. (1996). *The Bayview Hunters Point Foundation for Community Improvement, Inc.* [Brochure]. San Francisco: Author.

Bernal, G., Munoz, R., Perez-Stable, E.J., & Ying, Y.-W. (1995). Prevention of depression with primary care patients. *American Journal of Community Psychology, 23*(2), 199–222.

Broadhead, W.E. (1994). Presentation of psychiatric symptomatology in primary care. In J. Miranda, A.A. Hohmann, C.C. Attkisson, & D.B. Larson (Eds.), *Mental disorders in primary care* (pp. 139–162). San Francisco: Jossey-Bass.

Castillo, R., Escobar, J.I., & Waitzkin, H. (1994). Somatic symptoms and mental health disorders in immigrant and refugee populations. In J. Miranda, A.A. Hohmann, C.C. Attkisson, & D.B. Larson (Eds.), *Mental disorders in primary care* (pp. 163–185). San Francisco: Jossey-Bass.

Cross, T., Bazron, B., Dennis, K., & Isaacs, M.R. (1989). *Towards a culturally competent system of care: A monograph on effective services for minority children who are severely emotionally disturbed.* Washington, DC: Georgetown University, Child Development Center, Child and Adolescent Service System Program, Technical Assistance Center.

Dobrof, J., Rocha, L., Silverton, M., & Umpierre, M. (1990). Group work in primary care medical setting. *Journal of Applied Psychology, 15*(1), 32–37.

Garnaccia, P., Parra, P., Deschamps, A., & Millstein, G. (1992, June). Sí, dios quiere [Yes, God willing]: Hispanic families' experiences of caring for a seriously mentally ill family member. *Culture, Medicine and Psychiatry, 16*(2), 187–215.

Hayes-Roizner, M. (1996). Strategies for culturally competent evaluations in children's mental health. *TABrief, 2*(2), 10–11.

Institute for Human and Social Development, Inc. (1996). *San Mateo County Head Start Program: 1995–1996 demographic report.* South San Francisco, CA: Author.

Macro International Inc. (1996). *The national comprehensive community mental health for children and families program evaluation: Report from Year 1.* Atlanta: Author.

Murphy, J.M., Ichinose, C., Hicks, R., Kingdon, D., Crist-Whitzel, J., Jordan, P., Feldman, R., & Jellinek, M.S. (1996). Utility of the Pediatric Symptom Checklist as a psychosocial screen in EPSDT: A pilot study. *Journal of Pediatrics, 129*(6), 864–869.

Pagano, M., Murphy, J.M., Pederson, M., Mosbachr, D., Crist-Whitzel, J., Jordan, P., Rodas, C., & Jellinek, M.S. (1996). Screening for psychological problems in 4–5-year-olds during routine EPSDT examinations: Validity and reliability in a Mexican-American sample. *Clinical Pediatrics, 35*(3), 139–146.

Peninsula Children's Center/Zonta. (1996, July). *Progress report on project ABC: Early intervention mental health services under the San Mateo County mental health managed care plan.* Palo Alto, CA: Author.

Pumariega, A.J. (1996). Culturally competent evaluation of outcomes in systems of care for children's mental health. *TABrief, 2*(2), 1, 3–5.

Romero, J.T. (1982). Hispanic support systems: Health–mental health promotion strategies. In R. Valle & W. Vega (Eds.), *Hispanic natural support systems* (pp. 103–111). Sacramento: State of California, Department of Mental Health.

Rosenblatt, A., Attkisson, C.C., & Fernandez, A. (1992). Integrating systems of care in California for youth with severe emotional disturbance: II. Initial group home expenditure and utilization findings from the California AB 373 evaluation project. *Journal of Child and Family Studies, 1*(3), 263–286.

San Mateo County Mental Health Services. (1987). *Assembly Bill 377 system of care grant application submitted to the California State Department of Mental Health.* San Mateo, CA: Author.

San Mateo County Mental Health Services. (1995). *San Mateo mental health Medicaid managed care plan.* San Mateo, CA: Author.

San Mateo County Mental Health Services. (1996). *Cultural competence plan for San Mateo County Mental Health Services, 1996–1998.* San Mateo, CA: Author.

Shusta, R., Harris, P., Levine, D., & Wong, H.Z. (1995). *Multicultural law enforcement: Strategies for peacekeeping in a diverse society.* Upper Saddle River, NJ: Prentice-Hall.

SRI International. (1996). *California's Healthy Start school-linked services initiative: Results for children and families.* Menlo Park, CA: Author.

State of California, Department of Finance. (1995). *California statistical abstract.* Sacramento: Author.

State of California, Department of Health Services. (1994). *Health data summaries for California counties: 1994 report.* Sacramento: Author.

State of California, Department of Mental Health. (1993). *The California comprehensive system of care: A new model for children and youth with serious emotional disturbances* (Federal grant application submitted to the Center for Mental Health Services, Substance Abuse and Mental Health Services Administration, U.S. Department of Health and Human Services). Sacramento: Author.

State of California, Department of Mental Health. (1994). *Client data system reports submitted by counties to State Department of Mental Health.* Sacramento: Author.

Szapoznik, J., Scopetta, M., & King, O. (1978). Theory and practice in matching treatment to the specific characteristics and problems of Cuban immigrants. *Journal of Community Psychology, 6,* 112–122.

Valle, R., & Vega, W. (Eds.). (1982). *Hispanic natural support systems.* Sacramento: State of California, Department of Mental Health.

Wong, H.Z. (1982). Community mental health services for Asian and Pacific Americans. In L. Snowden (Ed.), *Annual review of community mental health* (Vol. 3, pp. 184–204). Thousand Oaks, CA: Sage Publications.

Neighborhoods and Communities as Partners in Mental Health Services

The Role of Ethnography in Creating Linkages with Communities

Identifying and Assessing Neighborhoods' Needs and Strengths

Susan D. Greenbaum

Ethnography offers concepts and tools that can illuminate the cultural values, belief systems, and customs that affect the manner in which different groups interpret and respond to program initiatives. One of the fundamental principles of cultural competence is the need to identify and work in concert with natural support systems in communities in which services are provided. Such systems, however, are rarely evident to outsiders, and they may follow many different patterns. In some places, the people who live close to each other may know each other well and may have developed a variety of ways to help each other cope with shared problems such as child care, transportation, surveillance, and information. In other environments, neighbors may be aloof or even hostile toward each other, and the support systems that exist may follow lines of kinship or ethnicity that are diffused across a much wider geographic area. The extent to which support networks exist can vary considerably from one context to another. Major challenges in designing culturally competent service delivery systems are learning how to reconnoiter the community and understand its indigenous structure and determining the most effective ways of making contact with and gaining the trust of its inhabitants.

Ethnography offers methods by which these processes can be carried out. *Ethnography* refers to a combination of techniques used in studying small populations. These include participant observation, interviewing key informants, mapping spatial relationships within and significant features of the community, and developing measures of formal and informal social relationships. Participant observation is the most basic tool of ethnography. It is carried out by direct involvement in the day-to-day life of the community being examined—that is, in activities and events that reveal what it means to be part of the community in question. Ethnographers strive to obtain an insider's perspective on the problems and capacities of communities.

In practical terms, achieving this level of comfort and understanding often takes a long time, so this dimension of ethnography has proved to be too costly for many kinds of projects aimed at improving services. In response to this difficulty, applied anthropologists have developed what are called *rapid assessment techniques* for shortening the period of participant observation and making strategic choices about how it will be implemented (Chambers, 1985; Van Willigen, 1986). One approach is to increase reliance on key informants. Key informants are individuals who are knowledgeable about particular aspects of the community, who already possess an insider's understanding, and who are willing and able to articulate that knowledge. Projects that are collaborative and that promise community residents both improvements in their quality of life and a larger role in decision making are well suited to the involvement of key informants because they offer community residents incentives to participate that are often lacking in basic ethnographic research. In other words, the nature of applied and program-related research lends itself to the rapid identification and cooperation of key informants, thus overcoming one of the standard reasons why ethnography takes so long to accomplish. Focus groups, in which several key informants are interviewed at the same time, can bring additional efficiency to the data collection process because a group's responses may supply interactive information that interviews conducted individually would not reveal.

Interviews and observations provide largely qualitative data, but quantitative data and analyses also are used in ethnography. Census data, epidemiological studies, and the numerical results of previous survey research in a given community can supply important contextual information. For studies in defined geographic areas, city directories provide a variety of data that are amenable to quantification with regard to the people who live there. Collection of new data based on sampling or quantitative indicators is frequently part of an ethnographic research design. Qualitative observations may generate hypotheses that can be tested with quantitative data and vice versa. The product of ethnographic research is an integrated description of a community that can be used to identify local leadership, cultural issues, social support systems, and organizational capacities. Ethnographic research offers a means by which to understand cultural and social differences within and among communities. Planners and community developers have begun to recognize that cultural values and traditions do have relevance to designing community programs and that programs designed by people from outside the community as well as those designed by people familiar with the local community often do not work in diverse environments. The virtues of ethnography, especially for research on ethnic communities, derive from ethnography's inductive approach in combination with anthropological concepts regarding culture. Inductive approaches are exploratory and open minded. Although general research plans are developed in advance, no prior judgments are made about what will be found; and the researcher expects to be surprised. The knowledge base of anthropology is based on wide-ranging inquiries into the patterns and processes of cultural adaptation to every conceivable combination of environmental, social, and political conditions. It offers a compendium of data on how humans use their unique capacities for social learning to solve problems and search for meaning. Local culture is more than food and festivals; it is everyday life—the customs, conventions, strategies, and habits that people in communities devise in the course of interacting with each other and with external agencies. It draws from both tradition and contingencies, from the ways in which space is organized and the nature of opportunities that exist or that are lacking in particular areas.

Ethnography, which is designed to elucidate culture, is a *grounded enterprise* in two relatively distinctive meanings of that term. First, it is an exploration designed to be free of preconceived ideas. This aspect is particularly important for research on ethnic communities because distorted stereotypes about cultural practices and outright racism are woven into the conventional wisdom that is often unconsciously incorporated into existing literature about the problems of ethnic communities. Second, ethnographers approach their work from the "ground level"; that is, they become personally acquainted with the people whom they study. They let people speak for themselves rather than rendering their experiences through the dispassionate and often distorted lens of aggregate statistics.

Ethnographic approaches are especially suited to the aims of neighborhood-based intervention strategies. Programs designed to capitalize on natural, or preexisting, support systems need a clear understanding of how these systems are actually configured. Moreover, neighborhood social relationships are not always supportive or constructive. Service area boundaries often enclose subpopulations that are mutually antagonistic, based on class or ethnic differences. Facilities or activities located in one section of a neighborhood may be unacceptable to residents in other sections of the neighborhood for reasons that are not obvious to outside observers. Differing cultural values and group traditions can exert a powerful influence on how residents respond to particular interventions. Service providers' prior knowledge of such conditions can do much to avoid problems in program implementation. Ethnography offers a kind of road map of salient features and relevant conditions within local communities, a tool that planners can use in developing authentically collaborative programs and projects. Growing numbers of politicians and policy makers contend that resources and decision making should be devolved to local levels, where there is both knowledge of local conditions and appropriate accountability. Within that context, however, ethnic minorities living in inner-city neighborhoods are often portrayed as being significantly less capable of determining their own needs or devising solutions to the problems that they face. Social programs, some people believe, have nurtured dependency to such a degree that they have produced an underclass who cannot function in society. Availing to the wisdom of localities is apparently to be reserved for those groups who are already most able to influence the courses of action in their own communities and whose problems are the least in need of attention. The truly disadvantaged are not really included in this framework because others assume that they have little to offer and cannot be trusted.

Since the mid-1960s, literature on urban planning and problems has produced a succession of theories and slogans that portray "ghetto" dwellers in highly pejorative terms. In the 1950s, they were viewed as pathetically unprepared migrants from the South who in the 1960s spawned a culture of poverty that by the 1980s had grown into a vast and menacing underclass. A particularly disturbing trend in analyses of African American culture in the 1990s is to argue that African Americans' historical traditions and communal values are fundamentally dysfunctional and are a leading cause of the persistent poverty of inner-city African American communities (D'Souza, 1995). This perspective is both venomous and misinformed. In a 1992 article, Newman reviewed findings of urban anthropologists that contradict these portrayals and urged anthropologists to become more actively involved in the critical debate about the culture of the urban poor. In spite of large expenditures of public resources aimed at improving the living conditions of inner cities, the living conditions in these areas have gotten worse since the early 1980s. Statistics related to crime, unemployment, urban decay, homelessness, welfare dependency, drugs, violence, and maltreatment of children have increased during this period. Political conservatives have concluded that the programs designed to alleviate these problems ironically must have caused them to worsen. Such facile assessments overlook the tandem effects of, for example, deindustrialization, falling wages, reductions in the stock of low-income housing, relative decreases in resources allocated for services and programs, and the failure to curb the flow of drugs across U.S. borders—all of which offer more direct explanations for these growing miseries.

It is nonetheless true, however, that many programs designed to develop and improve distressed communities have not achieved their objectives. There has been a kind of self-fulfilling failure built into interventions that purport to involve residents and clients but instead offer patronizing and sometimes punitive remedies for problems that are not properly conceived. With rare and fleeting exceptions, policy makers and shapers have tended to view the poor as behaviorally responsible for their own lamentable condition. The political advantages of a model that blames the victim are outweighed by its lack of predictive or explanatory power. Most of the research on which these perspectives are based rely on large-scale statistics; they pose the wrong questions and mistake consequences for causes. For example, Greenbaum's (1993) analysis of housing problems in a midwestern city revealed that explanations of blight based on alleged shortcomings of African American housing consumers are fundamentally erroneous and, in fact, have led to discriminatory policies that only make the problem worse. Recent immigrants who live in inner-city areas, especially those from politically unstable and impoverished countries, reflect additional patterns of response to a different set of problems that include language barriers, emotional trauma, unfamiliarity with local customs and services, and lack of education or marketable skills. Drawing on cultural knowledge, individuals in localities often band together in immigrant associations, establish broad support systems of interlocking family networks, identify new niches in the economy, and find other means of adjustment based on accumulated group traditions. Most authors who purport to examine the social conditions of inner-city neighborhoods fail to measure or to acknowledge the successes of indigenous self-help initiatives that have emerged in spite of or in opposition to the destructive influences of state intervention in poor communities. Important exceptions are Medoff and Sklar (1994), whose book *Streets of Hope* details the extraordinary accomplishments of ordinary people who live in the Roxbury section of Boston. Their narrative about the Dudley Street Neighborhood Initiative, a broad multi-ethnic coalition of grass roots organizations, disabuses myths about race and poverty, discloses the historical factors that have precipitated the decline of city neighborhoods, and clearly demonstrates the practical value of bottom-up approaches to redevelopment. Although Dudley Street is somewhat unique in the extent to which community activists were able to mobilize internal resources and external capital, the histories of most inner-city neighborhoods are replete with personal accomplishments and collective struggles; successful businesses; large churches; rich cultural developments; voluntary associations; mutual aid societies; civil rights activism; and a host of local leaders, many of whom became prominent activists in causes such as urban renewal, model cities, and scores of other programs that have required at least the infrastructure of citizen participation. Against a backdrop of poverty and despair are the survivors and strugglers and the networks and institutions laid down by those who went before.

The poor, both immigrants to and those who were born in the United States, have firsthand experience in devising means to cope with their problems, wisdom that should be studied rather than ignored. However, social programs intended for inner-city communities are typically built on an image of a client population that is problem-ridden and incapable. This perspective is to a great extent inevitable. The severity of the clients' problems is precisely what justifies the intervention, along with the perceived unlikelihood that these individuals can solve their own problems. However, the emphasis on needs and problems creates underestimates of clients' capacities and resources. Human capital is wasted because it is discounted, and the apparent enormity of clients' problems encourages acceptance of limited success or outright failure. Needs assessments, which inventory and correlate pathological indicators, inadvertently support this image. To complement the needs assessment, McKnight and Kretzmann recommended that planners also conduct a resource assessment, arguing that

> The starting point for any serious development effort is the opposite of an accounting of deficiencies. Instead there must be an opportunity for individuals to use their own abilities to produce. Identifying the variety and richness of skills, talents, knowledge, and experience of people in low-income neighborhoods provides a base upon which to build new approaches and enterprises. (1990, p. 4)

McKnight suggested that a new kind of map be constructed, in which the positive features and historical strengths of communities are inventoried. Ethnographic research offers an appropriate paradigm for creating this map and provides an analytical framework that can infuse meaning into such a listing. In identifying resources, one should gain an understanding of the particular context and its unique history. Ethnography can supply this added dimension. There are some common features of ethnographic research that can guide this enterprise and help define appropriate research methods and data to be gathered.

History

Ethnographic approaches often begin with history. Older inner-city neighborhoods tend to be far more stable than most people imagine.

People with fewer housing options also are less mobile, especially those who manage to buy the homes in which they live. The research of the author of this chapter involving many different neighborhoods revealed unexpectedly high proportions of residents who had lived at the same addresses for more than 20 years (Greenbaum, 1986, 1993). Many residents come from families who have lived in the same neighborhoods for several generations. This level of commitment and historical continuity represents an uncounted resource. History itself is a resource (see Greenbaum, 1986, 1990, 1995). In even the most depressed areas, many residents have a deep affection for their home territories. Older residents have experienced many changes and have witnessed singular events that contain important lessons for future efforts. In constructing neighborhood histories, these lessons come forth; and such accounts give credit to people who have been neglected in more traditional histories. They make the residents and their forebears central actors in a narrative that dignifies and documents the importance of their lives and contributions.

Diversity

Inner-city communities are internally diverse. In mapping resources, it is important to capture that diversity and understand its significance. There is a tendency to homogenize the social characteristics of "ghettos" and neglect ethnic differences in African American communities, where many residents may be of Caribbean, Latin American, or recent African ancestry. Similarities in appearance do not automatically signal identity of interest. More obvious ethnic conflicts may exist between native-born residents and immigrants from Asia or Latin America. There also may be wide class differences, especially when the so-called target area encompasses many small neighborhoods (Gregory, 1992). Diversity can be a resource, or it can be an obstacle. Finding ways to overcome hostilities and engender trust based on common goals requires particular skill and must begin with a grounded appreciation of the particular circumstances that exist in specific places. Participation strategies need to account for multiple constituencies and ensure that local involvement is authentically representative.

Organizational Capacity

Contrary to popular views, poor people are not inert or disorganized. Struggling requires effort and ingenuity. The strategies devised to deal with adversity are often submerged, and the results are hard to detect (see Sharff, 1987). Another way of viewing life in these communities is to look for the reasons why people's misery is less than what objective observers believe it should be, given the grim statistics on the income of welfare recipients and the many obstacles that poor working families face. Anthropologists who study urban kinship have reached conclusions far different from those of Moynihan (1965) and his successors, who have declared that the family is a dying institution among the poor (see Rapp, 1987; Smith, 1987; Stack, 1974). There is also no dearth of leadership or of organizations in poor communities (Drake & Cayton, 1945; Goode & Schneider, 1994; Greenbaum, 1991; Gregory, 1992; Jones, 1987; King, 1981). Churches and social clubs exist in abundance. Block clubs and civic associations can be found in most poor neighborhoods. Mutual aid societies and rotating credit associations provide credit and capital to individuals who are barred from obtaining loans from conventional sources. These organizations offer direct relief for many problems and provide individuals with valuable leadership experiences. Some of the most effective leaders are those who are not known outside their immediate areas but rather are long-term residents of the community who understand local conditions and families and have the respect and confidence of their neighbors. To assess resources, it is necessary to penetrate the local culture of neighborhoods, reframe definitions of problems and assets, and rethink stereotypes that have led to the self-defeating conclusion that poor people are the cause of poverty.

Casey Ethnographies

A project carried out in connection with the Annie E. Casey Mental Health Initiative for Urban Children illustrates the foregoing discussion. The initiative was conducted at four sites nationally (through December 31, 1998) and was designed to reform systems of care in mental health services, strengthen preventive measures, and reinforce local involvement and decision making in the design and delivery of children's mental health services. The sites selected for the Casey project were the East End in Richmond, the Third Ward in Houston, East Little Havana in Miami, and part of the Roxbury section of Boston. These districts include some of the worst conditions of poverty, violence, neglect, and drug abuse in the cities in which they are located; they are places where children confront serious challenges to their physical well-being and mental health. A major component of the Casey approach in these areas was the establishment of neighborhood governance structures that were intended to play a major role in securing the success of the intervention.

The Casey sites were not, however, *neighborhoods* in the conventional sense of the term. They were large districts of approximately 25,000 people each. Within the boundaries of these areas were included numerous small neighborhoods and considerable diversity in social and housing conditions. The task of creating effective neighborhood governance within such broad and variable populations is challenging. To aid in understanding the cultural differences and social diversity within these districts, the Florida Mental Health Institute, which had the contract for evaluating the Annie E. Casey Mental Health Initiative for Urban Children, included an ethnographic component. The ethnographic component of the Casey project was conducted at two of the four sites: Richmond and Houston. Limited funding was the principal reason why ethnographic research at only two sites was covered. These two areas are quite similar in a number of respects. Both are old neighborhoods in which nearly 90% of residents are African Americans. African American occupancy in these areas is long established, although both areas experienced high degrees of ethnic succession prior to the 1990s. African American sections of these areas have expanded in response to both "white flight" to the suburbs and urban renewal activities. However, urban renewal undermined and reduced thriving commercial districts of the 1950s. In the late 1990s, many of the contemporary businesses in both areas are operated by Asian immigrants. Housing in these districts is extremely diverse. Both contain public housing projects and deteriorated single-family homes, as well as solid middle-class housing and areas that are targets of gentrification. Large and small churches, social services agencies, and schools anchor the institutional life of these areas. Many of the people who live there have deep roots and highly intertwined life experiences. In the East End and Third Ward, there are significant social resources that should be mobilized in pursuit of the goals of the Casey initiative. The research was designed to identify and analyze these assets and to contextualize the historical conditions that have both nurtured and discounted them. The studies were ethnographic surveys of the history, traditions, leadership, institutions, and local networks of the communities in which services were being delivered. Research was extensive rather than intensive because of the large size of the areas involved. Although the study was designed and coordinated in Tampa, Florida (the location of the Florida Mental Health Institute), the actual research was conducted by local subcontractor investigators, each of whom had considerable knowledge of and experience in these communities. Ethnographic researchers must be able to gain acceptance among the community they are studying and must have sufficient familiarity with the community to formulate an efficient research strategy. Both of these processes take time that can rarely be afforded in applied research, and outsiders have a much harder time in achieving the rapport needed to produce trustworthy data and interpretations.

The methodology used in the Casey studies included the following components:

1. A summary of the neighborhood's history, changes in population and housing quality, factors shaping the characteristics of residents, the sense of neighborhood identity, and ethnic and class diversity within the boundaries of the project site
2. A topographic description of locations of the neighborhood's significant places and institutions, internal boundaries and subareas, geographic distribution of data on risk factors related to children's mental health (stated in terms of combination mapping and narrative keyed to location coordinates)
3. Interviews with approximately 20 key informants about leadership, conflicts among groups in the area, socially defined boundaries around and within the area, the extent of social cohesion among the residents, existing self-help neighborhood organizations (and their efficacy), other existing organizations and institutions, barriers to and advantages of increasing parents' and community members' participation, and estimates of the likelihood of successful participation by area residents
4. Field observations of the project site, including windshield surveys of physical conditions and indicators of blight and distress, observations of street-level activity in terms of both apparent levels of neighborly socializing and potentially inhibiting conditions, and attendance at public meetings and other accessible neighborhood gathering points

Each of these data collection activities was designed to provide descriptive information about the nature of the project sites and the people who lived there. In combination, they drew a picture, or, in McKnight and Kretzmann's (1990) terms, a *map,* of the social and institutional resources available in the community being studied.

The results of the research in the two areas studied in the Casey initiative revealed a high level of social and spatial diversity in spite of apparent ethnic homogeneity. The study also found a rich array of assets that were not considered in the narratives initially composed in the applications for the Casey funding. Both the complexity of these two areas and the untapped social and cultural resources suggested a need for alterations in the program structure of the Casey initiatives. Four recommendations were offered based on the research results, as described in the following paragraphs. These recommendations were specific to the Casey project; however, they have more general applicability in other neighborhood-based projects.

1. *Involve civic associations in the governance process.* Both areas studied had many active civic associations. The importance of civic

associations—in both single-family, predominantly owner-occupied sections and public housing areas—was a major theme of the responses in the interviews and of the other information that was obtained. The East End and the Third Ward both are large districts, larger than many small cities. The internal organization of these areas is a patchwork of small neighborhoods, virtually all of which have some kind of tenant's or homeowner's organizations. These associations are formed and staffed by the residents of the community themselves. They function in a variety of ways to provide a forum for shared concerns and a collective framework for finding solutions. They are the nexus of the many overlapping networks of neighborliness that form the social fabric of these areas. Levels of participation in these groups vary; a great many residents have no direct involvement in these associations. Those who do participate, however, tend to be aware of what is going on within their own blocks and small areas and are able to speak with far more knowledge and authority about local needs and issues than individuals who live outside the neighborhoods. To the extent that neighborhood governance requires informed representation, civic associations are ideal bodies to involve in the process.

2. *Decentralize neighborhood governance board structure to accommodate the size and diversity of the area being studied.* This recommendation was directly related to the preceding one. Because of the considerable diversity of populations within the sites studied in the Casey initiative, devising a systematic method of ensuring that the different sections were represented directly in the composition of the board membership was important. The Casey initiative's criteria for selecting resident members needed to be revised to incorporate more attention to the areas' geographic breadth and their differing housing and economic conditions.

3. *Focus more attention on the positive aspects of the East End and Third Ward.* Many of the problems of the areas studied in the Casey initiatives and in most inner-city neighborhoods are distorted and exaggerated by media attention focused heavily on incidents of violence and abuse. Virtually all news stories about these communities reflect either a negative or a patronizing perspective. The cumulative effect of this image of the Third Ward and East End as "ghettos" with few redeeming qualities has had direct consequences for the mental health of children living in these areas, who struggle with their identities and senses of self-worth. Indirectly, these image problems have contributed to inappropriate attitudes on the part of service providers. Activities such as the Casey project could help to rectify these negative images, both through the success of programs to help individuals and through public relations

campaigns that present positive information about the institutional strengths and constructive activities that always have been a significant part of the social and civic organizations of these areas.

4. *Incorporate heritage and culture into youth programs.* The foregoing issue of negative media images and community perceptions has been compounded by the fact that few young people ever learn about the history of communities like the Third Ward and East End. The present generation, which had grown up after the end of segregation, had a particularly fragmented view of past struggles faced by African Americans and of accomplishments of the people who had built the neighborhoods in which they lived. Many of the older residents who were interviewed were extremely discouraged by the lack of connectedness they perceived in the young people who lived around them. They painted nostalgic pictures of the past in their neighborhoods, of times when there was a sense of pride and a common understanding of the need to work together against the problems imposed on them by discrimination and unfair laws. Heritage projects in which youth are exposed to information about the history and contributions of their own neighbors and ancestors and that involve youth in collecting family history data and creating projects that focus on their local African American heritage should be incorporated as elements in preventive mental health programs. Alienation and low self-esteem are among the causes of many of the current problems that confront poor children. There is an abundance of untapped historical resources and exemplary role models in both of these areas that can help ameliorate some of these underlying identity problems among youth.

CONCLUSIONS

The Casey ethnographies offer one example of how this kind of research strategy may be employed to improve the cultural competence of programs and staff. Planners, implementers, and evaluators of services in ethnically diverse communities must recognize the limitations of their own cultural perspectives and take affirmative steps to eliminate any obstacles to appropriate practice that these present. The overburden of generations of social scientists who failed to reconcile these basic paradigmatic problems in their research has valorized distorted assumptions and led to wrongheaded and counterproductive approaches. African Americans especially have suffered from this phenomenon, a negative predisposition in American society that is deeply rooted in its history. More recent immigrant communities also suffer from the unexamined stereotypes, both positive and negative, that have emerged in American popular thinking. Ethnography provides an alternative mode of gathering information and data that is deliberately and systematically non-ethnocentric, enabling communities to participate directly in fashioning an understanding of what they need, what they will accept, and how they can best facilitate their own problem solving. Linkages with communities, to be effective, must be both bilateral and mutually respectful.

REFERENCES

Chambers, E. (1985). *Applied anthropology: A practical guide.* Upper Saddle River, NJ: Prentice-Hall.

Drake, St.C., & Cayton, H. (1945). *Black metropolis: A study of Negro life in a northern city.* New York: HarperCollins.

D'Souza, D. (1995). *The end of racism: Principles for a multiracial society.* New York: Free Press.

Goode, J., & Schneider, J. (1994). *Reshaping ethnic and racial relations in Philadelphia: Immigrants in a divided city.* Philadelphia: Temple University Press.

Greenbaum, S.D. (1986). *Afro-Cubans in Ybor City: A centennial history.* Tampa, FL: La Union Martí-Maceo.

Greenbaum, S.D. (1990). Marketing Ybor City: Race, ethnicity, and historic preservation in the Sunbelt. *City and Society, 4*(1), 58–76.

Greenbaum, S.D. (1991). A comparison of African American and Euro-American mutual aid societies in 19th century America. *Journal of Ethnic Studies, 19*(3), 95–120.

Greenbaum, S.D. (1993). Housing abandonment in inner-city black neighborhoods: A case study of the effects of the dual housing market. In R. Rotenburg & G. McDonogh (Eds.), *The cultural meaning of urban space* (pp. 139–156). Westport, CT: Bergin & Garvey.

Greenbaum, S.D. (1995). *Ethnographic overview of Houston's Third Ward and Richmond's East End* (Final report on research supporting the Annie E. Casey Mental Health Initiative for Urban Children). Tampa: Florida Mental Health Institute.

Gregory, S. (1992). The changing significance of race and class in an African-American community. *American Ethnologist, 19*(2), 255–274.

Jones, D. (1987). The "community" and organizations in the community. In L. Mullings (Ed.), *Cities of the United States: Studies in urban anthropology* (pp. 99–121). New York: Columbia University Press.

King, M. (1981). *Chain of change: Struggles for black community development.* Boston: South End Press.

McKnight, J.L., & Kretzmann, J. (1990). *Mapping community capacity* (Report of the Neighborhood Innovations Network). Chicago: Chicago Community Trust.

Medoff, P., & Sklar, H. (1994). *Streets of hope: The fall and rise of an urban neighborhood.* Boston: South End Press.

Moynihan, D.P. (1965). *The Negro family.* Washington, DC: U.S. Government Printing Office.

Newman, K.S. (1992). Culture and structure in the "truly disadvantaged." *City and Society, 6*(1), 3–25.

Rapp, R. (1987). Urban kinship in contemporary America: Families, classes, and ideology. In L. Mullings (Ed.), *Cities of the United States: Studies in urban anthropology* (pp. 219–242). New York: Columbia University Press.

Sharff, J. (1987). The underground economy of a poor neighborhood. In L. Mullings (Ed.), *Cities of the United States: Studies in urban anthropology* (pp. 19–50). New York: Columbia University Press.

Smith, R.T. (1987). Kinship and class in Chicago. In L. Mullings (Ed.), *Cities of the United States: Studies in urban anthropology* (pp. 292–316). New York: Columbia University Press.

Stack, C. (1974). *All our kin.* New York: HarperCollins.

Van Willigen, J. (1986). *Applied anthropology: An introduction.* Westport, CT: Bergin & Garvey.

A Culturally Receptive Approach to Community Participation in System Reform

Marcela Gutiérrez-Mayka
and Ricardo Contreras-Neira

In the opening paragraph of *Towards a Culturally Competent System of Care: Programs Which Utilize Culturally Competent Principles*, Isaacs and Benjamin (1991) referred to the 1990s as the decade of the *cultural imperative* in human services delivery. Their use of that term was based on the argument that U.S. institutions ranging from large government agencies to small, community-based organizations are involved in debate about issues of cultural diversity, multiculturalism, pluralism, and what constitutes cultural competence. Moreover, human services providers are faced with overwhelming evidence about the heart of U.S. cities, where minority populations are concentrating in larger and larger numbers, and are confronted with the hardships with which their clients must cope, such as poverty, unsafe environments, and disintegrating families. Thus, they have realized that they can no longer continue to do business as usual and ignore the role that ethnicity plays in their clients' experiences as well as their own.

INTRODUCTION

Although much has been written about cultural competence since the publication of Isaacs and Benjamin's (1991) monograph, emphasis has been placed on the development of service providers' understanding of the cultural values and beliefs held by individual children and families in order to overcome cultural barriers to effective service delivery and

The authors thank Angela Gomez, Teresa Nesman, and Joko Sengova for revising preliminary drafts of this chapter.

maximize the client–provider therapeutic relationship. The field of children's mental health, however, has recognized the needs to move beyond a "client versus system" focus in cultural competence and to look at the roles that communities play in their responses to systems of care (Bernard, Cablas, Hanley, Hernandez, & Romero, 1996; M. Hernandez, personal communication, May 1997; Hernandez & Benjamin, 1994).

The cultural competence literature of the mid- to late 1990s unfortunately does not address the new emphasis on inclusion of residents and implementation of more culturally responsive children's mental health services approaches. This omission takes on greater significance when one considers that the return to decentralization, power devolution, and local governance political philosophies among government and private funding sources has delegated more policy and management responsibilities to communities and that the neediest communities in terms of social change are those made up of minority individuals living in inner-city areas.

This chapter addresses the vacuum in the literature on cultural competence as it pertains to community participation. Cultural competence as applied to community participation translates into a culturally receptive approach on the part of service providers, program designers, or researchers, and the effectiveness of any given approach is linked to outsiders' knowledge of the community, their attitude about their partnership with residents, and their perceived role vis-à-vis members of the community. The chapter begins with a review of the different conceptions and implications of community and citizen participation in systems reform. Next, the components of a culturally competent strategy for engaging minority communities in reform efforts are described, including

- Knowledge as an ethnographic and ecological approach to learning about the community and the cultural norms by which its members behave
- An attitude that is open, receptive, respectful, and unbiased toward engaging in partnerships with the community
- A role that represents the willingness of outsiders to come into the community as learners and facilitators rather than as teachers and overseers

This culturally competent strategy is illustrated in the following sections by an example from an intervention involving resident participation in a predominantly Hispanic community in which a mental health reform initiative was being implemented. Finally, the implications of failing to involve community residents in the debate and decision-making process that leads to program and evaluation designs, systems reform, and policy development are discussed.

Community

The literature talks about two ways of defining *community:* geographically bound and not geographically bound. Agudelo (1983) defined *community* as a group of people who live in the same geographic area, share similar values and similar cultural patterns, and experience similar social problems. Geographic proximity encourages residents to interact more intensely with each other than with outsiders. The conception of community in geographic terms is consistent with the urban concept of *neighborhood,* which is a geographically bound area grouping individuals who have similar characteristics (e.g., socioeconomic status, level of education, ethnic origin). Chaskin and Garg (1994) added that a neighborhood is the primary context in which family life occurs and in which informal relationships and activities, as well as the provision of different goods and services, take place. In this sense, Berger and Neuhaus (1977) viewed the neighborhood as an institution that mediates between individuals and the institutions of the larger society.

The other definition of *community* departs from the geographic focus and centers on the shared characteristics, interests, or issues of a group of people who do not necessarily live close to each other. For instance, for Kinne, Thompson, Chrisman, and Hanley (1989), an ethnic community (e.g., the African American community), a professional community (e.g., the medical community), or an issue group (e.g., parents of children with disabilities) constitute communities that are not spatially bound. It is not unusual for these two types of communities to overlap, creating a situation in which an interest group exists within an ethnic community as well as within a geographic area.

These classifications of communities have important implications when one studies cultural competence in the context of community participation. The choice of strategies to involve community members should vary depending on whether members of the group are physically close to each other and whether there are particular issues about which the group is concerned. For instance, among ethnic groups, particularly recent immigrants, geographic proximity to others of the same ethnic background is sometimes paramount in their effort to define their place in society. This aspect of community is reflected in the composition of many inner-city neighborhoods in which ethnic groups cluster together and become communities within communities. Failure to recognize the existence of embedded communities would lead to approaches to service provision that might be meaningful for one group but totally inappropriate for another. Geographically dispersed ethnic communities may share a common racial background, but variables such as socioeconomic and educational status may create a class identity that is stronger than the communities' ethnic identification. When interest and issue groups develop in an ethnic community that is geographically bound (i.e., in a neighborhood), the challenge becomes to develop an approach that is both sensitive to the cultural issues of the group and significant in terms of their common interest.

Participation

There are many elements of community participation, including community members' voluntary participation in associations (e.g., Everitt, 1996; Perkins & Poole, 1996; Smith, 1975), political participation and decision making (e.g., Alford & Friedland, 1975; Clark, 1975; Leighley, 1996; Mollenkopf, 1979), federally mandated citizen participation in government-originated programs (e.g., Hessler & Beavert, 1982; Mott, 1977; Redburn, Buss, Foster, & Binning, 1980), community residents' participation in community organizations (e.g., Cnaan, 1991; Dubow & Podolefsky, 1982; Wandersman, 1981), and community power (e.g., Abrahams, 1996; Murphree, Wright, & Ebaugh, 1996; Pardo, 1990). This chapter discusses the community residents' involvement in planning and decision making regarding service provision. Barber (1984) defined citizen participation in policy making and service delivery as the recognition of the rights and responsibilities of citizens to have some control over the policies that will have an impact on their lives. Inherent in this recognition of community residents' rights and responsibilities is the belief that people have the capacity to define themselves as opposed to being defined by others. Giddens (1984) referred to this capacity in terms of the concept of *agency* and considered it the antithesis of dependency.

In the context of geographically bound ethnic communities, participation requires special consideration. In these neighborhoods, the experiences of members of ethnic minority groups are tied to the ethnic minority group's development of a self-identity (Maldonado, 1975), which includes language, values, self-concept, and motivation. These elements combine to form what Berger and Luckman (1966) called a social construction of reality by which people understand, perceive, and give meaning to life and significant events. In terms of participation, the group's social construction of reality can act as an incentive or a disincentive to individuals' participation in community activities.

A clear understanding of what is meant by *community* and how narrowly or broadly *participation* is defined is only the first step in the effective involvement of residents in the processes that lead to system of care reform, from program planning and implementation to evaluation and policy debate. The next crucial step is a self-examination by partners from outside the community of their individual approaches to achieving community participation. That step involves the type of knowledge that the outsider acquires of the neighborhood, his or her attitude toward neighborhood residents' social constructions of reality, and the role that the outsider chooses to play in his or her relationship with the community residents.

A CULTURALLY RECEPTIVE APPROACH TO PROMOTING PARTICIPATION IN MINORITY COMMUNITIES

Based on the experiences of the authors of this chapter in human services program evaluation, including involvement in the evaluation of a comprehensive multisite system's reform project with a significant community involvement component, a culturally receptive approach to the promotion of community participation has been identified that is consistent with the tenets of cultural competence (see Table 1).

In the field of children's mental health services, cultural competence has focused primarily on the ability of a system, an agency, or a professional to assess cross-cultural relationships, acknowledge the importance of culture, and incorporate specific knowledge to adapt services to meet culturally unique needs of the client population (Cross, Bazron, Dennis, & Isaacs, 1989). In terms of the community's participation in the system of care, however, the focus needs to fall on the outside players' ability to receive—that is, to be receptive and responsive—to ideas, impressions, or suggestions coming from community residents and to have a reciprocal relationship in research and program development. A culturally receptive approach to community participation is represented by the cultural knowledge; attitudes; and roles acquired, held, and played by those seeking to engage communities and their residents in reform efforts at various levels.

Knowledge

The acquisition of knowledge about a community and its residents is necessary prior to planning and developing intervention strategies that require residents' participation. Under a culturally receptive approach, the knowledge to be acquired is ethnographic. Ethnographic knowledge is acquired in an ongoing manner and transcends the initial stages of collecting baseline statistics about the community; it entails learning about the community holistically in terms of its history, economics, politics, racial relations, social and organizational structures, family structure, acculturation patterns of recent immigrants, and standard sociodemographic indicators and census data. This knowledge is also

Table 1. Approaches to promotion of community participation

Approaches	Culturally receptive	Non–culturally receptive
Knowledge	Ethnographic knowledge of community	Sociodemographic knowledge of community
Attitude	• Recognize lack of knowledge • Recognize possibility of learning • Allow competent member of culture to teach us • Everyone has a culture, including us • Respect residents' opinions, beliefs, and styles	• Knowledge of culture is comprehensive and sufficient • Overvaluing expert knowledge of culture • Devaluing local knowledge • Only members of minority groups have culture • Make community residents think and behave like us
Roles	Learner/facilitator	Teacher/expert

ecological; that is, it seeks to understand the interaction between 1) macro-level variables such as changes in the political arena, employment, or housing availability; and 2) micro-level indicators such as family functioning or rates of access to and use of available children's mental health system of care services.

Information about the community and its residents is collected from a variety of sources, including historical records and previous studies; interviews with community leaders, older residents, parents, and children; community asset–mapping techniques; and census data of the community. Moreover, the approach to gathering this information is participatory, involving residents as data collectors and interpreters of the findings. Finally, the type of knowledge sought is not limited to a priori impairment-based categories of inquiry. Rather, it is open to incorporating what the community itself, through its members, defines as important needs and strengths.

When culturally receptive knowledge of the community is not sought, information is acquired solely as an introductory prerequisite and as a planning and accountability tool. During the planning period, information is actively pursued on key sociodemographic indicators of community need such as the number of families receiving public assistance, the number of single-parent households, crime statistics, school dropout rates, and teen pregnancy prevalence rates. Through the implementation phase, statistics are collected periodically to document any changes in key indicators as a source of outcome data. Throughout the implementation and research process, emphasis is on the micro level rather than on the macro level, with limited attention being paid to the interactions between the two. In addition, when a culturally receptive approach is not sought, residents are viewed as the subjects of study rather than as partners in the research.

Attitude

In addition to knowledge, the promotion of community residents' involvement in the design, implementation, and evaluation of a system of care's reform efforts calls for outside players to examine their own attitudes regarding the partnership that they are pursuing. Outside players working from a culturally receptive framework approach the development of community partnerships with an attitude that recognizes their own lack of knowledge about the community's social construction of reality, recognizes their need to learn about it, and allows competent members of the community or members who understand its culture to teach them about the community's own reality.

Culturally receptive attitudes arise from the acquisition of ethnographic knowledge combined with the outside players' willingness to be learners rather than experts. Their attitudes as learners allow outside players to work within the context of the community and to understand and accept the community residents' abilities and desires to participate in processes of change. The residents' styles of participation are embedded in "the commonsensical though unarticulated understanding carried by virtually all members of a group" (Van Maanen, 1979, p. 541).

Three additional aspects of culturally receptive attitudes are a respect for differences, the dignity inherent in every set of customs, and the recognition that all human groups (e.g., ethnic, religious, social, occupational) are culture bound. In anthropology, these aspects of culturally receptive attitudes are related to the philosophy of cultural relativism. Herskovits (1955) described *cultural relativism* as a philosophy that emphasizes the worth of many ways of life, affirms the values of each culture, and seeks to understand the goals of different societies. This way of thinking is also consistent with one of the main premises of community participation—namely, the recognition that people have the capacity to define themselves as opposed to being defined by others and that community residents have the right and the responsibility to have some control over the policies that affect their lives.

Many outside players are less receptive. They still approach communities believing that their knowledge of the area and its culture is comprehensive and sufficient. In this, they tend to rely on the knowledge of outside "experts" and to devalue local knowledge. These outside players' assumption is that an extensive collection of community statistics is sufficient to gain an understanding of the nature of a community and that these data reflect the behavior of its residents.

The attitude that the ultimate goal of community participation is to make residents agree with outside players' views and adopt outside players' behavioral codes and values is rooted in what Cross et al. described as "a push toward assimilation, typically based on a pathology model rather than on cultural pluralism" (1989, p. 2). The weakness in the concept of cultural competence in systems of care is that it focuses attention on the culture of the client population as the one in which providers should be competent (D. Uzzel, personal communication, March 1997). Uzzel argued that the culture of service providers—including front-line practitioners and professionals—as well as that of bureaucrats and policy makers are equally in need of understanding and examination because they represent models of reality that are different from and sometimes in conflict with those of the people whom they serve. Furthermore, he proposed that the attitude that the only cultures worth studying and understanding are those of ethnic minority groups is narrow minded.

Role

The last determinant of the outcome of community participation in system of care reform efforts is related to the role performed by the outside player. That role in turn is influenced by the type of knowledge sought and the attitudes held regarding the nature of the relationship with community partners. In a culturally receptive framework, outside players are involved as learners and facilitators. Their relationship with residents is established first on the basis of their recognition that, as outsiders, their knowledge of the community is limited and superficial and second on the basis of their willingness to learn from residents who are knowledgeable about the community.

As parties who value the right of community residents to shape and influence the programs and policies that will directly affect them, the outside players will only act as facilitators to harmonize the goals of the different sectors of the community so that a common vision can be achieved. E. Cortés (personal communication, June 1997) proposed the additional role of activist that outside players can perform to promote community involvement. The role of the activist is to identify individuals recognized by their neighbors as community leaders, or, as Cortés calls them, "people with a following," and link them with a cause that his or her peers recognize as worthwhile.

The role played by outside players who lack a culturally receptive approach becomes akin to that of a teacher. The teacher enters the community unsolicited with a set of lessons to be taught and a list of skills that community residents need to master in order to successfully apply the lessons. The outside player's relationship with residents thus is paternalistic and protective on the one hand and punitive on the other in this type of approach. The rules for community engagement are narrowly defined by the teacher, who also establishes the timelines for task completion based on priorities established outside the community. Last, the teacher's performance is judged by the quality of the students' performance. In a community environment, the outside players' performance is judged by the community's outcomes and, to a large extent, by the degree of the community's commitment to and acceptance of externally imposed goals.

Case examples of both a culturally receptive and a non–culturally receptive approach to the promotion of residents' participation in a community-based initiative are presented in the following sections. These examples were drawn from a system of care reform pilot project in a predominantly Hispanic neighborhood in Florida.

CULTURALLY RECEPTIVE AND NON–CULTURALLY RECEPTIVE APPROACHES TO COMMUNITY PARTICIPATION

Through the work of the authors of this chapter in the evaluation of a comprehensive mental health reform initiative with a strong emphasis on community participation in the design and implementation of services, one example that illustrates the culturally receptive approach to community involvement described in this chapter and one example illustrating the absence of that approach were identified.

The community in which the project was implemented was a neighborhood in a Florida metropolitan area, the population of which was 90% Hispanic. The residents were immigrants from many different countries in Central America, South America, and the Caribbean. The residents' lengths of residency in the community ranged from a few months to more than 30 years. Social and economic indicators depicted an urban area with high levels of poverty; in fact, 50% of all children in the community lived below the poverty level. Focus groups conducted with residents from the neighborhood captured their concerns over increasing violence and gang activity, lack of employment opportunities, inadequate housing and recreation facilities, and educational constraints faced by Hispanic children in the local schools.

The project evaluated was designed to address some of the factors that put children, particularly children with emotional and behavior problems, at risk of being removed from their families and the community. The main premise of the project was consistent with the system of care philosophy, which states that services should be individualized, family centered, community based, culturally sensitive, and integrated and coordinated (Stroul & Friedman, 1986). If children with severe emotional and behavior problems received these types of services, they could be maintained in the community with their families or in the least restrictive environment and close to their homes and communities. An additional postulate of the project was that, to be effective, the intervention had to be shaped and guided by residents of the target community, especially parents of children who had been in or were at risk for out-of-home placements. The belief in the benefits of residents' participation was crystallized by the formation of a governing body composed of residents and clients, service providers, and local and state stakeholders with the capacity to facilitate the reforms necessary to achieve the desired outcomes for children, families, and communities.

Culturally Receptive Strategy for Community Participation

The example of how this project involved community residents in a culturally sensitive manner relates to its service design strategy. As part of the project strategy, a neighborhood family resource center was established. The purpose of the center was to provide a continuum of services from information and referral to promotion, prevention, service coordination, and therapeutic intervention, given the multiple needs of community residents. Several service providers were collocated in the facility to improve access and convenience for families. In addition to services, the family resource center provided a space for socialization and recreation activities for children and families from the community.

To support the activities of the family resource center and to attract families and encourage them to avail themselves of the services being offered, a strategy was implemented whereby volunteer residents were trained to conduct outreach activities and link neighbors to the center. These "link people" were called *madrinas* (godmothers) and *padrinos* (godfathers), and their training enabled them to provide information and referral, serve as family advocates, clarify residents' needs, and provide guidance about basic issues. In addition, *madrinas* and *padrinos* linked families to the neighborhood social network, facilitated the development and use of natural support networks, explained how various government systems work, and brokered communication between service providers and families.

The outreach model described in the preceding paragraphs is culturally receptive for several reasons. First, the knowledge on which it is based is consistent with the ethnographic type of knowledge proposed in this chapter. For instance, the project implementers were aware of and understood the role that the extended family plays as a support mechanism for Hispanics. According to Marín and VanOss Marín (1991), the significance ascribed to values such as familialism (the importance that people assign to relatives as referents and providers of emotional support) and to social scripts such as *simpatía* (i.e., the preference for positive interpersonal interaction) is shared by most Hispanics regardless of their national origin, birthplace, dominant language, or any other sociodemographic characteristics. An application of the value of familialism is the extension of the status of relative to close family friends who become the *madrinas*, or *comadres*, and *padrinos*, or *compadres*, either through their friendships or through their involvement in the raising of children (e.g., as godparents). The system of *compadrazgo* (co-parenthood) has a long and complex history as a viable social support network among Hispanics (Berruecos, 1972; Mintz & Wolf, 1950; Sotomayor, 1971; Vega, 1980). The *compadre*, or *padrino*, is seen as a forerunner of the "link person," and he acts as an extension of the person in need by providing knowledge of resources, assessment of need, and personal referral, either voluntarily or for nominal compensation (Vega, 1980).

A second reason why this model is consistent with a culturally receptive approach to residents' involvement is that outreach models that are taught by outsiders and based on expert knowledge at the expense of a sound cultural knowledge of the community go against the goal of residents' involvement and participation. The project's cultural receptivity is demonstrated in the assignment of the outreach role to community residents. In doing so, the individuals participating in the project recognize, value, and respect the residents' expertise and their own ways of reaching out to their neighbors. This is consistent with the belief that one of the goals of participation is self-empowerment. Zimmerman and Rappaport suggested that, just as is likely to occur with the *madrinas* and *padrinos* in the community used as a case study in this chapter, "participation may be an important mechanism for the development of psychological empowerment because participants can gain experience organizing people, identifying resources, and developing strategies for achieving goals" (1988, p. 727).

Non–Culturally Receptive Strategy for Community Participation

The same project that effectively incorporated the culturally receptive model of *madrinas* and *padrinos* also offered an example of the converse approach. This example comes from the neighborhood governance component of the initiative. Neighborhood governance was designed as the mechanism to involve residents and clients in the decision-making process that would shape the array of services offered to children and families in the neighborhood. The governing structure is a board made up of residents and mostly professional nonresidents, including service providers and representatives of public agencies such as schools, the police department, the city, and the health department. This governing approach is based on the assumption that all members will participate fully and as equals. In practice, this assumption has been proved wrong and has hindered the effective involvement of residents in the project for various reasons.

First, the approach is not based on ethnographic knowledge of the cultural background of the community and therefore does not reflect the cultural construct of power distance among residents. *Power distance* is defined as a measure of interpersonal power or influence that exists between two individuals or two groups (e.g., residents, professionals) (Hofstede, 1980, cited in Marín & VanOss Marín, 1991). In the context of community participation in children's mental health services systems of care, power distance implies a tendency among resident members of the governing board not to openly challenge the points of view of the professionals who also are members of the board.

Second, this approach is tied to an ethnocentric view of the world that attempts to make ethnic minority community residents think and behave like members of outside, nonminority groups. In the implementation of the governance component of the project, an attempt was made to use the American democratic system of government and citizen participation as a model. This effort failed because it did not take into consideration the various degrees of acculturation among the residents, who in many cases were recent immigrants to the United States, which plays an important role in facilitating or impeding this type of participation. It was observed that community residents became frustrated and felt powerless when faced with a process that asked for their participation but did not share the rules of engagement with them. In other words, participation was neither an effective nor a fulfilling experience for these community residents, because they did not share with professional members of the board the same knowledge and experiences of democratic participation.

Finally, project staff and nonresident members of the governance board often assumed the role of teacher to resident board members and proceeded with plans that did not incorporate residents' full input. In a non–culturally receptive approach to community participation, the temptation to play the expert's or teacher's role is related to a lack of recognition of the potential contributions that people without formal or professional education can make to system of care reform efforts. In immigrant communities such as the one in this case study, the resiliency that most families exhibit in their ability to survive under economic, social, and political pressures in their own countries as well as in the United States makes these residents the real experts. Unfortunately, their skills are undervalued or are not even considered relevant to the types of tasks involved in the process of system of care reform, which has traditionally been in the hands of professionals.

CONCLUSIONS

This chapter addresses a gap identified in the cultural competence literature related to systems of care—namely, the need to expand the application of cultural competence concepts beyond issues of service provider–client relations and into the arena of community residents' participation in the design, planning, and implementation of community-based systems of care. The implications of the foregoing discussion in this chapter in an environment of decentralization, devolution of power to the local level, and an emphasis on self-determination and self-empowerment, together with the increasing complexity of issues facing minority communities, led to the conclusion that a failure to engage communities in the system of care reform process in a culturally receptive manner would result in unrealistic program designs and planning. As a direct consequence of this failure to engage community members in the reform process, assumptions about the community are based on statistics that are focused on what the community and its residents lack rather than on ethnographically based knowledge. Through an ethnographic approach, variables that are likely to truly affect the process are taken into consideration. Some of these variables are the history and nature of relationships between the neighborhood and local and state governments, the ethnic mix of community residents and the nature of interracial relationships within the community that will either facilitate or hinder their working together, and the degree of acculturation of community residents who have recently arrived in the United States.

Another conclusion to be drawn from this chapter is that any attempt by outsiders to involve the community in system of care reform through an instructional approach that does not take into consideration community residents' knowledge is likely to be rejected by the community residents, who have experienced too many disappointments from expert-generated, expert-driven projects that have come and gone without having any impact on their community. A culturally arrogant attitude also precludes the identification of local experts and natural leaders in the community who can attract a strong and effective following and find support among their neighbors for the reform agenda. It also hinders the development of effective collaboration and partnership between those who have knowledge and can gain access to mechanisms by which to effect change at the system of care level and those who can ensure that the end product of reform fits the community's needs and responds to its priorities.

Finally, the role that outside players perform in fostering residents' participation is a reflection of both their knowledge and their attitude toward the community. Those who come in to teach the utility and applicability of a particular model based on evidence from a similar community encounter either passive acceptance among community representatives who are reluctant to question outsiders' expertise or active opposition from those who, knowing their community from the inside, question the assumptions being made by outside experts. Either way, the result of a culturally arrogant attitude will be to stifle residents' initiative and creativity in finding culturally meaningful adaptations of programs and remove residents' real and perceived barriers to service utilization. Furthermore, it precludes the necessary exchange of ideas that allows the community to shape its own goals.

The culturally receptive counterparts to the teacher's attitude and role are those of the facilitator. In this role, the outside player helps to broker information around which community leaders need to organize, present different models as options from which to choose and adapt to local circumstances, and provide advice and clarification of issues. Moreover, the facilitator can be useful in ensuring that partners acknowledge each other's cultural frames of reference and communicate in a respectful and productive manner. Without that kind of communication, the partnership fails to turn the reform agenda into a reality.

No one will deny that the task of reforming systems of care is hard. The challenge is magnified when the task is approached by involving residents of communities that, because of their structural and social characteristics, are most in need of the types of flexible, accessible, individualized, and culturally relevant services that reform would generate. Progress has been made in teaching professionals about the importance of understanding the cultural paradigms of clients of the mental health services system to provide more effective services. That message needs to be expanded to convey the urgency of examining the ways in which to seek community residents' involvement and participation in the process of system of care reform. A culturally receptive approach is a necessary paradigm for guiding the involvement of residents in this endeavor.

REFERENCES

Abrahams, N. (1996). Negotiating power, identity, family, and community: Women's community participation. *Gender and Society, 10*(6), 768–796.

Agudelo, C.A. (1983). Community participation in health activities: Some concepts and appraisal criteria. *Bulletin of the Pan American Health Organization, 17*(4), 375–386.

Alford, R.R., & Friedland, R. (1975). Political participation and public policy. In A. Inkels, J. Coleman, & N. Smelser (Eds.), *Annual review of sociology* (Vol. 1, pp. 429–479). Palo Alto, CA: Annual Reviews.

Barber, B.R. (1984). *Strong democracy: Participatory politics for a new age.* Berkeley: University of California Press.

Berger, P., & Luckman, T. (1966). *The social construction of reality.* New York: Doubleday.

Berger, P., & Neuhaus, R.J. (1977). *To empower people: The roles of mediating structures in public policy.* Washington, DC: American Enterprise Institute for Public Policy Research.

Bernard, J., Cablas, A., Hanley, J.H., Hernandez, M., & Romero, J.T. (1996, June). *Operationalizing cultural competence.* Paper presented at the Child and Adolescent Service System Program Institute on Developing Local Systems of Care Training Institutes, Traverse City, MI.

Berruecos, L. (1972). *Comparative analysis of Latin American compadrazgo* [co-parenthood]. Unpublished master's thesis, Michigan State University, Lansing.

Chaskin, R.J., & Garg, S. (1994). *The issues of governance in neighborhood-based initiatives.* Chicago: University of Chicago, Chapin Hall Center for Children.

Clark, T.N. (1975). Community power. In A. Inkels, J. Coleman, & N. Smelser (Eds.), *Annual review of sociology* (Vol. 1, pp. 271–295). Palo Alto, CA: Annual Reviews.

Cnaan, R.A. (1991, December). Neighborhood-representing organizations: How democratic are they? *Social Service Review, 65*(4), 614–634.

Cross, T.L., Bazron, B.J., Dennis, K.W., & Isaacs, M.R. (1989). *Towards a culturally competent system of care: Vol. I. A monograph on effective services for minority children who are emotionally disturbed.* Washington, DC: Georgetown University, Child Development Center, Child and Adolescent Service System Program, Technical Assistance Center.

Dubow, F., & Podolefsky, A. (1982). Citizen participation in community crime prevention. *Human Organization, 41*(4), 307–314.

Everitt, A. (1996). An introduction to the voluntary sector. *Youth and Policy, 53,* 106–108.

Giddens, A. (1984). *The constitution of society.* Berkeley: University of California Press.

Hernandez, M., & Benjamin, M.P. (1994, September). *Achieving cultural competence and changing your organization.* Paper presented at the Third Annual Wraparound Reunion, Fort Lauderdale, FL.

Herskovits, M. (1955). *Man and his works.* New York: Alfred A. Knopf.

Hessler, R.M., & Beavert, C.S. (1982). Citizen participation in neighborhood health centers for the poor: The politics of reform organizational change, 1965–1977. *Human Organization, 41*(3), 245–254.

Hofstede, G. (1980). *Cultural consequences.* Thousand Oaks, CA: Sage Publications.

Isaacs, M.R., & Benjamin, M.P. (1991). *Towards a culturally competent system of care: Volume II. Programs which utilize culturally competent principles.* Washington, DC: Georgetown University, Child Development Center, Child and Adolescent Service System Program, Technical Assistance Center.

Kinne, S., Thompson, B., Chrisman, N., & Hanley, J. (1989). Community organization to enhance the delivery of preventive health services. *American Journal of Preventive Medicine, 5*(4), 225–229.

Leighley, J. (1996). Group membership and the mobilization of political participation. *Journal of Politics, 58*(2), 447–463.

Maldonado, D. (1975). Ethnic self-identity and self-understanding. *Social Casework, 56,* 618–622.

Marín, G., & VanOss Marín, B. (1991). *Research with Hispanic populations.* Thousand Oaks, CA: Sage Publications.

Mintz, S., & Wolf, E. (1950). An analysis of ritual co-parenthood (compadrazgo). *Southwestern Journal of Anthropology, 6*(4), 341–368.

Mollenkopf, J. (1979, September/October). Neighborhood politics for the 1980s. *Social Policy, 10*(2), 24–27.

Mott, A.H. (1977). The future of citizen involvement in community development. In P. Marshall (Ed.), *Citizen participation certification for community development: A reader on the citizen participation process* (pp. 24–29). Washington, DC: National Association of Housing and Redevelopment Officials.

Murphree, D.W., Wright, S.A., & Ebaugh, H.R. (1996). Toxic waste siting and community resistance: How cooptation of local citizen opposition failed. *Sociological Perspectives, 39*(4), 447–463.

Pardo, M. (1990). Mexican American women grassroots community activists: "Mothers of East Los Angeles." *Frontiers, 11*(1), 1–7.

Perkins, K.B., & Poole, D.G. (1996). Oligarchy and adaptation to mass society in all volunteer organizations: Implications for understanding leadership, participation and change. *Nonprofit and Voluntary Sector Quarterly, 25*(1), 73–88.

Redburn, S., Buss, T.F., Foster, S.K., & Binning, W.C. (1980). How representative are mandated citizen participation processes. *Urban Affairs Quarterly, 15*(3), 345–352.

Smith, D.H. (1975). Voluntary action and voluntary groups. In A. Inkels, J. Coleman, & N. Smelser (Eds.), *Annual review of sociology* (Vol. 1, pp. 247–270). Palo Alto, CA: Annual Reviews.

Sotomayor, M. (1971). Mexican American interaction with social systems. *Social Casework, 52*(5), 316–324.

Stroul, B.A., & Friedman, R.M. (1986). *A system of care for severely emotionally disturbed children and youth.* Washington, DC: Georgetown University, Child Development Center, Child and Adolescent Service System Program, Technical Assistance Center.

Van Maanen, J. (1979). Reclaiming qualitative methods for organizational research: A preface. *Administrative Science Quarterly, 24,* 520–550.

Vega, W. (1980). Mental health research and north American Hispanic populations: A review and critique of the literature and a proposed research strategy. In R. Valle & W. Vega (Eds.), *Hispanic natural support systems: Mental health promotion perspectives* (pp. 3–12). Sacramento: State of California, Department of Mental Health.

Wandersman, A. (1981). A framework of participation in community organizations. *Journal of Applied Behavioral Science, 17*(1), 27–58.

Zimmerman, M.A., & Rappaport, J. (1988). Citizen participation, perceived control, and psychological empowerment. *American Journal of Community Psychology, 16,* 725–750.

Involving People of Color in Family Organizations

A Family Perspective

Velva Taylor Spriggs and Mary Telesford

In the 1990s, family members and family advocates have successfully created family organizations and support groups in most states to address the problems of children and adolescents with serious emotional disabilities and their families. Most of these efforts have been the result of a nationwide movement shaped by 1) a new consciousness of the roles and values of families in addressing the needs of their children and 2) advocacy on behalf of children with special needs. This movement, largely reflected in white, middle-class advocacy organizations, has been either in concert with or in conflict with service providers, agency administrators, policy makers, and legislators. Although people of color are involved in many of these organizations at the local and national levels, the predominant constituencies of the organizations are white. Nevertheless, most of these organizations have adopted policies of cultural competence, and some have designed strategies to implement these policies.

Still, many of these organizations have not been able to attract or to sustain the membership and involvement of families of color in numbers that are at least consistent with their proportionate representation in the general population. When authorities are pressed to explain why

---

Although standard references to racial minorities in the United States reflect a people's origin as an integral part of being American, such as *African American* and *Native American*, the term popularized in mental health literature on cultural competence tends to include all such groups in the term *people of color*, contrasting them with the dominant racial group of white people, who together are multiethnic but are not racial minorities within the American social context of race and ethnicity. Thus, references to the racial identity of these groups in this chapter are *people of color* and *whites*.

more people of color are not involved in such organizations, the consistently offered replies are that people of color cannot be found easily or that outreach is problematic for myriad reasons having mostly to do with an alleged passivity or resistance of families of color and the internal tensions provoked within these organizations by the inclusion effort. Some groups simply profess ignorance about how to be more inclusive (Harry, 1992).

The view posited in this chapter is that racism is a significant, often intractable barrier to increasing the participation of people of color in these organizations and thus is the source of tension associated with the persistent demand for racial and cultural diversity, parity, and harmony. This chapter briefly explores one theory of the roots and manifestations of racism and how they might affect family organizations that are mostly white and the people of color that these organizations seek to attract. The chapter also discusses the demonstrated merits of including, valuing, and building on the advocacy capabilities of people of color.

RACISM AS AN AMERICAN PHENOMENON

In a perusal of various definitions of *racism*, the authors of this chapter came across one definition that seemed best suited to understanding the barriers to advocacy for families of color and the difficulties surrounding the participation of families of color in predominantly white family organizations and support groups: "Racism is . . . an ideology of racial domination or exploitation that 1) incorporates beliefs in a particular race's cultural and/or inherent biological inferiority and 2) uses such beliefs to justify and prescribe inferior or unequal treatment for that group" (Wilson, 1976, p. 34). In the United States, racism not only reinforces the idea of the intrinsic inferiority of people of color but also assumes an inherent claim to rights, power, privileges, and superior intelligence for those who are classified as white. Furthermore, racism invokes the fear of encroachment by people of color on this claim (Wilson, 1976). Why else was the Civil Rights movement of the 1950s and 1960s threatening to so many whites, who resisted the dismantling of a segregated society? The prospect of granting to people of color rights and privileges that were previously unattainable by them and reserved for whites only provoked feelings of fear for millions of white people, who had become accustomed to American social mores that restricted positions of privilege on the basis of skin color. For example, prior to the Civil Rights era, at the beginning of the 20th century, European immigrants arriving in the United States acquired advantages over African Americans, who had been brought forcibly to the American continent centuries earlier, and over Native Americans, who had lived in North America for thousands of years prior to the arrival of Christopher Columbus.

No one in the United States is exempt from the impact of racism, which exists in all U.S. social and economic institutions, either through standard beliefs and practices or through victimization by racially motivated events and circumstances. For that reason, racism of necessity also affects family organizations nationwide as they address the needs and aspirations of all children and adolescents, including children and adolescents of color with emotional disabilities and their families.

Racism is an intrinsic part of the American experience and value system. West commented in the Afterword of Lubiano's book *The House That Race Built* that

> The very construction of "race" is a European creation rooted in attempts to rationalize European superiority in oceanic transportation, military technology, and capitalistic expansion resulting in imperial conquests and colonial subordination of many non-European peoples. The distinctive feature of the precious experiment in democracy called the United States of America was its profound and pervasive investment in white supremacy—in the expropriation of indigenous peoples' land and African peoples' labor. And one glaring aspect of our present-day society is the depth and breadth of racial polarization, balkanization, and de facto segregation. (1997, p. 301)

Franklin, distinguished historian, scholar, and chair of President Clinton's Commission on Race, stated in his book *Race and History* that "This nation tolerated and, indeed, nurtured the cultivation of a racism that has been as insidious as it has been pervasive" (1989, p. 161). Admitting unwelcome truths about the historical and contemporary existence of racism is a critical first step in the process of addressing it as a barrier to the full participation of people of color in advocating for rights and privileges and equal access to services. The United States has come some distance from its pernicious history of slavery, annexation of Mexican lands, the conquest of the islands of the Pacific, and massacres and imprisonment on reservations of Native Americans, events triggered by unconscionable political and economic forces and celebrated as part of U.S. history. Still, people of color, as well as many whites, decry acts of racism and discrimination and emerging policies of retrenchment from national commitments to open doors to all U.S. citizens.

References to racism as the "R word" trivialize the reality of the continued existence of racism, which is still pervasive but subtle and disguised in phrases such as *reverse discrimination*. Clever references by journalistic scholars to the "R word" transform the response to racism into an intellectual, academic discussion; the "R word" thus becomes a code phrase for something considered out of date, anachronistic, and out of step with "progressive" thought espoused by those who advocate colorblindness and "kinder, gentler" approaches to responding to the needs of racial minorities in the United States. References to racism are publicly discouraged in pronouncements such as "How long are people going to live in the past?" "Move on," and "Stop whining and using racism as an excuse." Thus voices are muted, and racist policies and practices persist in a nation that "moves on."

Briggs and Paulson, in their chapter on racism in Mattain and Thyers's book *Finding Solutions to Social Problems: Behavioral Strategies for Change,* stated that

> Most white Americans are aware that our democracy is less than perfect. Historically, white citizens have discriminated against minority groups and attempted to exclude them from the mainstream of American life. Today, however, many whites tend to see the problem of racial discrimination as either having been perpetrated in the past, or in terms of prejudices held by people we would now refer to as racist in their ideas (whom they assume to be either Southerners or blue-collar workers). Few white Americans appreciate the fact that well into the 20th century the bulk of scientific, psychological, and social theories supported racist arguments. . . . Nor do they realize that liberals tended to use these arguments, too. At all levels of society, many people—including writers, scientists, presidents, statesmen, and educators—subscribed to beliefs of white superiority in one form or another. Furthermore, many of today's so-called enlightened explanations for social problems, which are accepted by much of white society, are little more than subtle forms of the same line of reasoning. . . . [T]hese explanations have a strong historical continuity with ideas promoted earlier in our history by people we would now call racist in their ideological and behavioral expressions. (1996, p. 147)

Frances Cress Welsing (1992), a child and general psychiatrist, linked racism to a basic instinct for white people's survival on the planet, with skin color serving as the key to ensuring this survival through the domination and control of people of color who constitute the majority of the world population. In *The Isis Papers: The Keys to the Colors,* Welsing invited the reader to consider this theory for the creation and maintenance of racism in the United States: "[T]he goal of the white supremacy system is none other than the establishment, maintenance, explanation and refinement of world domination by members of a group that classifies itself as the white 'race'" (1992, p. 3).

In the Cress Theory of Color Confrontation and Racism (White Supremacy), the conceptual basis of which was developed in 1969 by Fuller, Welsing dissected the racism construct. She stated straightforwardly that people who classify themselves as white are both intrigued by and fearful of the "color-producing capacity" of nonwhites, contending that, through the process of intermarriage between whites and people of color, whites as a group might eventually face annihilation as a result of the loss of "whiteness" among their offspring. Thus, to combat the potential for annihilation of their race, whites continually engage in activities to organize and maintain a system of white domination and control, from the smallest social units to large-scale, complex organizations, systems, and institutions, to prevent the loss of influence of their race and to maintain their position of power and control (Blauner, 1972; Comer, 1969; Fuller, 1969; Gullattee, 1969; Welsing, 1992).

The Cress theory, though not widely known in mental health circles, provides an intriguing explanation of behavior that is motivated by racism. Might there be a fear that people of color will destabilize the family organization, erode its power base, diminish attention to white interests, or substantially alter its focus, to the detriment of whites? Rarely is there theoretical discussion of the motivations underlying racism and how they have historically driven and currently direct the behavior of whites, both consciously and subconsciously, to be generally and sometimes individually hostile toward people of color. Academic discussions of racism more generally tend to focus on its impact on people of color—the victims. For example, the triumphs of golfer Tiger Woods (whose father is African American and whose mother is Asian American), though highly celebrated, are also confusing to those who believe that a person of color cannot exhibit superior skills in golf. Thus, discussions about the composition of Woods's racial makeup seem to be an act of desperation to confirm that his mixture of racial backgrounds, which also includes some European ancestry, helps to justify his victories. Nevertheless, Woods has joined the long line of celebrities, such as baseball great Jackie Robinson, Olympic gold medalist Jesse Owens, world boxing champions Joe Louis and Muhammad Ali, former Miss America and current actress and singer Vanessa Williams, and many others who have experienced a negative reaction to their great feats. They all were subjected to discussions of race and endured derision and death threats associated with their race ("Tiger Woods' Death Threats Continue," 1997) along with the accolades following their successes. Their victories remained incomprehensible and generally intolerable to holders of racist views.

According to Welsing (1992), racism is a powerful tool used to maintain the status quo of whites' domination over people of color. In the case of children's mental health services and related family-centered organizations, racism becomes a barrier to advocacy and support for children and adolescents of color with emotional disabilities and their families. Racism places this population at greater risk than white children and their families of not receiving culturally competent interventions and support. This inequality is especially important in view of the overrepresentation of children and adolescents of color in the institutional care of child welfare and juvenile justice authorities throughout the country, and it is an issue that receives only limited attention. The problems faced by these children and adolescents of color and their families are pervasive and require urgent attention within their own communities and the larger society.

MOVING TOWARD SOLUTIONS

Coping with differences is never easy, but not to do so will result in broadening the racial divide in the United States, thereby limiting opportunities for Americans to work together to improve the quality of life for all people, regardless of ancestry. Not doing so will result in continuing the myth within white-controlled institutions, including family organizations, that people of color naturally lack crucial competencies with rare exceptions, whereas whites naturally possess superior intellect and skills in whatever activities they undertake. If differences are not dealt with in a comprehensive, sustained way, families of color will continue to be overlooked as a valuable resource in local and national advocacy efforts to generate policies, programs, and initiatives aimed at helping all children with emotional disabilities and their families. The family movement will have lost an opportunity for its own enrichment and empowerment. There is strength in numbers and diversity. The leadership of the Federation of Families for Children's Mental Health has discovered this gem of organizational development, even though the outreach to families of color was not a prominent feature of its earliest vision. The commitment of the Federation in this area has grown in spite of the naysayers, who prefer to adopt policies of colorblindness.

In April 1992, The Annie E. Casey Foundation funded the Federation to implement Casey's Urban Children's Mental Health Initiative for the purpose of promoting family involvement among families of color whose children had or were at risk of having emotional disturbances in urban centers. The four sites chosen were Little Havana in Miami; Roxbury in Boston; East Richmond, Virginia; and Houston. This initiative sparked controversy within the Federation because of its focus on impoverished communities of color. Those in the leadership of the Federation, however, envisioned opportunities to heighten and enrich efforts to create a national family organization that was truly diverse racially and culturally. The Federation faced challenges by its own membership about the fairness and appropriateness of focusing on these populations of color on the basis that the Federation did not prohibit the involvement of any family, regardless of racial or cultural association, and that color should not be a special consideration. The Federation nevertheless accepted the grant from The Annie E. Casey Foundation and, after enduring a tumultuous history on this issue, has become one of the most racially diverse family organizations in the United States that is concerned with children's mental health.

Within mental health advocacy groups, there is recognition that children with emotional disabilities come to the attention of various children's services authorities in school systems, child welfare, juvenile justice systems, and mental health systems. Yet, in spite of the overrepresentation of children of color in the child welfare and juvenile justice systems, most of the attention in children's mental health services does not focus consistently on these two systems, except in academic circles and sporadic volunteer and governmental programs.

When reaching out to people of color to encourage their involvement in the family movement, many probably select those few who may be considered representative of their racial or cultural group and who are viewed as nonthreatening to whites in their appearance, thoughts, speech, and actions. More flexibility is required to include family members whose lifestyles may vary considerably and whose racial background is different from that of the mainstream. Cultural competence, the mechanism by which an operational understanding of racism, racial and ethnic knowledge, and skills in the mental health field is achieved, is frequently an afterthought or a side issue of family support or professional practice in systems of care, even for those who have incorporated it into larger program efforts. Inclusion of cultural competence may be viewed as an added burden to an already weighted struggle of advocacy on behalf of children and adolescents with serious emotional disabilities. Still, the inclusion of both mainstream and unique concerns of diverse racial groups in this protracted struggle of advocacy and family involvement cannot be delayed or addressed as an afterthought without significant cost to these populations and the society at large. The Federation can attest to that conclusion.

Family organizations that support initiatives to include more families of color in their activities may face allegations of reverse racism or of promoting affirmative action, when it is politically unpopular to do so. Detractors may attempt to sanitize such allegations by declaring that the organization should be colorblind and open to serving all in the same way. Rosenthal and Carty put it succinctly: "It is a bitter fact that many of those who champion justice and equality for people with disabilities seem unconcerned about the injustice facing minority citizens with disabilities" (1996, p. 3). Similarly, Isaacs and Benjamin (1991) suggested a historical context for that view. Individuals tend to personalize racism and oppression and cannot objectively view society and its institutions from such perspectives. Thus, there is a natural American tendency to dismiss racial differences or cultural variations as key factors to be addressed by American institutions and service providers. A major precept of the American value system is that an individual can overcome any condition—that is, to use a once-popular expression, that everyone should be able to pull oneself up by one's own bootstraps. The Civil Rights movement of the 1950s and 1960s, many white Americans believe, took care of all racial and ethnic problems. The resurgence of cries of institutional racism and cultural dominance in the 1990s has created questions that had been buried since the civil rights era and thus generated renewed hostility. Often there are concerns that outreach to and inclusion of people of color is really a form of reverse discrimination, especially when the issues of affirmative action, quotas, and preferential treatment are brought into the discussion.

Family organizations that profess a desire for inclusion but cannot find effective ways to create bridges to people of color may need to examine their own internal views toward this subject to surface reactions that either inhibit or support outreach to people of color in their organizations. To do so puts one in the position of going against the grain of the system of racism. As Welsing wrote, "Despite all kinds of programs and pronouncements to the contrary, for the past several hundred years, white supremacist social conditions have remained intact as the dominant social reality" (1992, p. 5; see also Wilson, 1976). Welsing's characterization of historical and contemporary American attitudes toward people of color describes racism as being both normalizing and prescriptive in individuals', groups', and institutions' behaviors that attempt to maintain the power differential between whites and others.

BURDENS AND BLESSINGS

Because of institutional resistance to more inclusion of people of color in the family movement, people of color have had to be demanding about their issues and insistent that their concerns be given attention equal to those of their white counterparts. This posture of competition and solicitation is burdensome. It adds another layer of difficulty to a situation in which services are frequently inadequate, inappropriate, and inaccessible. In addition, people of color must bear the brunt of the irritation of some white Americans who perceive them as gaining preferential treatment. In such an environment, they are faced with the exigencies of "triculturalism" in that they are simultaneously confronted with issues of race, culture, and the diagnosis of serious emotional disabilities in their children.

In addition, if a service provider or family organization is inclined to consider the relevance of the impact of race and culture on children and their families, most often the burden is thrust upon the family member to be the expert in matters of race. This circumstance frequently occurs when one is called upon to be a token participant to deliver a particular point of view. Tokenism is stressful and unproductive. Parents of color may share their experiences involving their race in dealing with emotional disabilities in their children, but rarely are white parents expected to discuss their experiences as beneficiaries of racism.

In the arena of advocacy, family members are called upon to petition the courts, social workers, psychiatrists, teachers, and a host of others for appropriate services, including culturally competent services, for their children. Many people of color have gained skills that allow them to maneuver within complex bureaucratic structures that may not be suited to their world views; they have learned how to obtain support for themselves, and, if they are members of a family organization that values their participation, they are able to participate in ways that are culturally meaningful and productive for themselves and their children. When organizations are flexible and value the dynamics of diversity among their local populations, instead of viewing them as competitive and potentially threatening, they will be better positioned to accept the unique experiences of various racial and ethnic groups and manage cross-cultural interactions with greater predictability of success. That is a situation in which everyone benefits.

Racism need not be a barrier to the development of advocacy organizations. What is certain, however, is that white, African American, Hispanic or Latino, Native American, Asian American, and Pacific Islander families must agree that racism is dysfunctional and lends nothing to their collective efforts to work on behalf of children and adolescents with emotional disabilities. They must value each other for their experiences, their cultural uniqueness, and their strengths. Blending their efforts strengthens their cause. These ideals can replace notions of racial fear, ignorance, and competition.

People of color are challenged every day by racism. Consequently, they have learned of necessity to be bicultural. They have had to develop creative strategies to cope with powerlessness and the devaluation of their cultures and themselves to secure what they need for their children (Isaacs & Benjamin, 1991). White Americans who care for children with emotional disabilities also know feelings of powerlessness and the effects of stigma. Through pooling their knowledge, whites and people of color can strengthen their efforts to obtain the best results for all children.

In the absence of Eurocentric organizing practices, people of color have helped to build organizations, staff committees, contribute to the development of projects, and write and deliver testimonies before Congress and state and local governments. Because so many of their children end up in the courts and prisons instead of in mental health programs as large numbers of white children do (Cross, Bazron, Dennis, & Isaacs, 1989), parents of color have helped to bring attention to juvenile justice issues within the mental health arena. In spite of racism, people of color are an asset to the children's mental health field and must be viewed as such to help break down the barriers of racism and its concomitant destructive behaviors.

Parents of color have begun to formalize their advocacy efforts and in turn affect the appropriateness of service design and delivery, especially in the children's mental health arena. Even though the dynamics of racism add another dimension to concerns that must be overcome by advocacy, parents of color have developed strategies that allow for a healthy resistance to racism and the power differentials that continue to result in a denial of adequate and appropriate services for their children. White family members and families of color can benefit together from this knowledge base.

Throwing off the cloak of racism will require formidable courage and vision only possible among those willing to go against the grain of racism's insulating, normalizing practices, beliefs, and values while recognizing that the benefits to families and systems of care collectively include a stronger advocacy voice and enlightened family organizations. Only then can new human values and strategies emerge to dismantle the institutionalized forces of white supremacy, a major barrier to making the essential human connection across the racial divide that presently results in differential treatment of Native American, Asian American, African American, and Hispanic children and adolescents who are more often removed legally and geographically from their families, disproportionately diagnosed with character disorders and schizophrenia, more likely to be assessed in a language or culture other than their own, and too frequently diverted to the juvenile justice system. All families together can make a difference for all families if they are aware of and avoid the traps of racism (Cross et al., 1989).

ROLES OF FAMILIES OF COLOR IN ADVOCACY

Historically, parent advocates, especially those in the children's mental health services system, have been white, middle class, and not initially dependent on the public social services system when seeking care for their children. These parents have been effective in advocating for better services for their own children as well as others' children and have been instrumental in effecting change in the mental health care system. They clearly have been able to articulate the needs and some valuable solutions to problems related to appropriateness of and access to services. Many parents have used their personal resources to advocate for their children and assist other families, not only while advocating for their children but also while engaging in activities promoting systems change. In addition to using their personal resources to support advocacy, these parents most often have had the support of their spouses, significant others, other family members, and friends.

However, for parents who have to rely on the public social services system, many of whom are poor and people of color, the advocacy path has not been so easily traveled. Many families of color, especially those receiving public assistance or the working poor, lack appropriate resources (e.g., telephone, car, bus fare, child care, proper clothing) to support volunteer advocacy efforts. In addition, many of these parents do not have the support networks necessary to help address the everyday needs of maintaining their families in their absence if they were to engage in advocacy. Therefore, many families of color are precluded from engaging in volunteer advocacy efforts because of lack of resources and support.

Some may question why it is necessary to have parents of color as advocates. The answer is simple but not simplistic. In the second author's 5 years of experience in working with families of color with the Federation of Families for Children's Mental Health as a technical advisor on the Mental Health Initiative for Urban Children, three reasons supporting the necessity of having people of color as advocates have become apparent:

1. People of color are critical in organizing advocacy efforts in communities composed of people of color.
2. The input of people of color is critical to the development of linguistically and culturally appropriate service design and delivery as many public systems, especially children's mental health, address issues of reform and recommended practice.
3. People of color love and value their children, and, when encouraged and inspired to operate from a base of strength in spite of obstacles, they contribute as much as anyone to the children's mental health movement.

ORGANIZING ADVOCACY EFFORTS
IN COMMUNITIES COMPOSED OF PEOPLE OF COLOR

People of color in many poor communities have been helped for many years by various social programs and systems that were supposed to make a difference. After all of the "help," however, the communities still look the same. There is still an overwhelming preponderance of community and personal poverty, illicit drug activity, alcoholism, low-income families, and dropouts and teenage mothers. Most households continue to be headed by minority, single females with limited education and job skills who are dependent on public assistance to maintain their families. In addition, high rates of violent crime permeate the whole environment, making neighborhoods unsafe, especially for African American and Latino or Hispanic males. Furthermore, because of the environments in which they live, these families have learned to be distrustful and suspicious of those who advocate for change from outside the social services system. Combating this suspicion is the major obstacle of the parent advocate as he or she tries to elicit the support of parents and other community residents in advocacy efforts. In addition, it is an added plus if the parent of color organizing the other parents is from the same or from a similar community or neighborhood. This type of parent is particularly instrumental in breaking through the barrier of mistrust because many times he or she shares common experiences and frustrations, and the parents in the community are more apt to trust one of their own and consequently are more likely to support the advocacy activities. In addition, the parent advocate is key to identifying resources in the community that would support families. Many times these types of supports include the following:

1. *Churches:* In many neighborhoods, churches provide not only religious training and spiritual uplift but also food and clothing banks; soup kitchens; care centers for older adults; child care services for working mothers; recreation programs; and a safe haven for homeless families, individuals, and children. Clergy and church elders are often community leaders and can be sources of information about the history of a community, as well as able to make basic assessments of the needs, wants, and fears and strengths of community residents. Moreover, churches represent organized constituency bases in many of these communities.

2. *Community-based organizations:* Throughout neighborhoods, community-based organizations provide various direct services to residents of the community. These services include substance abuse clinics and counseling, parenting skills education, tutoring, and various other types of training ranging from literacy to employment preparedness. These organizations are funded both privately and publicly. Many of them serve as beacons of hope for the most unserved and underserved community residents. These organizations regularly hire local community members; because of the community-based organizations' proximity to and long history of

working with community residents, they strive to provide culturally and linguistically appropriate services.

3. *Schools:* Schools are the optimal setting for assessing the well-being
of children. Often, it is at school that the problems of a child or a
child's home life are noticed, particularly if the child is coming to
school unkempt, hungry, sleepy, withdrawn, or uncommunicative
or if the child is frequently absent. These and other problems can
result in the child's poor behavior and poor classroom performance.
Strong schools cultivate trust among parents and have strong parent and family input bonds and parent–teacher–administrator relationships. The schools in some of these communities support other
activities, especially recreational activities, that are sorely lacking
in the rest of the community. Schools are also sites for adult education and parenting classes, especially classes designed for teenage
mothers. Some schools also serve as clothing and food distribution
centers.

Although the parent advocate can identify tangible resources that
may support parents in the community, it is just as important for the
parent advocate to assist in identifying community leaders and other
parents who would be most receptive to organizing and engaging in
advocacy activities. This identification process incorporates the values
of the community in which the parent advocate is working. More
specifically, unlike in mainstream American culture, where value is
often attached to one's net financial worth, in poorer communities of
color, one's net worth is not the standard by which people are valued.
There is more value placed on the relationships that a person has with
his or her own family, the neighborhood, the church, and other community groups. In addition, there is strong value placed on parents,
especially on women who, despite the odds, are coping well.

IDENTIFICATION OF COMMUNITY LEADERS

The parent advocate from the neighborhood is key in identifying community leaders who can help organize and support parents. Each community has natural leaders. Many times, these community leaders are
neither particularly well educated nor particularly worldly beyond
knowledge of their own communities. Nevertheless, they are trusted
and well known in their respective communities and therefore, once
their support for a program is obtained, are valuable in encouraging
others in the community to participate in advocacy efforts. These natural leaders can be found in various places, including churches, schools,
residents' councils of public housing complexes, Head Start and child

care programs (especially those that address the needs of teenage parents), and the homes of Good Samaritans (e.g., mothers who watch others' children in addition to their own or who participate in community crime watch patrols).

Women of Strength

In addition to being key in identifying community leaders, the parent advocate can seek out strong community residents who historically have been the backbone of advocacy efforts in poor communities. These communities are overwhelmingly composed of households headed by women. Many of these women live in public housing communities and rely on public assistance to maintain their families. Many had their secondary education interrupted by starting their families as teenagers. Despite these hardships, some of these women exhibit personal strengths that are to be commended. They should be encouraged to help similarly situated women who are not coping as well as they are. A parent advocate would be remiss if these women of strength were not sought out to participate in advocacy efforts. Usually, these women have some common characteristics, including the following:

1. *Spiritual base:* Whether they are affiliated with churches or mosques, women of color for whom spirituality plays an important role seem to be able to meet the challenges of maintaining themselves and their families. This spirituality sustains their optimism and keeps them striving.

2. *Strong support systems:* A strong support system affords many women of color an extra pair of hands for child care or a shoulder to cry on when situations get tough. Their support network may include biological relatives but most likely comprises an extended family network including friends and neighbors.

3. *Value of education:* Education is highly valued in communities made up of people of color. Realizing the dire consequences of not obtaining or delaying their own education, women of color insist that their children do well in school. They have come to understand that education is the ticket out of poverty, not only for their children but also for themselves as they strive to obtain their own high school diplomas, general equivalency diplomas, or additional job training.

4. *Employment possibilities:* Along with valuing an education is their concomitant desire to obtain a job. Women of color want not just any position but one that leads to a career opportunity that offers a wage or salary sufficient to cover all of their living expenses, including child care, food, housing, and health insurance.

5. *Involvement in the community:* Involvement in community activities provides women of color an opportunity to give something back to

their communities and helps to raise their self-esteem. They are involved in school and church activities. Many of their homes become safe havens for neighborhood children. Some women of color are part of informal neighborhood crime watch groups that assist police in addressing violent crime and illegal drug activity.

6. *Sobriety:* Sobriety plays a part in enhancing the coping skills of women of color as they maintain themselves and families. A clear mind obviously is better than one clouded by substance abuse. Despite the prevalence of alcohol and other drug abuse in communities composed of people of color, most of the women in these communities have never had a problem with alcohol and other drug abuse. The ability of women to recover from such addictions and achieve and sustain abstinence means that they can successfully maintain themselves and their families. A driving incentive for substance-abusing parents to help themselves is their desire to take care of their children. The dilemma, however, is that overcoming their substance abuse may involve hospitalization for an extended time, forcing them to confront questions of child care and child custody. Many substance-abusing parents do not want to relinquish their children to the foster care system because of their fear that their children will be lost or abused. Parents' simply admitting a substance abuse problem also carries a stigma and the overriding concern of losing custody of their children. Involvement in designing foster care arrangements while retaining some control of their children's eventual home and community settings seems to ameliorate parents' fears. These arrangements can include placing children with biological family members or in the parents' extended family networks. These arrangements allow parents to address their substance abuse issues in earnest while their children remain in a familiar and caring environment. The unification of the family upon completion of a rehabilitation program or effort is most successful when parents follow up their recovery by attending Alcoholics Anonymous or Narcotics Anonymous meetings. Once the parent advocate has identified and assembled community residents and parents as a core group, an effort can be made to support the core group as it negotiates the advocacy process.

Parent Advocate

Without support, a volunteer parent advocate from a poorer community would be unlikely to be able to engage in advocacy efforts to assist children and families being served by the public services systems. It is therefore incumbent upon service providers and community-based organizations that are committed to promoting parent involvement and systems change to include a paid parent advocate position on their staffs. In addition, these positions must be described and advertised in such a way that residents of the community are encouraged to apply and compete for placement in this position. To achieve this goal, the job description should be written so that the values of the community are reflected. Credentials alone would not ensure job placement; in fact, connection with the community; experience in working with people, especially community residents; and understanding the strengths of the community in terms of material and human resources should be highly valued when selecting a person to fill the parent advocate position. An applicant's status as a parent, especially if she or he has had experience with public child services agencies, would be another plus.

In addition, training in office operations areas (e.g., administrative tasks, personnel procedures) can be built into on-the-job training if necessary. Evaluation and instruction can be delivered in a format that encourages improved performance rather than highlighting mistakes and problems. Conferences, seminars, and other training in leadership development, community organizing, communication skills, and pro-family practices also may prove helpful. It should go without saying that, as a staff member, the parent advocate should enjoy all of the privileges that other staff members enjoy (e.g., access to photocopy machines, postage meters, credit cards, petty cash, office space, educational opportunities as appropriate to enhance job performance). Unfortunately, some of these privileges are denied to parent advocates after they are hired as part of the staff, leading to a feeling that, as a community resident, he or she is not valued by other staff members.

Community Residents and Parents

Because many parents of color, especially in poor communities, do not have the resources to support advocacy efforts, they should be provided with transportation to meetings, child care, and food. In this way, the community resident will not incur expenses to be a part of the advocacy process. Ideally, a stipend for participation should also be offered. In addition, parents should have the opportunity to learn through training, conferences, seminars, and workshops. The parents should not bear the cost of these educational experiences. A parent who is required to travel for training or for a conference should make babysitting arrangements and payments before departing, and expense money should be given to the parent before he or she leaves. To expect a parent to travel and then wait 6–8 weeks upon his or her return for repayment of babysitting expenses is unrealistic because many of these parents are poor and lack money for unbudgeted expenses.

Parent Involvement in Children's Services System Reform

In most public children's services agencies, there are advisory panels as well as some paraprofessional positions that can easily be filled by parent advocates working in communities composed of people of color, where many of the residents rely on public services agencies. In the era of managed care, cost containment, and cost-effectiveness, children's services agencies would be prudent in aggressively recruiting parent advocates of color in order to learn what services would best serve their clients. This commitment by agencies would be a win-win situation because parents of color would acquire meaningful employment as they met personal goals while assisting their communities, and children's services agencies would have a lifeline to community resources. Together, they could design and deploy more linguistically and culturally appropriate services.

CONCLUSIONS

Parents of color have an obligation to their communities to organize, identify, and advocate for better services for themselves and their children. They, like their white counterparts, are invested in their children's well-being and have consistently demonstrated the experience and skills necessary to undertake this charge within their own communities as well as within white-controlled family organizations and the broader systems of care when provided with the opportunity to do so. Agencies have a responsibility to provide linguistically and culturally appropriate services to families and children, regardless of people's socioeconomic status. Clearly, without the efforts of a parent advocate for and from communities of color and without the proper support of the parents and parent advocates in the advocacy process, the marriage of parent obligation and agency responsibility will be a dream deferred as the reality of inappropriate provision of services to families and children of color continues.

REFERENCES

Blauner, R. (1972). *Racial oppression in America.* New York: HarperCollins.

Briggs, H.E., & Paulson, R.I. (1996). Racism. M.A. Mattani & B.A. Thyer (Eds.), *Finding solutions to social problems: Behavioral strategies for change* (pp. 147–177). Washington, DC: American Psychological Association.

Comer, J.P. (1969). White racism: Its roots, form and function. *American Journal of Psychiatry, 126*(6), 802–806.

Cross, T.L., Bazron, B.J., Dennis, K.W., & Isaacs, M.R. (Eds.). (1989). *Towards a culturally competent system of care: Vol. I. A monograph on effective services for minority children who are severely emotionally disturbed.* Washington, DC:

Georgetown University, Child Development Center, Child and Adolescent Service System Program, Technical Assistance Center.

Franklin, J.H. (1989). *Race and history: Selected essays 1938–1988.* Baton Rouge: Louisiana State University Press.

Fuller, N. (1969). *The united independent compensatory code/system/concept: A textbook/workbook for thought, speech, and/or action for victims of racism (white supremacy).* Unpublished manuscript.

Gullattee, A.C. (1969, May). *The subtleties of white racism.* Paper presented at the American Psychiatric Association annual meeting, Miami Beach, FL.

Harry, B. (1992). *Cultural diversity, families, and the special education system: Communication and empowerment.* New York: Teachers College Press.

Isaacs, M.R., & Benjamin, M.P. (1991). *Toward a culturally competent system of care: Volume II. Programs which utilize culturally competent principles.* Washington, DC: Georgetown University, Child Development Center, Child and Adolescent Service System Program, Technical Assistance Center.

Rosenthal, E., & Carty, L.A. (1996). *Impediments to services and advocacy for black and Hispanic people with mental illness.* Washington, DC: Mental Health Law Project/National Institute of Mental Health.

Tiger Woods' death threats continue. (1997, November 24). *Jet, 93*(1).

Welsing, F.C. (1992). *The Isis papers: The keys to the colors.* Chicago: Third World Press.

West, C. (1997). Afterword. In W. Lubiano, *The house that race built: Black Americans, U.S. terrain.* New York: Pantheon.

Wilson, W.J. (1976). *Power, racism, and privilege.* New York: Free Press.

Special Issues in Serving Culturally Diverse Populations

The Psychological Impact of Violence on Children and Families

Assessment and Service System Strategies

Marva P. Benjamin

System of care experts widely acknowledge that violence among youth and families is one of the United States' most pressing public health problems. Its effects include not only the perpetuation of acts of violence but also the internalized psychological scars that affect millions of children and family members of all ages (Benjamin, 1995). Rates of criminal violence involving children and adolescents had reached unparalleled high levels in American society by the early 1990s (Kelly, Huizinga, Thornberry, & Loeber, 1997). For example, according to the U.S. Department of Justice's National Crime Survey, 130,000 youth ages 10–17 were arrested for rape, robbery, homicide, or aggravated assault in 1991. This figure represented a 48% increase in such youth arrests since 1986 (Grayson, Childress, & McNulty, 1994). Fortunately, however, juvenile arrests for violent crimes in the United States declined in 1995 for the first year in nearly a decade. This decline included a 3% overall decrease in arrests, comprising a 14% decline in juvenile arrests for murder and nonnegligent manslaughter, a 4% decline in forcible rape, a 1% decline in robbery, and a 3% decline in aggravated assault from 1994 to 1995 (Kelly et al., 1997).

Nevertheless, in *Injury to Children and Teenagers: State by State Mortality Facts*, Baker, Fingerhut, Higgins, Chen, and Braver (1996) concluded that injuries are the leading cause of death among children and teenagers in the United States. During the 20th century, trauma replaced infectious disease as the most serious threat to children. Figure 1 shows that injuries claimed a total of almost 20,000 lives of children and youth from birth to age 19 years in 1992 (Baker et al., 1996). Further-

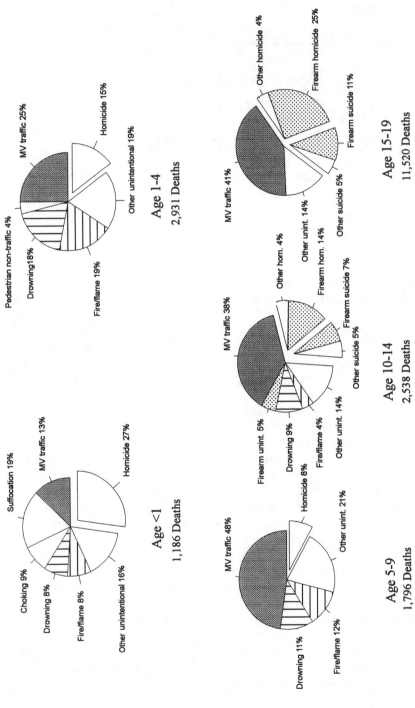

Figure 1. U.S. injury deaths by age, intent, and cause, 1992. (MV, motor vehicle.) (From Baker, S.P., Fingerhut, L.A., Higgins, L., Chen, L.-H., & Braver, E.R. [1996]. *Injury to children and teenagers: State-by-state mortality facts.* Baltimore: The Johns Hopkins Center for Injury Research and Policy.)

more, according to Cohen and Swift (1993), the rates of interpersonal violence are higher in the United States than in any other industrialized nation. In comparison with 21 other countries, the U.S. homicide rate (8.7 per 100,000 people) was 2.6 times greater than the nation with the next-highest rate (Finland, 3.3 per 100,000 people) and 4–8 times greater than the rates in most other countries. An American 17-year-old is 10 times more likely to commit murder than his or her Canadian counterpart (Blumstein, 1994; Kelly et al., 1997; Silverman & Kennedy, 1993).

Although violence in the United States is a serious societal problem, it is not evenly distributed across neighborhoods or across demographic groups. For example, a young African American male is 6 times more likely to be murdered than a young African American female, 9 times more likely to be murdered than a young Caucasian male, and 26 times more likely to be murdered than a young Caucasian female (Centers for Disease Control and Prevention, 1990; Isaacs, 1992). Homicide is also the leading cause of death among African American youth between ages 15 and 19 (Jenkins & Bell, 1992). Furthermore, homicides committed by African American youth with firearms more than doubled from 1979 to 1989 (Kelly et al., 1997). Indeed, youth of color, especially African American and Hispanic and Latino youth, are disproportionately both victims and perpetrators of violent crimes. Significantly, some of these youth grow up in poor neighborhoods and, as such, are exposed to problems such as chronic violence, high unemployment rates, poor housing, inadequate schools, substance abuse, and poor medical and dental care. They are also confronted with social forces such as racism and economic inequality. These conditions increase the probability that youth will become involved in delinquent and violent behavior. Moreover, economically disadvantaged and distressed environments provide youth with opportunities for learning about and engaging in delinquent and violent behavior. Some of the characteristics of these environments are the presence of gangs, illegal markets, violent role models, single-parent families, and high school dropout rates (Benjamin, 1997).

IMPACT OF VIOLENCE

According to Isaacs (1992), the published research suggests that children exposed to violence often experience a range of physical, social, educational, and emotional problems. Although research in this area is sparse, initial studies involving African American youth, for example, suggest that exposure to community and family violence dramatically and negatively influences African American youth's ability to experience and modulate their states of emotional arousal, their images of themselves as individuals, their beliefs about the likelihood of surviving into adulthood, their willingness and ability to form positive relationships, their sense of morality or beliefs in a just and benevolent world, and other areas central and germane to typical or adaptive development (Isaacs, 1992). Serious developmental consequences for youth who have been exposed to chronic violence include psychological disorders, grief and loss reactions, and posttraumatic stress disorder (PTSD). Other consequences include intellectual development impairments and problems in school, truncated moral development, pathological adaptations to violence, identification with aggressors, and lowered self-esteem (Bell & Jenkins, 1991; McCart, 1994; Warner & Weist, 1996).

In addition, some of these children are often angry and have difficulty in getting along with others, and their anger is likely to be incorporated into their personalities. Carrying this extra load of anger makes it difficult for them to control their behavior and therefore increases their risk of resorting to violence (Wallach, 1994). Furthermore, research and clinical experiences on the effects of exposure to violence reveals that these children are deeply affected by violence and that they often show symptoms of PTSD. For example, in Pynoos's (Pynoos & Eth, 1985; Pynoos & Nader, 1988) work with children who had witnessed the murder of a parent and who were exposed to community violence, he found that the children displayed the following classic PTSD symptoms: reexperiencing the event in play, in dreams, or in intrusive images and sounds associated with the event; psychic numbing characterized by subdued behavior and inactive, constricted affect and diminished interest in activities; sleep disorders; avoidance behaviors; and startle reactions (Bell & Jenkins, 1991). In addition, these children are often plagued by fears of recurrence of violence and guilt about their behavior during the violent incident, they may have a pessimistic attitude toward their futures, and they may experience difficulty in forming and maintaining relationships. Furthermore, when these youth have access to firearms, are involved with alcohol and other drugs, become gang members, and are exposed to violence in the mass media, their risk of involvement with violence increases. By age 16, most North Americans have already witnessed 200,000 acts of violence on television, ranging from fights to murders (Cohen & Swift, 1993). According to Stutman and Benjamin (1994), violence is often portrayed on American television as the only option for resolving conflict, and the barrage of violent images on television serves to reinforce negative and limited approaches to problem solving. In addition, social forces such as racism, economic inequality, and attitudes toward violence in American culture interact with the influences of childhood, consequently fostering the expression of violence (American Psychological Association, Commission on Violence and Youth, 1993).

FACTORS THAT CONTRIBUTE TO VIOLENCE

Although there are many contributing factors to violence in various combinations, these factors may decrease or increase the likelihood that violence will occur; there is no combination of variables that can predict with certainty which individuals will commit violent acts or which interventions will prevent violence or reduce the incidence of repeated offenses (Earls, 1994). Violence, however, is a learned behavior; as such, the strongest developmental predictor of a child's future involvement in violence is the child's history of previous violence (American Psychological Association, Commission on Violence and Youth, 1993). Unfortunately, some young people view violence as either the only way or the most effective way to achieve status and respect and to attain basic social and personal needs (Elliot, 1994). Like money and knowledge, violence is a form of power, and some youth may perceive violence as the only form of power available to them.

It is therefore not surprising that young people who grow up in poor, disorganized neighborhoods that are rife with drug dealers and that offer limited opportunities for employment, recreation, socialization, and support do not experience a typical course of adolescent development, and thus the likelihood that such youth will engage in violent behavior increases. Indeed, as stated previously, these neighborhoods provide opportunities for learning about and engaging in violent behavior. One critical feature of such neighborhoods is the relative absence of any effective social or cultural organization (Elliot, 1994). Moreover, individuals residing in these neighborhoods may change residences frequently, which disconnects them from their support systems and causes a sense of isolation in the individuals and makes it difficult for such neighborhoods to develop common values, norms of behavior, and effective social controls. Most acts of violence (which are often fueled by anger and emotion), however, occur between family, friends, and acquaintances. Lacking skills for defusing violence, some individuals get locked into an escalating situation from which it is difficult to extricate themselves without loss of face (Holinger, Offer, Barter, & Bell, 1994).

Children's mental health services experts acknowledge that the most important source of acts of violence committed by and among children is exposure to family violence and the breakdown of the family. Some of these experts believe that family disintegration is at the root of many of the social and economic problems present in American society at the end of the 20th century (Zinsmeister, 1990). For example, the American Psychological Association Presidential Task Force on Violence and the Family took the position that family violence creates a breeding ground for social problems, resulting in outcomes such as

- Physical damage caused by repeated abuse, putting children and adolescents at risk of developmental and neuropsychological problems as well as physical health problems beyond the immediate injuries caused by violence
- Increased contact with the legal system and higher rates of incarceration among individuals and families with histories of violence
- Posttraumatic stress, with after-effects lasting many years after the original causative incidents of violence, and a lifetime of risk for psychological disorders as a result of incest or sexual abuse
- Rates of suicide and attempted suicide that are higher than those of the general population and a higher lifetime risk of substance abuse problems compared with that of the general population
- Increased risk for poor or impaired school and job performance as well as higher incidence of destructive relationships among family members
- A greater economic toll on the family and society (1996, pp. 22–24)

As a consequence of all of the factors just listed, among others, significant advances in improving the outcomes for youth and families exposed to violence cannot be made until service providers focus on childhood abuse and family violence issues (Geffner, 1992). Certainly, children who witness chronic family violence may exhibit atypical development patterns and impaired cognitive, emotional, and/or behavioral adjustment. These children and their families are in need of services from the service delivery system.

SERVICE DELIVERY SYSTEM CHALLENGE

The challenge for the service delivery system and for American society as a whole is to ensure that all children and adolescents, especially those deemed to be at high risk for engaging in delinquent or violent behavior and who are from culturally diverse backgrounds, have access to supportive environments that facilitate healthy growth and development. Physical safety and psychological security are the foundations—indeed, the essential preconditions—for a child's health, education, and overall development (Zinsmeister, 1990). Moreover, a child's abilities to acquire a sense of trust in him- or herself and in the outside world are dependent on the extent to which his or her critical early relationships have created an environment of predictability, safety, and security (Hill, 1991, cited in Isaacs, 1992). Nevertheless, there are some children whose environments are not safe and secure yet who are still able to triumph over some of their numerous stressors and grow up to be healthy adults. Some of the protective mechanisms that researchers have observed in some of these seemingly unsafe and insecure situations are

- Early bonding in the child's primary relationships with a caring adult that promote social development

- An adult who can buffer the child from violence
- Experiences that promote the child's positive development
- An explicit value system that eschews violence
- Promotion of cultural awareness and a positive cultural identity (Hill, 1991, cited in Isaacs, 1992)

These factors suggest that families and communities that are able to promote an active understanding and appreciation of culture as well as a positive cultural identity can instill a sense of self-protection and value in their children, which seems to mitigate youth involvement in violence and juvenile delinquent behavior (Hill, 1991, cited in Isaacs, 1992). Moreover, when public and private youth services organizations share the common mission of developing supportive environments for healthy growth and development, young people are better able to move successfully through adolescence and into adulthood. Building a positive base of operation for youth and their families on the one hand and linking them with a collaborative service delivery system that is culturally competent on the other are steps in the right direction.

If the service delivery system is to be successful in preventing and reducing violence, attention must be focused on developing ways to train, develop, and help both the victims and the perpetrators of violence; to better understand why individuals become violent; and to work collaboratively to change many of the situations that lead to violence. Toward that end, the rest of this chapter highlights and outlines some local service system strategies to prevent and reduce youth violence (Benjamin, 1995).

SERVICE SYSTEM AND VIOLENCE
PREVENTION STRATEGIES WITHIN A CULTURAL CONTEXT

Service system and violence prevention strategies that are likely to reduce the psychological impact of violence on children and families of diverse cultural backgrounds include identifying and putting to constructive use an understanding of the naturally occurring coping mechanisms available to children and families exposed to violence. This process must include using state-of-the-art cultural knowledge as well as technical expertise to help children exposed to violence build on their individual strengths to triumph over their violence-related stressors. Fostering skills, status, and respect for the individual as well as building pathways to economic resources are also necessary strategies for addressing issues related to youth and family violence (Hill, 1991; Hill, Soriano, Chen, & La Fromboise, 1994).

A community-based system of care involving a strong mental health component that is committed to violence prevention is in a good position to effectively use its understanding of the psychosocial and mental health needs of youth to help reduce and prevent violence (Benjamin, 1995). This process includes using strategies such as 1) providing leadership in carrying out collaborative programs designed to prevent violence, 2) using a systems approach to service delivery, 3) involving families in every aspect of violence prevention strategies, and 4) promoting culturally competent approaches to service delivery. (For a summary of these strategies, see Benjamin, 1995.)

Recognizing that the mental health system must become more involved in efforts across children's mental health services agencies to prevent and reduce youth violence, state mental health representatives for children and youth agree that effective collaboration is the key to understanding and reducing youth violence (Benjamin, 1995). They also agree that the children's mental health services system should move quickly toward establishing partnerships with families that respect each entity's involvement and commitment to developing the best and most responsive child and family policies and services possible in an effort to reduce and prevent violence. This type of partnership calls for the inclusion of families in all aspects of the development, management, funding, and implementation of violence prevention programs and strategies. Also of importance is that cultural competence in service development and provision is emerging as a major priority in implementing violence prevention programs. Equally important is the need to redirect the children's mental health services system and other children's services systems toward responsiveness to the needs of children and families from diverse cultural backgrounds and to provide violence prevention services within a cultural context. This approach requires that mental health and other services systems understand that ethnic cultures can protect children and youth who are vulnerable to social risk factors by providing them with a pattern of living, specific values, social support, and affirmation of themselves and their ethnic groups. Conversely, ethnic minority cultures can fail to protect against mounting risk factors when they are weakened by negative forces in society and when they are overwhelmed by the demands of the dominant culture. For example, when an ethnic minority culture's values and modes of behavior are denigrated by the dominant culture, it may lose its power to serve as a positive socialization guide for both young people and adults (American Psychological Association, Commission on Violence and Youth, 1993; Hill, Soriano, Chen, & La Fromboise, 1994).

Many mental health professionals believe that the strengths of an individual's culture of origin can be incorporated into mental health or other interventions with children and that these strengths should be used to reinforce children's cultural identity and integrity. They believe that using strategies based on culture is likely to have a powerful impact on preventing violence among young people from culturally diverse backgrounds. To be truly successful in preventing violence, however, community-based strategies that involve the entire children's mental health services system in partnership with families is essential. There are at least four key elements of effective violence prevention approaches that should be considered:

1. Prevention and early intervention
2. Respect for cultural differences
3. Support for families and development of communitywide approaches and approaches developed by communities
4. Promotion of interagency collaboration

Emphasizing prevention and early intervention as a children's mental health services system strategy requires detecting the early signs of violence in children, targeting youth and families for early intervention, responding quickly to incidents of violence, and involving survivors and victims of violence in violence prevention efforts.

Respecting cultural differences requires an understanding of culture and a determination to foster a positive sense of cultural identity (Hill, 1991, cited in Isaacs, 1992). Putting a human face on issues, regardless of the racial or cultural makeup of the community within which the violence occurs, is a valuable approach to employ in promoting violence prevention strategies as well. In addition, in any effective violence prevention and intervention effort, one should involve the natural support networks that exist within communities and carefully match intervention strategies to the cultures of the families and communities involved.

Supporting family and community approaches to violence prevention requires an understanding of the community and family contexts in which specific incidents of violence occur. In addition, mobilizing entire communities to face violence-related issues and using the community's strengths (e.g., organizations, resources, leaders) to combat problems is a service system strategy that has been known to work in some communities. Such a strategy requires effective communication among all of those affected by violence in the community. Using family-centered prevention and intervention strategies and giving parents the tools that they need to be advocates for programs and resources required to support their children is an effective violence prevention strategy. Interagency service system strategies that are viewed as effective in addressing violence include identifying and engaging key players in different organizations and agencies in these efforts, overcoming agency turf issues, and taking actions that promote interagency communication and encourage joint initiatives in the community.

OTHER ACTIONS AND
STRATEGIES FOR VIOLENCE PREVENTION

Some other service system and violence prevention strategies that need to be considered and adopted within a cultural context are

- Conducting needs assessments
- Improving communication
- Using creative fund-raising strategies
- Developing violence prevention curricula
- Including violence prevention programs in planning and implementation strategies
- Changing policies as needed
- Encouraging the broad-based participation of families and community members
- Advocating for issues that strengthen families
- Fostering interagency collaboration

The preceding strategies are sometimes used as specific action steps designed to increase the effectiveness of violence prevention programs. If collaborative and holistic, such action steps will likely lead to an increase in the repertoire of families, service providers, community organizations, and youth themselves as they search for effective ways to prevent and reduce the violence that so strongly affects youth.

Conducting Needs Assessments

The following assessment activities have proved helpful in developing and implementing effective violence prevention programs in some communities:

- Carrying out communitywide assessments of youth violence and determining its causes, incidence, and responses
- Determining which resources (e.g., plans, private and public programs, leaders) already exist in the community
- Assessing the situations of local populations who are at risk of becoming involved with violent behaviors
- Designing and using screening forms or tools to identify victims of violence
- Identifying in emergency rooms the causes and nature of incidents of violence that result in injuries
- Exploring the long-term effects of violence, such as its cumulative stress on young people
- Identifying differences between rural and urban violence and among various forms of violence found in different communities in different states

- Finding resource centers that can provide information on violence prevention strategies, approaches, programs, and models

Improving Communication

In order for families, children's services agencies, and other community organizations to strengthen their abilities to prevent violence and in order to reduce the mortality and injury rates from violence, it is necessary that they identify and use effective methods of communication, including activities such as

- Encouraging the media to publicize positive violence prevention programs and approaches
- Increasing public awareness about risk factors that can lead to youth violence
- Helping victim's rights advocates be heard through various media outlets at the state and local levels
- Pressing for communication among separate parts of the youth corrections system
- Removing roadblocks brought about by agencies', providers', and community members' not sharing information
- Promoting the establishment of a common database in communities to identify youth at risk of becoming involved with violent behavior

Using Creative Fund-Raising Strategies

Financial resources must be made available to families and communities of diverse cultural backgrounds to assist them with the cost of developing programs for reducing the impact of violence on their children and families. Such strategies include

- Identifying new public and private funding sources to support violence prevention programs
- Investigating new resources that may be available through block grants
- Using newsletters to disseminate information about successful funding strategies employed with local, state, and regional organizations, both public and private
- Setting aside a percentage of block grant funds for violence prevention efforts
- Encouraging funding for violence prevention demonstration programs with definitive outcomes

Developing Violence Prevention Curricula

Measures that can be taken to reduce the probability that a young person will become involved in violent behavior include developing and implementing violence prevention curricula. These curricula are designed to teach social skills, behavior recognition and management, and socially acceptable problem-solving skills. In developing violence prevention curricula, consideration should be given to

- Offering violence prevention curricula in local schools
- Including in violence prevention curricula ways to promote and model alternatives to gangs, such as Boys and Girls Clubs and other recreational and socialization organizations
- Sponsoring training programs to develop positive leadership skills among youth at risk of becoming involved with violence

Including Violence Prevention Programs in Planning and Implementation Strategies

Some activities that can be undertaken to ensure that violence prevention programs are a part of planning and implementation strategies include

- Creating opportunities for federal, state, and local children's mental health services systems to address issues of violence within already-established planning processes
- Committing staff resources to focus on violence prevention efforts
- Planning early intervention violence prevention strategies that involve infants, toddlers, and preschool-age children

Changing Policies as Needed

Changing policies as appropriate to support a mission of planning, developing, implementing, and evaluating violence prevention programs for youth at risk of engaging in violence within a cultural context could include activities such as

- Conducting local policy design academies to develop strategies for meeting the needs of youth exposed to violence
- Identifying mechanisms to get violence prevention issues to the top of the political agenda at all levels of government

Encouraging the Broad-Based Participation of Families and Community Members

Because violence is a community problem, solutions to this problem require the broad-based participation of families and community members residing in a particular community. Some of the activities that can be undertaken to encourage broad-based participation include

- Reaching out to adult victims of violence to sit on parent advisory boards

- Providing information about violence prevention approaches and efforts to family members
- Encouraging the broad participation of community members in violence prevention efforts
- Getting representative young people and families to participate in planning violence prevention and intervention programs
- Developing peer leadership groups

Advocating for Issues that Strengthen Families

Because violence is a learned behavior and because most children grow up in families in which learning takes place, it follows that the prevention of violence is more likely to occur if families are strong and if children are taught problem-solving skills that do not include the use of violence. Thus, advocacy for issues that strengthen families and that provide assistance to them in their efforts to provide a clear set of positive values can be viewed as an effective violence prevention activity, including

- Advocating for changes in policies and laws to make it possible for grandparents to receive financial assistance when they are called on to raise their grandchildren
- Providing job opportunities for youth and their families

Fostering Interagency Collaboration

Violence prevention involving culturally diverse populations requires effective collaboration among neighborhood groups, community agencies, public and private organizations, the service delivery system, the natural support system, and family members affected by violence. Fostering interagency collaboration is an essential ingredient for reducing or preventing violence and for reducing the psychological impact of violence on children and families. Some activities designed to foster interagency collaboration include

- Getting all parties involved in violence prevention efforts to communicate with each other as a first step toward collaboration
- Getting to know local child abuse and domestic violence programs to determine whether early-warning systems can be developed
- Considering youth programs in junior high and high schools as potential resources
- Linking hospital emergency rooms with children's mental health services
- Promoting contacts between juvenile justice agencies and children's mental health organizations
- Collaborating with court systems that are dealing with young people

- Analyzing the resources available to juvenile justice facilities, especially resources that will help in dealing constructively with the stress factors experienced by the young people in the juvenile justice system
- Identifying ways to share pertinent information about youth and violence with various children's and family mental health services providers
- Identifying a lead agency for violence prevention efforts
- Bringing together multi-agency teams from several states within regions to find common issues and violence prevention strategies

CONCLUSIONS

Because violence is a family and community problem that has serious psychological consequences for children and their families and communities, assessment and children's mental health services system strategies to prevent violence must be identified and implemented. In order for young people who have been exposed to violence to move successfully through adolescence and into adulthood in American society, all of the children's services systems must work together to develop and provide comprehensive, community-based, culturally competent, family-centered violence prevention and intervention services.

REFERENCES

American Psychological Association. (1996). *Violence and the family* (Report of the American Psychological Association Presidential Task Force on Violence and the Family). Washington, DC: Author.

American Psychological Association, Commission on Violence and Youth. (1993). *Summary report of the American Psychological Association Commission on Violence and Youth: Vol. I. Psychology's response.* Washington, DC: Author.

Baker, S.P., Fingerhut, L.A., Higgins, L., Chen, L.-H., & Braver, E.R. (1996). *Injury to children and teenagers: State-by-state mortality facts* (pp. 1–9). Baltimore: The John Hopkins University, Center for Injury Research and Policy.

Bell, C.C., & Jenkins, E.J. (1991). Traumatic stress and children. *Journal of Health Care for the Poor and Underserved, 2*(1), 175–188.

Benjamin, M.P. (1995). *Effective collaboration as the key to understanding and reducing youth violence: A mental health perspective.* Washington, DC: Georgetown University, Child Development Center, National Technical Assistance Center for Children's Mental Health.

Benjamin, M.P. (1997). Overrepresentation of youth of color in the juvenile justice system: Culturally competent service system strategies. *Focal Point: The Bulletin of the Research and Training Center on Family Support and Children's Mental Health, 11*(1), 12–15.

Blumstein, A. (1994). *Youth violence, guns and the illicit drug industry* (Working paper series). Pittsburgh, PA: Carnegie Mellon University, H. John Henry III School of Public Policy and Management.

Centers for Disease Control and Prevention. (1990). Homicide among young black males: United States, 1978–1987. *Morbidity and Mortality Weekly Report, 39*(48), 869–873.

Cohen, L., & Swift, S. (1993). A public health approach to the violence epidemic in the United States. *Environment and Urbanization, 5*(2), 50–66.

Earls, F.J. (1994). Violence and today's youth: Critical health issues for children and youth. *The Future of Children, 4*(3), 4–23.

Elliot, D.S. (1994). *Youth violence: An overview.* Boulder: University of Colorado, Center for the Study and Prevention of Violence.

Geffner, R. (Ed.). (1992). Politics, families, and values. *Family Violence and Sexual Assault Bulletin, 8*(2), 1.

Grayson, J., Childress, A., & McNulty, C. (Eds.). (1994). Youth violence: The child abuse connection. *Virginia Child Protection Newsletter, 42,* 1, 3–7, 10–11, 16.

Hill, H. (1991, June). *Violence: The impact of community violence on African American children and families: Collaborative approaches for prevention and intervention.* Paper presented at the National Center for Education in Maternal and Child Health conference, New York City.

Hill, H., Soriano, F., Chen, A., & La Fromboise, T. (1994). Psychocultural factors in the etiology and prevention of violence among ethnic minority youth. In L. Eron, J. Gentry, & M. Schlegal (Eds.), *A reason to hope: A psychosocial perspective on violence and youth* (pp. 59–104). Washington, DC: American Psychological Association.

Holinger, P., Offer, D., Barter, J.T., & Bell, C.C. (1994). *Suicide and homicide among adolescents.* New York: Guilford Press.

Isaacs, M.R. (1992). *The impact of community violence on African American children and families.* Arlington, VA: National Center for Education in Maternal and Child Health.

Jenkins, E.J., & Bell, C.C. (1992). Adolescent violence: Can it be curbed? *Adolescent Medicine: State of the Art Reviews, 3*(1), 71–86.

Kelly, B.T., Huizinga, D., Thornberry, T.P., & Loeber, R. (1997, June). Epidemiology of serious violence. *Juvenile Justice Bulletin,* 1–11.

McCart, L. (Ed.). (1994). *Kids and violence.* Washington, DC: National Governors Association.

Pynoos, R., & Eth, S. (1985). Developmental perspectives on psychic trauma in childhood. In R. Figley (Ed.), *Trauma and its wake* (pp. 36–52). New York: Brunner/Mazel.

Pynoos, R., & Nader, K. (1988). Psychological first aid and treatment approaches to children exposed to community violence: Research implications. *Journal of Traumatic Stress, 1,* 445–473.

Silverman, R.A., & Kennedy, L. (1993). *Deadly deeds: Murder in Canada.* Scarborough, Ontario, Canada: Nelson Canada.

Stutman, S., & Benjamin, M. (1994, October). *An opportunity to prevent violence: A culturally competent media.* Paper presented at the Eighth Annual Conference on Counseling and Treating People of Color, San Juan, Puerto Rico.

Wallach, L.B. (1994). *Violence and young children's development.* University of Illinois, Urbana. (ERIC Document Reproduction Service No. EDO-PS-94-7)

Warner, B.S., & Weist, M.D. (1996). Urban youth as witnesses to violence: Beginning assessment and treatment efforts. *Journal of Youth and Adolescence, 25,* 361–377.

Zinsmeister, K. (1990, June). Growing up scared. *Atlantic Monthly, 265*(6), 49–66.

CHAPTER 11

Clinical Issues in Assessment and Intervention with Children and Adolescents Exposed to Homicide

Linda N. Freeman

Serving the profound and unmet needs of surviving siblings and family members of youth homicide victims requires coordination among human services agencies. Because homicide disproportionately affects youth who are members of minority groups, understanding the nature and effects of grief after the homicide of a child or an adolescent is particularly important for establishing culturally competent systems of care that focus on minority families. This chapter focuses on the problem of youth homicide and summarizes the literature related to children who lose young relatives to homicide. In addition, the chapter is based on the experiences of a group of 17 children and adolescents who are involved in a longitudinal study of sibling death by homicide. Specifically, the chapter addresses the questions of which people become murder victims, which people commit murders, where murders take place, the needs of survivors of a sibling's homicide, the barriers to gaining access to needed care, and how the needs of the survivors of youth homicide can be better served within systems of care such as mental health, criminal justice, and schools.

THE PROBLEM OF YOUTH HOMICIDE

The following sections consider youth homicide in the United States, specifically the higher homicide rates among African American and

This chapter was supported by a grant from the Lowenstein Foundation to the Lowenstein Center for the Study and Prevention of Disruptive Disorders and by the American Academy of Child and Adolescent Psychiatry, National Institute of Mental Health K–12 Award.

Latino youth than among youth from the dominant culture, possible reasons for these higher rates, and the demographic data on homicide victims and perpetrators.

The High Rate of Homicide Among African American and Latino Youth

The United States leads the developed world in rates of homicide (Fingerhut & Kleinman, 1990). In 1990, the overall rate of homicide among people 15–24 years old was nearly 37 per 100,000 individuals, or more than seven times that of the next most violent nation in the world (Italy). The rate of homicide among African American males ages 15–24 years is particularly alarming (Centers for Disease Control and Prevention, 1991a). The homicide rate for African American males, 158 per 100,000 population, was seven times greater than that for American Caucasian males of similar age (Fingerhut & Kleinman, 1990). Although infrequently reported, the homicide rate among young Latino males in the United States is almost as high as that of African American males (National Center for Health Statistics, 1990).

Two factors are associated with the increase in homicides of African American and Latino youth: drug use and the increased availability and deadliness of firearms. Drug use, particularly cocaine use, may be related to high rates of homicide among African American and Latino youth, not because young homicide victims use cocaine (the proportion of homicide victims younger than age 25 who use cocaine 48 hours or less before their deaths is small) but because homicides result from the business of cocaine trafficking (Tardiff et al., 1994). Violence is often used to control a drug sales territory or in retaliation for drug trade violations (Fagan & Chin, 1990; Hamid, 1990). Many youth, both those involved in the drug trade and those who are bystanders, can be victimized.

The increased availability and deadliness of firearms are also responsible for the increase in homicides. The rate of homicides committed with firearms among young African Americans has increased since 1985 (Centers for Disease Control and Prevention, 1991a). Homicides committed with firearms account for three fourths of all homicides and for an even greater proportion of homicides involving African American and Latino youth. A 1993 Louis Harris/Joyce Foundation Poll (Moran, 1994) of sixth- and twelfth-grade students found that 59% of schoolchildren could get a handgun if they wanted one. Of that population, 15% had carried a handgun in the 30 days preceding the poll, 4% had carried a gun to school, and 9% said that they had fired a gun at someone. A 1990 national survey of high school students (Centers for Disease Control and Prevention, 1991b) reported gun carrying by 20% of the students. Of those who carried guns in high school, the majority were African Americans (39%) and Latinos (41%). Callahan and Rivera

(1992) suggested that low socioeconomic status rather than race accounts for greater access to firearms among youth. Nonetheless, many disputes among African American and Latino youth that prior to the 1990s would have been settled with fist fights or with nonlethal weapons involve firearms and homicide in the late 1990s.

Victims of Youth Homicide

In 1988, there were 1,432 adolescent homicide victims in the United States between the ages of 10 and 18 years. In fact, homicide was the leading cause of death among 10- to 18-year-olds in 1988 (Earls, 1994). Victimization by homicide and other acts of violence is unequally distributed by race, class, and location of residence. The high homicide rates within disadvantaged populations suggest that psychosocial variables related to homicide are confounded by factors related to socioeconomic status and by racial inequity (Griffith & Bell, 1989). Youth in urban areas who are poor and members of an ethnic minority group may be disproportionately affected by homicide because vulnerability to violence is associated with lower economic status (Messner & Tardiff, 1986) and because the overwhelming majority of children living in poor urban neighborhoods are members of minority groups, reflecting the high level of residential segregation in the United States (O'Hare, 1994).

Most homicides occur in large, urban areas (Earls, 1994), and they tend to occur in the working-class and other neighborhoods affected by poverty (Getzel & Masters, 1984). Cultural and subcultural norms governing the appropriate responses to words and actions influence adolescent individuals from these neighborhoods to engage in violent behavior. Among African American and Latino youth, issues of respect and disrespect in words and actions are particularly salient. Murders often result from disputes between young men about property or money that escalate either to fist fighting or to shooting if a firearm is present. Often, after winning the fist fight, the winner may be shot to "even the score."

Perpetrators of Youth Homicide

Youth violence, more commonly than violence against adults, involves victims and offenders of the same race, sex, and age (U.S. Department of Justice, 1991). Offenders are often casual acquaintances of the victims. The perpetrators of youth homicide tend to be young, male, poor, and frequently unemployed. Perpetrators are most likely to murder someone like themselves. The offender in one homicide is likely to be the victim in another (Benjamin, 1995). Gang-related violence accounts for some homicides. In one study, 25% of youth between the ages of 15 and 19 years who were murdered were killed by gangs (Benjamin, 1995). Some homicides are attributable to drug trafficking (Tardiff et al., 1994), but most homicides occur during interpersonal altercations (Moran, 1994).

IMPACT OF YOUTH HOMICIDE ON SURVIVING SIBLINGS

The murder of a sibling is not only the loss of a brother or sister in an act of sudden, horrifying violence but also the simultaneous loss of parents to deep and long-lasting grief. Sensational news media stories reported to the community may label the deceased sibling as a crime victim or as a criminal who deserved to become a victim. Interactions with the criminal justice system can be painful and demeaning for surviving siblings and often do not lead to a feeling of vindication of their loss. Although there are cultural customs for consoling the parents of a dead child, the emotional needs of young siblings of homicide victims are often overlooked; their experiences of loss and of trauma are often ignored or minimized. Few systems of care provide services for the young siblings of homicide victims, and few sibling survivors of homicide victims are even identified as needing support or services (Freeman, Shaffer, & Smith, 1996). Yet, homicide is the leading cause of death among minority youth, and often young homicide victims leave sibling survivors.

Sibling Bereavement Study

The Sibling Bereavement Study (Freeman et al., 1996) is an ongoing research project designed to prospectively examine developmental differences in the bereavement reactions of children and adolescents who have lost a sibling to homicide. Those who are being studied are young siblings of homicide victims who were ages 19 years and younger at death and who were killed by non–family members. Homicide victims are identified through contact with the New York Police Department and the Office of the Chief Medical Examiner of New York City. Cases are selected consecutively. Letters are sent to the family of the victim explaining the study and requesting the participation of eligible siblings. Siblings are eligible if they are between the ages of 7 and 18 years and had lived at home with the homicide victim. Individuals in the control group are New York City public school students who have not lost a sibling in a homicide; they are matched by age, gender, and ethnicity. To date, the siblings ($N = 17$, mean age = 14.2 years) of 11 homicide victims and their mothers have been intensively interviewed over the course of 1 year after their loss. The victims were mostly male and older than their siblings. The siblings all are African Americans (71%) and Latinos (29%). Most are poor, with annual family incomes of less than $10,000 (63%). Nine siblings are male, and eight are female.

The first interview occurs, on average, 5 months after the homicide; the second interview occurs 6 months after the homicide; the third, 12 months after the homicide; and the last, 18 months after the homicide. After obtaining written consent from the victims' mothers and their siblings, interviews are conducted in the families' homes by teams of two interviewers. The teams' interviewers are drawn from a pool of two child psychiatrists, both of whom are African American; three bilingual Latino interviewers; and a Caucasian doctoral-level graduate student in social work. The interview combines an open-ended clinical interview with structured interviews and self-report questionnaires. The interviews are tape recorded, transcribed, and abstracted for qualitative analyses of themes. The following case example and the observations of bereaved siblings' reactions to homicide are derived from the Sibling Bereavement Study.

Saundra

The case study of Saundra provides a view of the reality of youth homicide from the perspective of one sibling survivor. It illustrates the particular ways in which youth homicide influences the symptoms and the functioning of a sibling survivor and points to areas that are important for understanding the psychological stresses of young siblings of homicide victims. Saundra was age 17 years and Mike, her brother, was age 20 years when Mike was murdered. Mike was murdered after a dispute with two young men. No drugs were involved. They had "jumped him" earlier on the day on which he was murdered, and he had beaten them both. They went away, got a gun, and later that day shot him.

Saundra and Mike lived at home with their mother, a 44-year-old homemaker; their stepfather, age 46 years, who was unemployed; and four younger siblings. They had only intermittent contact with their biological father. Their mother and stepfather had been together since Saundra's infancy. The family's annual income was less than $10,000.

Saundra had quit high school during the eleventh grade and had been working as a clerk in a shop for 1 year. She had asthma and a lifelong simple phobia of bridges but no other medical or psychiatric history. She worked regularly and consistently and was popular and socially active. She had had a steady boyfriend for 2 years.

She and her brother, Mike, were close. He had had no medical or psychiatric history. His father had taught him to box, and Mike was known as a good fighter. His family and friends looked up to him as a protector. "Everybody liked my brother. Nobody would mess with me or my friends if he was around," Saundra said. The family denied that Mike had been a gang member.

Saundra's first thought after the murder was guilt. She said, "Nothing would have happened if I was there. I would have told him not to fight." Her thoughts about revenge were intense. "For about a month, I thought about killing them." Because of this vengeful anger and her fear for her own safety, she bought a .25-caliber pistol. A friend informed the police of her purchase, and Saundra was arrested for illegal gun possession a few weeks after she had lost her brother to homicide. Her arrest was fortuitous because her attorney sent her to a court social worker so that he could petition the court to reduce her sentence to probation. The social worker discovered that she had recently been bereaved and counseled her for grief during the months until her case was settled.

Saundra described her fear of going outside: "I never wanted to come out of the building. I thought something would happen to me." Adding to her fear, the murderer had come to the family's apartment to apologize for committing the murder. Saundra stopped going to work for 7 weeks because, she said, "I was afraid to go out. I just wanted to be with my parents."

Saundra reported significant changes in her mood after her brother's murder. She became depressed and socially withdrawn. At first she said she was "mad and angry" all the time. During the first month after the homicide, her feelings changed to predominately fear and sadness. "I used to like to talk to my mother and sister, take my friends shopping and stuff; but now I don't feel happy no more. Now if anybody says something smart, it pisses me off and I curse them out. I feel real depressed. I feel alone. I can't get happy anymore." She also described a number of other symptoms of depression that had an onset within the first month after Mike's murder and had persisted for 10 months.

When interviewed 10 months after the murder, she said, "At first I blamed myself; but now so many people get killed, I think that's just a part of life." Even after the perpetrator had himself been murdered, her anxiety remained intense. "Every day, I'm afraid something is going to happen. If it can happen to my brother, it can happen to anybody. Some days I think I'm going to die, for no reason." Her social activity has been strikingly curtailed because of her anxiety, depression, and suspicion of her friends that developed after the murder. "I don't go nowhere except to work. Nowhere! You never know what might happen when you go somewhere." When she is away from home, she experiences trouble with catching her breath, a smothering feeling, and heart palpitations. She said, "I still hung with my friends for about 3 weeks after, then no more. Enough is enough. I don't have no more friends. I don't trust nobody."

She reported symptoms of posttraumatic stress, including intrusive and distressing thoughts, avoidance of going places and doing things that make her think about Mike, loss of interest in activities, avoidance of people who knew Mike, a sense of numbing ("I don't care about nothing anymore"), irritability and frequent loss of temper, and jumpiness.

She described signs of pathological mourning with symptoms of denial, yearning and searching, and avoidance. "I don't think he is dead. I try to think he's gone away out of town somewhere." Searching (i.e., mistaking men on the street for being Mike) is an almost daily experience. She tries to avoid reminders of him. About a bag of his belongings kept at home, she said, "I'm scared to touch it. I don't like nobody else to touch it neither. If I did, it might make me want to do things to myself—like go crazy." She got rid of all her necklaces because Mike had liked to wear them. She said, "I'll just buy everything new."

She ruminates a lot. "Life now is thinking, thinking, thinking. I think so hard I can't stop. I just stay alone, watch TV, and go to bed early."

Emotional Reactions to Loss of a Sibling to Homicide

Mourning The terms *grief, mourning,* and *bereavement* are often used interchangeably. *Grief* refers to the dysphoric feeling or affective response to death of a loved one. For children as well as for adults, normal grieving can continue even after 1 year (Pynoos, Nader, Frederick, Gonda, & Stuber, 1987). *Mourning* describes the internal process of adaptation to death that leads to appropriate or maladaptive adjustment. Mourning also includes the cultural rituals and other social expression of grief. *Bereavement* is an overarching term that encompasses both feelings of grief and the process of mourning (Osterweiss, Solomon, & Greene, 1984). Mourning involves four tasks:

1. *Accepting the reality of the death:* The child's task here is to overcome symptoms of denial, shock, and isolation.
2. *Experiencing the pain of the grief:* The child's task here is to allow him- or herself to feel the anger, guilt, and resentment associated with the loss.
3. *Adjusting to a world in which the loved one is missing:* The child's task here is to adapt to and resolve the loss.

4. *Withdrawing emotional energy from the grieving process and reinvesting it into another relationship or activity:* The child's task here is to be able to think about the deceased sibling without experiencing physical or emotional pain (Worden, 1982).

In contrast to typical mourning, anecdotal reports and clinical surveys suggest that children exposed to loss and homicide can develop a range of serious problems such as posttraumatic stress disorder (PTSD) (American Psychiatric Association, 1994) and other anxiety disorders (Pynoos & Nader, 1988), depression (Weller, Weller, Fristad, & Bowes, 1991), and disruptive behaviors (Raphael, 1983). In addition, *pathological grief*, defined as intense and prolonged depressive symptoms and psychosocial impairment (Lundin, 1984), is more likely to occur when the bereaved is poor (Vachon et al., 1982), when the sibling's death is sudden (Lundin, 1984), or when the circumstances of the sibling's death are unclear (Balk, 1983), all of which represent the usual circumstances in which siblings of young homicide victims find themselves.

Risk of Pathological Mourning   Young siblings of homicide victims are at risk for pathological mourning and poor outcomes (Freeman et al., 1996). They are at increased risk for pathological mourning not only because their siblings' deaths are sudden but also because the deaths often involve physical mutilation (Danto, 1982) and may be complicated by the surviving siblings' PTSD. The comorbidity of grief and PTSD inhibits the development of typical mourning (Pynoos & Nader, 1990). In addition, social support may be reduced because the community reaction to homicide often stigmatizes the surviving sibling. The surviving sibling can be further isolated because it is painful for those around the sibling to listen to the sibling's expressions of grief. If their expressions of loss evoke feelings of sadness, horror, and rage in listeners, the surviving sibling is often compelled to be silent. Surviving siblings can have feelings similar to adult members of the family, who typically find themselves vulnerable and isolated (Miller, Moore, & Lexius, 1985). They may feel rejected by society and powerless in the face of the complexities of the criminal justice system, which is often unsympathetic to the catastrophic loss that they have suffered.

Difficulties with Accepting the Sibling's Death   The circumstances of violent death can be more confusing for a child or an adolescent than any other form of death. For children and adolescents, understanding death is a part of the initial work of accepting the reality of the death and coping with loss (Osterweiss et al., 1984). Parents often have difficulties with discussing violent deaths with surviving children and often give misleading information or do not discuss the death at all.

At the same time, the news media and neighbors may distort information through inaccurate or sensational reporting or rumors. The lack of congruence between what the children are told and what they know about the death can contribute to ongoing confusion and inability to accept the loss.

Inability to accept the loss can lead to pathological mourning (Parkes, 1972). Like Saundra, many of the siblings of murdered youth report persistent difficulties with accepting the reality of the death. Instead, they disbelieve that the murder happened and think that the death is a bad dream from which they will one day wake up. One teenage sibling interviewed 6 months after his brother's death said, "It's only sunk in a little bit that he is dead. I like to think he's gone away to school." Another teenager interviewed 6 months after her brother's death said, "I'm not in a mourning phase yet, because I can't accept it."

However, cultural variations of typical mourning responses should not be labeled as pathological. Many grieving children and adolescents in the Sibling Bereavement Study, as well as their parents, experienced vivid dreams about and awake illusions of the deceased siblings. In contrast to reports on bereaved Caucasian widows (Parkes, 1970), who considered these experiences to be illusions or hallucinations indicating their own wish to find or reunite with the deceased, participants in the Sibling Bereavement Study considered these reactions to indicate the actual return of the deceased. Often the deceased would "ask" the dreaming or hallucinating sibling to "be good" or to "watch out for" certain family members. Similarly, several families, both Latino and African American, reported prescient illusions. For example, immediately before he received the call announcing that his son had been shot, Mike's father said that he was looking out his window for Mike because he had heard someone was knocking on his window. He and the surviving family believe that Mike's spirit was making contact with them. Rarely were these visitations described as frightening, which would indicate denial of the death; instead, they were described as reassuring, suggesting that it may be culturally harmonious among some ethnic minority groups for the dead to reappear and speak to survivors.

Avoiding the Pain of Grief In addition to difficulties with accepting the reality of the sibling's death, many siblings describe their attempts to avoid experiencing the intense pain, anger, and resentment associated with their thoughts about their sibling's murder. This avoidance curtails their ability to talk about their loss and reminisce about their sibling with family and friends. For example, in order to avoid reminders of her murdered brother, Saundra gave away all of her gold necklaces that her brother had liked to wear. This inability to recollect even pleasant experiences about the deceased can prolong the grief process (Pynoos & Nader, 1990) and causes grieving siblings to endure their reactions without the support of family or friends.

Posttraumatic stress symptoms also contribute to this avoidance. Studies of children and adolescents who are bereaved as a result of loss of a sibling or friend to homicide (Freeman et al., 1996; Pynoos, Nader, et al., 1987), suicide (Brent et al., 1995), and accidents (Applebaum & Burns, 1991) found that these bereaved youth often exhibited posttraumatic stress reactions that may have complicated or delayed their grieving processes. These posttraumatic stress reactions can occur without the child's having directly witnessed the murder (Applebaum & Burns, 1991; Rynearson, 1984). PTSD acts in synergy with grief (Rynearson & McCreery, 1993) to delay grief recovery (Pynoos & Nader, 1990). The intense traumatic response of intrusive thoughts and images and avoidance of reminders coexists with the grief response of longing and sadness. Surviving siblings' striving not to think about the homicide and to avoid reminders of what happened interferes with their reminiscing and memorializing of the loved one, which is part of the typical mourning process. Burgess (1975) observed this phenomenon in adult survivors of violent crime who had lost a family member. He stated that horror over the manner of death interferes with survivors' typical capacity to address the reality of their loss. In Pynoos, Frederick, and colleagues' (1987) study of children whose classmate was killed by a sniper, two distinct syndromes, one related to trauma and the other related to grief, can be distinguished among children exposed to homicide: intrusive and dissociative thought patterns (Pynoos, Nader, et al., 1987). Pynoos and colleagues found that posttraumatic stress reactions disappeared sooner than grief reactions among children who did not witness the homicide but that trauma reactions persisted among children who did witness the homicide and were physically close to the homicide victim. Similarly, the Sibling Bereavement Study found that bereaved siblings most often reported dreams of seeing their brother or sister alive and intact. Those bereaved siblings who witnessed their siblings' murders or saw their siblings' mutilated bodies reported having had dreams about their siblings' murders.

Surviving siblings' efforts to cope with anxiety associated with posttraumatic stress appear to take psychological precedence over the mourning process (Pynoos & Nader, 1988). Children who lose a sibling or a friend to violence should be assessed for PTSD. Appropriate treatment of children with PTSD requires the treatment of PTSD anxiety prior to proceeding with interventions for their grief reactions (Eth & Pynoos, 1985). Failure to identify surviving siblings' PTSD reactions can result in service providers' delivering inadequate or incomplete interventions.

Difficulties with Adapting to the Loss

Many survivors experience difficulties with adapting to sibling loss because of other intense emotional responses to the homicide, social isolation after the homicide, or behavior problems.

Anger, Reminders, and Fear Homicide is different from other losses of life caused by violence (e.g., suicide, accidental death) because it involves a perpetrator, usually a youth of similar age and ethnicity who intentionally and often premeditatedly injured the victim, as well as the victim him- or herself. In addition, families often feel revictimized by the media's sensationalizing of murders, by police investigations, and by either the lack of or delays in the prosecution of the perpetrator. These circumstances elicit not only feelings of rage in the surviving family members but also feelings of violation, helplessness, loss of safety, and heightened vulnerability.

Of course, families express rage at the perpetrators; but much of their anger is directed toward the criminal justice system. Few families are able to establish satisfactory communication with the police while police are investigating the homicide (Freeman et al., 1996). Families often feel dissatisfied with the responses of court personnel and with what appears to them to be injustice in the criminal justice system. The families feel helpless, vulnerable, and pushed aside by law enforcement procedures. One mother said, "[Since] they took us down to the station and questioned us, I haven't heard from them. It seems like all they cared about was if he dealt drugs or not." Families expect the police and the courts to acknowledge the wrong done against their murdered loved one, but the expected expressions of regret and concern from these entities are not delivered. The system of inner-city justice does not place high priority on the dissatisfaction of the victim's relatives. Families are frequently not informed of suspects or of arrests made or indictments or charges filed, nor are they often informed of who are the police detectives or assistant district attorneys assigned to the murder victims' cases. At best, the families see the criminal justice system as indifferent and demeaning. One mother said, "I guess because I'm black and poor, they don't think they have to deal with me. I don't think [the police] are trying to find [the perpetrator]." Many ethnic minority families eventually feel even greater mistrust of law enforcement officials after these experiences with the criminal justice system after their loss and find it difficult to believe that an ethnic minority can receive help from the institutions that they believe are working against them (Benjamin, 1995). Their mistrust is accentuated by the lack of information and poor communication commonly experienced by victims' families.

Sometimes young perpetrators of homicide were acquainted with their victims and the victims' families prior to the homicide. The victims' surviving family members often think perpetrators will commit acts of violence against them as well because of the perpetrators' fears that the family members wish for retaliation. When surviving family members do not know who the perpetrator is, many of them worry that their physical resemblance to the murder victim makes them vulnerable to the perpetrator(s), who might have the ability to recognize them as the victim's relative, whereas the family members cannot recognize the perpetrator. Often perpetrators are not arrested or are released after their arrest because of a lack of evidence or as a result of making bail or the courts' acceptance of their plea bargains, so perpetrators and their accomplices often remain in the neighborhood. Many parents and children express fear of the perpetrator's harming other family members. The perpetrators of two of the homicides in the Sibling Bereavement Study actually returned to the families' homes to threaten other family members.

In addition, the murder of a family member often occurs close to the family's home or in the apartment building where the family lives. Thus, families must repeatedly and vividly experience trauma every time that they pass by or through the scene of the crime. Most families want to move to a new home subsequent to the murder for that reason; but because many of these families are poor or receive public assistance, they experience difficulties with obtaining subsidized or affordable housing and are unable to move. Issues of safety and security are often realistic concerns that give rise to excessive anxiety. The family's ongoing rage, fear, and traumatization reduce siblings' abilities to adapt to and resolve their loss.

Difficulties with Reinvesting in Relationships and Activities
Surviving siblings report impairments in both family and peer relationships after loss of their sibling to homicide (Freeman et al., 1996). Surviving siblings must cope with living with their parents, who are grieving, often depressed, and less emotionally available. They are concerned about their parents' intense suffering and active, unabating, and deep mourning that can continue for many months. Frequently, the grieving parents do not receive much social support from friends or family. As time passes, the parents' friends and relatives become uncomfortable and even exasperated by their prolonged and intense mourning, particularly when their admonitions to try to live for themselves and go on with their lives go unheeded. Grieving parents are then faced with additional loneliness. Some siblings are afraid to add to their parents' grief and anxiety, so they suppress their own feelings. Other parents become less attentive to their surviving children and monitor their activities less. One 14-year-old sibling survivor whose mother became depressed and was abusing alcohol after the family member's murder

said, "I hang out more . . . to keep away from how she acts. She worries a lot about me, but she don't bother me about going out."

Many bereaved surviving siblings avoid their peers because of the intrusiveness they experience when their peers discuss news stories written about their siblings' homicides. In particular, when peers discuss news stories that implicate their sibling in illegal activities, siblings report distress. One adolescent male said, "They talk about him like they knew him. They don't know him. He never did the things [the peers quoting a news report] said." Some surviving siblings become suspicious of their peers, believing that their peers may have been involved in the homicide. An adolescent brother of a homicide victim said, "You don't know. They might act nice to you; but they might have been one of [the perpetrators of the homicide]." Adolescents' social withdrawal from their peers is not uncommon after the loss of one of their siblings to homicide (Freeman et al., 1996).

Behavior Problems and Mourning Reactions The major distress reactions (grief, pathological mourning, comorbid depression, posttraumatic stress, and anxiety disorders) experienced by bereaved siblings are internalized (Freeman et al., 1996). Few children or adolescents who have lost a sibling to homicide receive treatment for their internalized distress, however. Even children who are subjectively distressed enough to seek help from school guidance counselors and school social workers are not provided needed counseling (Freeman et al., 1996). By contrast, children are most often identified as troubled when they exhibit aggressive or other acting-out behaviors. Rarely is their aggression or behavior problem assessed as part of a bereavement reaction.

Some children and adolescents with externalizing behavior disorders exhibit exacerbated behavior problems after the murder when their parents' supervision and monitoring may be reduced because of mourning. Sometimes, as in the case of Saundra and Mike, fear and rage lead to surviving siblings' obtaining a firearm and breaking laws in other ways. In addition, irritability, a symptom of depression and posttraumatic stress, can contribute to surviving siblings' impulsive and aggressive behaviors. For example, after a 13-year-old girl's brother was murdered, she was remanded to a group home by juvenile court for violating the local curfew and for snatching a girl's necklace. The surviving sibling's mother, who was suffering intense grief, depression, and migraine headaches, felt overwhelmed by her daughter's behavior and requested that the court place her in a group home. While in custody, the girl's depression deepened to the point that she was frequently tearful and developed suicidal thoughts. The corrections staff did not assess her behavior as being a symptom of bereavement and depression, so she received no treatment. Predictably, she was deeply depressed and irritable on the day of the anniversary of her brother's murder. She got into a fight with another resident of the group home who had been teasing her. Instead of anticipating her anniversary reaction and offering support or providing intervention for her pathological mourning, the agency punished her. The girl was transferred, without her family's knowledge, to a secured facility that was about 300 miles from her family's home.

BARRIERS TO CARE

Barriers to survivors' gaining access to needed care include the fear induced by murder and the lack of comprehensive services that coordinate needed systems of care. The fear evoked by murder frightens many victims' families away from getting involved with the formal systems of care around them. Fear may also deter some service providers from reaching out to the victims. The families fear reprisal and retaliation, and their fear and suspicion can be pervasive. One mother said, upon receiving the letter introducing the Sibling Bereavement Study, "I thought it might have come from [the perpetrators]." In addition, friends and acquaintances fear that close association with the victims' families might be dangerous. This fear of "contagion" isolates families from their acquaintances (Miller et al., 1985). Similarly, many service providers are fearful of working with victims of violence because such assignments often involve outreach to families that live in violent neighborhoods. The challenge is to link families and children who live in increasingly isolated, violent communities with the professionals who have the skills and services that the families need. Because families often cannot move out of their communities, professionals must be willing to find ways to work with families in their neighborhoods.

Instead, the needs of victims' families are often neglected by all systems of care (Freeman et al., 1996). A homicide victim's surviving family members must bear intense emotional, social, and economic stresses that take years to overcome, if indeed they can be overcome. Few mental health agencies are prepared to provide the necessary outreach services to these families who face such long-term trauma and isolation. Many families are not aware of the government-funded supportive services to which they are entitled as crime victims. Rarely do families seek out formal mental health services. When treatment is sought, it is sought late in the bereavement process, after families' maladaptive responses to the traumatic event have become entrenched (Black & Kaplan, 1988).

Few school personnel are trained to understand the needs of sibling survivors of homicide victims. Sibling survivors can be ignored by school personnel (Freeman et al., 1996), or schools may avoid the controversy associated with youth homicide by discouraging the sibling from attending classes. For example, the mother of a 7-year-old survivor of a sibling's homicide was told to keep her daughter at home after the homicide for the 3 months until the school year ended. She said, "My daughter saw what happened. We're in Witness Protection. I don't think [the school officials] want to deal with it, so they told me to keep her home."

The criminal justice and juvenile justice systems remain primarily involved in prosecution and have little concern for young homicide victims' surviving siblings. Youth and the their families may feel ignored and betrayed by the criminal justice system. Similarly, the posttraumatic stress and pathological mourning reactions of juvenile offenders are frequently ignored despite the possibility that treatment of this distress might aid the youthful offenders' rehabilitation.

Although some cities have specialized coordinated services for the adult surviving family members of homicide victims, there are few services for young siblings of homicide victims (L.-A. Campbell, personal communication, January 1995). The few victims' services that involve young surviving family members of homicide victims are new, and they operate on a commonsense basis without much guidance from the professional literature about what works for young crime victims and why. Despite the renewed interest in the subject of homicide for social investigation because of the increase in youth homicide rates in the 1990s, the ways of helping young surviving family members of homicide victims is still a neglected area of study. Little has been written about approaches to interventions with child and adolescent surviving family members of youth homicide, so the principles discussed in the following section are based on the findings of the Sibling Bereavement Study.

SERVICE APPROACHES AND TREATMENT

Loss of a child or an adolescent to homicide affects families of all cultural backgrounds; but minority families, particularly poor African American and Latino families, are predominantly affected. Systems of care involved in supporting and helping these families must be able to understand and empower minority families and communities. To avoid reinforcing their sense of helplessness, services for homicide survivors should include all interested family members and extended kin to the maximum degree possible in the design of the intervention. When available, services from natural, informal support and helping networks within the community, such as churches, spiritual leaders, and healers, should be integrated into the intervention. Such approaches may include case advocacy for needed services and entitlements while the family is in disarray, short- and long-term counseling to help the family members cope with the acute and enduring effects of homicide on the individuals and the kinship system, individual and group support for parents and siblings of homicide victims to reduce their social isolation, and social action activities to address families' criticisms of the procedures of the criminal justice system and to empower their communities' action against violence (Benjamin, 1995; Getzel & Masters, 1984).

Needs and Problems

Getzel and Masters's (1984) analysis of the needs of families of homicide victims served by Victim Services Agency, a multiservice agency funded by the federal, New York state, and New York City governments, indicated the range of services requested by victims' families. More than 60% of service requests were for financial entitlement, advocacy, and benefits in kind such as crime victims' compensation, public assistance, public housing, food stamps, assistance with utility bills, and medical care. About 30% of the problems were related to acute grief reactions to the homicide and behavior problems of children. The depth of the emotional problems was overwhelming. Families were dealing with shock and apathy induced by their feelings of helplessness, fear, intense rage, guilt, and yearning for their lost love one. Their active and deep mourning often continued for many months. Finally, 10% of presenting problems involved direct assistance from the criminal justice system. Families receive little information about justice system procedures, yet information from law enforcement is necessary for survivors' mourning process and their ability to renew their sense of safety and trust. Bereavement counselors believe that the ability to understand and face the circumstances of the murder is essential as the first step in grieving a homicide loss (V. Torres, personal communication, January 1995).

Case Advocacy

Case advocates may be based in the mental health system of the criminal justice system, or they may provide specialized services for crime victims. The primary needs of many families who are overwhelmed by the loss of their loved one to homicide and the unforeseen economic, social, and emotional consequences thereof may involve help in managing a financial emergency. The money required for burial of the victim can exhaust a family's resources, leaving them behind in paying their rent and making credit payments. Families can be educated about the operation of victims' entitlement programs and encouraged to advocate on their own behalf. Often, however, the emotional toll of the event leaves the family unable to take on the complex bureaucracies that handle such matters. In such situations, case advocates should intervene on behalf of families that cannot afford to wait indefinitely for services to which they are entitled.

Family, Individual, and Group Treatment

After a homicide, the family system is thrown into chaos. Families must learn to accept the death and reorganize their kinship system so that their life cycles can continue (Parkes, 1963). Getzel and Masters (1984) and Miller and colleagues (1985) described effective group, individual, and family approaches to interventions with adult family members who have lost loved ones to homicide.

Crisis intervention can minimize posttraumatic reactions of children and adolescents (Pynoos & Eth, 1986b) and may reduce the risk of pathological mourning. Pynoos and Eth (1986a) described the benefits of a crisis intervention approach that encourages children to recount the traumatic aspects of the homicide and their feelings about it as comprehensively as possible. This affect-laden storytelling method, which can incorporate the use of drawing and other creative expression, may be particularly useful among African American youth who are familiar with oral traditions. Rapid intervention, administered within the first 24 hours of the homicide, is recommended because memories of the events are soon lost to recall and maladaptive responses may become entrenched.

Crisis intervention for young survivors of homicide might involve mental health professionals who work in conjunction with the police investigating a youth's homicide, with members of the ambulance crew who were at the murder scene, or with those who provide specialized victims' services for youth. Crisis workers might accompany the police personnel who notify and question the family after the homicide or might meet the family in the hospital emergency room. Soon after their initial contact with the family, crisis workers could meet with all of the children and adolescents, not just the homicide victim's biological siblings, who live in the family's home, regardless of whether they were witnesses to the murder. Prior to this meeting, crisis workers should consult with the district attorney's office to determine whether there has been an indictment and to ensure that the crisis interviews do not disrupt the murder investigation. In addition, if a family member is a suspect or a witness in the homicide, crisis workers should consult with authorities with regard to the limits within which they can assist the family. Crisis intervention, however, does not preclude the need, in the longer term, for bereavement counseling and perhaps psychotherapy.

Bereavement counseling may be needed to address the homicide victim's surviving siblings' abilities to accept the death, provide social role valorization for their grief responses, provide social and emotional support for the long-term mourning process, and help the surviving siblings reestablish a belief in the social order so that they can move on toward grief recovery. Bereavement counseling may need to be combined with posttraumatic stress interventions to address children's fear and trauma and the impairments associated with it; restore their sense of safety; and help them understand the meaning of their feelings of rage, helplessness, and guilt. PTSD anxiety should be addressed before bereavement counseling proceeds.

Youth may prefer that their interventions be handled separately from those performed with their parents because of concerns about overburdening their parents with their problems. Group support treatments can be useful (L.-A. Campbell, personal communication, January 1995). Because survivors often believe that they have been violated by a peer, however, they become suspicious of their peers; thus, some may not tolerate group intervention approaches.

Young homicide survivors may need interventions that are different from those provided for children who experience the nonviolent death of a family member. Coordination with the criminal justice system may improve bereavement outcomes. First, children may benefit from understanding what is happening as the criminal investigation evolves, such as the reason for the homicide and the identification and legal status of the perpetrator. Second, finding ways to ensure surviving youth's safety may reduce their subsequent anxiety reactions. Finally, siblings may need support to manage the shame associated with discovering the victim's criminal involvement if that was the case. Integrating the truth about the reason for the homicide can improve surviving siblings' grief recovery process (M. Batista, personal communication, January 1995).

Social Action

Siblings must cope with feelings of rage and helplessness after the loss. Survivors' groups can evolve a social action focus that might help youth reconceptualize their negative views of society and find an outlet for their grief through activism. Just as many adults who have lost children to homicide choose to become socially active to improve the sensitivity of the criminal justice system toward victims (Getzel & Masters, 1984) and to prevent violence (Benjamin, 1995), youth can also emotionally benefit from reinvesting energy in social action (M. Batista, personal communication, January 1995).

Schools

Much of bereaved children's psychosocial impairment is due to depression, poor concentration, social withdrawal, and anxiety, all of which can affect school performance and behavior in school. School personnel may or may not be aware of the homicide but can be exposed to the impact of the homicide on the student. Many youth homicides receive considerable media attention and are widely discussed in the neighborhoods where they occur, but many adolescents attend high schools that are some distance away from their homes, so school personnel may not hear of the homicide on an informal basis. Of course, the confidentiality of any student who loses a loved one to homicide must be protected; but frequently the homicide and siblings' relationships to the homicide victim is common knowledge in schools. Bereaved students may seek help from teachers, guidance personnel, and school social workers. School staff may need training to understand the signs, symptoms, and long duration of bereavement, as well as to be aware of appropriate referral sources for sibling survivors of homicide victims who experience pathological mourning.

CONCLUSIONS

The many needs of young survivors of adolescent homicide are frequently overlooked by the systems of care that serve them. Interventions with siblings of homicide victims should begin soon after the homicide and might include

- Assisting the surviving siblings' parents with economic concerns and with effectively communicating with police and district attorneys about the reasons for the family member's homicide and about the identification and prosecution of the perpetrator(s)
- Helping surviving siblings cope with the trauma of having witnessed the homicide or death of the victim
- Screening surviving siblings for psychiatric sequelae such as posttraumatic stress, anxiety, depression, and acting-out behaviors
- Recognizing the rage and fear that children and adolescents feel after a sibling's murder and the behavioral sequelae that they may develop, such as carrying weapons, fighting, and aggression toward peers

- Helping surviving siblings to integrate and accept knowledge of the victim's criminal activities if they had not been aware of them before the homicide
- Helping surviving siblings to develop effective defensive strategies to cope with their fears of the perpetrators, including helping families to relocate if necessary to ensure their safety from the perpetrators
- Helping the surviving siblings and family members anticipate and prepare for intensification of their sense of loss on the first holidays and birthdays after the murder and on the anniversary of the murder
- Educating teachers and school personnel about the grief and post-traumatic processes and recovery if the surviving siblings consent

Community-based intervention approaches that coordinate and include families, schools, and criminal justice systems in the intervention may reduce suffering and empower youth to engage in positive social action.

REFERENCES

American Psychiatric Association. (1994). *Diagnostic and statistical manual of mental disorders* (4th ed.). Washington, DC: Author.

Applebaum, D.R., & Burns, G. (1991). Unexpected childhood death: Posttraumatic stress disorder in surviving siblings and parents. *Journal of Clinical Child Psychology, 20,* 114–120.

Balk, D. (1983). Effects of sibling death on teenagers. *Journal of School Health, 58,* 14–18.

Benjamin, M.P. (1995). *Effective collaboration as the key to understanding and reducing youth violence: A mental health perspective.* Washington, DC: National Technical Assistance Center for Children's Mental Health.

Black, D., & Kaplan, T. (1988). When father kills mother: Issues and problems encountered by a child psychiatric team. *British Journal of Psychiatry, 153,* 624–630.

Brent, D.A., Perper, J.A., Moritz, G., Liotus, L., Richardson, D., Canobbio, R., Schweers, J., & Roth, C. (1995). Posttraumatic stress disorder in peers of adolescent suicide victims: Predisposing factors and phenomenology. *Journal of the American Academy of Child and Adolescent Psychiatry, 43*(2), 209–215.

Burgess, A.W. (1975). Family reaction to homicide. *American Journal of Orthopsychiatry, 45,* 391–398.

Callahan, C.M., & Rivera, F.P. (1992). Urban high school youth and handguns: A school-based survey. *Journal of the American Medical Association, 267,* 3038–3042.

Centers for Disease Control and Prevention. (1991a). Homicides among young black males: United States, 1978–1987. *Journal of the American Medical Association, 265,* 183–184.

Centers for Disease Control and Prevention. (1991b). Weapon-carrying among high school students: United States, 1990. *Morbidity and Mortality Weekly Report, 40,* 681–684.

Danto, B.L. (1982). Survivors of homicide. In B.L. Danto, J. Bruhns, & A.H. Kutscher (Eds.), *The human side of homicide* (pp. 36–58). New York: Columbia University Press.

Earls, F.J. (1994). Violence and today's youth. *The Future of Children: Critical Issues for Children and Youth, 4*(3), 4–23.

Eth, S., & Pynoos, R.S. (1985). Interaction of trauma and grief. In S. Eth & R.S. Pynoos (Eds.), *Post-traumatic stress disorder in children* (pp. 169–186). Washington, DC: American Psychiatric Press.

Fagan, J., & Chin, K. (1990). Violence as regulation and social control in the distribution of crack. In M. De La Rosa, E.Y. Lambert, & B. Gropper (Eds.), *Drugs and violence: Causes, correlates, and consequences* (pp. 8–43) (National Institute on Drug Abuse Research Monograph No. 103). Washington, DC: U.S. Government Printing Office.

Fingerhut, L.A., & Kleinman, J.C. (1990). International and interstate comparisons of homicide among young males. *Journal of the American Medical Association, 263,* 3292–3295.

Freeman, L.N., Shaffer, D., & Smith, H.I. (1996). Neglected victims of homicide: The needs of young siblings of murder victims. *American Journal of Orthopsychiatry, 66,* 337–345.

Getzel, G.S., & Masters, R. (1984). Serving families who survive homicide. *Social Casework, 65,* 138–144.

Griffith, E.E.H., & Bell, C.C. (1989). Recent trends in suicide and homicide among blacks. *JAMA: The Journal of the American Medical Association, 262,* 2265–2268.

Hamid, A. (1990). The political economy of crack related violence. *Contemporary Drug Problems, 17,* 31–78.

Lundin, T. (1984). Morbidity following sudden unexpected bereavement. *British Journal of Psychiatry, 144,* 84–88.

Messner, S.F., & Tardiff, K. (1986). Economic inequality and levels of homicide: An analysis of urban neighborhoods. *Criminology, 24,* 297–317.

Miller, K., Moore, N., & Lexius, C. (1985, September). A group for families of homicide victims: An evaluation. *Social Casework, 66,* 432-436.

Moran, M. (1994, November 18). Public health strategies urged to prevent violence. *Psychiatric News, 6*–7.

National Center for Health Statistics. (1990). Mortality: Part A. *Vital Health Statistics, 11,* 11.

O'Hare, W.P. (1994, September). 3.9 million U.S. children in distressed neighborhoods. *Population Today, 4*–5.

Osterweiss, M., Solomon, F., & Greene, M. (1984). *Bereavement: Reactions, consequences, and care.* Washington, DC: National Academy Press.

Parkes, C.M. (1963). *Bereavement: Studies of grief in adult life.* Hammondsworth, England: Pelican Books.

Parkes, C.M. (1970). The first year of bereavement: A longitudinal study of reactions of London widows to the death of their husbands. *Psychiatry, 33,* 444–467.

Parkes, C.M. (1972). *Bereavement.* London: Tavistock.

Pynoos, R.S., & Eth, S. (1986a). Witness to violence: The child interview. *Journal of the American Academy of Child Psychiatry, 25,* 306–319.

Pynoos, R.S., & Eth, S. (1986b). Witnessing violence: Special interventions with children. In M. Lasted (Ed.), *Violence and the family* (pp. 193–216). New York: Brunner/Mazel.

Pynoos, R.S., Frederick, C., Nader, K., Arroyo, W., Sternberg, A., Eth, S., Nunez, F., & Fairbanks, L. (1987). Life threat and post-traumatic stress in school-age children. *Archives of General Psychiatry, 44*, 1057–1063.

Pynoos, R.S., & Nader, K. (1988). Psychological first aid and treatment approach to children exposed to community violence: Research implications. *Journal of Traumatic Stress, 1*, 445–473.

Pynoos, R.S., & Nader, K. (1990). Children's exposure to violence and traumatic death. *Psychiatric Annals, 20*, 334–344.

Pynoos, R.S., Nader, K., Frederick, C., Gonda, L., & Stuber, C. (1987). Grief reactions in school-aged children following a sniper attack at school. *Israeli Journal of Psychiatry and Related Science, 24*, 53–63.

Raphael, B. (1983). *The anatomy of bereavement*. New York: Basic Books.

Rynearson, E.K.G. (1984). Bereavement after homicide: A descriptive study. *American Journal of Psychiatry, 141*, 1452–1454.

Rynearson, E.K.G., & McCreery, J.M. (1993). Bereavement after homicide: A synergism of trauma and loss. *American Journal of Psychiatry, 150*, 258–261.

Tardiff, K., Marzuk, P.M., Leon, A.C., Hirsch, C.S., Stajic, J., Portera, L., & Hartwell, N. (1994). Homicide in New York City: Cocaine use and firearms. *Journal of the American Medical Association, 272*, 43–46.

U.S. Department of Justice. (1991). *Crime victimization in the United States: Teenage victims*. Washington, DC: Author.

Vachon, M.L.S., Sheldon, A.R., Lancee, W.J., Lyall, W.A.L., Rogers, J., & Freeman, S.J.J. (1982). Correlates of enduring distress patterns following bereavement: Social network life situations and personality. *Psychological Medicine, 12*, 783–788.

Weller, R.A., Weller, E.B., Fristad, M.A., & Bowes, J.M. (1991). Depression in recently bereaved prepubertal children. *American Journal of Psychiatry, 148*, 1536–1540.

Worden, W.J. (1982). *Grief counseling and grief therapy: A handbook for the mental health practitioner*. New York: Springer.

Substance Abuse
Services in Systems of Care

Linkages and Issues in Serving
Culturally Diverse Populations

H. Westley Clark,
Terry Michael McClanahan, and Karen Lea Sees

Substance abuse has reached epidemic proportions in contemporary American society and well may be postmodernism's pandemic. The number of current illicit substance users was at its apex around 1979 and then declined steadily until 1991 (Substance Abuse and Mental Health Services Administration [SAMHSA], 1997). The resurgence in drug abuse in the 1990s surpassed the level reached in the 1960s. For example, in 1996, there were an estimated 13 million current illicit drug abusers in the United States (SAMHSA, 1997). Nine percent of American youth reported abusing illegal drugs during the preceding month (SAMHSA, 1997). SAMHSA (1997) reported that, with regard to abusers' drugs of choice, 1.7 million were cocaine abusers and 2.3 million were marijuana abusers. Although the number of Americans using heroin in 1995 was substantially lower than those using marijuana and cocaine, the impact of individuals' heroin use on communities cannot be minimized. In 1995 alone, the Drug Abuse Warning Network (DAWN) reported 76,023 emergency room mentions of heroin or morphine use (SAMHSA, 1996). These numbers may seem trivial when taken as a percentage of the total U.S. population; but when the substance abuse problem is extrapolated, these numbers have numerous far-reaching implications.

Although unlikely, some segments of American society may be shielded from illicit drug abuse; but tobacco and alcohol use dominate

This chapter was supported in part by National Institutes on Drug Abuse Grant 1P50-DA09253.

American society, which has a direct effect on all Americans. In 1996, 109 million Americans ages 12 and older had used alcohol in the past month, constituting 51% of the population older than age 12 and 60% of those ages 21 and older (SAMHSA, 1997). Drinking among youth is problematic, especially from a developmental perspective. Approximately 32 million youth engaged in binge drinking in 1996, with approximately 11 million reporting heavy drinking. *Heavy drinking* is defined as consuming five or more drinks on five or more separate occasions in the immediately preceding 30 days. Similarly, in 1995, there were an estimated 62 million Americans who were current tobacco smokers, a significant number in light of the fact that smokers are more likely than nonsmokers to engage in heavy drinking and illicit drug use (National Household Survey on Drug Abuse [NHSDA], 1996). The implications for substance abuse among youth and the disadvantaged are especially alarming, given that the daily experiences of these individuals are problematic enough without the impact of drugs— either licit or illicit.

The sections that follow provide an overview of cultural diversity, pointing out the complexity of the terms and then detailing some of the specifics of substance abuse among broad categories of cultural groups. The discussion includes coverage of women and gays and lesbians, not because these groups of individuals are more prone to substance abuse problems per se but because their unique needs with regard to the provision of culturally competent services must be considered. Naturally, women of color and gays and lesbians of color who have substance abuse problems as well as either physical or mental health problems may encounter even more barriers in their quest for services. A section on youth is included because, as a cultural paradigm, American youth represent a category in and of themselves, despite their attachment to their parents and adult caregivers. The chapter concludes with a discussion of treatment for substance use.

SUBSTANCE ABUSE AMONG CULTURALLY DIVERSE POPULATIONS

The experience of an individual is defined by a spectrum of factors: race, age, gender, sexual orientation, physical status, psychiatric status, culture, subculture, language, social status, economic status, and religion. Any one of these factors can mistakenly be perceived as defining the entire context of individuals' lives. Consequently, if such a generalized view is applied to an individual who uses or abuses psychoactive substances, clinicians and system of care service delivery systems can erroneously conclude that a given characteristic of an individual is either relevant or irrelevant to that individual's substance abuse. The clinician must exercise caution in pursuing the provision of care, guarding against defining the experiences of the intended recipients of that care in narrow, restrictive terms; thus, cultural diversity can easily be underemphasized or overemphasized to the detriment of the patient.

The key to understanding diversity from a systems perspective is by expanding broad categories into specifics. In order for there to be linkages in a service delivery system that strives for effectiveness, clinicians must recognize that ethnic groups are not monolithic. The tendency to lump individuals into broad categories instead of splitting them into more relevant experiential groups often is at the core of racism and clinical misunderstanding. African Americans raised in various geographic locations (e.g., Bermuda, Brazil, Minnesota, New York) have had different life experiences; yet all will share certain cultural experiences that transcend geography, and all may encounter certain barriers that are borne of characterizations in the mass media and popular societal assumptions. The same can be said of Latinos, whose geographic origins are equally diverse (e.g., Cuba, El Salvador, Guatemala, New York, Puerto Rico, Texas). Although the Spanish language may be a common thread that runs through each Latino subcultural group, Latinos' common language alone cannot be said to be their defining ethnic characteristic.

Native Americans are members of or are descendants of members of many different tribes, each tribe having its own traditions. Their identities and traditions come from their tribes of origin, such as the Nez Percé, Cherokee, Navajo, Seminole, and Kickapoo. The broad Native American ethnic category used for the U.S. census similarly includes Native Hawaiians and Native Samoans. As a result, solely assigning an individual the label *Native American* lacks clarity and specific reference to the individual's cultural origins. The solitary label "Indian" may do more harm than good by evoking stereotypic images rather than providing service providers with useful cultural information.

Asian Americans and Pacific Islander Americans also come from a broad spectrum of countries, including Japan, Vietnam, People's Republic of China, Taiwan, Guam, American Samoa, Laos, the Philippines, Thailand, and India. The relationships among these groups may be remote, yet the U.S. Census category of Asian/Pacific Islander suggests a more proximate relationship among these groups and may evoke similarities that do not exist in the minds of those who do not know better.

Caucasians also have a spectrum of origins. They are not merely Europeans or, in the case of Americans, European Americans. Not all Caucasians regard themselves as "generic Americans." Irish Americans, German Americans, English Americans, Polish Americans, Arab

Americans, French Americans, and Turkish Americans are examples of Caucasians who share similar characteristics yet represent different subcultures within the Caucasian ethnicity category.

Treatment systems must also consider religion as a defining cultural characteristic. In the United States, the spectrum of religions encompasses all of the major world religions. To the degree that religion contributes to the cultural matrix out of which an individual grows, it is important to consider the influence of religion in any discourse about cultural diversity. Furthermore, to the extent that religion and spiritual matters are bound to issues of individuals' access to services, use of services, and responses to services, consideration of religious and spiritual matters in an analysis of cultural competence is essential.

Similarly, an individual's sexual orientation cannot be separated from the notion of the developmental cultural matrix. Gays and lesbians have experiences that are not shared by heterosexuals. They experience barriers and limitations of cultural expression imposed by society's biases and prejudices, which exacerbate these individuals' feelings of shame and guilt. A substance abuse service provider errs when he or she assumes that the issue of sexual orientation is completely subordinate to the issue of substance abuse.

Ethnicity and culture provide a sense of identity but can also bring with them stressors that are related to oppression, overt or covert racism, and other barriers. Overcoming these barriers is much more difficult for a person who is in a culturally distinct class than it is for a Caucasian who may experience some of the same barriers. As Clark and Zweben (1994) stated, an "ethnic experience" is defined by race, culture, economics, and religion. Another experience that defines the ethnic experience is language (Sue & Sue, 1990). Other factors can also lead to an individual's classification as a minority. For instance, women are in a majority status as a percentage of the total U.S. population; but, because of their relative lack of political and economic power, they find themselves in a minority position.

Raw statistics with regard to the levels of alcohol use among Caucasians and some people of color as a percentage of the total populations of these groups appear to be similar. There are different patterns of use and abuse and varying degrees of the prevalence of alcohol-related problems, however, among Caucasians, African Americans, Latinos, American Indians, and Pacific Islanders. Substance abuse–related medical problems also indicate that substance abuse affects people of color differently from the way in which it affects Caucasians. For instance, Sutocky, Shultz, and Kizer (1993) reported that African Americans and Latinos have higher mortality rates from alcoholic cirrhosis of the liver than do Caucasians or Asian Americans.

There are differences among ethnic groups with regard to the use of drugs. There are also differences between ethnic groups and the majority culture and within generations of the majority culture with regard to the symbolic meanings assigned to drugs. The discussion in this chapter highlights some of the differences in patterns of drug use among various ethnic cultures. From the perspective of the mental health service delivery system, these use differences are important. From the perspective of the client, these use differences may reflect efforts to self-medicate their psychological states, or they may be the result of peer pressure or escapism. Therefore, mental health services systems of care may find that clients who suffer from major psychiatric disorders are resistant to abandoning the drugs that are favored by their respective social or ethnic group. Hence, service providers must understand the use patterns of clients who present for treatment and clients' rationales for their substance use.

African Americans

African Americans as a group experience and suffer from serious problems related to substance use, including illicit substances, alcohol, and tobacco. In 1995, the rate of current (i.e., within the immediately preceding month) illicit drug use by African Americans (7.5% of all African Americans) was higher than that for Caucasians (6.1% of all Caucasians) (SAMHSA, 1997). African Americans' rate of current use of cocaine was 1% compared with 1.1% of Hispanics and .8% of Caucasians. The statistics with regard to cocaine do not tell the whole story. The DAWN reports indicated that 54.2% of all individuals (142,494) who presented in emergency rooms with cocaine-related presentations were African Americans, 29.3% were Caucasians, and 8.1% were Hispanics. In addition, 1993 data indicated that among non-Hispanic African Americans who were admitted for substance abuse treatment, 42% reported cocaine as their primary substance of abuse compared with 9.6% for Caucasians, 41.1% for Cubans, 17.9% for Puerto Ricans, 8.2% for Mexicans, 12.4% for Asians and Pacific Islanders, and 4.8% for Native Americans (SAMHSA, 1996).

Of the percentage of individuals reporting current marijuana use in 1995, 5.9% were African Americans, 4.7% were Caucasians, and 3.9% were Hispanics. The statistics are different for alcohol: 16.6% of Caucasians reported binge drinking of alcohol on at least one occasion in the immediately preceding month compared with 11.2% of African Americans and 17.2% of Hispanics. Furthermore, 5.7% of Caucasians reported heavy alcohol use in the immediately preceding month compared with 4.6% of African Americans and 6.3% of Hispanics. *Heavy alcohol use* is defined as five or more drinks on five or more occasions during the immediately preceding 30 days (SAMHSA, 1997).

The NHSDA did not provide data with regard to heroin use. However, DAWN data for 1995 showed an approximately equal number of total emergency room mentions of heroin or morphine use among Caucasians and African Americans (29,397 and 28,787, respectively). Considering the proportionate representation of these two groups in the total U.S. population, with Caucasians representing 83.9% and African Americans representing only 12.3%, one can extrapolate from these data that there is a disproportionate representation of African Americans.

Numerous studies reported that the incidence of fetal alcohol syndrome (FAS) among African Americans is approximately seven times higher than that among Caucasians (Chavez, Cordero, & Becerra, 1989; Herd, 1989; Sokol, Ager, & Martier, 1986). This finding is paradoxical, given that African American women generally abstain from drinking alcohol more than Caucasian women, and fewer African American women than Caucasian women are high-quantity drinkers. Thus, the question remains with regard to which specific factors cause higher rates of FAS among African Americans; but it is clear that alcohol affects African Americans differently than it affects Caucasians.

SAMHSA (1996) data indicated that though African Americans compose about 12% of the total U.S. population, they compose 21% of the substance abuse client population in systems of care. Furthermore, 9.7% of African American clients who were admitted to inpatient facilities specializing in mental health in 1986 had a diagnosis of drug abuse/dependence, and 19.2% of the same population had a diagnosis of alcohol abuse/dependence. Of African American clients in these facilities, 34.2% were diagnosed as having schizophrenia. This disparity indicates the propensity to disproportinately diagnose African Americans with schizophrenia.

The issues raised in the previous paragraph are paralleled in the ambulatory care environment, with 14% of African Americans presenting with diagnoses of alcohol or drug abuse/dependence and 22% presenting with diagnoses of schizophrenia (SAMHSA, 1996). Although one can acknowledge that race bias may affect diagnoses, including the tendency of clinicians to disproportionately diagnose African Americans as having schizophrenia, alcohol and drug abuse contribute to problems of diagnosis. Also contributing to diagnosis problems is that African American and Caucasian clients with schizophrenia present differently. African Americans with schizophrenia present more frequently than Caucasians as disoriented, thereby increasing their risk of misdiagnosis (Chu, Sallach, Zakeria, & Klein, 1985).

The risk for substance use and abuse is believed to be increased by an impoverished, deprived environment (Brown & Alterman, 1992). To the extent that African Americans continue to be impoverished and deprived of many of the resources and benefits of American society, one would expect to find higher rates of substance abuse and more severe consequences of drug use among African Americans than among the rest of the U.S. population (Brown & Alterman, 1992). It would be an error, however, to classify the contemporary experiences of all African Americans as impoverished or deprived. Indeed, there is a substantial African American middle class. Regardless of color, the middle class is not immune to the ravages of alcohol and drug abuse. Clinical programs are in short supply for those African Americans of varied socioeconomic status, especially those in the lower, working, and middle-socioeconomic classes. Furthermore, shame and guilt related to substance use may be much greater among working- and middle-class African Americans.

Although there is relatively sparse literature regarding how factors such as insurance coverage and service availability affect ethnic groups who seek outpatient mental health services, these factors impinge on all groups; but ethnic minorities are affected in different ways and at disproportionate rates compared with Caucasians. In an examination of 1.2 million federal employees insured by Blue Cross/Blue Shield, Padgett, Patrick, Burns, and Schlesinger (1994) reported that both African Americans and Latinos had lower probabilities and amounts of use of outpatient mental health services than Caucasians. In fact, Caucasians were 1.7 times more likely than African Americans and Hispanics to use mental health services. Padgett and colleagues studied nonpoor ethnic populations whose different levels of acculturation were minimized. In light of those facts, the study showed, even in the context of people who were not poor, that there are cultural barriers that impinge on ethnic groups' seeking mental health services.

Latinos

Mexican Americans, a subgroup of the Hispanic and Latino population, represent one of the fastest-growing segments of American society (Boles, Casas, Furlong, Gonzalez, & Morrison, 1994). The Mexican American population increased by 45.2% between 1980 and 1989, and demographic trends indicate that this growth rate will continue in the 21st century (Boles et al., 1994). The National Institute on Alcohol Abuse and Alcoholism (NIAAA) (1994) reported that, among those who have immigrated to the United States, individuals' levels of acculturation have a dramatic effect on their drinking patterns. Likewise, comparisons of alcohol consumption among first-, second-, and third-generation Mexican American women reveal that drinking rates of successive generations approach those of the general population of American women (NIAAA, 1994).

The SAMHSA (1997) reported an estimated 1.1 million current illicit drug users among Latinos in 1996. The rate of marijuana use among Caucasian, African American, and Latino youth ages 12–17 more than doubled between 1992 and 1995 (SAMHSA, 1997). The SAMHSA (1997) reported that, in 1996, 43% of Latinos used alcohol, with 6.2% using it heavily. The 1996 figures represented the highest percentage of heavy users to date among Latinos, African Americans, and Caucasians. Binge drinking was also higher among Latinos (16.7%) than among African Americans (13.1%) or Caucasians (16.1%).

In a 1996 study, SAMHSA found that Hispanics accounted for 8.1% of the 142,494 total emergency room mentions of cocaine use, 12.9% of the 76,023 total emergency room mentions of heroin and morphine use, and 7.7% of the 47,069 total emergency room mentions of marijuana and hashish use. These seemingly low percentages do not reflect the degree of the problems that substance use and abuse cause Latinos. The intersection of the increasing Latino population with the percentage of illicit substance abuse within the total U.S. population lends itself to closer examination of the Latino's experience with substance abuse.

Boles et al. (1994), in a study of 8,000 southern California ninth and eleventh graders, found that male and female Mexican American youth reported alcohol and drug use rates similar to those of Caucasian students. These results contradicted the findings of Padilla, Padilla, Morales, Olmedo, and Ramirez (1979); but the Padilla et al. study used an opportunity sample, whereas the Boles et al. study was essentially a census. Boles and colleagues also reported that Mexican American females reported a lower rate of alcohol and drug use than Mexican American males or Caucasian males and females.

American Indians[1]

Westermeyer (1996) and others reported findings that alcohol consumption is significantly lower for American Indians in general than for other ethnic groups in the United States. In general, female American Indians reported that they abstain from drinking and are less likely than male American Indians to report drinking more than once per month (11% versus 30%) (Barker & Kramer, 1996). Although these findings may be true, the fact is that alcoholism affects American Indians in ways that significantly and negatively affect their mortality. For instance, the Indian Health Service (1993) reported that the age-specific death rate

---

[1]The term *Native American* typically encompasses American Indians, Native Hawaiians, and Native Samoans. As such, the term *Native American* is more accurately a political classification than an ethnic category, whereas the term *American Indian* has cultural and ethnic connotations to which many American Indians are more receptive, and thus that term is used in the remainder of this chapter.

due to alcohol-related disorders among American Indians ages 55 years and older is more than four times that of the same age group in the U.S. general population.

Culture-specific norms and mores operate within all ethnicities, some of which in the American Indian culture encourage alcohol consumption. One such more is that drinking is considered a social event. Since the 1980s, American Indians have migrated to urban areas, and, as of 1984, more than half of all Native Americans reside in U.S. cities (U.S. Department of Commerce, 1984). Social drinking in this context functions as a major component of American Indians' establishing and maintaining ties to their clans, tribes, or nations (Barker & Kramer, 1996). Alcohol use varies with age among American Indians; for example, Barker and Kramer found that American Indians ages 61 years and older were more likely to abstain from drinking (79%) than those ages 60 years and younger (68%). Barker and Kramer also reported that American Indians who lived in a multigenerational household were less likely to drink more than once per month. These findings are similar to other literature indicating that American Indians reduce their alcohol consumption as they get older. Barker and Kramer suggested that some reasons for American Indians' shift from alcohol consumption to abstinence or reduced consumption were that they became disgusted with their drinking habits, saw friends becoming disabled or dying because of their chronic alcoholism, or became grandparents.

Women

The NHSDA (1996) reported that 7.3% (4.3 million) of women ages 15–44 had used an illicit drug during the immediately preceding month compared with 11.6% of men in the same age category. Of those 4.3 million women, more than 1.6 million had children living with them. Of the women surveyed, 45% reported that they were users of alcohol in the immediately preceding month. Only 2.3% of pregnant women were current drug users, which suggests that women reduce their drug use when they are pregnant. However, the rate of illicit drug use was 5.5% among women who had recently given birth, suggesting that women resume their drug use immediately after giving birth. Similar use patterns among women were reported with regard to alcohol and tobacco. Rates of substance abuse among pregnant women were higher for those who were ages 15–25, unmarried, and in their first trimester than for other subgroups of women.

Surveys of women's alcohol and drug use have found that women consume alcohol and illegal drugs less frequently than men and are more frequent abusers of psychoactive prescription drugs than males (Blume, 1992). Williams, Grant, Harford, and Noble (1989) estimated that in 1990 there were 1.8 million adult women (ages 18 and older) in the United States who could be diagnosed as suffering from alcohol abuse and that 2.8 million men had been diagnosed with alcohol abuse or dependence during the previous 12 months. This ratio of male-to-female alcohol dependence or abuse is almost 2:1.

Women's illegal drug use patterns and problems are greatly influenced by their partners' patterns of use (Blume, 1992). Evidence also suggests that genetically inherited traits in women are strongly influenced by their environment (Cloninger et al., 1988). Boyd (1993) reported a significant correlation between family drug use and children's age of first sexual abuse, age of first depressive symptoms, and age of first illicit drug use. Unfortunately, because so few studies of illicit drug use have focused on females, environmental, psychological, and biological factors and their relationships to drug use are not well understood (Boyd, 1993).

Youth

A 1997 SAMHSA report revealed that, compared with African Americans and Hispanic Americans, Caucasians have a higher lifetime rate of use of marijuana, inhalants, hallucinogens, stimulants, sedatives, tranquilizers, analgesics, alcohol, cigarettes, and phencyclidine (commonly known as PCP or "angel dust"). Latinos reported greater use of cocaine than other ethnic groups, and African Americans reported greater use of crack cocaine and heroin than other ethnic groups.

The SAMHSA (1997) also reported that, in 1996, 109 million Americans ages 12 and older had used alcohol in the previous month, representing a full 51% of the U.S. population. There were approximately 9.5 million current drinkers who were under the age of 21 years, the legal drinking age in most states. The rate of alcohol use of Americans over the age of 21 years was greater than 60%. The age group that reported the highest usage of any illicit drug in the previous month were those ages 18–20, 20% of whom reported using drugs during that time frame. Youth ages 12–17 years reported the most significant increase in previous-month drug use between 1992 and 1995 (NHSDA, 1996). Between 1992 and 1995, the rate of marijuana use more than doubled to 8.2% among youth ages 12–17 years. As in previous years, SAMHSA (1997) reported the highest rate of cocaine abuse among people ages 18–25 years. Approximately 4.1 million youth ages 12–17 years were current tobacco smokers in 1996 (SAMHSA, 1997). These youth were nine times as likely as nonsmokers to use illicit drugs and 16 times as likely as youth who did not smoke to drink heavily.

According to Kandel and Logan (1984), the most important trends among youth are the onset of experimentation with licit and illicit drugs in early adolescence, the substantial increase in their abuse of psychoactive prescription drugs during their middle 20s, and the apparent peaking in their use of illicit drugs between the ages of 18 and 22. Kandel and Logan (1984) interviewed 1,325 tenth and eleventh graders in New York state. They reported that, among this age group, males' use of illicit drugs was twice the rate of females'. They also reported that their sample's rate of marijuana use exceeded their use of both alcohol and tobacco beginning at age 13.5 and continuing until age 18, when alcohol use was their most frequently used substance.

In a follow-up study of the same sample, Yamaguchi and Kandel (1984a) tested a progression sequence of alcohol, tobacco cigarettes, marijuana, other illicit drugs, and psychoactive prescription drugs. They reported that these youth's sequence of involvement with drugs progressed from the use of at least one legal drug (alcohol and/or tobacco cigarettes) to marijuana and from marijuana to other illicit drugs and/or to prescribed psychoactive prescription medications. In a follow-up study, Yamaguchi and Kandel (1984b) reported that individuals 20 years of age and older are much less likely to initiate marijuana use than those under the age of 20. Likewise, the probability that individuals who never use marijuana will initiate the use of other illicit drugs is low (Yamaguchi & Kandel, 1984b).

Stanton and Galbraith (1994) found that approximately 10% of male, urban, African American early adolescents reported that they had engaged in drug trafficking. A higher percentage of those studied indicated that they had been asked to sell drugs. Perceived social pressures from family members and/or peers to engage in drug trafficking were highly correlated with individuals' involvement in drug trafficking. These findings were consistent with those of Li and Feigelman (1994), who found that of 351 African Americans between the ages of 9 and 15, 6% reported selling or delivering drugs during the previous 6 months and 12% indicated that they expected to engage in these activities during the next 6 months. These authors also found that drug trafficking was highly associated with the use of alcohol, tobacco cigarettes, and illicit drugs. Social influences strongly affected both recent and intended future involvement with drug trafficking, especially among the male adolescents studied. Li and Feigelman (1994) reported that 41% of those involved in recent drug trafficking expected to be involved in future drug trafficking.

Activities such as drug trafficking are perceived as opportunities for economic advancement and as ways to establish power bases for individuals who have been denied access to legal opportunities (Whitehead, Peterson, & Kaljee, 1994). Youth who perceive these benefits are at an increased risk of engaging in drug trafficking. Youth's attitudes toward employment and the legal system seem to be highly correlated with whether they become involved in drug trafficking. Youth realize that it is important to earn money, and drug trafficking may be the only way for youth to earn money. An additional factor is that being arrested may make youth more respected by their peer groups (Stanton & Galbraith, 1994). These perceptions have enabled drug kingpins to engage youth in illegal drug trafficking. Youth typically work for lower wages than adults who engage in drug trafficking, and the structure of the juvenile justice system enables their rapid return from incarceration back to their neighborhoods for continued service in the illegal drug trade (Leviton, Schindler, & Orleans, 1994). For early adolescents, the drug kingpin offers an economic avenue by which they can achieve their ambitions.

Education

Education level is also highly correlated with illicit drug use. Among adults ages 18–34, those who had not completed high school had the highest rate of illicit drug use (16.8%). In contrast, the rate of illicit drug use by college graduates was just 6.9% (SAMHSA, 1997). In contrast with illicit drug use patterns, the higher an individual's level of education, the more likely the person is to report current use of alcohol (SAMHSA, 1997). In 1996, 66% of adults with college degrees reported that they were current drinkers compared with 39% of those having less than a high school education. The statistics for heavy alcohol use do not follow this pattern, however. Among those who had completed college, 3.7% were heavy drinkers compared with 6.8% of those who had not completed high school (SAMHSA, 1997).

Employment

Employment status is also a key variable in illicit drug use. In 1996, 12.5% of unemployed adults ages 18 and older were currently using illicit drugs compared with 6.2% of adults who were employed full time. However, 73% (8.1 million) of all current illicit drug users ages 18 and older were employed. Of these 8.1 million individuals, 6.2 million were employed full time and 1.9 million were employed part time (SAMHSA, 1997).

INTERVENTIONS

The epidemiological data presented in this chapter reveal differences in substance use patterns. Many drugs of abuse are simply ubiquitous. Alcohol is one such drug: It is almost universally accepted and championed by the corner bar, the package liquor store, and the local supermarket. The mass media have been enlisted by the alcoholic beverage industry to promote consumption of alcohol by appealing to youth, normalcy, sexuality, and any other common desire or basic emotion that will generate a sale. The same can be said about the tobacco industry's promotion of cigarette smoking. Although American society's attitudes toward tobacco and especially the tobacco industry have become increasingly negative in the late 1990s, the media continue to promote its use. For instance, advertisements in Turkey advocate the health benefits of drinking.

Clients who strive to conform to the cultural norm may find that the use of alcohol is both reassuring and seemingly therapeutic. Socially inhibited individuals may claim that alcohol makes it easier for them to congress. Socially phobic individuals may claim that alcohol decreases their levels of anxiety. An individual's ability to have social interactions, regardless of whether they are fueled or facilitated by alcohol, is an important social need. Socially isolated clients who drink alcohol with their "drinking friends" may find it difficult to give up their "social lubricant" even if their alcohol use exacerbates other psychiatric symptoms. Likewise, clients with schizophrenia who use cocaine to barter for sex may be reluctant to give up their "social currency."

These use patterns affect how a client presents to the service delivery system. A cocaine-using African American male may simply be classified as having paranoid schizophrenia when in fact he is experiencing a substance-induced psychosis. The treatment for that individual's psychosis might be the same regardless of whether service providers realized the reason for the diagnosis; however, the individual's potential for recovery might be different. The diagnosis of both the substance use disorder (at the level of either dependence or abuse) and any comorbid psychiatric disorder unrelated to substance use can be influenced by the clinicians' views of the clients. Hence, the clinicians' or service delivery systems' expectations are affected by the clients' perspectives.

Many mood disorders and psychoses tend to be recurrent. The same can be said for the natural course of alcohol and drug use disorders, especially among people with severe mental disorders. Data indicate that clients who experience mental illness and are drug users and thus receive interventions from two separate service delivery systems (a substance abuse intervention system and a mental health services system) do not fare well. From the perspective of cultural responsiveness, a parallel service delivery system is unlikely to be able to meet individual clients' unique cultural needs.

Treating clients who present with dual diagnoses through parallel systems of care have been proved to be ineffective (National Institute on Drug Abuse, 1997). Treatment delivered through parallel systems of care results in clients' slipping through the cracks of the systems or in their being passed from one system to the other. The end result is the same: The clients do not get better. An integrated treatment approach is clearly preferred. *Integrated treatment* means that both the clients' psychological issues and the clients' substance abuse issues are treated simultaneously by the same professional, team, or organization rather than separately through parallel systems of care. Some fundamental components of an integrative approach include service coordination, assertive outreach, group interventions, education, motivational techniques, behavioral strategies, attention to family and social factors, stagewise treatment, and an overall treatment approach that is long term in nature.

The rationale that treatment should be provided by the same professional team or organization is that it is important to avoid sending mixed messages and failing to provide essential treatment. Clearly, having treatment conducted by one system of care should alleviate the occurrence of and the pitfalls associated with clients' slipping through the cracks or clients' being passed from one system of care to another. Clients with dual diagnoses frequently have clinical, housing, social, and other needs that are necessary for their survival as well as their recovery. Service coordination should be designed to address these issues. From the perspective of cultural diversity, parallel systems of care are particularly problematic for the reasons described previously: Language barriers, mistrust, stereotypic approaches to clients, elitism, and resistance are more easily fostered and perpetuated by the existence of parallel systems of care.

There are generally insufficient resources in the parallel provision of both mental health services and substance abuse treatment. Cultural diversity in the service delivery system, although it is most likely cost effective in the long run, requires the reallocation of resources in terms of staff training and the approach to client care. As a result, there is a natural tendency to resist such changes. Having to address needed changes in two different systems rather than in one integrated system simply creates an opportunity to fail in creating and sustaining necessary links between the systems.

Developing a social support network is an essential ingredient to an integrated approach to service delivery. The social support network is critical to both clients' recovery from the pernicious effects of mental illness and their recovery from substance abuse. Assertive outreach is designed to develop a social support network that helps substance abusers during their recoveries by providing services to the community, providing group interventions such as peer support for the recovery process, and fostering family and social networks to bolster clients' resistance to relapses. These macro-level system interventions often overlap with each other, further enhancing the possibility of clients' successful treatment and recovery.

Families in Treatment

Including clients' families in the treatment process is another essential element of effective treatment. Education of both clients with mental health and substance abuse problems and their families should include informing clients of the nature of both the psychiatric disorders and the substance abuse. This education process should highlight the negative effects of alcohol and other substances. Behavioral strategies should involve training in social and coping skills, to assist clients in avoiding high-risk situations and managing their symptoms.

Although specific epidemiological data on the children of substance abusers are not provided in this chapter, it is important to recognize that these children are a unique concern. The children of active substance users are at risk of being abused and neglected by their parents. Furthermore, they are at risk of developmental delays in growth and cognitive functioning. These children are also at increased risk of becoming substance abusers or drug dealers later as adolescents. Children are generally revered; however, this reverence does not prevent them from being at risk or from being abused. Nevertheless, clinicians can leverage parental concern for the welfare of their children to engage the parents in the treatment.

Parents who are substance users or are diagnosed with mental illnesses may fail as providers or nurturers. Parents who are substance users may require a necessary respite from parenting to stabilize their own lives so that they do not endanger the lives of their children. In such cases, the extended family or the extended social networks common to many people of color become critical to the children, the parents, and the service delivery system.

An integrated service delivery system, then, is more effective when it is able to incorporate the extended family into treatment. Intakes and assessments should focus not simply on the identified parent and children but also on the other trusted caregivers on whom the substance-using parent relies for support and child care. When the substance-using parent makes excessive demands on members of the extended family, often the mothers of substance users who are themselves parents, the integrated service delivery system may have to provide assistance to the extended family. The academic and popular literature have periodically addressed the issue of grandmothers who raise toddlers in the absence of substance-abusing parents. There has been much discussion concerning introducing the grandmother as the primary caregiver in such situations, but the grandmother herself in such circumstances needs support from the service delivery system in performing her new duties. By determining whether clients have extended families, clinicians working in an integrated service delivery system can provide a safety net for substance-abusing parents, children of substance abusers, and extended-family members. Many communities of color have conservative views on drug abuse. Hence, clients often experience shame, guilt, and recrimination that are not easily shared with clinicians. Clinicians must understand this reaction and manage their client interactions with great care.

Unique Views of Clients

Understanding the unique views of clients served by a particular service delivery system makes the development of social support networks not only more feasible but also more desirable. Psychiatrists, psychologists, social workers, counselors, and outreach workers need to be trained to become culturally competent (Wallace, 1996). Efforts must be undertaken to ensure adequate preparation for cross-cultural interventions and service delivery. Traditional parallel system of care models encourage either superiority over clients of color or fear of them, and both of these attitudes are barriers to effective treatment. An integrated system of care affords systems of care an opportunity to provide the necessary training and supervision to militate against cross-cultural conflicts between service providers and clients. An integrated system of care diminishes the creation of stress, distrust, and resistance among clients who present for interventions.

Individuals with Dual Diagnoses

Individuals with dual diagnoses are often homeless or live alone in single-room-occupancy hotels, making them vulnerable to exploitation and violence. In urban areas, where political and funding concerns may foster an adherence to a traditional parallel service delivery system, comorbid diagnoses may be overlooked or underaddressed. For instance, many African Americans and Hispanic Americans may experience posttraumatic stress disorder (PTSD) because they have been the victims of violence that exists in these urban, high-risk neighborhoods. PTSD can easily cause hyperarousal symptoms of anger, irritability, and hypervigilance that could be mistaken for paranoia, as well as insomnia. An approach that views such symptoms strictly in terms of formulating a mental illness diagnosis may actually miss or dismiss the PTSD symptoms, especially if the evaluators do not appreciate the cultural context in which their clients live. A strictly substance abuse approach may also miss or dismiss the PTSD symptoms by attributing all of the clients' problems to their substance use. An integrated treatment approach that is culturally competent takes into consideration the clients' cultural context and explores the therapeutic possibilities in clients' presentation.

Culturally Competent Clinicians

Cultural barriers are less critical to a client who trusts the therapist. However, because of these cultural issues, trust may take longer to form. When trust is established, the fact that the service providers do not share the same ethnicities or cultures of their clients is less critical to providing their clients with successful interventions. An integrated treatment system that employs culturally competent service coordinators is in a unique position to foster transcultural trust. However, a client who is angry with a society that rejects him or her and misunderstands that his or her condition is likely to test the service provider's commitment to him or her and to the intervention process. In the absence of real threats to person or property, for example, non–African American and non-Hispanic service providers must be willing to make a commitment to the treatment process and must not view the client as a potential threat.

In both the integrated service delivery system and the traditional parallel system, it may not be possible to match clients with service providers who are members of the same culture, ethnic group, or gender or are of the same sexual orientation. The wealth of extant material that provides insight into the medical, psychological, cultural, and social experiences of different groups of clients should be helpful in understanding a particular client who presents for treatment (American Psychological Association, Office of Ethnic Minority Affairs, 1993). Treatment programs need to avail themselves of only that information.

It is difficult in traditional parallel systems of care for clinicians to effect trust across cultural lines. An African American client may expect disparaging remarks or disapproving comments or attitudes from non–African American service providers and clinicians. A Hispanic client may find trust difficult to establish across the language barrier or may expect to confront service providers' negative attitudes toward his or her country of origin, especially if the client is a first- or second-generation immigrant. An Asian American client may find it difficult to overcome shame and humiliation. Any of these clients may present with these expectations but may display them differently. Hence, the Asian American client may be angry, the Hispanic client may be hypersensitive to remarks, and the African American client may be filled with shame and humiliation. Any clients who experience a comorbid psychiatric illness may have had previous experiences with either substance abuse or a mental health system of care that discounted their unique conflicts or experiences. An integrated treatment system of care is conducive to service providers' resisting their temptation to lump dual-diagnosis clients into the amorphous categories of "average" alcoholic, drug addict, or client with a mental illness.

There may be clients with whom it is critical to match a clinician by ethnicity, sexual orientation, gender, language, or culture. One indicator of the necessity of assigning clients to service providers of similar backgrounds is the clients' desires to be seen by someone of the same ethnic group or cultural background. Such a request should be honored whenever possible. If it is not possible to assign such a client to a clinician of similar background, the service provider should address the specific concerns of the client. It is important not to mistreat clients' psychiatric symptoms or misattribute clients' symptoms of distress and pathology to their culture and thus leave the client at greater risk of experiencing a relapse or exacerbation of preexisting symptoms. An integrated service delivery system or a traditional parallel system with effective linkages should be able to accommodate any needs of a patient with a substance abuse problem and other comorbid condition.

CONCLUSIONS

Every clinician who treats clients who are ethnically and culturally diverse and have dual diagnoses should permit them to articulate their concerns. These concerns may include confusion, anger, shame, or even hope and pride. The service delivery system itself must be structured to permit both the clinician and the service provider to address clients' concerns. The traditional parallel system of care, marked by poor communication with clients and inefficient use of resources, may actually impair the service delivery system's ability to address the needs of substance-abusing clients who also need mental health services. Clinicians who operate within parallel systems of care have almost as many barriers as their clients to surmount.

An integrated service delivery system allows individual practitioners, community mental health centers, public substance abuse programs, and any other entity concerned with the treatment of clients of diverse ethnic and cultural backgrounds to aid in their clients' recoveries. The integrated system of care can facilitate the access to community resources to aid in recovery. If a language barrier exists, a translator might be hired or 12-step group meetings conducted in the client's primary language might be identified. In the absence of a specific community group, a mental health center at which medications are dispensed or prescribed may collaborate with a substance abuse program by holding a communitywide recovery group meeting addressing the specific issues in question, regardless of whether they involve language, sexual orientation, human immunodeficiency virus status, medication compliance issues, or any other issues. An integrated service delivery system should be able to more easily involve family and cultural supports in the clients' willingness to accept medication. Clinicians should be able to explain the importance of medication to family or community members in order to aid the client's stability and to counter any tendency by them to oppose the maintenance use of medications.

No model of service delivery is a panacea. In order to effectively address the issues of cultural diversity in a service delivery system, there has to be a willingness and commitment in all parts of that system: clinicians, outreach workers, administrators, planners, and politicians. A lack of commitment to diversity only foreshadows failure in addressing the needs of clients.

REFERENCES

American Psychological Association, Office of Ethnic Minority Affairs. (1993). Guidelines for providers of psychological services to ethnic, linguistic, and culturally diverse populations. *American Psychologist, 48*, 45–48.

Barker, J.C., & Kramer, B.J. (1996). Alcohol consumption among older urban American Indians. *Journal of Studies on Alcohol, 57*(2), 119–124.

Blume, S.B. (1992). Alcohol and other drug problems in women. In J.H. Lowinson, P. Ruiz, R.B. Milman, & J.G. Langrod (Eds.), *Substance abuse: A comprehensive textbook* (2nd ed., pp. 794–807). Baltimore: Williams & Wilkins.

Boles, S., Casas, J.M., Furlong, M., Gonzalez, G., & Morrison, G. (1994). Alcohol and other drug use patterns among Mexican American, Mexican, and Caucasian adolescents: New directions for assessment and research. *Journal of Clinical Child Psychology, 23*(1), 39–46.

Boyd, C.J. (1993). The antecedents of women's crack cocaine abuse: Family substance abuse, sexual abuse, depression and illicit drug use. *Journal of Substance Abuse Treatment, 10*, 433–438.

Brown, L.S., & Alterman, A.I. (1992). African Americans. In J.H. Lowinson, P. Ruiz, R.B. Milman, & J.G. Langrod (Eds.), *Substance abuse: A comprehensive textbook* (2nd ed., pp. 861–867). Baltimore: Williams & Wilkins.

Chavez, G.F., Cordero, J.F., & Becerra, J.E. (1989). Leading major congenial malformations among minority groups in the United States: 1981–1986. *Journal of the American Medical Association, 261*(2), 205–209.

Chu, C.C., Sallach, H.S., Zakeria, S.A., & Klein, H.E. (1985). Differences in psychopathology between black and white schizophrenics. *International Journal of Social Psychiatry, 31*(4), 252–257.

Clark, H.W., & Zweben, J.E. (1994). Dual diagnosis, minority populations, and women. In N.S. Miller (Ed.), *Treating coexisting psychiatric and addictive disorders* (pp. 111–126). Center City, MN: Hazelden Foundation.

Cloninger, R.J., Sigvardson, S., Gilligan, S.B., von Knorring, A.L., Reich, T., & Bohman, M. (1988). Genetic heterogeneity and the classification of alcoholism. *Advancements in Alcohol and Substance Abuse, 3*(4), 3–16.

Herd, D. (1989). The epidemiology of drinking patterns and alcohol related problems among U.S. blacks. In *Alcohol use among U.S. ethnic minorities* (pp. 3–50) (National Institute on Alcohol Abuse and Alcoholism Research

Monograph No. 18). Washington, DC: U.S. Government Printing Office. (DHHS Pub. No. [ADM] 89-1435)

Indian Health Service. (1993). *Trends in Indian Health: 1993*. Washington, DC: U.S. Department of Health and Human Services.

Kandel, D.B., & Logan, J.A. (1984). Patterns of drug use from adolescence to young adulthood: 1. Periods of risk for initiation, continued use, and discontinuation. *American Journal of Public Health, 74*(7), 660–666.

Leviton, S., Schindler, M.A., & Orleans, R.S. (1994). African American youth: Drug trafficking and the justice system. *Pediatrics, 93*(6), 1078–1084.

Li, X., & Feigelman, S. (1994). Recent and intended drug trafficking among male and female urban African American early adolescents. *Pediatrics, 93*(6), 1044–1049.

National Household Survey on Drug Abuse (NHSDA). (1996). *Advance report 18: Preliminary estimates*. Washington, DC: Alcohol, Drug Abuse, and Mental Health Administration. (DHHS Pub. No. [ADM] 89-1636)

National Institute on Alcohol Abuse and Alcoholism (NIAAA). (1994). *Alcohol alert 23: Alcohol and minorities*. Washington, DC: U.S. Department of Health and Human Services. (Rep. No. 23 PH 347)

National Institute on Drug Abuse (NIDA). (1997). *Treatment of drug-dependent individuals with comorbid mental disorders* (NIDA Research Monograph 172). Washington, DC: National Institutes of Health. (NIH Publication No. 97-4172)

Padgett, D.K., Patrick, C., Burns, B.J., & Schlesinger, H.J. (1994). Ethnicity and the use of outpatient mental health services in a national insured population. *American Journal of Public Health, 84*(2), 222–226.

Padilla, E.R., Padilla, A.M., Morales, A., Olmedo, E., & Ramirez, R. (1979). Inhalant, marijuana, and alcohol abuse among barrio children and adolescents. *International Journal of the Addictions, 14*, 945–964.

Sokol, R.J., Ager, J., & Martier, S. (1986). Significant determinants of susceptibility to alcohol teratogenicity. *Annals of the New York Academy of Sciences, 477*, 87–102.

Stanton, B., & Galbraith, J. (1994). Drug trafficking among African American early adolescents: Prevalence, consequences, and associated behaviors and beliefs. *Pediatrics, 93*(6), 1039–1043.

Substance Abuse and Mental Health Services Administration (SAMHSA). (1996). *Preliminary estimates from the Drug Abuse Warning Network: 1995 preliminary estimates of drug-related emergency department episodes*. Rockville, MD: Office of Applied Studies. (Advance Rep. No. 17)

Substance Abuse and Mental Health Services Administration (SAMHSA). (1997). *Substance abuse among women in the United States* (Analytic Series A-3). Rockville, MD: Office of Applied Studies.

Sue, D.W., & Sue, D. (1990). *Counseling the culturally different*. New York: John Wiley & Sons.

Sutocky, J.W., Shultz, J.M., & Kizer, K.W. (1993). Alcohol-related mortality in California: 1980 to 1989. *American Journal of Public Health, 83*(6), 817–823.

U.S. Department of Commerce. (1984). *1980 census of population and housing, American Indian areas and Alaskan native villages: Supplementary report*. Washington, DC: U.S. Bureau of the Census. (Rep. PC 80-S1-13)

Wallace, B.C. (1996). *Adult children of dysfunctional families*. Westport, CT: Praeger.

Westermeyer, J. (1996). Alcohol and older American Indians. *Journal of Studies on Alcohol, 57*(2), 117–118.

Whitehead, T.L., Peterson, J., & Kaljee, L. (1994). The hustle: Socioeconomic deprivation, urban drug trafficking, and low-income, African American male gender identity. *Pediatrics, 93*(6), 1050–1054.

Williams, G.D., Grant, B.F., Harford, T.C., & Noble, J. (1989). Population projections using DSM-III criteria, alcohol abuse and dependence: 1990–2000. *Alcohol Health and Research World, 13,* 366–370.

Yamaguchi, K., & Kandel, D.B. (1984a). Patterns of drug use from adolescence to young adulthood: II. Sequences of progression. *American Journal of Public Health, 74*(7), 668–672.

Yamaguchi, K., & Kandel, D.B. (1984b). Patterns of drug use from adolescence to young adulthood: III. Predictors of progression. *American Journal of Public Health, 74*(7), 673–681.

Service Approaches for Infants, Toddlers, and Preschoolers

Implications for Systems of Care

Harry H. Wright and Tami V. Leonhardt

In 1982, Knitzer documented the failure of the mental health services system of care to adequately serve children and adolescents who are in need of mental health care. Partially in response to Knitzer's work, the Child and Adolescent Service System Program (CASSP) was established by the National Institute of Mental Health to promote the development of a comprehensive array of services, collaboration among children's services agencies, and family involvement in planning interventions for youth with serious emotional disturbances. In addition, the planned services were to be community based and delivered in a culturally competent manner (Stroul & Friedman, 1986).

In most states across the United States, systems of care focused first on the adolescent population and later on school-age populations. In the 1990s, after more than 10 years of system development, many state systems of care have begun to consider providing mental health services for children younger than 6 years of age. As with the older children in the 1980s, a consensus is developing that the way in which mental health services are usually provided to young children is inadequate (Bickman, Heflinger, Lambert, & Summerfelt, 1996). In fact, the majority of the population younger than 6 years of age who are in need of mental health services receive no services at all, and those who do receive services are frequently treated inappropriately by providers who have no training or experience in providing interventions with young children (Costello, Burns, Angold, & Leaf, 1993; Duchnowski & Friedman, 1990).

Many people at the local level, including mental health providers, continue to believe that young children do not develop mental health

problems and therefore do not need mental health services, despite tes-
timonial evidence and statistical and clinical data that provide evidence
to the contrary. For example, Osofsky (1996) reported that infants, toddlers, and preschoolers often experience or witness violence; but many
adults, including parents, police, and members of the media, think that
these children are too young to know what happened or will not remember what happened. However, it has become clear that young
children experience significant distress after being involved with or
witnessing violence and that most of them need mental health interventions that frequently are not available (Zeanah & Scheeringa, 1996).

Young children and families face many difficulties in what has been
called a quiet crisis (Feinberg & Fenichel, 1996). Nearly all reports indicate that only a small percentage of infants and preschool children with
emotional, developmental, and behavior disorders are provided with
assessments and interventions. Mental health services for infants and
toddlers and their families have their roots in parent support and education programs and physical health–oriented systems of care. Service
delivery strategies and approaches for this population have existed in
various forms and have been shaped by religious values and political,
economic, and social trends throughout history. In the United States,
parent education evolved from an informal process of sharing child-
rearing information to an organized approach to parenting and advocacy for child welfare (Weissbourd, 1987).

Head Start was established in the 1960s to provide early intervention services to children from disadvantaged socioeconomic backgrounds as a means of improving their chances for success in school and
afterward. Parent support and education programs burgeoned in the
1970s, with an increased emphasis on providing expanded services
through parent–child development centers to families with children ages
3 years and younger as a means of enhancing opportunities for these
children's school and social success. The 1980s brought new knowledge
regarding the capacities of infants. In the 1990s, new understanding of
the critical importance of the first weeks and months of children's lives
has also led to an increased emphasis on early parent–child interactions
and growth of programs aimed at parents and their young children.

Despite these efforts, health and social services for young children
in the United States have tended to be fragmented and often lacking in
depth and comprehensiveness. Although the system of care reform concerns for older children have focused on services that were uncoordi-
nated and too restrictive, the system of care concerns for young children
include too much focus on children and not enough on the caregivers,
the sociocultural contexts in which children live, and the interactions

between children and their sociocultural contexts. Only in the late 1990s has there been a more concerted effort to develop comprehensive child- and family-centered service delivery approaches to enhance the health and well-being of young children and their families.

CULTURALLY COMPETENT
SYSTEMS OF CARE FOR YOUNG CHILDREN

The 1990s saw the development of systems of care for youth with emotional and behavior disorders in most states. Systems of care emphasize the role of families, the intensity of services, the delivery of culturally competent services, and the building of a community-based service system. Tannen (1996) described the role of families in systems of care development. Others (Stroul & Friedman, 1986) have described the array and intensity of services. A model community-based system of care and the continuum of services for youth with emotional disturbances have been described in detail (Stroul & Friedman, 1986). *System of care* usually refers to a comprehensive array of services that address youth's physical, emotional, social, and educational needs; *continuum of care* generally refers to a comprehensive and coordinated range of residential and nonresidential services within the mental health services system. Unfortunately, the population of children younger than age 6 years is frequently left out of both systems and continuums of care. When they are included, many of the services offered are not relevant to their age group, as illustrated in Table 1.

To effectively intervene with young children, service providers must deal with young children's numerous developmental issues within a broader ecological context emphasizing a cultural framework. Both developmental and cultural competence are essential for service providers' effective assessments and diagnoses of and interventions with young children and the children's families. The increasing number of young children and families with serious problems, combined with the increasing cultural diversity of the U.S. population, has created the need for a large number of clinicians with developmental and cultural competence to provide adequate mental health care for young children and their families. Unfortunately, there is a dearth of well-trained clinicians available to provide such services, and little consideration of or planning for appropriately trained children's mental health services professionals has been included in system of care development efforts around the United States (Hanley & Wright, 1995). Producing culturally and developmentally competent clinicians should be a major goal of system of care development.

Table 1. Systems of care and the continuum of mental health services for young children

System component	Relevance of service for birth–3 age group	Comment
Mental health services	***	
Prevention	***	Usually the goal of intervention with young children
Early identification and intervention	***	Requires specific competence for this age group
Assessment	***	Requires specific competence for this age group
Outpatient intervention	**	Requires specific competence for this age group
Home-based services	**	Frequently used with this age group
Day treatment	**	Underused with this age group
Therapeutic foster care	*	Sometimes used with this age group
Independent living services	N/A	Not an issue with this age group
Residential intervention	N/A	Every effort is made to avoid residential intervention
Crisis services	*	Preventive focus decreases need for crisis services
Inpatient hospitalization	N/A	Every effort is made to avoid psychiatric hospitalization
Health services	***	Significant interaction between physical health and mental health
Social services	**	Many young children receiving mental health services in systems of care are in social service agencies' custody because of abuse and neglect
Education services	**	Many 3-year-olds with special needs are enrolled in public schools
Vocational services	N/A	Not an issue with this age group
Recreation services	*	Generally not a major focus
Operational services	**	Service coordination is important with this age group

N/A, not relevant; *, relevant; **, very relevant; ***, extremely relevant

Cultural competence is clinicians' abilities to serve individuals from diverse cultural backgrounds in an appropriate, effective, and efficient manner. The culturally competent clinician

1. Values diversity
2. Has developed the capacity for cultural self-assessment

3. Is aware of the dynamics that are inherent when people from different cultures interact
4. Has developed adaptations to diversity
5. Has cultural knowledge (Cross, Bazron, Dennis, & Isaacs, 1989)

Culturally competent services are family centered. That is, the family is recognized as the child's primary system of support, and family input is considered essential in designing appropriate interventions. Assessment incorporates strategies and questions designed to obtain information regarding family background, including the family's cultural values, preferences, traditions, and level of acculturation and assimilation into American society (Cross et al., 1989). According to Davis and Voegtle, the following five factors are critical components of a culturally competent health-related assessment:

1. Ethnic origin and identification
2. Language preference
3. Family structure and dynamics
4. Cultural health beliefs and practices
5. Socioeconomic influences (1994, p. 28)

These five factors are also essential for conducting culturally competent mental health assessments. Culturally competent interventions aim to strengthen the family as well as other informal support and helping networks and are intentionally designed to be responsive to family needs and choices. Clinicians and institutions alike need to be culturally competent to effectively and efficiently assess, diagnose, and intervene with the culturally diverse population of young children and families that they encounter.

To implement a culturally competent model, clinicians must first avoid stereotyping any individuals belonging to any particular group. Avoiding stereotypes can be accomplished first by establishing a framework that promotes an understanding that people think differently and make different choices based on individual as well as cultural traditions and experiences. Second, clinicians must achieve a historical understanding of the forces of racism, discrimination, and subsequent poverty that reinforce many cultural differences and have adverse effects on children and families who are members of ethnic minority groups. Third, clinicians must be aware of and sensitive to mental health issues stemming from biculturalism, such as conflict and ambivalence related to identity and the need to function in cross-cultural contexts (Garbarino, Stott, & Faculty of the Ericksonian Institute, 1992). Fourth, clinicians must recognize their own cultural values and beliefs to avoid misinterpretations that are based on ethnocentric thinking.

Developmental competence is also an essential skill when working with young children and their families. Frequently, clinicians working with young children are assumed to have developmental competence because they have completed a basic mental health education program; more often than not, however, that is not the case (Hanley & Wright, 1995). In thinking about providing care for young children, mental health service providers must consider multisystem involvement just as they do with older children. However, as shown in Table 1, health and social services are of greater importance with the younger age group.

In public mental health systems of care, two major factors have had a significant influence on the delivery of mental health services for young children: ethnicity and poverty. Clearly, U.S. demographics with respect to ethnicity are rapidly changing. According to the 1990 U.S. census data, 20% of the U.S. population was considered to have ethnic minority status. Among children, however, the proportion with ethnic minority status was 33%. By 2010, approximately 42% of children will be members of ethnic minority families. The number of ethnic minority families who are poor and have young children also appears to be increasing. These families tend to be concentrated in urban centers and rural areas across the United States. Poverty is a major stressor for families and must be considered in developing clinical interventions for young children and their families. In 1991, the Children's Defense Fund estimated that of the more than 12 million children younger than age 3 years in the United States, one in four, or nearly 3 million, of them lived in families with incomes below the federal poverty level.

Both epidemiological studies and clinical impressions suggest that the number and the intensity of behavior problems in young children are increasing (Achenbach & Howell, 1993). Richman, Stevenson, and Graham (1975) estimated that 7% of 3-year-old children have moderate to severe behavior problems. Stallard (1993) reported a behavior problem prevalence of 10% in 3-year-old children using a parent report methodology. There have been few reports on the prevalence of behavior problems in infants and toddlers, but one study suggested that 3 out of 100 children younger than age 3 years had emotional problems and needed help (Luk, Leung, Bacon-Shone, & Lieh-Mak, 1991). Accumulated stressors such as discrimination, poverty, and violence make it more likely for infants and their families to experience serious emotional difficulties.

In addition, few studies have followed infants and preschool children longitudinally; yet the accumulating body of evidence suggests that a significant number of young children with emotional and behavior problems continue to have difficulties during their school-age years and afterward. Moreover, despite the accumulating evidence that mental health issues are prevalent and enduring among young children, few mental health agencies or organizations offer services that are specifically designed to assess and address the developmental and functional needs of young children or to work effectively with their families from a biopsychosocial and cultural mental health perspective.

CLINICAL INFANT MENTAL HEALTH CARE: A BIOPSYCHOSOCIAL AND CULTURAL MODEL

The discipline of clinical infant mental health care has emerged in the 1990s. Professional organizations interested in infants' mental health care, such as the World Association of Infant Mental Health (WAIMH) and ZERO TO THREE/National Center for Infants, Toddlers, and Families, have matured in the 1990s. The scientific journals sponsored by these organizations, *Infant Mental Health Journal* (WAIMH) and *The Bulletin of Zero to Three* (ZERO TO THREE), have published an increasing number of articles addressing the cultural aspects of children's development and the need for culturally competent children's mental health care in the latter part of the 1990s. Although these organizations and others have recognized the need to train clinicians to work with young children, little action has occurred. The requirement under the Education of the Handicapped Act Amendments of 1986 (PL 99-457) that services for children with disabilities include a multidisciplinary assessment and a written individualized family service plan calls for an approach that emphasizes comprehensive integrated services that involve the family (Bondurant-Utz & Luciano, 1994; Eggbeer & Fenichel, 1995) and are delivered on the basis of a biopsychosocial cultural perspective.

The importance of early intervention with infants and their families as a means of decreasing the incidence of emotional and behavior disorders in later childhood has long been recognized. However, the establishment of clinical infant mental health intervention environments is relatively new, having evolved in the 1990s along with increases in research on infant development and interventions. Similarly, programs that emphasize cultural competence are fairly new and continually evolving. Several program models have emerged, one of which is discussed in the next section.

CLINICAL INFANT MENTAL HEALTH PROGRAM

A multidisciplinary, collaborative model aimed at developing a continuum for infant mental health services within a system of care that emphasizes developmentally and culturally competent services for young children and their families is presented and discussed in the sections that follow.

Introduction

A publicly supported research and training psychiatric hospital developed a program that it calls the Clinical Infant Mental Health Program in response to an increasing demand for services specifically targeting multi-ethnic infants and children in the birth–3 years age group and to its growing realization that the pool of available service providers trained to meet the needs of these infants and young children and their culturally diverse families was inadequate. The program is well integrated with other primary systems of care and community agencies serving children ages birth–3 years.

Target Client Population

A culturally diverse group of young children and their families are seen in the Clinical Infant Mental Health Program. The majority are males (70%); the ethnic and racial distributions are African Americans, 54%; Caucasians, 36%; Latinos/Hispanics, 6%; and mixed race, 4%. Referrals for infants and toddlers younger than age 3 years are accepted from caregivers and service providers who identify one or more presenting problems within the following categories of problems or concerns:

1. *Regulatory disturbances:* Examples include sleep disturbances, excessive crying or irritability, limited capacity for self-soothing, eating difficulties, low frustration tolerance, self-stimulatory behavior or unusual movements, and hyperactivity or recklessness
2. *Social and environmental disturbances:* Examples include blunted affect; apathetic expression; social withdrawal; either limited interest in or avoidance of social interactions; excessive negativism or aggressiveness; excessive fearfulness, clinginess, or separation anxiety; limited interest in objects or play; and a history of multiple attachment disruptions as a result of repeated or prolonged separations or multiple placements
3. *Psychophysiological disturbances:* Examples include failure to thrive; recurrent vomiting, dermatitis, or breathing problems; and chronic constipation or diarrhea
4. *Other:* Examples include a caregiver with a mental illness or a substance abuse problem

A representative year of referrals to the Clinical Infant Mental Health Program showed that more than 25% of the young children were referred for evaluation of aggressive behaviors, temper tantrums, self-abusive behaviors, or sleep difficulties. In addition, more than 20% were referred for evaluation of excessive crying or irritability, hyperactivity, speech-language difficulties, and various other developmental difficulties. Referrals for evaluation of young children with suspected or evident developmental delays, history of child maltreatment, or typical pediatric problems in addition to one or more of the problems described previously are accepted; but the focus of the program is not exclusively on developmental problems, issues of child maltreatment, or standard pediatric problems.

Staffing

The Clinical Infant Mental Health Program was developed and staffed by a multi-ethnic group of professionals from various disciplines and community agencies who were willing to volunteer their time, interest, and/or expertise in working with infants and youth ages birth–3 years and their families who needed mental health services. Infant mental health care is complex, given the biological, psychological, social, and cultural dynamics involved. Thus, the Clinical Infant Mental Health Program has made a conscious effort to recruit a multidisciplinary team with a broad range of complementary skills. The initial core staff consisted of three males and four females: one African American, two Asian American, and four Caucasian professionals. Although ideally the cultural composition of the assessment team would be as similar as possible to the population of clients served, that goal often is neither possible nor practical.

Referral, Assessment, and Follow-Up Process

Referrals to the Clinical Infant Mental Health Program come from a variety of sources, including the state early intervention system, local health department clinics, social services agencies, community mental health providers, community pediatricians, infant and child care centers, and parents and other primary caregivers. Relevant background and referral information is obtained through an initial telephone intake process and acquisition of pertinent case records. Family members are interviewed to obtain pertinent developmental, cultural, educational, and health history information as well as information about the family's needs, language preferences, and prior help-seeking experiences. An informational packet is sent to the referring party with various background assessment forms to be completed prior to the family's clinic appointment. Assistance in completing background forms and other paper-and-pencil measures is offered in situations in which language differences, reading or comprehension problems, or other barriers may be present.

The assessment team gathers prior to seeing the child and family to review the available information and formulate questions for the initial interview session. All significant parties in the child's life (e.g., parents, guardians, caregivers, grandparents or other extended-family members, service providers) are invited to attend. During the initial assessment session, significant adults are interviewed to clarify the family's concerns, gather additional background information, and begin to identify the family's strengths and needs.

A comprehensive health and social history of the family is taken that focuses on the child's prenatal and neonatal experiences; the family's ethnicity and socioeconomic status, language preferences and practices, psychosocial history and context, living arrangements, family composition, and child-rearing practices; the role of extended-family members; the family's prior experiences with and expectations regarding social and health service providers; and the family's cultural customs, religious beliefs, and family traditions. A participant-observer technique is used, with family members and assessment team members acting in partnership to observe and interpret the young child's behavior in the assessment session as well as to piece together valid anecdotal records of the child's behavior repertoire across various settings. The nature of the problem(s) resulting in the referral is clarified, and family issues are explored in detail. Family members serve as consultants during the process of data collection and interpretation.

Observations of the child's behavior are recorded and discussed with family members. Information recorded includes the child's non-verbal communication; language and verbal communication attempts; social responsiveness and interaction style; capacity for age-appropriate play; attention span; problem-solving strategies; activity level; anxiety level; and general affect during formal assessment, unstructured time, feeding, and free play. Parent–child interactions and observations of the child's response to strangers are also noted and discussed.

The Denver Developmental Screening Test II (Denver II) (Frankenburg et al., 1992) is routinely administered to children during assessments to screen for possible developmental problems and identify the need for more in-depth assessments. This brief screening also serves as a baseline by which to monitor young children at risk of developmental problems. The Denver II was selected because of its relatively high level of sensitivity to cultural factors and young children (Evans, 1985; Patton, 1992). In general, as compared with assessment instruments used with older children, assessment instruments for infants and toddlers, such as the Denver II, usually show less variation in results between children from culturally diverse backgrounds and those from the dominant culture. The explanations for this phenomenon include that measures used with young children are able to tap more accurately the breadth of skills that culturally diverse children can demonstrate, that patterns of development among culturally diverse children vary increasingly with age, and that the effects of cultural factors as well as genetic and environmental influences may also increase with age (Bergen & Mosley-Howard, 1994).

It is always important to inquire whether observed behavior is typical for the infant or toddler in other, similar situations and to assess how his or her behavior may differ in other environments, contexts, or situations. Behavioral observations across time and environments (e.g., home, clinic, with siblings, with peers) are often necessary to elicit a valid picture of the young child's behavior repertoire and competencies. Context and knowledge of relevant cultural issues need to be taken into consideration throughout the assessment process and when designing interventions. For example, the following are some of the issues often associated with poverty and with culturally diverse populations that must be considered: illiteracy in either the native language or English, mistrust of professionals and programs resulting from past negative experiences or current community views, lack of a social support system, and geographic isolation within cities and rural environments.

These clients' definitions of *family* may vary from those of traditional, Caucasian, middle-class standards; and variations in their expression of emotions or in their decision-making patterns may be present. Culture influences socialization and child-rearing practices, which in turn interact with developmental processes such as cognitive, language, and social-emotional competencies and may affect the young child's ability to demonstrate those competencies in the context of an assessment situation (Bergen & Mosley-Howard, 1994). Thus, the clinician must strive to distinguish through culturally sensitive inquiry the degree to which observations and assessment findings represent culturally diverse but normal variations in development or practice versus evidence of more significant problems or impairments.

At the end of the initial session, the assessment team gathers once again. At that time, a biopsychosocial-cultural formulation is made and additional assessment and intervention recommendations are discussed with parents and/or guardians in an interpretive dialogue format. Recommendations for additional assessments or interventions are also discussed, and a mutually agreed-on plan of action is developed. Follow-up may include referrals for more comprehensive diagnostic assessment, referrals to other community agencies, and in-home early intervention services through the state's early intervention program. A summary report is sent to involved agencies as requested and consented to by the parent or guardian, and the family is sent an interpretive letter summarizing the clinician's diagnostic impressions and recommendations.

Clinical Education and Training

Clinical education and training are provided to child and adolescent psychiatry residents, predoctoral psychology interns, master's-level social work interns, and graduate-level nursing students. General training goals include increased knowledge and skill in the assessment, diagnosis, and intervention with infants and toddlers from a biopsychosocial-cultural perspective; increased awareness of and linkage with other resources in the community available to meet the needs of infants and toddlers and their families; and formal training in clinical assessment and evaluation methods for infants and toddlers within a multidisciplinary team framework. Child psychiatry residents are required and other trainees have the option to participate in a seminar series on cultural issues that serves to build their awareness and knowledge base of critical issues such as the dynamics of biculturalism; socioeconomic influences; and the aspects of one's own background, beliefs, values, and practices that are likely to influence clinical practice. Cultural variations in typical development as well as child-rearing practices are examined. Cultural diversity related to regional differences across the state are highlighted. In addition, continuing education is offered to staff and trainees on a monthly basis through a series of lectures and seminars on a wide range of topics relevant to infants' mental health. Invited speakers represent diverse disciplines and sectors of the community, and topics covered represent a broad range of developmental and cultural aspects of care for infants and toddlers and their families.

The Clinical Infant Mental Health Program

The following case study may best illustrate issues of cultural and developmental competence, which can influence the assessment, diagnosis, and treatment process in clinical infant mental health programs.

Background Twelve-month-old male Hispanic twins, Miguel and Pedro, were referred to the Clinical Infant Mental Health Program for evaluation of the children's development and functioning because of concerns regarding the children's history of being physically abused and possibly neglected, their suspected developmental delays, and their current social situation. The twins were taken into foster care subsequent to their substantiated abuse and neglect by their birth mother. The children's mother was from Mexico, and their father was from Guatemala. The parents had left their respective native countries and entered the United States as illegal aliens. The parents had never married and did not live together.

Neither parent spoke English. The twins had been in the primary custody of their mother; but at the time of the children's referral, their mother was in the custody of legal authorities on charges of felony child abuse. In addition, there were issues of paternity regarding the identified father.

The children were taken into the custody of child protective services when they were 8 months old, following an incident in which their mother attempted to leave the children with their father. After discovering that the children's father was not at home, the children's mother left them with their father's neighbor. One of the children, Pedro, appeared to be hurt. He was badly bruised and cried when he moved. When the children's father returned, the father's neighbor suggested that the father call the child protective services authorities; and the twins were taken to a hospital. Pedro was found to have numerous fractures and bilateral subdural hematomas. Miguel had no physical injuries and was soon released to a foster home. The twins were placed in separate non–Spanish-speaking foster homes, and, at 14 months of age, shortly after their initial assessment, they were reunited in a non–Spanish-speaking preadoptive foster home.

Assessment and Intervention   A multifaceted assessment was conducted during a period of 2 months. The children's mother, father, maternal grandfather, previous foster parents, and current preadoptive foster parents were interviewed separately, and developmental and social histories were obtained. Because neither birth parent spoke English and none of the clinic staff spoke Spanish proficiently, the aid of an interpreter was needed. The father's neighbor and friend served as the interpreter between him and the intervention team. The mother was incarcerated in a facility in which no one spoke Spanish and no social support was available. Thus, the possibilities for an interpreter within the mother's social context were limited. Consequently, someone from outside the mother's culture—a well-educated, Spanish-speaking professional who was on the mental health agency's list of volunteers—acted as interpreter for the mother in jail.

The foster parents were interviewed with respect to the twins' developmental status, progress, and adjustment since entering their care. Evaluation of each child's social-emotional functioning within the preadoptive home was monitored during a 2-month period and reassessed at 4-month and 1-year follow-ups. The maternal grandfather was interviewed during the course of the evaluation. He had not had any contact or relationship with the twins but expressed a desire to have some type of relationship with them in the future. He had neither seen nor spoken to his daughter in more than 1 year.

Results of the initial assessment indicated that both twins exhibited significant delays in gross motor skills and in receptive and expressive language skills. Despite the fact that Pedro was the twin who had sustained severe physical injuries, he was more socially engaging and had brighter affect than Miguel. However, he was smaller and displayed greater developmental delays in gross motor skills than his brother. Occupational and physical therapy were recommended, along with follow-up neurological and orthopedic consultations.

Miguel presented with blunted affect. He was slow to warm up to people. He remained passive throughout the assessment session, and his interpersonal interactions were restricted. His preadoptive mother reported that Miguel's passivity had been an ongoing concern. She also expressed concern that Miguel screamed day and night, demonstrated poor balance and coordination, and seemed excessively scared and fearful. Miguel's ability to make attachments appeared fragile. Like Pedro, Miguel was referred for occupational and physical therapy. He also was referred for a hearing test and comprehensive speech-language evaluation.

At 4-month follow-up, both boys were making dramatic gains in all areas of their development. Pedro's speech-language skills, though still lagging, had substantially improved. He was receiving physical therapy on a monthly basis and was making good progress. He also had been linked with an ophthalmologist. Miguel was vocalizing more and was more socially interactive, both at home and in the assessment environment. He was working on his self-feeding skills and making good progress. He was feeding himself by hand and learning to use a spoon. Reevaluation of the twins' speech-language development was recommended for both boys in 6 months.

At 1-year follow-up, Pedro was no longer receiving physical therapy but was on a yearly follow-up schedule with an orthopedist. He also was scheduled to see an ophthalmologist for yearly follow-up assessments. Pedro's slow growth pattern and short, round stature raised some concern regarding possible growth hormone impairment, and a referral to a pediatric endocrinologist was made. Miguel continued to exhibit severe expressive language delays and moderate delays in his receptive language. His social-emotional development also continued to be delayed. He continued to be less interactive and engaging than Pedro and neither pointed to objects nor used his hands or arms as freely as would typically be expected in a child at his age. Both boys were continuing to receive speech-language therapy on a weekly basis.

CASE STUDY DISCUSSION

The preceding case study highlights a number of difficult developmental, clinical, cultural, and service delivery system issues that may confront professionals in the assessment of and intervention with ethnically diverse infants and young children with special problems and needs. The case study raises a number of concerns for the multidisciplinary team, including the impact of including cultural differences, language barriers, and systems issues on the assessment process and the validity of assessment results. The challenges presented to the families, professionals, and systems involved with these young children were the complex interplay of biological, social, environmental, and cultural influences on the developing child; dilemmas regarding custody and placement; and boundary considerations for multiagency communication and involvement.

The process of assessment and intervention planning in the preceding case study was fraught with difficulties. Multiple agencies in addition to the infant assessment team were involved in the intervention-planning process for these infants, including the Department of Social Services, the statewide early intervention program, the lay guardian ad litem program, and the hospital's department of pediatrics. The sharing of information and coordination of intervention recommendations were difficult, particularly because of the multiple needs of the twins and the complexity of systems issues and cultural factors affecting treatment decisions and placement options. The following are some of the challenging issues posed by the preceding case study with regard to providing mental health services to children and families in systems of care:

Children's issues

Developmental risks and current developmental delays
The children's history of early deprivation and maltreatment
Issues of attachment, separation, and loss
Placement outside the children's culture of birth

Families' issues

The illegal alien status of both parents
The parents' unfamiliarity with and inaccessibility of the system of care because of legal, language, and cultural barriers
The mother's history of losing children to the foster care system and her current incarceration

> The maternal grandfather is interested in seeking custody of the
> boys and raising them in the state; the father is interested in ob-
> taining custody and having his family raise the boys in his coun-
> try of origin

Both the children's issues and the family's issues in the preceding case
study highlight the need for significant developmental and cultural
competence on the part of the clinician.

A major goal of any clinical encounter between clinician and child
is the valid, reliable, and comprehensive assessment of the child's emotional, behavioral, medical, and psychological state, as well as the child's
developmental, social, educational, and recreational functioning. A
comprehensive biopsychosocial-cultural assessment examines at least
five domains of a child's functioning: individual level of psychosocial
adjustment and biological functioning, family relationships, school adjustment and achievement, peer relationships, and community adaptation. In general, the assessment compares each child's functioning in
these areas with that of other children of similar age and attributes who
are living in similar circumstances. The focus should include an assessment of the child's individual strengths and the family's strengths and
resources in addition to any impairments and liabilities of the child and
the family. In addition, diversity among ethnic minority families, an
issue that is often overlooked or misunderstood, must be taken into
account. There has been—and there continues to be—a tendency to char-
acterize ethnic minority families according to stereotypes. In reality,
however, there is great diversity in values, lifestyles, and characteristics
of ethnic minority families that emerge from a number of different environmental and social factors, including geographic origin, current residence, level of assimilation and acculturation, socioeconomic status,
educational background, religious background, and health status. After
assessment and diagnosis, effective intervention for any debilitating conditions should be initiated within the child's cultural context.

Clearly, the case study described in this chapter points to significant
cultural issues. One of the more subtle interactions between culture and
language involved the use of an interpreter whose background in terms
of geographic origin, education, and socioeconomic status was different
from that of the children and their original and foster families. In situations such as the one described in this chapter's case study, in which there
is a need for an interpreter, the evaluators need to be aware of potential
biases involved because of the cultural diversity among individuals who
share a common language. Similarly, the process of assessment and information obtained from each of the boys' prior foster parents appeared to
be influenced by individual as well as cultural factors.

Randall-David (1989, cited in Davis & Voegtle, 1994) offered guidelines for service providers' use of interpreters, including tips for choosing an interpreter and working with an interpreter to facilitate cross-cultural communication. According to Randall-David, interpreters ideally should be trained in cross-cultural interpretation and relevant health and mental health issues and should be proficient in the languages of both the client and the provider. If a trained interpreter is not available, a volunteer should be selected, keeping in mind issues of clients' privacy and confidentiality, rapport-building capacity, and ability to bridge the culture gap.

An additional language issue that affected the assessment process in the previous case study was the interpretation of apparent language delays in light of the boys' change in primary home language from Spanish to English when they entered foster care. The children's developmental age made a language assessment of them even more complicated. These issues clearly indicate the importance of ongoing assessment of young children's functioning across contexts and over time.

There are many developmental and cultural issues related to the short- and long-term placement of the twins in the previous case study. These issues and other considerations led the team to a variety of systems of care issues involving the following questions:

- Should twins always be placed together?
- What are the circumstances influencing placement decisions? For example, should a child be adopted outside his or her family and culture if there are people from within the family and culture who are willing to take custody?
- What are the main considerations in assessing birth family members when a child has been removed and termination of parental rights is being considered?
- What are the legal issues with regard to children born in the United States to unmarried parents who are in the United States illegally?
- Should a child be moved from a foster home to preadoptive placement before legal issues are resolved?

The complexity of the infant mental health case study presented in this chapter, though focusing on just one decision from only the developmental and cultural perspectives, illustrates the difficulties of providing culturally competent children's mental health services in systems of care. The twins' grandfather was the only biological relative in the United States who was eligible to assume custody or guardianship of the children, yet he had no contact with the twins and had never even seen them prior to the evaluation conducted by the infant mental health team. He expressed a desire to establish a relationship with his grandchildren and possibly have them live with him at some point in the future. From a developmental perspective, placing the twins in temporary foster care for months to years while waiting for the grandfather to establish a relationship with them and make a decision about seeking custody and then waiting for the authorities to evaluate and approve such a placement may have had an adverse impact on the twins' development. From a cultural perspective, however, the possibility of the twins' eventual placement with their grandfather, which might offer the twins a positive cultural context for their development and keep them within their own extended family, may have justified the wait. Of course, many other factors must also be considered when making such placement decisions.

Other systems of care questions raised by the case study presented in this chapter include the following: How can information be shared across systems effectively? How can intervention goals be coordinated effectively? How can professionals resolve issues that stem from differing perspectives and responsibilities, such as the need to balance the psychological needs of the child, the rights of the child's biological family, the responsibilities of the social services agency, and legal considerations? One issue in response to the last question stems from the identified father's report that, in the past, he had attempted to have but was unsuccessful at completing a paternity test, which was a prerequisite for his trying to obtain custody of his children. He indicated that he had missed his appointment because of an unanticipated event and that he had been waiting for the social services agency to recontact him. His assumption was that that was the expected procedure for the situation. Thus, the father's unsuccessful attempt to establish his paternity of the twins was in part due to his cultural expectations of who should initiate the next step, which differed from service delivery systems procedures.

Although system of care issues are discussed in this chapter only as they are related to infants and toddlers and their families, the system of care issues for preschool children and their families are essentially the same. In general, however, more systems are involved, and with greater intensity, with preschoolers and their families. The model service approach described in this chapter requires appropriately trained children's mental health services professionals who are both developmentally and culturally competent. Because the Clinical Infant Mental Health Program is situated in an education facility, education and training are additional components of the program. In this component, the program specifically focuses on highlighting developmental and cultural issues as they relate to the program's multicultural population. The program's approach to teaching development from a multicultural perspective exposes trainees and clinicians to some of the realities of the everyday world of people who may live differently from them. The goal is to help trainees and clinicians be adaptive so that they are open to making more appropriate assumptions and decisions about children's development and families' cultures using models other than the impairment model. As an outcome of this teaching, the program's instructors expect trainees and clinicians to approach each infant and each child as a member of a specific culture, one that has its own developmental pathways and pitfalls, culturally determined symptomatic expressions of dysfunction, and culturally specific pathways of influence.

Professionals who have participated in training programs that focus specifically on issues related to young children and their families have described the benefits of such participation on their subsequent work with this population. Some of these benefits include

1. Skill development for assessing children and families from a biopsychosocial-cultural perspective
2. Enhanced knowledge regarding developmentally appropriate assessments and short-term interventions for the young children within a cultural context
3. Enhanced knowledge regarding utilization of consultative services from other disciplines
4. Enhanced understanding of multidisciplinary teamwork within a cultural context

Clinicians, agencies, and institutions that work with young children and their families must be aware that both culture and context can powerfully shape the values, beliefs, and attitudes that families convey to young children. Studies of parents' child-rearing expectations have found that the definition of appropriate or desirable behavior of children of various ages depends on one's ethnocultural heritage (National Advisory Mental Health Council, 1996). Furthermore, it is within the family that all children first learn the traditions, values, behaviors, and beliefs of their families' cultures. The family also interprets and modifies the culture based on their unique experiences. The family is responsible for much of the diversity that is observed within a given cultural group (Davis & Voegtle, 1994). Because young children are dependent on their families, assessing and providing interventions for infants and toddlers without focusing on their families and sociocultural contexts are unthinkable.

All aspects of the Clinical Infant Mental Health Program described in this chapter were designed with the goal of improving the developmental and cultural competence of mental health professionals and trainees serving an ethnically and culturally diverse population of infants and toddlers and their families. The case study described herein highlights the complexity of issues involved in conducting developmentally and culturally competent assessments as well as the need for clinicians and program planners within the field of children's mental health services systems of care to continually strive toward further refinements in their design and implementation of culturally competent systems of care for infants, toddlers, and preschoolers.

REFERENCES

Achenbach, T.M., & Howell, C.T. (1993). Are American children's problems getting worse? A 13-year comparison. *Journal of the American Academy of Child and Adolescent Psychiatry, 32,* 1145–1154.

Bergen, D., & Mosley-Howard, S. (1994). Assessment perspectives for culturally diverse young children. In D. Bergen (Ed.), *Assessment methods for infants and toddlers: Transdisciplinary team approaches* (pp. 190–206). New York: Teachers College Press.

Bickman, L., Heflinger, C.A., Lambert, E.W., & Summerfelt, W.T. (1996). The Fort Bragg managed care experiment: Short-term impact on psychopathology. *Journal of Child and Family Studies, 5,* 137–160.

Bondurant-Utz, J.A., & Luciano, L.B. (Eds.). (1994). *A practical guide to infant and preschool assessment in special education.* Needham Heights, MA: Allyn & Bacon.

Children's Defense Fund. (1991). *The state of America's children.* Washington, DC: Author.

Costello, E.J., Burns, B.J., Angold, A., & Leaf, P. (1993). How can epidemiology improve mental health services for children and adolescents? *Journal of the American Academy of Child and Adolescent Psychiatry, 32,* 1106–1116.

Cross, T.L., Bazron, B.J., Dennis, K.W., & Isaacs, M.R. (Eds.). (1989). *Towards a culturally competent system of care: Vol. I. A monograph on effective services for minority children who are severely emotionally disturbed.* Washington, DC: Georgetown University, Child Development Center, Child and Adolescent Service System Program, Technical Assistance Center.

Davis, B.A., & Voegtle, K.H. (1994). *Culturally competent health care for adolescents: A guide for primary care providers.* Chicago: American Medical Association, Department of Adolescent Health.

Duchnowski, A.J., & Friedman, R.M. (1990). Children's mental health: Challenges for the nineties. *Children's Mental Health, 17,* 3.

Education of the Handicapped Act Amendments of 1986, PL 99-457, 20 U.S.C. §§ 1400 *et seq.*

Eggbeer, L., & Fenichel, E. (Eds.). (1995). Educating and supporting the infant/family workforce: Models, methods, and materials. *Zero to Three, 25,* 1–72.

Evans, E.D. (1985). Longitudinal follow-up assessment of differential preschool experience for low-income minority children. *Journal of Educational Research, 78*(4), 197–202.

Feinberg, E., & Fenichel, F. (1996). *Who will hear my cry?* Washington, DC: National Technical Assistance Center for Children's Mental Health.

Frankenburg, W.K., Dodds, J.B., Archer, P., Bresnick, B., Maschka, P., Edelman, N., & Shapiro, H. (1992). *Denver Developmental Screening Test II* (Denver II). Denver: Denver Developmental Materials.

Garbarino, J., Stott, M., & Faculty of the Ericksonian Institute. (1992). *What children can tell us.* San Francisco: Jossey-Bass.

Hanley, J.H., & Wright, H.H. (1995). Child mental health professionals: The missing link in child mental health reform. *Journal of Child and Family Studies, 4,* 383–388.

Knitzer, J. (1982). *Unclaimed children: The failure of public responsibility to children and adolescents in need of mental health service.* Washington, DC: Children's Defense Fund.

Luk, S., Leung, P.W., Bacon-Shone, J., & Lieh-Mak, F. (1991). Behavior disorders in pre-school children in Hong Kong: A two-stage epidemiological study. *British Journal of Psychology, 158,* 213–221.

National Advisory Mental Health Council. (1996). Basic behavioral science task force report. *American Psychologist, 51,* 627.

Osofsky, J.D. (1996). Introduction: Islands of safety: Assessing and treating young victims of violence. *Zero to Three, 16,* 5–8.

Patton, J.M. (1992). Assessment and identification of African American learners with gifts and talents. *Exceptional Children, 59*(2), 150–159.

Randall-David, E. (1989). *Strategies for working with culturally diverse communities and clients.* Bethesda, MD: Association for the Care of Children's Health, as cited in B.A. Davis & Voegtle, K.H. (1994). *Culturally competent health care for adolescents: A guide for primary care providers.* Chicago: American Medical Association, Department of Adolescent Health.

Richman, N., Stevenson, J.E., & Graham, D.J. (1975). Prevalence of behavior problems in 3-year-old children: An epidemiological study in a London borough. *Journal of Child Psychology and Psychiatry, 16,* 277–287.

Stallard, P. (1993). The behavior of 3-year-old children: Prevalence and perception of problem behavior: A research note. *Journal of Child Psychology and Psychiatry, 34,* 413–421.

Stroul, B.A., & Friedman, R.M. (1986). *A system of care for children and youth with severe emotional disturbance.* Washington, DC: Georgetown University, Child Development Center, Child and Adolescent Service System Program, Technical Assistance Center.

Tannen, N. (1996). *Families at the center of the development of a systems of care.* Washington, DC: Georgetown University, Child Development Center.

Weissbourd, B. (1987). A brief history of family support programs. In S.L. Kagan, D.R. Powell, B. Weissbourd, & E.F. Zigler (Eds.), *America's family support programs* (pp. 38–56). New Haven, CT: Yale University Press.

Zeanah, C.H., & Scheeringa, M. (1996). Evaluation of post-traumatic symptomatology in infants and young children exposed to violence. *Zero to Three, 16,* 9–14.

CHAPTER 14

Immigrant Children and Families

William Arroyo

This chapter addresses the unique challenges that mental health clinicians, children's mental health services agencies, and systems of care face in their efforts to provide mental health and related services to culturally diverse children and families who have recently emigrated to the United States. Children's mental health services agencies and systems of care are nonexistent in many of the countries from which immigrants come. For purposes of this chapter, the term *immigrant* refers to anyone residing in the United States who was not born in the United States. Although immigrants can be further classified into several subcategories, including refugees and undocumented groups, there are commonalities found among these various subcategories. Several aspects of immigration as it pertains to the mental health of children and families are addressed. Immigration status as determined by the federal government has social services implications; some of these implications are also addressed. Some of the federal subcategories of immigrants are *legal immigrant, illegal alien* (referred to in this chapter as undocumented immigrants), and *refugee.*

The impact of immigrants on American society caused controversy throughout the late 19th century and much of the 20th century. The erroneous belief that immigrants were more "mentally defective" than native members of American society was particularly prevalent during the second half of the 19th century. During the second half of the 19th century, almost 80% of individuals admitted to the New York City Lunatic Asylum, as the main local psychiatric hospital was called, were immigrants. Popular opinion at the end of the 19th century, among both mental health professionals and society at large, was that the influx of lower-class immigrants from southern and eastern Europe would taint the mental development of the northern Europeans who had previously settled in the United States (Thielman, 1985) by intermarriage with Americans who were immigrants from or descendants of immigrants from northern Europe. More recent literature related to the impact of immigration on adults does not conclude that the immigration experience accounts for the psychological problems of immigrants.

The body of literature regarding the impact of immigration on children is limited and contradictory and suffers from dissimilar methodologies. Although two studies (Mena, Padilla, & Maldonado, 1987; Padilla, Alvarez, & Lindholm, 1986) concluded that immigrants experienced greater acculturation-related stress than individuals in succeeding generations, Hovey and King (1996) did not find that generational status to be a predictor of acculturation-related stress among immigrant Latino adolescents in the United States. Non-American literature reviews (Aronowitz, 1984; Canadian Task Force on Mental Health Issues Affecting Immigrants and Refugees, 1988) and studies from Sweden (Ekstrand, 1976) and the United Kingdom (Rutter et al., 1974) suggested that immigrant children have more emotional and behavior problems than native-born children, whereas Cochrane (1979), Fichter et al. (1988), Kallarackal and Herbert (1976), and Klimidis, Stuart, Minas, and Ata (1994) did not find a higher prevalence of disturbance among immigrant children.

The influx of immigrants into the United States since the 1960s has shifted; today, immigrants are primarily Latin American and Asian rather than European. The 1995 data released by the U.S. Bureau of the Census indicated that the top three regions from which legal immigrants came to the United States were, in decreasing order, Asia (37% of all immigrants), Latin America (32%), and Europe (17%).These three regions accounted for 86% (638,000 immigrants) of all legal immigrants admitted to the United States. The top 10 countries from which legal immigrants entered the United States in 1995 were Mexico (12.5% of all legal immigrants), the Philippines (7.1%), Vietnam (5.8%), the Dominican Republic (5.3%), Republic of China (Taiwan) (4.9%), India (4.8%), Cuba (2.5%), Ukraine (2.4%), Jamaica (2.3%), and the Republic of Korea (2.2%). Thus, the top three countries of origin of immigrants accounted for about 25% of all legal immigration to the United States in 1995.

The U.S. Immigration and Naturalization Service (INS) (1996) reported that in fiscal year 1995, immigration to the United States decreased by 10.4%, which followed a decline in fiscal year 1994 of 9.3% from the previous year. People who come to the United States from Puerto Rico and other United States territories are not considered or counted as immigrants by the federal government; however, cultural and racial diversity exists among people from these territories. Some Native American groups may also share similarities with these latter nonimmigrant groups. The federal government does not systematically collect data related to undocumented (i.e., illegal) immigration; but the leading source of undocumented immigration to the United States is

believed to be Mexico, with estimates of the total number of undocumented emigrants arriving from Mexico ranging from a few thousand
to at least the tens of thousands in fiscal year 1995.

In 1990, more than 2.3 million immigrant children and youth in the
United States attended schools and colleges; they accounted for nearly
5% of all U.S. students (Vernez & Abrahamse, 1996). About 75% of these
newcomers were concentrated in California, Florida, Illinois, New York,
and Texas; California is home to 40% of all children who have recently
immigrated to the United States. Such data should be integral to any
planning or restructuring of children's mental health services or systems of care on a nationwide basis and, in particular, in those states
and communities that have had the largest influxes of immigrants.
Determination of financial responsibility for public services provided to
immigrant populations is an issue that polarized debate in the 1990s in
Congress and in state legislatures.

CLINICAL CONSIDERATIONS

The discussion in this section is meant to serve as a guide for evaluations of immigrant children and their families. This guide is not
intended to be used in lieu of a standard child and family intake interview; it is intended to supplement the standard interview to assist a
clinician or an investigator in the integration of all relevant information
to formulate a meaningful service plan. The enumerated domains are
not mutually exclusive. Some of this information may not be elicited
during the initial meeting with the child and the family; disclosure by a
child and/or a family may be dictated by cultural socialization patterns
(e.g., when a person from a particular culture is likely to disclose personal information to a stranger).

Generally speaking, the less exposure that immigrant children and
families have had to American culture, the more likely it is that they will
continue to abide by the tenets of their culture of origin. Those immigrant families that have had more prolonged exposure to American
culture adhere to their cultural tenets in a more variable fashion. With
increasing international industrialization, travel, and various modes of
communication, however, some argue that a gradual blurring of differences among cultures is occurring.

The definition of *refugee* by the federal government (see 8 U.S.C.
§ 101[a][42][A]) may differ from that understood by the American public. According to the Illegal Immigration Reform and Immigration
Responsibility Act of 1996 (PL 104-208), aliens must have a "well-
founded fear of persecution" in their countries of origin to be able
to establish their eligibility for asylum in the United States. Once their

eligibility for asylum is established, these aliens are considered "refugees." In addition, that legislation expanded the definition of *refugee* to include those people who have been subjected to or have a well-founded fear of being subjected to coercive population control methods such as forced abortions or involuntary sterilizations. If the federal definition of *refugee* is conferred on an individual, then that individual qualifies for certain types of services provided by federal refugee assistance programs.

Cultural Context

It is beyond the scope of this chapter to fully discuss the cultures of all immigrant groups in the United States. It should also be recognized that, though it may seem as if the elements of a culture are stable, cultures constantly undergo changes, if only minor. A lot of variation exists within a single culture. Nevertheless, clinicians and investigators are confronted with the fact that an individual's mental condition or presenting problem is often influenced by that person's culture.

Typical Help-Seeking Patterns Many non–European American cultural groups commonly provide direct care for any family member who is suffering from mental illness and often first seek professional assistance from mental health agencies at what is, by American standards, a relatively late date. Prior to seeking help from a mental health services agency, if at all, a family from a non–European American culture would likely seek help from several other sources. In many cultures, people may seek help from their traditional health services providers, acupuncturists, local herbalists, faith healers, magnetic healers (among Pilipinos) (Araneta, 1993), community elders, religious leaders, and/or local healers (e.g., *espiritistas* among certain Caribbean groups, shamans among certain East Asian cultures [Kim, 1997], *curandero* among Mexicans). Many immigrant groups do not view health and mental health issues separately as professionals, service providers, and American people in general commonly do. If an immigrant receives help from natural or traditional healers, it is important for service providers to determine whether they experienced any relief of their symptoms or conditions by doing so. It would also be important for service providers to determine whether any of the medications or substances provided by these natural and traditional healers had unique and beneficial psychotropic effects.

Attitudes U.S. immigrants' cultural attitudes vary toward life, mental illness, "the way things are done in the United States," and particular types of services, including mental health services. With regard to seeking mental health services, an immigrant family may experience feelings of shame (Kim, 1997). In some cases, these feelings are largely influenced by their limited exposure to Western-style mental health services; but they may also be influenced by a report from a relative or a friend of a similar cultural background who has sought or has had experience with Western-style mental health services.

Religion Religion often systematically prescribes people's values, certain patterns of socialization of children and adults, gender roles, parental roles, and certain behaviors. Buddhism, Confucianism, and Islam often prescribe beliefs that conflict with Christian beliefs; however, some immigrants, such as those from East Asia, may in fact have been influenced by both an Eastern and a Western religion. A unilateral dismissal of immigrant clients' religious beliefs may undermine otherwise effective interventions. Many religions have unique rituals (e.g., circumcision, baptism) as well as days of celebration that must be respected.

Language Preference and Fluency Although many immigrants to the United States have learned some English either formally or through their exposure to it through the media, most are more fluent in their native tongues. Some immigrants may in fact be multilingual because they are fluent in the official language of their country of origin, a local dialect of their country of origin, and English. Some of the implications of immigrants' language fluency for providing services are obvious; others, such as the use of an interpreter, are discussed in a subsequent section of this chapter. Members of an immigrant family settling into a new community will learn English at different rates, so levels of English fluency within the family may vary widely. It is often tempting to resort to the use of English in these situations, but doing so may undermine service providers' rapport with parents and may be interpreted by the parents as a dismissal of their culture of origin.

Socialization Patterns Various aspects of socialization are critical to any service plan offered by children's mental health services agencies. Typical behavior for a particular child from a particular cultural group is often dictated by the family's religion and by other culturally consistent social influences that may be different from those of American culture. Children's presenting problems may be manifested by a breakdown of their families' cultural practices, perhaps due to their families' new economic circumstances and sometimes to intercultural conflicts.

Although child-rearing practices vary among Western countries, they vary to a greater extent between European American and non–European American countries. For example, Arab (Hajal, 1997), Chinese (Tsai, 1997), and Mexican (Arroyo & Cervantes, 1997) parents often value and promote dependency among their children and strongly encourage them to rely primarily on the family. Developing autonomy is not as highly valued in these cultural groups as it is in American culture. Various cultural groups strongly encourage children to maintain close ties to their family of origin. Children from various non-Western cultures are taught to be grateful to their parents, to have *respeto* (Pumariega & Ruiz, 1997), and to feel obligated to them throughout their lives. Corporal punishment is commonly used by parents among various immigrant groups; new arrivals to the United States generally do not have knowledge of American child protection laws. Discussing these laws with immigrant families is imperative for clinicians.

Gender role differences tend to be much more sharply drawn among various immigrant groups. Males are often given more authority in other cultures than they are in American society. Sons are more valued than daughters among many immigrant groups in the United States. Public displays of affection among family members is strongly discouraged among certain East Asian groups (Tsai, 1997), unlike other groups such as some Latin American cultures. Economic factors also shape customs among some cultural subgroups that nominally are from the same cultural group (Dillon & Ichikawa, 1997). The institution of marriage differs somewhat across cultures; for example, in some Middle Eastern cultures, marriages are prearranged. Children often serve as the primary requisite for viable marriages in various cultural groups. Dating patterns are also strongly culturally influenced.

Idioms of Distress　The expression of a group of symptoms or a sign that communicates a need for social support is often strongly culturally influenced. Explanations of illness are also significantly culturally rooted. There are various constellations of symptoms that are acknowledged as illnesses by different cultural groups that have immigrated to the United States; these culture-bound syndromes (Simons & Hughes, 1993) are not included in the main section of the *Diagnostic and Statistical Manual of Mental Disorders, Fourth Edition* (DSM-IV) (American Psychiatric Association, 1994) but are added in an appendix to it.

Cross-Cultural Dynamics　Immigrants' perceptions of American society may be influenced by the historical political relationships not only between their country of origin and the United States but also between their country of origin and the national origin that they perceive in their service providers. These historical political relationships may serve as a framework for ongoing service delivery with immigrant clients. In addition, service providers' perceptions of American society and of their clients may similarly be influenced by such historical political relationships between countries; therefore, it is imperative that service providers examine their perceptions of the cultural backgrounds of their clients who are children and the children's families.

Immigration Factors

Various factors that directly relate to immigrants' immigration experiences can be etiologically relevant to their psychological problems. This section addresses unique psychosocial circumstances that are relevant to the process of immigration. The temporal sequence of premigration, immigration, and postimmigration experiences is used as a framework for the discussion. Immigrants' reasons for immigrating to the United States, which often range from economic to social to political or a combination of these, provide the discussion with another contextual dimension. As in every mental health evaluation of a child, it is important to assess potential stressors from the perspective of the child and with regard to the child's developmental context and, especially in the case of young children, the reaction of the child's caregivers. Service providers should bear in mind that potential stressors also may often provide opportunities for children's and families' further psychological development (e.g., development of better coping skills).

Premigration Factors that may be relevant to the premigration phase of immigrants' migration experiences are those circumstances that converge to cause their decision to emigrate from their countries of origin to the United States. These circumstances may vary substantially from one family to another and from one individual to another. In the majority of cases, the family's actual migration is preceded by planning. Immigrant children and families have had time to psychologically prepare for their transition as well as their resettlement experiences. Many immigrant individuals and families have previously established social networks in the United States. Many older children and adolescents immigrate to the United States alone, which presents unique challenges for these youth and their families. Additional premigration considerations are that individuals and families may be fleeing persecution in their countries of origin (e.g., immigrants from countries in Southeast Asia, the Caribbean, Central America, and Eastern Europe).

Refugee families may have experienced numerous sources of stress. Families' potential stressors during the premigration phase may include the process and duration of preparations for emigration, their degree of fear or their children's terror, their witnessing of war-related violence, their own experiences of war-related assaults, or their abrupt separation from their primary support systems and social networks. It is not uncommon for some young refugees from war-torn countries to eventually admit to having personally perpetrated acts of war-related violence; this experience has served as a great source of stress, if not psychological trauma, for many of them.

Immigration   The actual immigration experience is quite variable among immigrant families. Those immigrant families who have the necessary financial means are processed through the respective immigration agencies of their countries of origin, are granted formal permission by the federal government to enter the United States, and generally have uneventful *admissions* (a legal term that was formerly referred to as *entry*) to the United States. These immigrants constitute the majority of newcomers to the United States.

Those immigrant children and families that are not processed through the aforementioned route have more challenging and, in some cases, life-threatening immigration experiences (Arroyo, 1997; Urrutia-Rojas & Rodriguez, 1997). Many such immigrant families are from Mexico or Central or South America and must negotiate the sometimes dangerous trip to and across the U.S.–Mexico border. It is also not unusual for adolescents to attempt this type of immigration independently of their families. Many undocumented immigrant children and families have reported that they enlisted the services of people who, in the course of crossing the U.S.–Mexico border, robbed or physically and/or sexually assaulted them. Some such immigrants have developed psychological traumas as a result of these assaults. Many of these undocumented children and families have subsequently survived in the United States in a clandestine fashion. Others may have taken risks via unpredictable sea routes from the Caribbean. Numerous suspected undocumented immigrants have experienced life-threatening automobile chases by the U.S. Border Patrol just north of the U.S.–Mexico border, and some of the chases have resulted in their deaths.

Postimmigration   The potential stressors in the postimmigration phase are also quite variable. Those immigrants who have family members or other relatives to receive them in the United States often have an easier initial transition than those who do not or than those who do not have shelter. From a developmental perspective, younger children fare better if a familiar and dependable caregiver, preferably a parent, accompanies them or is readily available. A common phenomenon is families' immigrating to the United States in a piecemeal fashion whereby children may precede their parents or vice versa during a period of from a few months to several years. Sometimes the eventual reunion of such family members has complex psychological consequences and adverse implications for these families' functioning. In a minority of cases, immigrant and refugee families who are undocumented immigrants may have been apprehended by the INS and placed in a designated detention center for a period ranging from a few days to a few months. Such situations have resulted in at least a few lawsuits being filed against the federal government, such as *Flóres v. Meese* (1990), a case in which conditions in the INS detention centers were found not to be conducive to the typical development of children.

If one or both immigrant parents are employed, the family's well-being is enhanced, especially during the early part of the resettlement phase. Although some parents have arranged for their employment prior to their arrival in the United States, most have not. In almost all situations, immigrants' levels of education, especially among professionals, are not recognized by prospective U.S. employers. Immigrant parents must frequently settle for low-paying jobs that tend to require limited or no skills. Those immigrant parents who have the federal government's permission for admission to the United States are more readily employable than those who do not. Many families' older children, especially in Latino families, seek employment to help support their families.

The reception of immigrants to the United States by the local and general community also has implications for immigrant families. It is not uncommon for either the local or general community to harbor resentment against new or even more established immigrants, especially if a population of U.S.-born citizens are already marginalized in the community and fear that they must compete with the new arrivals for limited community resources (Board of Children and Families, 1995). In California, a 1996 ballot initiative, Proposition 287, that passed by a 59% majority sought to bar undocumented immigrant children from public schools and to require agencies to report undocumented immigrants to the state attorney general. This initiative triggered various lawsuits; in 1998, it was declared unconstitutional. At times, immigrants may even be resented by people who were born in the United States but share the same or a similar cultural background. Immigrant families who are well received by their local communities are more likely to establish the social support system that is necessary for them to become acclimated to those communities.

Diagnostic Considerations

Many authors (Cervantes & Arroyo, 1995; Fabrega, 1990; Rogler, 1993) have inquired about the cultural relevance of the DSM-IV diagnostic classification systems. Lewis-Fernandez and Kleinman strongly suggested that the DSM-IV's emphasis on "psychologized" (1995, p. 437) presentations to categorize psychiatric disorders is erroneous in light of much cross-cultural research indicating that somatic symptomatology is much more prevalent on a worldwide basis than in the United States. Lewis-Fernandez and Kleinman also suggested that some of the fundamental constructs of the DSM-IV are themselves products of Western culture. These and other related issues may be particularly germane to the diagnostic assessment of immigrant children. The American Psychiatric Association's Group on Culture and Diagnosis recommended to its DSM-IV Task Force the inclusion of a cultural formulation that would ensure that cultural factors were systematically considered as part of the routine diagnostic process. An outline of that formulation is provided in the DSM-IV. DSM-IV diagnoses that are common among young immigrant and refugee populations are discussed elsewhere (Arroyo & Eth, 1996; Westermeyer & Wahmanholm, 1996).

A discussion with the immigrant family that includes the family's perception of the mental condition of their child is imperative. Also important is that the family indicate whether the prescribed intervention benefits the child. A successful medical workup and subsequent intervention may be a function of how culturally competent the service provider's procedures and interventions are. Some authors (e.g., Hiegel, 1981; Mull & Mull, 1981) investigated mental health service providers' belief systems; they often have implications for children's mental health services. Such belief systems may not be culturally consistent with those of culturally diverse populations.

Many newly arrived immigrant populations in the United States come from countries where medical care is poor at best. Some new arrivals may have infections that are endemic to their countries or regions of origin, and some of these infections may have psychological manifestations or implications for mental health interventions. Appropriate inquiry and medical examination are essential.

Service System Plans

Culturally competent intervention considerations are discussed elsewhere (Cross, Bazron, Dennis, & Isaacs, 1989). Similar to the underpinnings of so many elements of American society, human service systems of care are designed in a manner that is culturally competent in providing services to European Americans. A system of care that serves immigrant children and families must reflect their cultures to be effective. Immigrant children and families are ideally served by a service system approach tailored especially for those recent arrivals who have a limited understanding of the service system in their new community.

A discussion of the broad spectrum of mental health interventions is beyond the scope of this chapter; therefore, only some of the salient issues are addressed in this section. Immigrants generally follow the cultural norms of their country of origin more than their U.S.-born cultural counterparts. Although the general approach to clinical assessment tends to approximate an impairment model, a service provider should also attempt to assess the strengths of the child and family in planning an approach to services.

The clinical use of interpreters with immigrant children and their families can be a special challenge for any mental health care agency. Interpreters may fill a complex role in interventions with immigrant children and families. They do not merely translate words but also interpret cultural norms. Arroyo (in press) cautioned clinicians to use interpreters who are trained in mental health concepts; to avoid using family members, especially children, as interpreters, despite their convenience; to understand that certain concepts and terminology commonly used in U.S. mental health services cannot be translated or communicated accurately in some other languages (Fujii, Fukushima, & Yamamoto, 1993; Westermeyer, 1993); and to avoid the assumption that an interpreter who speaks the same language as the family fully understands the family's culture.

The principles, constructs, and various forms of psychotherapy are often an enigma to many U.S. immigrants, especially if they are from non-Western cultures (Kim, 1993; Kinzie & Leung, 1993). Family therapy is more culturally congruent for many of the new arrivals. Refugees may warrant more specialized types of psychotherapy (Arroyo & Eth, 1985; Kinzie, 1981). With regard to training parents in parenting, Forehand and Kotchick (1996) urged clinicians to "wake up" to the various beliefs about parenting that parents from diverse cultural backgrounds hold. They warned clinicians and behavioral researchers that parents of different cultural backgrounds have varying parenting practices that are rooted in their cultures of origin and advised clinicians and researchers to modify their practices and theories to become culturally competent.

Psychological testing of immigrant children is another challenge, especially for mental health services and education agencies. Some of the pitfalls of testing children who have limited English proficiency, as in the case of new, young émigrés, are discussed by several authors (e.g., Cervantes & Acosta, 1992; Cervantes & Arroyo, 1995). In general, it is most appropriate that these youth be assessed in their own primary languages and that the assessment instruments be culturally relevant to them.

Research on the effectiveness of psychotropic medications with children lags behind similar research conducted with regard to adults. The effectiveness of psychotropic medications among people of different racial and ethnic backgrounds is still in its infancy; there is, however, an increasing amount of literature on the different metabolic effects of certain psychotropic medications and their side effects among different racial groups in adult populations (Kishimoto & Hollister, 1984; Lin, Lau, & Smith, 1988; Lin, Poland, & Nuccio, 1989). Similar studies among children and youth have not been completed. Judicious use of psychotropic medications with immigrant children is therefore strongly urged. Furthermore, it is not uncommon for immigrant families to resort to the use of remedies that are considered to be traditional healing methods in their cultures of origin; herbs and other substances that are psychoactive agents may be self-administered. An inquiry regarding their ingestion of such substances should be routinely made of all immigrant families.

Immigrant children are often placed in an academic environment that is commensurate with their age upon their arrival in the United States despite their prior educational achievement. Vernez and Abrahamse (1996) studied more than 21,000 immigrant children from four major racial and ethnic groups (Asian Americans, African Americans, Latinos, and Caucasians) in U.S. educational institutions. They found that enrollment rates among all four groups of immigrant children and youth were comparable to their U.S.-born counterparts in primary and middle schools. However, immigrant children were less likely than U.S.-born children to attend high school. In 1990, high school enrollment rates were 87% for immigrant youth and 93% for U.S.-born youth, with the entire differential being accounted for by immigrant youth of Latino origin. In 1990, one of every four immigrants from Mexico in the 15–17 years age group was not enrolled in high school. The enrollment rate of Mexican immigrants in this age group was approximately 20% lower than that for any other immigrant group and 17% lower than that for U.S.-born youth of Mexican origin in the same age group. These statistics suggested that Mexican immigrants of high school age simply were not registering for school. Some of them do not enroll because they must support themselves and their families.

The Vernez and Abrahamse study further indicated that those immigrant students who were enrolled in school by the tenth grade were more likely than their U.S.-born counterparts to eventually strive to pursue a college education. These immigrant students were more likely to follow an academic track and to take advanced mathematics and science courses. This pattern was found in the aggregate for immigrant students as well as for each racial and ethnic group that Vernez and Abrahamse studied. The variations among the ethnic groups were that immigrant students from Asia performed best on indicators of preparation for college. They were followed in overall academic achievement by, in order of achievement level, Caucasians, African Americans, and Latinos. Vernez and Abrahamse reported that immigrant children's parents had higher expectations of their children than U.S.-born parents with regard to educational achievement. Immigrant children and their parents in all four of the racial and ethnic groups that Vernez and Abrahamse studied were found to have higher educational aspirations than their U.S.-born counterparts. The difference in level of aspiration was three times greater between Latino immigrants and U.S.-born Latinos than it was between immigrants and those U.S.-born youth of the same racial or ethnic background in the other three groups.

Whatever difficulties immigrant children have in adjusting to life in the United States, their educational attainment has equaled if not exceeded that of U.S.-born children and youth. Vernez and Abrahamse found that immigrant high school graduates were more likely than their U.S.-born counterparts across the four racial and ethnic groups they studied to pursue their college studies continuously for 4 years. Vernez and Abrahamse did find differences, however, between the four immigrant racial and ethnic groups and the four U.S.-born groups of the same cultural backgrounds. Asian immigrants and U.S.-born Asian Americans generally scored the highest on all indicators of college enrollment and achievement, and Latino immigrants and U.S.-born Latinos scored consistently the lowest on indicators in that area. Caucasians and African Americans were ranked in the middle. Vernez and Abrahamse also found that the individual and family factors associated with going to college were generally the same for immigrants and U.S.-born youth of the same or similar cultural backgrounds across all four groups. High school graduates whose parents had higher incomes, higher levels of education, and higher expectations of them with regard to educational achievement were more likely to pursue a college education than others were. These investigators suggested that, given the increasing size of the Latino population in American society, education strategies should be implemented to enhance Latino children's educational achievement. In studies that focused on East Asian children, academic success was found to be more highly valued among some East Asian immigrant groups (Tsai, 1997) than among those East Asian groups who had become more assimilated to American life (Butterfield, 1990).

The immigration status of each child and family member is important because it may often dictate the types of services, especially those that are publicly funded and might be available. There are many types of visas and special permissions given to people who immigrate to the United States from other countries. The strong national anti-immigrant sentiments in the United States in the 1990s are not unlike those of earlier eras. The 1990s immigration backlash focuses largely on Latino immigrants. The common and arguable reasoning for these sentiments are that Latino immigrants are draining a great amount of resources that should be available for the benefit of U.S. citizens, that they are primarily interested in handouts, and that they do not contribute their fair share to the U.S. economy. Latino immigrant children and their families are often resentful of these sentiments. Some states have considered but have not yet passed legislation that would prevent U.S.-born children of undocumented immigrants from automatically becoming U.S. citizens as allowed by federal law. Thus, eliciting information related to an immigrant client's immigration status should be conducted in a sensitive manner. Such elicitation that occurs without assurances to the immigrant individual that the information will not be shared with local or federal authorities may discourage such important information disclosures.

It behooves all mental health service providers who work with immigrants to be aware of evolving legislation related to immigration. Changes in federal laws affecting immigrants have triggered a flood of applications by immigrants for naturalization. Some of the restrictions on the immigrants' naturalization are related to certain mental conditions, especially those that are ongoing or recurrent. The application for naturalization of a person with a mental disorder, who may need to rely on the government for financial support, is likely to be denied.

Immigration advocacy resources are often found in communities with large populations of immigrants. These resources may serve as a useful resource not only for immigrants but also for agencies that serve immigrants. In addition, national advocacy agencies can be found on the Internet. Federally funded welfare services for legal and undocumented immigrants have been curtailed considerably by the Personal Responsibility and Work Opportunity Reconciliation Act of 1996 (PL 104-193) (more commonly known as the Welfare Reform Act) (Bazelon Center for Mental Health, 1996). Legal immigrants are no longer routinely eligible for nonemergency Medicaid; Temporary Assistance for Needy Families (TANF), formerly called Aid to Families with Dependent Children (AFDC); and Supplemental Security Income (SSI) for those with disabilities, including those with mental disabilities.

The Congressional Budget Office (CBO) (Bazelon Center for Mental Health, 1996) opined that under the Personal Responsibility and Work Opportunity Reconciliation Act of 1996, 44% of the federal government's budget savings in fiscal year 1997 would be realized by denying benefits to legal immigrants. The CBO estimated that 140,000 legal immigrant children would lose their Medicaid benefits (Bazelon Center for Mental Health, 1996). Legal immigrant children younger than age 7 years were eligible to receive Medicaid. In addition, under the 1996 federal legislation, 300,000 legal immigrant children were at risk of losing their eligibility to receive food stamps.

The federal programs serving immigrants affected by the 1996 Act included the former AFDC program (replaced by TANF), SSI (which serves children with emotional disturbances), Medicaid, food stamps, social services block grants, and child care block grants. The legislation affected undocumented immigrants (so-called illegal aliens) more extensively than documented immigrants. Most states have opted not to make available routine publicly funded medical services, including mental health services, to undocumented immigrants. In some states, undocumented adolescent and adult women do not have access to prenatal care. Some states have exercised their option to make emergency room services available to undocumented immigrants. Each state has the option to continue to provide some of these welfare services to legal immigrants by shifting a small amount of federal funds to these funding areas or by using their own state-generated funds. Refugee assistance programs were not affected by the Personal Responsibility and Work Opportunity Reconciliation Act of 1996. Foster care children who are legal immigrants remained eligible for most services that they had received prior to the Act (Bazelon Center for Mental Health, 1996).

The Illegal Immigration Reform and Immigration Responsibility Act of 1996 included increases in criminal penalties for immigration-related offenses, an increase in INS enforcement personnel, enhanced INS enforcement authority, and restrictions on the undocumented aliens' eligibility for public benefits. In addition, it imposed new requirements on sponsors of undocumented relatives for immigration.

Nearly anyone who is found to be an undocumented person in the United States is subject to removal—that is, deportation—from the United States. There are certain exceptions to the deportation laws that pertain to children. If an undocumented immigrant or his or her child has been "battered or subject[ed] to extreme cruelty" (8 U.S.C. § 1641[c][2]), the child may not be subjected to this removal procedure. Another exception applies to cases in which the removal of an undocumented immigrant who is the spouse or child of a U.S. citizen or lawful permanent resident would cause the U.S. citizen or resident "extreme hardship" (8 U.S.C. § 240A[b]). Presumedly, the child would be allowed to stay with his or her guardian in the United States with certain stipulations.

CONCLUSIONS

Immigrant children and families from diverse cultural backgrounds may have a broad range of needs for mental health services at the time of their arrival in the United States. Although the majority gradually make the transition to American society, many need assistance, if only temporarily, from various mental health services agencies. Service agency personnel can prepare to meet these needs effectively by acknowledging the immigrant families' unique cultural attributes and providing mental health services accordingly. Providing immigrants with responsive care ultimately benefits all of American society.

REFERENCES

American Psychiatric Association. (1994). *Diagnostic and statistical manual of mental disorders* (4th ed.). Washington, DC: Author.

Araneta, E.G. (1993). Psychiatric care of Filipino Americans. In A.C. Gaw (Ed.), *Culture, ethnicity, and mental illness* (pp. 377–412). Washington, DC: American Psychiatric Press.

Aronowitz, M. (1984). The social and emotional adjustment of immigrant children: A review of the literature. *International Migration Review, 18,* 237–257.

Arroyo, W. (1997). The Central American child in the United States. In G. Johnson-Powell & J. Yamamoto (Eds.), *Transcultural child psychiatry: A portrait of America's children* (pp. 80–91). New York: John Wiley & Sons.

Arroyo, W. (in press). Clinical use of interpreters. In J.D. Noshpitz (Ed.), *Handbook of child and adolescent psychiatry.* New York: John Wiley & Sons.

Arroyo, W., & Cervantes, R.C. (1997). The Mexican-American child. In J.D. Noshpitz (Ed.), *Handbook of child and adolescent psychiatry* (Vol. 4, pp. 532–542). New York: John Wiley & Sons.

Arroyo, W., & Eth, S. (1985). Children traumatized by Central American warfare. In S. Eth & R. Pynoos (Eds.), *Posttraumatic stress disorder in children* (pp. 103–120). Washington, DC: American Psychiatric Press.

Arroyo, W., & Eth, S. (1996). Post-traumatic stress disorder and other stress reactions. In R.J. Apfel & B. Simon (Eds.), *Minefields in their hearts: The mental health of children in war and communal violence* (pp. 52–74). New Haven, CT: Yale University Press.

Bazelon Center for Mental Health. (1996). *An uncertain future: How the new welfare law affects children with serious emotional disturbance and their families.* Washington, DC: Author.

Board of Children and Families. (1995). Immigrant children and their families: Issues for research and policy: The future of children. *Critical Issues for Children and Youth, 5,* 72–91.

Butterfield, F. (1990, January). Why they excel. *Parade,* 4–6.

Canadian Task Force on Mental Health Issues Affecting Immigrants and Refugees. (1988). *Review of the literature on migrant mental health* (Catalog No. Ci96-37/1988E). Ottawa, Ontario: Health and Welfare Canada, Minister of Supply and Services Canada.

Cervantes, R.C., & Acosta, F.X. (1992). Psychological testing for Hispanic Americans. *Journal of Applied and Preventive Psychology, 1,* 209–219.

Cervantes, R.C., & Arroyo, W. (1995). Cultural considerations in the use of DSM-IV with Hispanic children and adolescents. In A.M. Padilla (Ed.), *Hispanic psychology: Critical issues in theory and research* (pp. 131–147). Thousand Oaks, CA: Sage Publications.

Cochrane, R. (1979). Psychological and behavioral disturbance in West Indians, Indians, and Pakistanis in Britain: A comparison of rates among children and adults. *British Journal of Psychiatry, 134,* 201–210.

Cross, T.L., Bazron, B.J., Dennis, K.W., & Isaacs, M.R. (Eds.). (1989). *Towards a culturally competent system of care: Vol. I. A monograph on effective services for minority children who are severely emotionally disturbed.* Washington, DC:

Georgetown University, Child Development Center, Child and Adolescent Service System Program, Technical Assistance Center.

Dillon, J.E., & Ichikawa, V. (1997). Culture and psychopathology in Pacific/ Asian children. In J.D. Noshpitz (Ed.), *Handbook of child and adolescent psychiatry* (Vol. 4, pp. 586–599). New York: John Wiley & Sons.

Ekstrand, L.H. (1976). Adjustment among immigrant pupils in Sweden. *International Review of Applied Psychology, 25*, 167–187.

Fabrega, H. (1990). Hispanic mental health research: A case for cultural psychiatry. *Hispanic Journal of the Behavioral Sciences, 12*, 339–365.

Fichter, M.M., Elton, M., Diallina, M., Koptagel-Ilal, G., Fthenakis, W.E., & Weyerer, S. (1988). Mental illness in Greek and Turkish adolescents. *European Archives of Psychiatry and Neurological Sciences, 273*, 125–134.

Flóres v. Meese, 913 F.2d 1315 (9th Cir. 1990).

Forehand, R., & Kotchick, B.A. (1996). Cultural diversity: A wake-up call for parent training. *Behavior Therapy, 27*, 187–206.

Fujii, J.S., Fukushima, S.N., & Yamamoto, J. (1993). Psychiatric care of Japanese Americans. In A.C. Gaw (Ed.), *Culture, ethnicity, and mental illness* (pp. 305–346). Washington, DC: American Psychiatric Press.

Hajal, F. (1997). The Middle Eastern/Arabic child. In J.D. Noshpitz (Ed.), *Handbook of child and adolescent psychiatry* (Vol. 4, pp. 543–556). New York: John Wiley & Sons.

Hiegel, J.P. (1981). The ICRC and traditional Khmer medicine. *International Review of the Red Cross, 21*, 251–261.

Hovey, J.D., & King, C.A. (1996). Acculturative distress, depression, and suicidal ideation among immigrant and second-generation Latino adolescents. *Journal of the American Academy of Child and Adolescent Psychiatry, 35*, 1183–1192.

Illegal Immigration Reform and Immigration Responsibility Act of 1996, PL 104-208, 8 U.S.C. §§ 1101 *et seq.*

Kallarackal, A.M., & Herbert, M. (1976). The happiness of Indian immigrant children. *New Society, 35*, 422–424.

Kim, L.I.C. (1993). Psychiatric care of Korean Americans. In A.C. Gaw (Ed.), *Culture, ethnicity, and mental illness* (pp. 347–376). Washington, DC: American Psychiatric Press.

Kim, W.J. (1997). Korean immigrant children. In J.D. Noshpitz (Ed.), *Handbook of child and adolescent psychiatry* (Vol. 4, pp. 600–610). New York: John Wiley & Sons.

Kinzie, J.D. (1981). Evaluation and psychotherapy of Indochinese refugee patients. *American Journal of Psychotherapy, 35*, 251–261.

Kinzie, J.D., & Leung, P.K. (1993). Psychiatric care of Indochinese Americans. In A.C. Gaw (Ed.), *Culture, ethnicity and mental illness* (pp. 281–304). Washington, DC: American Psychiatric Press.

Kishimoto, A., & Hollister, L.E. (1984). Nortriptyline kinetics in Japanese and Americans [Letter]. *Journal of Clinical Psychopharmacology, 4*, 171–172.

Klimidis, S., Stuart, G., Minas, I.H., & Ata, A.N. (1994). Immigrant status and gender effects on psychopathology and self-concept in adolescents: A test of the migration-morbidity hypothesis. *Comprehensive Psychiatry, 35*, 393–404.

Lewis-Fernandez, R., & Kleinman, A. (1995). Cultural psychiatry: Theoretical, clinical, and research issues. *Psychiatric Clinics of North America, 18*, 433–438.

Lin, K.M., Lau, J.K., & Smith, R. (1988). Comparison of alprazolam plasma levels and behavioral effects in normal Asian and Caucasian male volunteers. *Psychopharmacology (Berlin), 96*, 365–369.

Lin, K.M., Poland, R.E., & Nuccio, I. (1989). A longitudinal assessment of haloperidol doses and serum concentration in Asian and Caucasian schizophrenic patients. *American Journal of Psychiatry, 146,* 1307–1311.

Mena, F.J., Padilla, A.M., & Maldonado, M. (1987). Acculturation-related stress and specific coping strategies among immigrant and later generation college students. *Hispanic Journal of the Behavioral Sciences, 9,* 207–225.

Mull, J.D., & Mull, D.S. (1981). Residents' awareness of folk medicine beliefs of their Mexican patients. *Journal of Medical Education, 56,* 520–522.

Padilla, A.M., Alvarez, M., & Lindholm, K.J. (1986). Generational status and personality factors as predictors of stress in students. *Hispanic Journal of the Behavioral Sciences, 8,* 275–288.

Personal Responsibility and Work Opportunity Reconciliation Act of 1996, PL 104-193, 8 U.S.C. §§ 1621 *et seq.*

Pumariega, A.J., & Ruiz, P. (1997). The Cuban American child. In J.D. Noshpitz (Ed.), *Handbook of child and adolescent psychiatry* (Vol. 4, pp. 515–521). New York: John Wiley & Sons.

Rogler, L.H. (1993). Culturally sensitizing psychiatric diagnosis. *Journal of Nervous and Mental Disease, 181,* 401–408.

Rutter, M., Yule, W., Berger, M., Yule, B., Morton, J., & Bagley, C. (1974). Children of West Indian immigrants: I. Rates of behavioral deviance and of psychiatric disorder. *Journal of Child Psychology and Psychiatry and Allied Disciplines, 15,* 241–262.

Simons, R.C., & Hughes, C.C. (1993). Culture-bound syndromes. In A.C. Gaw (Ed.), *Culture, ethnicity, and mental illness* (pp. 75–93). New York: John Wiley & Sons.

Thielman, S.B. (1985). Psychiatry and social values: The American Psychiatric Association and immigration restriction, 1880–1930. *Psychiatry, 48,* 299–310.

Tsai, L.Y. (1997). Mental health of Chinese American youths. In J.D. Noshpitz (Ed.), *Handbook of child and adolescent psychiatry* (Vol. 4, pp. 574–578). New York: John Wiley & Sons.

Urrutia-Rojas, X., & Rodriguez, N. (1997, December). *Unaccompanied migrant children from Central America: Socio-demographic characteristics and experiences with potentially traumatic events.* Paper presentation at Ethnographic Research on the Health and Well-Being of Immigrant Children and Families Conference, National Research Council of the Institute of Medicine, Irvine, CA.

U.S. Immigration and Naturalization Service. (1996). *Statistical yearbook* [Annual]. Washington, DC: U.S. Department of Justice.

Vernez, G., & Abrahamse, A. (1996). *How immigrants fare in United States education.* Santa Monica, CA: Rand Corporation.

Westermeyer, J. (1993). Cross-cultural psychiatric assessment. In A.C. Gaw (Ed.), *Culture, ethnicity, and mental illness* (pp. 125–146). Washington, DC: American Psychiatric Press.

Westermeyer, J., & Wahmanholm, K. (1996). Refugee children. In R.J. Appel & B. Simon (Eds.), *Minefield in their hearts: The mental health of children in war and communal violence* (pp. 75–103). New Haven, CT: Yale University Press.

Evaluation and Research Issues Facing the Development of Culturally Competent Services

The Importance of Children's Mental Health Epidemiological Research with Culturally Diverse Populations

Saundra H. Glover and Andres J. Pumariega

Epidemiology provides the framework for the study of patterns of illness and, ideally, guides planning decisions for prevention, interventions, and services. With regard to children's mental health services, the role of epidemiology becomes more complex. A number of obstacles can be identified that challenge the traditional epidemiological approach to the study of illness, even mental illness. The assessment of children's mental health must occur in a broader context that takes into account the contextual nature of children's behavior within their families and communities, the influence of children's developmental levels on their cognition and skill acquisition, and the subjective definition of behavior problems by informants (Costello, Burns, Angold, & Leaf, 1993). Culturally diverse children offer additional challenges to the epidemiological study of children's mental health.

The need for epidemiological research focusing on the unique characteristics, risk factors, and special needs of culturally diverse children and adolescents and their families is becoming more evident as the development of systems of care for children's mental health services progresses. Systems of care involve the coordination of different services and service delivery systems in the provision of individualized care at the community level for children with serious emotional disturbances. At the same time, these systems serve an increasing proportion of clients from underserved minority populations. This change in the client population is due to the increasing minority population in the United States, particularly among children and adolescents who are from ethnic minority groups, who, in aggregate numbers, are often in fact the majority. A significant proportion of this population receives public mental health and substance abuse services.

As the U.S. population continues to become more diverse, culturally diverse children will, in increasingly large numbers, be represented in communities and will demand more mental health services. Ethnic minorities in the aggregate represent 21% of the U.S. population, but they compose 40% of the public school population (Hoberman, 1992). By 2000, approximately 31% of the adolescent population in the United States will represent a racial or ethnic group, and by 2020 their representation will increase to 40%. African Americans constitute 12% of the U.S. population, one half of whom are younger than 18 years of age. Hispanics represent 7% of the U.S. population and are the fastest-growing ethnic minority group. By 2000, the number of Hispanics will have increased by 42%. A heterogeneous population, the Hispanic population is composed of Mexican Americans (60%), Puerto Ricans (14%), Cubans (6%), and people of other Hispanic origin (21%). Second to the rapid growth of the Hispanic population is that of the Asian American population, resulting from the influx of immigrants and refugees (U.S. Bureau of the Census, 1986). Far more heterogeneous than the Hispanics, the Asian American population is composed of more than 30 ethnic groups. About one third of the Asian American population are ages 17 years and younger (Hoberman, 1992). The Native American population, which had been in decline from the mid-1800s to the mid-1900s, is experiencing resurgent growth in the 1990s.

To adequately describe the mental health status of culturally diverse children, epidemiological research must go beyond its traditional functions of counting cases, identifying patterns of distribution, and noting trends. It must consider the historical, geographical, and socioeconomic characteristics of the ethnic groups to which these children belong and the areas in which they develop (Costello et al., 1993). In doing so, cross-cultural comparisons can be made, providing a basis for identifying the risk factors and determining which groups may be at high risk of developing mental illness. Such analysis also guides the planning, developing, and testing of interventions that are culturally effective (Rogler, 1989). Studies that both support (Canino, Rubio-Stipec, Canino, & Escobar, 1992) and refute (Shrout et al., 1992) higher levels of mental health symptomatology among culturally diverse populations reinforce the need for service providers to have a better understanding of the influence of cultural factors on children's mental health functioning and the prevention of, diagnosis of, and interventions for mental illnesses.

The first stage in significant epidemiological research for culturally diverse children is needs assessment, which links epidemiological research methods to improvement in children's mental health. Specifically, epidemiology can serve to clarify the distribution of mental illnesses across culturally diverse children. Once the issue of need for mental health services is determined, the second stage of epidemiological research involves assessing the extent to which children's needs have not been met. Issues of access to services and barriers to services for culturally diverse children then become important.

Children's need for services can be assessed in different ways and affects the methods used to measure service delivery. One way to define need is by studying those who receive interventions or use services. In doing so, a variety of environments must be considered, including the school system, social services, and juvenile justice. This is especially true of culturally diverse children, who often have limited access to formal mental health services and receive such services indirectly through their involvement in multiple children's services agencies (Canino & Spurlock, 1994; Costello et al., 1993). According to Burns (1994), only 1% of children actually received interventions in mental health services environments.

Need as a diagnosis assumes that every child with a need can be readily diagnosed (Costello et al., 1993). This definition of need has serious implications for culturally diverse children because diagnosis is dependent on a number of factors that pose problems for children who are economically disadvantaged, are unacculturated, and experience discrimination. Diagnosis can vary based on who is interviewed, who the interviewer is, which questions are asked, and how the questions are asked. It can also be influenced by culturally determined patterns of symptom aggregation, differential levels of threshold of distress, and terminology used by the child or the family to describe the child's behavior (Pumariega, 1996).

A child's experience of a functional impairment is a third method of assessing need that has received research attention only in the 1990s. Proponents of this definition of need argued that a child experiencing mental health problems experiences an impairment in activities of daily living as a direct consequence (Costello et al., 1993). Although this approach may be more adaptable to the assessment of culturally diverse children, cultural factors also enter into the definition of impairment (Pumariega, 1996).

Epidemiological research has provided the basis for identifying risk factors associated with children's mental health. Epidemiological studies have already provided evidence of prenatal and birth complications as risk factors. Studies have shown that African Americans and Hispanics tend to have a higher incidence of low birth weight, poor pregnancy outcomes, birth defects, and infant death, all of which are conditions related to their being socially and economically disadvantaged (Vega & Rumbaut, 1991).

Medical conditions that lead to developmental limitations such as prenatal and perinatal complications of iron deficiency and excessive blood lead levels disproportionately occur in children who are poor. Research has also found evidence of the prevalence of environmental risk factors among this population. Poverty, along with levels of education (particularly children's mothers' levels of education), families' structures (e.g., fathers' absence), and immigration and degree of acculturation pose problems for culturally diverse children. For a Hispanic group of children enrolled in Head Start programs, socioemotional problems were strongly related to their solitary play, negative peer interactions, and maternal reports of their children's temperament problems (Grossman & Shigaki, 1994).

Epidemiological studies have been equally as important in discerning protective factors for children at high risk of developing mental illness. Family cohesion and kinship networks tend to create an environment in which the positive self-esteem and sense of personal power of children at risk of developing mental illness build resilience. The confirmatory associations among children's mental health outcomes, generational effects, and length of residence in the United States in general have been established for risk factors and protective factors (Board on Children and Families, National Research Council, Institute of Medicine, 1995). Children's mental health researchers can broaden their understanding of the risk and protective factors of children at risk by developing an appreciation of the different values orientations of children who are at risk of developing mental illness (Dilworth-Anderson, Burton, & Turner, 1993).

LIMITATIONS OF MENTAL HEALTH EPIDEMIOLOGICAL RESEARCH ON CULTURALLY DIVERSE CHILDREN

Major issues limiting epidemiological research on children from diverse cultural backgrounds are discussed in the following sections. These issues must be addressed when conducting research on this highly vulnerable population.

Sampling and Demographic Issues

A complete picture of the mental health status of culturally diverse children has yet to be drawn. Recognizing that ethnic groups are not monolithic is the first priority. Epidemiological studies using racial comparisons often fail to consider the heterogeneity of the races (Canino et al., 1992). The identification of differences within the Asian,

Hispanic, African American, and Native American populations would assist in the design of intervention and prevention measures based on the adaptive or preventive factors and the risk factors associated with the subcultural groups of these races and ethnicities.

Ecological Factors

Equally as significant as sampling and demographic issues is how children from culturally diverse backgrounds interrelate with their environments. A number of issues support specific patterns of relationships between children from culturally diverse backgrounds who are at risk of developing mental illness and their environments.

Majority versus Minority Epidemiological research has been limited in the attention paid to how children view their ethnic identities (Canino & Spurlock, 1994). When and how children develop an awareness of their ethnic and cultural identities can have a bearing on their mental health status. The development of ethnic identification begins as early as age 3 years, with children's beginning awareness of color differences (Cross, Bazron, Dennis, & Isaacs, 1989). Children at that age often misidentify their own race, as shown by their tendency to select the wrong-color doll when asked to pick a doll most like themselves (Aboud, 1977). Minority children tend to confront the issue of racial or ethnic difference at an earlier age than majority children (Goodman, 1964). As children continue to develop, their sense of ethnic orientation strengthens through early latency (developmental stage experienced at ages 5–8 years), with a unique definition of self or identity occurring in adolescence. When race or ethnicity is visibly linked with skin color, children face additional challenges related to their racial or ethnic identities (Hoberman, 1992). Of particular importance for minority children is how they are perceived by members of the majority race. These perceptions play a role in the minority child's efforts to understand and create an external boundary of ethnic self-definition (Rosenthal, 1987). Also serving to reinforce these boundaries are the traditions and institutions of the child's ethnic group. Strong external reinforcers have been shown to heighten ethnic identity, resulting in a rejection of assimilation by minority adolescents.

Whether a minority child identifies more with the majority group than with her or his ethnic group is an issue that needs additional study relative to effective intervention, particularly with regard to whether this identification results from perceived or actual prejudicial or discriminatory practices that the minority child experiences. Native American children in particular understand the environment through intuitive, visual, and pictorial means, in direct contrast with the U.S. school system, in which success is dependent on auditory processing, abstract conceptualization, and language skills. This difference among Native American children, when compounded with their other risk factors (e.g., poverty, alienation, dislocation, depression, intergenerational conflict), can result in higher rates of symptomatology for this cultural group (Yates, 1987).

Urban versus Rural Additional research is needed that examines the place of residence of culturally diverse children. Limited research has suggested that a child's immediate environment can prove to be either a protective factor or a risk factor (Canino & Spurlock, 1994). Typically, children in urban areas and large communities have higher rates of psychopathology than children in rural areas and small communities. Urban areas tend to be rich in multiple stressors that can have an adverse impact on a child's mental health. Children in urban environments are exposed to violence and often live in buildings that are overcrowded and unsafe. Extreme economic deprivation can lead to homelessness for children and their parents. There is also growing concern in rural areas about minority adolescents' being accused of or being involved in serious juvenile crime and the appropriateness of traditionally urban interventions that may be less effective in a rural environment (Scherer, Brondino, Henggeler, Melton, & Hanley, 1994).

Border versus Inland Epidemiological research on culturally diverse children, particularly Hispanic children, must define patterns of behavior based on whether the children live near the U.S.–Mexico border, where the Hispanic culture is expressed in adjoining yet somewhat different social ecologies, or inland, where the influence of the American culture may be greater. The degree to which American culture impinges on Hispanic culture in the United States and the relationship of that impingement on the mental health status of Hispanic children needs to be addressed in order for epidemiological research to be culturally sensitive. In general, culturally diverse children struggle with adherence to contrasting values and standards between their culture and the culture of Caucasians and may perceive a loss of their personal identities as a natural result of acculturation (Pumariega, Swanson, Holzer, Linskey, & Quintero-Salinas, 1992).

Refugee versus Established Conflict occurs for refugees and immigrants to the United States who are confused about what is acceptable or appropriate behavior in American society. They also face the possibility of having to start over in occupations that may be of lower status than those to which they were accustomed in their countries of origin. Refugees often enter the majority culture after experiencing trauma prior to relocation (Clarke, Sack, & Goff, 1993). Once they relocate, they must learn a new language, find a place to live and work, and adapt to the majority culture. Clarke and colleagues suggested that the strongest relationship with depressive symptoms is related to the refugees' trauma associated with the relocation as opposed to their prior traumatic experiences. Posttraumatic stress disorder in refugees studied over time tends to persist, but refugees' symptoms have been shown to decrease in intensity (Sack et al., 1993). The transition that refugees and immigrants face, contrary to established members of the same race, can bias study results on the mental health status of culturally diverse populations (Malgady & Rogler, 1993; Shrout et al., 1992).

Socioeconomic Status

With the exception of some groups of Asian origin (Japanese, Indians, Koreans, Pilipinos, and Chinese), the educational and income levels of non-Caucasian Hispanics substantially exceed those of all other racial and ethnic minorities in the United States (Vega & Rumbaut, 1991). In concordance with this pattern, the highest rates of behavior disorders are evidenced to occur in the lowest socioeconomic status (SES) groups, particularly with regard to cognitive impairments and schizophrenia (Holzer et al., 1986). High levels of poverty and subsequent disparities in mental health outcomes have been noted among Puerto Ricans, Vietnamese, African Americans, Native Americans, Mexican Americans, and Pacific Islanders (Portes & Rumbaut, 1990). Of significance is the length of time that children spend in poverty. African American and Hispanic children generally have spent longer periods in poverty than non-Hispanic children. This persistent poverty yields increased levels of internalizing symptoms such as anxiety, unhappiness, and dependence that have evolved over a period of time and may have more significant implications for racial and ethnic differences than a static representation of poverty (e.g., current poverty) (McLeod & Shanahan, 1993). The challenge for epidemiological research is to determine the degree to which culture has an impact on the manifestation, perception, recognition, and salience of psychiatric symptoms independent of the impact of SES (Good & Good, 1985).

Considerable variation exists within cultural groups in terms of their mental health and sociodemographic risk factors (Neighbors, 1984). African Americans of low SES experience more distress than their counterparts of high SES when faced with economic crises or physical illnesses. African Americans of high SES, however, experience more distress than their counterparts of low SES when faced with emotional adjustment problems. Williams, Takeuchi, and Adair (1992) found an inverse relationship between SES and psychiatric disorders across racial groups, but less so for African American males, particularly with regard to alcohol abuse.

The impact of these differences for culturally diverse children warrants attention. Mexican American adolescents reportedly indicated more depressive symptoms than African Americans or nonminorities (Clarke et al., 1993; Roberts & Chen, 1995; Roberts & Sobhan, 1992). Higher rates of severe levels of alcohol and drug abuse have been found in Mexican Americans in small towns. Survey data showed that Chinese refugees are more likely to need mental health services than nonrefugee Chinese. Relative to other ethnic groups, Native Americans are characterized by higher rates of alcohol and drug abuse, earlier age of onset of alcohol and drug abuse, and higher rates of delinquency and arrests (Kinzie, Leung, Boehnlein, & Matsunaga, 1992).

Gender

Gender vulnerability to psychiatric illness varies across cultural groups as well. Mental health studies of African Americans generally have reported higher symptomatology in women than in men; however, some studies have shown no differences between African American men and women. Across other ethnic groups, studies have reported that gender differences vary based on whether the individuals studied are U.S. born, the length of individuals' residency in the United States, their levels of education, and their occupations, as well as on subcultural issues of family and friends of the same ethnicity (Roberts & Sobhan, 1992; Takeuchi, Roberts, & Suzuki, 1994).

Inherent biases in the assessment of mental illness among culturally diverse children in clinical populations versus typical populations relate to the factors leading to intervention selection. Studies have shown that minority children and adolescents often reflect higher levels of social aggression than nonminority children and adolescents. Such behavior may trigger premature intervention when actual clinical conditions have not fully evolved (Fabrega, Ulrich, & Mezzich, 1993; Rogler, Cortes, & Malgady, 1994). Hence, the threshold for minorities to receive clinical referrals may be lower than for nonminorities, and intervention selection may be influenced by a gatekeeper's discomfort or bias (Fabrega et al., 1993).

Hidden Populations

The noncoverage of African American males in most epidemiological surveys and their overrepresentation in institutional environments serving children who have been neglected or who are in the juvenile justice system are significant concerns and may bias the results and/or interpretations of the findings of these studies (Lindsey & Paul, 1989; Wierson & Forehand, 1995). Some research supports a referral bias, with African Americans placed in psychiatric facilities with lower levels of

standard clinical psychopathology but higher levels of social oppositional behavior (Fabrega et al., 1993). The underrepresentation of African
Americans in psychiatric hospitals can also be influenced by insurance
criteria, with a disproportionate number of non-Caucasians being supported by public funds (Mason & Gibbs, 1992).

Epidemiological research that ignores the child welfare and juvenile justice populations is not culturally sensitive research. Historically,
culturally diverse children are disproportionately found in these environments, and a high percentage of these youth require mental health
services. Both the child welfare and juvenile justice systems experience
high rates of recidivism, which may reflect their failure to properly
screen youth for significant mental health problems and their failure to
provide the necessary on-site mental health services (Pumariega, Johnson, & Cuffe, 1996; Wierson & Forehand, 1995). Studies have shown that
even when Caucasians and African Americans experience equal psychiatric impairments, African American adolescents are more likely to
be incarcerated and Caucasian adolescents are likely to be hospitalized
for psychiatric care (Cohen et al., 1990; Lewis, Balla, & Shanok, 1979;
Lewis, Shanok, Cohen, Kligfeld, & Frisone, 1980; Westendorp, Brink,
Roberson, & Ortiz, 1986). To achieve an accurate assessment of the mental health needs and unmet needs of culturally diverse children, data on
referral pathways that can lead children to different service systems
(e.g., minority children to child welfare and juvenile justice systems versus majority children to the mental health system) must be examined.

Instruments

Few normative studies (Achenbach et al., 1990; Bird, Gould, Rubio-
Stipec, Staghezza, & Canino, 1991) exist to assess the quality of instruments used to measure mental illness among culturally diverse children.
Landmark studies (Achenbach et al., 1990; Reiger et al., 1984) in psychiatric epidemiology have ignored ethnicity or have failed to include
sufficient numbers in the different ethnic groupings to make racial comparisons. The Midtown Manhattan Study (Srole, Langner, Michael,
Opler, & Rennie, 1962), one of the first studies of psychiatric impairments in an urban environment, was drawn from a population that was
99% Caucasian. Few instruments exist (Rogler, 1989) that have been
cross-culturally validated. Epidemiological research addressing the
appropriateness of different measures for different cultural groups
would be a significant contribution toward an improved understanding
of the mental health issues facing culturally diverse children.

A focus on cultural sensitivity in epidemiological research requires
a consideration of cultural components in the planning and pretesting
stages, the collection of data and translation of instruments, the instru-

mentation of measures, and the analysis and interpretation of data (Rogler, 1989). The pretesting and planning phases allow the researcher to gauge the appropriateness of a research concept to a particular cultural environment and to incorporate concepts in the research study that are unique to a particular cultural environment. In the instrumentation of measures, an awareness of how the cultural context can influence the variables under study enhances the cultural sensitivity of the research. The significance of culturally sensitive research instruments is apparent as researchers wrestle with issues of help-seeking behavior across cultures, the effectiveness or ineffectiveness of interventions across cultures, and patterns of mental illness diagnoses across cultures. For example, the interpretation of low scores of adolescent Puerto Rican girls on a personality measure (Eysenck Personality Inventory [Eysenck & Eysenck, 1968]) took into consideration the role distinctions for men and women in Puerto Rico, thereby reinforcing the importance of understanding the historical, psychological, social, and economic contexts in which their responses were provided. The girls' low scores were attributed to adolescent Puerto Rican girls' perception of the subjugated role of females in their culture (Porrata, 1995).

Studies to determine the effectiveness of the Center for Epidemiologic Studies Depression Scale (CES-D) (Radloff, 1977) for use with young adolescents have examined the scale's internal consistency, ability to detect cases of major depression and dysthymia, ability to discriminate between major depression and other psychiatric disorders, and the implications of these features for the scale's use with various gender racial groups (Garrison, Addy, Jackson, McKeown, & Waller, 1991; Garrison, Schoenbach, Schluchter, & Kaplan, 1989). An examination of variations across races when using the Child Depression Inventory (Kovacs, 1980/1981) with children and adolescents with emotional disturbances found no differences but attributed the lack of significant differences to the small number of African Americans in the sample. Evidence of the acceptability of the Diagnostic Interview Schedule for Children–Revised Version (DISC–R) (Shaffer et al., 1993) for assessing a comprehensive range of children's and adolescents' diagnoses in general has been found, but its cross-cultural validity has yet to be established (Shaffer et al., 1993). In fact, African Americans and Hispanics have been the normative samples largely used in the development of the DISC–R , with the instrument's validity among Caucasian majority populations being in question. This may be the case with many instruments because minority families of low SES are more easily recruited with small financial incentives than Caucasian middle-income families.

Considerable cross-ethnicity functional and scalar equivalence have been established for several mental health measures for children

(Child Depression Inventory Youth Hostility Scale [Cook, 1986], Global Self-Worth Scale [Harter, 1985]) for assessing depression, behavior disorder, and negative life events (Knight, Virdin, Ocampo, & Roosa, 1994). An assessment of the internal consistency and concurrent validity of the Child Behavior Checklist (CBCL) (Achenbach, 1991) indicated its applicability for use with Hispanic children (Rubio-Stipec, Bird, Canino, & Gould, 1990). The adaptation of the Thematic Apperception Test (Murray, 1943) to assess the cognitive, affective, and personality functions of minority versus nonminority children by using culturally sensitive stimuli is one attempt to address the cultural inadequacies of the psychological assessment and diagnosis of children of diverse ethnic and racial backgrounds (Costantino, Malgady, Casullo, & Castillo, 1991).

Translation: Language and Dialect

The data collection and translation of instrument phase, in a culturally sensitive framework, provides the opportunity to make language adaptations within the cultural context of the clients with whom the language-adapted instruments are to be used (i.e., interviewer and respondent similarity). Collecting data from a Hispanic population, for example, can be facilitated by having bilingual interviewers and allowing interviewees the option of responding in Spanish or in English (Malgady, Rogler, & Costantino, 1987). A second provision of culturally sensitive research is the translating of the study's instrument to the language of the respondent. Although back-translation is not completely free of cultural bias, it is the most-used procedure for translation and takes mental health research for culturally diverse populations a step closer to cultural sensitivity. In the strict language translation of instruments for culturally diverse populations, the emotional context is often lost; yet it is difficult to make language interpretation part of systematic measures.

Assessment Paradigms

When making interracial or cross-ethnicity comparisons for diagnosis, the fact that different cultures embody beliefs, values, and standards of acceptable behavior that differ from the norms of the dominant American culture cannot be ignored. The domains and clustering of symptoms that may define a particular disorder would most likely vary across the different cultural and racial groups. Most assessment paradigms developed to understand mental health problems have inherent biases toward the dominant American culture's norms of behavior.

The clinician's cultural and educational background can also result in intracultural diagnostic variations. The clinician's training, ideological orientation, patterns of diagnosis, and level of cultural competence influence his or her diagnostic behavior (Fabrega, Chul, Boster, & Mezzich, 1990). Clinicians' bias is implicated in psychiatric intakes in which African American adolescents are referred to psychiatric facilities with lower levels of standard clinical psychopathology but higher levels of social oppositional behavior (Fabrega et al., 1993).

The American Psychiatric Association developed and published the primary diagnostic system used in psychiatry and the mental health field in general, the *Diagnostic and Statistical Manual of Mental Disorders*, (DSM), which added a cultural formulation process in its fourth edition (DSM-IV) (American Psychiatric Association, 1994). Despite that addition, the constructs on which diagnoses are based remain constant and inflexible across cultural groups. This inflexibility is especially problematic with regard to disorders that are more psychologically based in which culture may have a major role. Although worldwide studies point to constant rates of certain biologically based disorders such as schizophrenia, these disorders often go untreated because of cultural differences in their manifestation. Furthermore, these paradigms do not yet address culture-bound systems unique to certain groups. Many studies do not include confound variables such as SES and religion (Leff, 1988).

Rogler (1996) provided a framework for organizing and focusing the cultural addenda in the DSM-IV when conducting research on cultural differences in psychiatric diagnoses. The framework was designed to support research on three levels: generation of hypotheses about the cultural influences on symptom assessment, translation of symptoms into disorders, and psychiatric diagnosis. Cervantes and Arroyo's (1994) comprehensive review of the literature yielded few empirical studies of the DSM-IV categories used with Hispanic children and adolescents, leading them to conclude that diagnostic classifications should incorporate culturally relevant patterns to achieve cross-cultural applicability and diagnostic accuracy.

Analyses

Epidemiologic multicultural research should begin with a thorough review of the theoretical premises and hypotheses to determine the implications of ethnicity for the data analysis process (Vega, 1992). If cultural variables are explicitly contained in the theoretical premises and the hypotheses, then the analysis and interpretation of the data should include operationalization of the cultural variables. Once the relevance of cultural factors to the theoretical formulations has been established, an awareness that those factors may influence the psychometric properties of the measurement instruments is warranted (Vega, 1992).

A major limitation of data analyses in epidemiological research on culturally diverse children is the lack of inclusion of ethnicity as a variable in examining risk factors for disorders. Studies that clearly included large minority population samples have failed to examine cross-ethnicity differences in their findings (Halfon, Berkowitz, & Klee, 1992). In studies in which the impact of ethnicity has been considered, the interactive effect of related factors such as SES, gender, and location is often excluded. Studies have indicated that different interpretation of some scales may be appropriate for racially and ethnically diverse populations, particularly for children and adolescents of low SES (Wrobel & Lachar, 1995).

A move beyond the usual correlational analyses of symptoms and sociodemographic variables to additional statistical approaches, such as regression analyses, is needed to study the effects of these variables (Pumariega, Holzer, & Nguyen, 1993). Researchers cannot assume that current statistical analysis (i.e., diagnostic cutoff scores) are valid across all groups. Further work is needed to test the power of various diagnostic cutoffs to discriminate between clinical and nonclinical samples in different cultures (Achenbach et al., 1990).

REVIEW OF STUDIES

Future children's mental health epidemiological research with culturally diverse populations must build on the research that has been conducted to date. A number of studies and their foci are summarized in the next sections as a precursor to making recommendations for future research.

Clinical/Descriptive

Kilgus, Pumariega, and Cuffe (1995) examined racial differences in the final discharge diagnoses of adolescents who had been hospitalized for psychiatric reasons. Significant racial differences among final diagnoses were found. Mood and anxiety disorders as well as substance abuse were more often diagnosed in Caucasians than in African Americans. Kilgus and colleagues also found that African American adolescents were more likely to be involuntarily committed to psychiatric hospitals than Caucasian adolescents and had significantly more organic and psychotic diagnoses than Caucasians.

The question of bias at psychiatric intake has also been addressed. Fabrega and colleagues (1993) found that African Americans were referred to a psychiatric facility with lower levels of standard clinical psychopathology but higher levels of social oppositional behavior than Caucasians who showed a higher number of Axis I definite diagnoses (clinical disorders) and level of symptoms. A study by Canino and colleagues (1992) of intergroup and intragroup differences in functional somatic symptoms found significant differences between Hispanic and non-Hispanic Caucasian adults independent of sociodemographic factors and suggested that the same may be true among children and adolescents in these ethnic groups.

Several studies have examined depression and suicide ideation among minority and nonminority adolescents. Suicidal behavior in minority female adolescents has been linked to psychiatric diagnoses other than major depressive disorder and borderline personality disorder. Of 61 minority females who had attempted suicide, major or minor depressive disorder was found in 42%, conduct disorder was found in 46%, multiple diagnoses were made in 38%, and no diagnosis was made in 13% (Trautman, Rotherram-Borus, Dopkins, & Lewin, 1991). In a sample of male minority and nonminority adolescents, African Americans had the highest prevalence of suicide ideation (20.5%), and Haitians had the highest number of suicide attempts (11.4%) (Vega, Gil, Warheit, Apospori, & Zimmerman, 1993). Drug abuse was consistently related to suicide attempts among both minority and nonminority adolescents in the sample, with the factors of acculturation strains interacting with drug abuse being a predictor of suicide attempts among Hispanic respondents (Vega et al., 1993). A national survey of adolescents ages 12–17 years showed differences in rates of depression for Caucasians, African Americans, and Hispanics. Among the ethnic groups, Mexican American adolescent males (and, to a lesser extent, Mexican American adolescent females) reported more depressive symptoms than other males (and other females) (Roberts & Sobhan, 1992). Using a translated version of the Todai Health Index Depression Scale (Aoki, Suzuki, & Yanai, 1974), Takeuchi et al. (1994) found significantly higher depression scores for Japanese boys than for Hispanic boys. Most of the studies have shown gender differences across ethnic groups for depression and suicidal ideation; however, questions remain concerning the interpretation of such findings. The differences noted can have a significant impact on the delivery of mental health services to adolescents. The study of factors, specifically cultural factors, that may be reflective of these differences is needed.

General Population Studies

Pumariega and colleagues (1992) proposed an approach for measuring cultural factors through the activity orientations that youth endorse. These researchers examined the recent drug abuse, long-term drug abuse, depressive symptomatology, and activity orientations of Mexican American and Mexican youth. Although the findings of Pumariega and colleagues showed that an increased risk of substance abuse significantly related to these youth's cultural activity orientations, a stronger effect was found between symptoms of distress or depression and sociodemographic factors.

Researchers examining the relationship of stressful life events and changes in substance abuse among multiracial adolescent boys recognized the important moderating influence of culture and ethnicity on the relationship between stress and substance abuse (Biafora, Warheit, Vega, & Gil, 1994). The findings of a second group of researchers showed the impact of acculturation on crack cocaine and cocaine abuse and suicide attempts among Hispanic respondents (Roberts & Chen, 1995; Vega et al., 1993). Swanson, Linskey, Quintero-Salinas, Pumariega, and Holzer (1992) showed a large proportion of "border youth" (48.08% of those on the U.S. side of the U.S.–Mexico border and 39.41% on the Mexican side) reporting high levels of psychological distress as measured by the CES-D cutoff score of 16 or higher. Chang, Morrissey, and Koplewicz (1995) investigated the impact of acculturation on the psychiatric symptoms of Chinese American children as measured by the CBCL. The findings, which reflected lower symptom scores on the total problem, internalizing, externalizing, total competence, activities, and social scores than Achenbach's (1991) American norms by age and race, were attributed to temperamental differences, underreporting, and cultural intolerance of misbehavior.

Hidden Populations

Studies have supported the importance of addressing the mental health needs of culturally diverse children and adolescents in hidden populations with serious emotional disturbance and serious mental illness in systems other than mental health systems of care (e.g., juvenile justice system, child welfare). The prevalence of clinically significant emotional disturbances and substance abuse among youth residing in residential group homes has been shown and is indicative of the need to provide mental health services in residential group home environments. A significant percentage of African American youth (51.7%) studied in residential group home programs scored above the conservative cutoff score of 16 for the CES-D (Pumariega, Johnson, & Sheridan, 1995). No significant differences were found in the mental health statuses of youth placed in psychiatric hospitals when compared with youth placed in correctional facilities (Cohen et al., 1990). The Cohen and colleagues study also raised the issue of race as a determining factor in placement because it found an overrepresentation of African American youth in the correctional facility involved in the study. However, the Caucasian youth placed in that correctional facility had the highest scores on the CBCL, raising additional issues of how to effectively serve the mental health needs of youth with serious behavior and emotional problems in nontherapeutic environments.

Other studies have also suggested racial bias in the disproportionate placement of nonminority youth in the juvenile justice system as opposed to the mental health system, regardless of their mental health needs. Kaplan and Busner (1992), in their study of the admission rates of youth to the juvenile justice system versus the mental health system, found no evidence to support racial bias in admission to the children's and adolescents' mental health system in New York state. Pumariega, Atkins, and colleagues (1996) found lower levels of psychopathology and symptomatology in incarcerated youth as compared with hospitalized youth, yet they found higher levels of psychopathology and symptomatology among these youth than are found among the general population. Their findings also supported the hypothesis that nonminority youth travel a path that leads them from school or social services into the juvenile justice system and bypasses the mental health services system.

Services Studies

Most of the children's mental health services research has been relegated to documenting differences in services provided to children of color. A comprehensive children's mental health services study would require an analysis of the relationship between race and service delivery across a range of services including those provided by the mental health, child welfare, and juvenile justice systems. However, studies to date have usually been limited to one service area. For example, studies of African American children tend to focus on one type of service delivery independent of the others. African American children have been shown to remain in foster care for longer periods of time and have more foster care placements than Caucasian children, who were more likely to be given family services and affective skills training (Finch & Fanshel, 1985; Mech, 1983; Seaberg & Tolley, 1986; Shyne, 1980; Shyne & Schroeder, 1978). However, these studies were limited in scope, and none of them examined mental health services for African American children in foster care or in the juvenile justice system. In Hawkins and Salisbury's (1983) study of service delivery to juvenile delinquents, minority youth were found to be more likely to receive academic and employment skills training, whereas Caucasian youth were more likely to be given family services and affective skills training.

Mental health services research has been sparse. The studies that have been conducted support the argument that significant differences in service delivery exist for culturally diverse children and Caucasian children. Studies have shown culturally diverse children to be under-represented in mental health institutions and overrepresented in child welfare and juvenile justice systems (Gruber, 1980). Other studies have shown that minority children are at higher risk of receiving mental health interventions than children from the dominant culture (Beiser & Attneave, 1982). One study that did examine the relationship between mental health service delivery and child welfare services found that, regardless of levels of symptomatology, culturally diverse children are less likely to have out-of-home placements (Eyman, Boroskin, & Hostetter, 1977). Longres and Torrecilha (1992) examined the effect of race on the delivery of mental health services and found a significant relationship between race and the service needs of racial and ethnic minorities.

More specifically, studies examining the relationships among psychiatric diagnosis, race, gender, SES, and service use have supported the need for placing a high priority on future research to address disparities in use of services by culturally diverse groups and the associated factors that contribute to the disparities (Bui & Takeuchi, 1992; Cuffe, Waller, Cuccaro, Pumariega, & Garrison, 1995). Cuffe and colleagues (1995) found possible referral bias, variations in intervention-seeking behavior, and instrumentation bias in assessing mental health services use among African American adolescents. African American adolescent females received interventions at one third the rate of Caucasian adolescent females, and African American adolescent males received interventions at one half the rate of Caucasian adolescent males, despite reports among both African American adolescent males and females of higher levels of symptomatology than were found among Caucasian adolescents. African Americans were also found to terminate interventions prematurely, failing at a higher percentage than Caucasians to continue interventions beyond two sessions.

Bui and Takeuchi (1992) suggested a different pattern of utilization of mental health services among minority adolescents compared with that of Caucasians. African American adolescents were overrepresented and Asian Americans and Mexican Americans were underrepresented in the population that uses mental health services. In addition, Asian Americans tended to continue their interventions for longer periods and African Americans tended to continue their interventions for shorter periods than Caucasians. African Americans have also been shown to have more outpatient episodes than Caucasians (Bui & Takeuchi, 1992; Pumariega et al., 1993).

Mason and Gibbs (1992) also examined patterns of mental health service utilitzation using Medicaid claims data for the state of California. Their analysis revealed the placement into private facilities of a high proportion of nonminority adolescents who were privately insured. Minority adolescents were overrepresented in the juvenile justice system. The Mason and Gibbs study directed attention to the need for standards in psychiatric admissions based on severity of illness, criteria for appropriate clinical interventions, and careful evaluation of interventions used with mental illnesses among minority adolescents. These considerations could prevent situations in which poor and minority youth are grossly underrepresented simply because they do not have equal access to inpatient treatment facilities.

Epidemiological assessment of the balance between children's mental health needs and the utilization of mental health services illustrates an imbalance that warrants the attention of policy makers (Zahner, Pawelkiewicz, DeFrancesco, & Adnopoz, 1992). Zahner and colleagues' survey of children in an urban environment found that 38.5% were at risk of developing psychiatric disturbances. Only 11% were receiving interventions in a mental health environment, which was less than those who were receiving mental health interventions in school and medical environments. These results underscore the importance of considering alternative intervention environments to meet the needs of a diverse population.

FUTURE DIRECTIONS AND RECOMMENDATIONS

Several recommendations emerge from the examination of major issues or concerns when considering epidemiological research with children from diverse cultural backgrounds that will improve the yield of future research.

Approaches to Epidemiological Research

The insights of minority investigators and field staff can be invaluable in expanding the knowledge base relevant to culturally diverse children and their need for mental health services. Recruitment efforts should be broadened to increase the number of minority researchers in proportion to the growing population of minority children and families and the unique needs and challenges that they bring to mental health interventions. Such efforts would serve to correct the dearth of studies of minorities in the mental health literature and enhance the data collection, interpretation, and analysis of psychiatric problems of minority children.

If systems of care are to effectively serve a major and increasing proportion of their clients, they must examine the impact of culture and cultural differences on their clients. Because mental health professionals face increasing challenges to the funding for such systems, they need data that identify the critical psychological, biological, and social aspects of serving culturally diverse populations. These data should drive the planning for systems of care and the evaluation of their overall effectiveness. They should help address questions about which services or interventions work for which culturally defined populations of children and families as well as identify essential components of model programs for replication. As managed care approaches are applied to systems of care, the importance of such data becomes more crucial because they can determine the allocation and management of clinical and financial resources.

The "cultural blindness" approach that American society has so frequently used is also reflected in mental health epidemiological research. This approach keeps mental health professionals from finding out important differences in the variety of needs and orientations to service utilization across ethnic groups. Identifying and addressing such cultural differences and how to accommodate them makes programs more clinically effective and cost effective. In any mental health epidemiological study, if there are any culturally diverse populations in the study sample, researchers have a responsibility to determine how these populations are similar to or different from the prevailing community population along whatever variables are being examined. This responsibility becomes the overarching goal of culturally competent epidemiological research and program and system evaluation. However, for such research to be effective and noninjurious to the populations being served, cultural competence principles must be applied in its implementation. The subsections that follow discuss recommendations to guide future research so that it achieves cultural competence in its implementation as well as in its interpretation.

Defining Population Characteristics and Related Indicators

As part of designing epidemiological studies, population, client, process, and outcome indicators or variables must be defined. These definitions allow the evaluation to answer the key questions of which risk factors are operant under which conditions or with respect to which problems, which interventions work, for whom those interventions work, and how those interventions work. Population and client indicators should include information about the race and ethnicity of the population as well as other key demographic characteristics that often interact with culture, such as gender, age, SES, and whether the population is urban or rural. Such data should be collected in conjunction with other clinical data. The inquiry approach, categorization, and coding of such data are important. Culturally diverse children and their parents often do not relate to these variables in the same manner as researchers do.

For example, Hispanic youth often respond to the question of race by indicating that they are Mexican Americans or Chicanos. In fact, the sociopolitical movement of the 1960s among migrant farm workers of Mexican origin reestablished traditional mestizo beliefs about a "cosmic race" (*la raza cosmica*) resulting from the ethnic mixture of Spanish and/or Portuguese colonists and American Indians, which the Virgin of Guadalupe came to symbolize through her apparition to American Indian followers while they were being conquered by the Spaniards in the 1600s (Jimenez, 1995). Similarly, there is often a high level of sensitivity to inquiries about information such as income, number of individuals in the household, and family lineage. Such questions have different meanings across different cultures, and such information about culturally diverse individuals and populations has been used for negative or destructive ends in the past. Its collection requires a sensitive approach as well as methods of inquiry that ensure that collection biases are reduced to a minimum.

Outcome indicators in any program or system evaluation study usually involve domains of symptom change, functional change, safety, cost, community tenure, level of restrictiveness, and clients' burden and satisfaction. All of these domains are largely culturally determined. For example, if emotional separation and autonomy are viewed as important aspects of psychological functioning, clinicians should ask themselves whether these aspects of functioning are an appropriate focus in interventions for a cultural group for which multigenerational closeness and communal dwelling are the norm. Another example might be that clinicians should ask themselves whether gainful employment should be viewed as an outcome for parents who live in an impoverished region.

Study Design and Sampling

The nature of the study design chosen can be a significant issue for culturally diverse groups. Pre–post or multiple baseline designs are often more acceptable than others. However, culturally diverse populations frequently change over time for reasons other than interventions provided, such as exposure to the dominant American culture, generational changes, and signal events in the life of the community. Keeping track of such intervening changes in these designs is important. Experimental designs with control groups and/or random assignment to different conditions are considered the scientific standard. However, these designs are hard to achieve in the reality of service provision as well as with regard to the limited willingness of different populations to serve as controls when the benefits from their involvement are not evident to them. They also lead to ethical problems when any particular ethnic group does not receive a worthwhile intervention, which reinforces their suspicions of bias in the service delivery system. Longitudinal designs following a cohort of clients over time to measure outcomes can be useful. Their drawback is that some behavior changes may be specific to certain cohort groups if they share many life experiences; thus, results may be hard to generalize to other groups.

Researchers who sample culturally diverse groups must ensure that the racial or ethnic, socioeconomic, age, and gender composition of any sample reflects that of the base population. However, sampling within a given region or cultural group or subgroup leads to limited applicability of the results to that group. Sampling across different regions or subgroups often requires a much larger sample. Oversampling or stratification of samples may be necessary if the samples of culturally diverse populations are too few in number to be representative.

Measurement Strategies

Instrumentation and measurement strategies require many cultural considerations. Few instruments have been normed or evaluated for validity and reliability across different cultural groups, and some have subtle but distinct cross-cultural biases (Pumariega, Holzer, & Swanson, 1991). This inherent limitation may require that researchers validate instruments with a small subsample upon initiating their studies as well as evaluate their item and subscale structures. Such pretesting should involve an overinclusive number of items to allow streamlining of the instrument by using factor analytic techniques if the data from such pretesting are to be included in the final analyses.

Instruments should ideally have all or most of the following characteristics if they are being used or compared across cultural groups:

1. *Conceptual equivalence:* The same theoretical construct is measured across different cultures (e.g., parental role functions are defined differently in different cultures).
2. *Semantic equivalence:* Not only translation across language but also idioms and expressions of the groups being studied are accounted for (e.g., the term *feeling blue* for low mood as used by Caucasians is nonsensical for Hispanics and has a historical context for African Americans). Bilingual versions for people in cultural transition are often necessary.
3. *Content equivalence:* The content of each item in the instrument is relevant to the phenomenon being studied in that culture (e.g., the

concept of being put upon may not have a comparable translation or idiom in a language other than English). Lack of familiarity with clinical jargon and different attributions or understandings of symptoms or illnesses and culturally bound presentations or syndromes (e.g., schizophrenia versus "being possessed") must be taken into account. It may be necessary to include descriptions of mental illnesses or behaviors in questions.

4. *Criterion equivalence:* Interpretation of the variable measured is given in reference to the norms for that culture (e.g., the level of depression and cutoff for significant depression are based on the normative responses for that culture). Measures of symptoms or behaviors need to account for culturally determined thresholds of dysfunction within the community. It may be necessary to develop different cutoff scores for different ethnic groups using culturally specific normative samples.

5. *Methodological equivalence:* Different methods of assessment may not yield comparable responses across cultures (e.g., some groups are more open in self-administered questionnaires, whereas others are more open when they interact with an interviewer). The cultural acceptability of answering on the extremes of a Likert-type question may vary among ethnic and cultural groups.

The environment in which the collection of data takes place can also influence results. A neutral site may be most desirable to preserve individuals' confidentiality and reduce the potential stigma that may be associated with their participation (Guillermin, Bombardier, & Beaton, 1993).

A common issue is using monocultural instruments versus cross-cultural instruments. Monocultural instruments may be necessary when specific aspects of a culture are being evaluated, such as ethnic pride and ethnic identification in a particular culture or in particular cultural beliefs and practices. Such instruments should be normed for the particular group or subgroup that is being studied. Cross-cultural instruments or instruments that theoretically can measure constructs cross-culturally are necessary when making comparisons across cultural and ethnic groups. It may be necessary to develop parallel versions of instruments that are specific for different groups or even to pilot-test instruments with community populations to obtain normative data and to identify problems with acceptability and response (Pumariega, Holliday, & Holzer, 1995).

Qualitative ethnographic approaches may also be useful in obtaining information about culturally related variables and eliciting important perceptions or attitudes without the stringent categorical limits of rating instruments (Thornton & Garret, 1995). These approaches are often consonant with cultural values and means of transmission of information in many communities, which include differences in traditions of oral versus written language and what types of information are to be shared, with whom, and when. Such methods include open-ended questions, questionnaires, interviews, or observational data. Focus groups of community members or community leaders can discuss certain problems to be addressed by interventions and develop associated themes. These can be compared with similar groups postintervention. Ethnographic measures can be used in combination with standardized instruments, especially using post hoc coding approaches, or to develop culturally sensitive standardized measures (Guillermin et al., 1993).

There are special issues to be considered around the measurement of specific culturally related variables. The measurement of cultural identification and cultural value orientation presents particular challenges. The construct that is most commonly endorsed in the cross-cultural mental health field is biculturality or multiculturality (that culturally diverse individuals by necessity are bicultural or multicultural in order to adapt successfully). The domain of cultural and ethnic identification must allow for this construct and must take into account a number of domains, such as self-identification, relational patterns, culture-related traditions and preferences (e.g., clothing, foods, language, media), and cultural value orientation (Cuellar, Harris, & Jasso, 1980). In order to measure culture-related traditions and preferences, one must decide on a model for value orientation and on which dimensions to measure (e.g., attitudes versus behaviors). For children and for many families, the measure of concrete behaviors or activity orientations (i.e., culturally related activities of daily living) is a valuable means of assessing cultural identification. These assessments include simple activities such as the amount of time spent with family, engaging in religious activities, and exposure to the media (Pumariega et al., 1992). As mentioned previously, the measure of functional status needs to differ socioecologically according to cultural expectations for role functioning. Measures of SES need to be nonintrusive to ensure cooperation and valid responses. The implementation of traditional cultural healing methods requires special measures and methods for certification of the appropriate application of interventions by a healer or practitioner as well as for the expected behavioral or attitudinal responses. The collaboration of spiritual healers in developing such measures may be crucial so that they are relevant as well as acceptable to the individuals studied (Robbins, 1994).

Use of Databases and Clinical Records

Important demographic information may be available from agency databases, which can be interlinked for more effective identification. Information defining the types of clinical conditions that clients usually present can be obtained either from agency databases or from other epidemiological studies. Researchers need to be aware of biases that may have been inherent in the manner in which such information was collected and coded, such as how issues of race, ethnicity, or income were asked and who was the informant. For example, there are common problems with the ratings of ethnicity/race identification in databases. Often clinicians do not ask individuals about their race or ethnicity directly but infer it from individuals' appearances or surnames. There are also problems with the coding categories used for cultural and ethnic groups, with insufficient or unclear categories (e.g., a single Hispanic category, Asian/Pacific Islander combined category). There are also problems with the coding of much culturally related information in databases, such as SES, diagnosis, and service utilization information. It may be important to develop rational coding categories for clinical database information, with instructions for clinical staff or other staff entering information (Flaskerud & Hu, 1992; Pumariega, 1996). Racial or ethnic bias in clinical diagnosis is well documented, especially by clinicians not familiar with the cultures of their clients (Kilgus et al., 1995). The diagnostic assessment of ethnic minority children with serious emotional disturbance often leads to a serious underestimation of comorbid affective and substance abuse disorders and an overestimation of psychotic and organic disorders by clinicians. It may be more valuable to have clinicians rate the presence of symptoms reported by the client or family, which would offer a better base of objectivity and would not be contaminated by the biases of classification systems. Methodology used to relate demographic characteristics to relevant variables for the region of residence, such as geocoding (mapping such characteristics by towns or by neighborhoods), can shed further light on factors that influence psychopathology and service delivery, such as the proximity of the population to natural stressors and physical access to services (Bean, 1996).

Participation by the Community and Cultural Providers

In order to begin implementing epidemiological or system studies with culturally diverse populations, cooperation and participation of the culturally defined community must be obtained and nurtured. Attitudes about evaluation and research in minority communities are often quite negative because of their prior negative experiences. They have often been exposed to much research without direct pay-off. There is also mistrust about whether evaluations can be used as a tool of government agencies, immigration, social services, and child welfare agencies for custody termination or termination of benefits. The methodology used often conflicts with cultural values, traditions, and accepted means of communication of sensitive information.

Attitudes about cross-cultural research and issues in service and policy agencies can also serve as barriers to addressing these issues in evaluations. Precompetence attitudes persist (e.g., "all people are the same") in mental health services agencies, with agency staff wanting to be perceived as politically correct and not being open about their attitudes, biases, and lack of cultural competence skills. There is also the fear that evaluation and research might frighten clients away from using services (Pumariega et al., 1995).

A number of approaches can be used to gain access to minority communities and to solicit the cooperation of minority clients and program staff. Actively seeking out advice, input, and endorsement from the minority community, particularly from the community's leaders and elders, is quite effective. Building community support for a system of care not only builds bridges of trust but also can serve to inform the selection of instruments, methods, and procedures that are more acceptable and more effective. Recruiting research and evaluation assistants from the community can also build in such community input and expertise. Cultural competence introduction and training for research staff as studies are initiated can heighten awareness for the need to examine issues relating to cultural diversity and reduce defensiveness. Integration of evaluation tools and indicators into existing processes in the community, including clinical care, helps to minimize burden on staff and time spent with clients. Informed consent procedures must also be easily understood and should involve appropriate family members when culturally indicated (Windle, Jacobs, & Sherman, 1986).

Needed Studies

Epidemiological research is ripe for studies of culturally diverse populations. Studies are needed to address the cross-ethnicity prevalence rates of emotional disturbance and psychopathology in culturally diverse children. It is important that these prevalence studies include multiple ecological and SES samples. Longitudinal studies are needed as well to adequately assess the predictors of later social, emotional, and behavior problems for minority children. These studies should incorporate genetic and environmental factors, which include a perspective toward adaptation and resiliency.

A second area of opportunity is to expand the knowledge base for understanding mental health issues unique to culturally diverse children by examining hidden populations with serious emotional disturbance and serious mental illness in systems other than mental health systems of care (e.g., juvenile justice system, child welfare). Examinations of the factors influencing the use of different venues for the delivery of mental health services for culturally diverse children are needed. Comparative analyses of the services provided to children outside and within the mental health system could possibly enhance the understanding of intervention outcomes from both environments. Additional studies are needed to identify risk and protective factors.

Epidemiological research is needed prior to the implementation of pilot service intervention programs. Of paramount importance is the development of cross-culturally valid instruments to be used in cross-cultural research. Reliance on a single psychiatric interview has not proved to be an effective means of collecting data for a culturally diverse population. Just as a researcher can expect different responses across age groups and developmental stages, different responses should be anticipated across and within different racial and ethnic groups; hence, researchers need to use reliable instrumentation that addresses cross-cultural measurement issues.

Research on the cost of care for culturally diverse children, given the unique characteristics of their mental health profiles, is an area warranting attention because of the current focus on cost accountability for mental health services in general and child mental health services in particular. Questions that address differences in cost of interventions for minority children by specific patterns of disorder and impairment need to be answered. In order to address issues of cost, however, reliable service use and service need data are required. Therefore, an effective means of assessing service use and service need using multiple informants would facilitate data collection. The cost impact of minority children's mental illness on the family or caregiver and the societal cost must also be considered to arrive at total cost of care. An interesting area of focus for such research could be the cost effectiveness of culturally competent clinical and preventive interventions, which make maximum use of original cultural values and community resources.

Epidemiological research on culturally diverse children can be instrumental in improving the mental health services received. Such research can help increase the understanding of the causes and development of mental health disorders in this special population. Epidemiological research must expand the focus to include gathering information on need, availability, and effectiveness of services for minority children. The prevalence and incidence data provided by epidemiological research involving minority children should be the basis for planning and designing culturally effective prevention services and interventions. The ultimate goal of epidemiological research should be prescriptive and relevant to policy making. The end results of focused research on culturally diverse children should be specific intervention modalities, the derivation of which is based on a consideration of unique socioecological and socioeconomic factors.

REFERENCES

Aboud, F. (1977). Interest in ethnic information: A cross-cultural developmental study. *Canadian Journal of Behavioral Science, 9*, 134–146.

Achenbach, T. (1991). *Achenbach 1991 manual for the Child Behavior Checklist and 1991 profile*. Burlington: University of Vermont, Department of Psychiatry.

Achenbach, T., Bird, H., Canino, G., Phares, V., Gould, M., & Rubio-Stipec, M. (1990). Epidemiological comparison of Puerto Rican and U.S. mainland children: Parent, teacher, and self-reports. *Journal of American Academy of Child and Adolescent Psychiatry, 29*(1), 84–93.

American Psychiatric Association. (1994). *Diagnostic and statistical manual of mental disorders* (4th ed.). Washington, DC: Author.

Aoki, S., Suzuki, S., & Yanai, H. (1974). A new trial of making a health and personality inventory: THPI. *Japanese Journal of Behavior Metrics, 2*, 41–53.

Bean, J. (1996, April). *Add maps to your data analysis tool kit*. Paper presentation at the 9th Annual Research Conference, Florida Mental Health Institute, Tampa.

Beiser, M., & Attneave, C. (1982). Mental disorders among Native American children: Rates and risk periods for entering treatment. *American Journal of Psychiatry, 139*(2), 193–198.

Biafora, F., Warheit, G., Vega, W., & Gil, A. (1994). Stressful life events and changes in substance use among a multiracial/ethnic sample of adolescent boys. *Journal of Community Psychology, 22*, 296–311.

Bird, H., Gould, M., Rubio-Stipec, M., Staghezza, B., & Canino, G. (1991). Screening for childhood psychopathology in the community using the Child Behavior Checklist. *Journal of American Academy of Child and Adolescent Psychiatry, 30*(1), 116–123.

Board on Children and Families, National Research Council, Institute of Medicine. (1995). Immigrant children and their families: Issues for research and policy. *Critical Issues for Children and Youths, 5*(2), 72–89.

Bui, K., & Takeuchi, D. (1992). Ethnic minority adolescents and the use of community mental health care services. *American Journal of Community Psychology, 20*(4), 403–417.

Burns, B. (1994). The challenge of child mental health services research. *Journal of Emotional and Behavioral Disorders, 2*(4), 254–259.

Canino, I., Rubio-Stipec, M., Canino, G., & Escobar, J. (1992). Functional somatic symptoms: A cross-ethnic comparison. *American Journal of Orthopsychiatry, 62*(4), 605–612.

Canino, I.A., & Spurlock, J. (1994). *Culturally diverse children and adolescents: Assessment, diagnosis, and treatment* (pp. 1–34). New York: Guilford Press.

Cervantes, R., & Arroyo, W. (1994). DSM-IV: Implications for Hispanic children and adolescents. *Hispanic Journal of Behavioral Sciences, 16*(1), 8–27.

Chang, L., Morrissey, R., & Koplewicz, H. (1995). Prevalence of psychiatric symptoms and their relation to adjustment among Chinese-American youth. *Journal of the American Academy of Child and Adolescent Psychiatry, 34*(1), 91–99.

Clarke, G., Sack, W., & Goff, B. (1993). Three forms of stress in Cambodian adolescent refugees. *Journal of Abnormal Child Psychology, 21*(1), 65–77.

Cohen, R., Parmelee, D., Irwin, L., Weisz, J., Howard, P., Purcell, P., & Best, A. (1990). Characteristics of children and adolescents in a psychiatric hospital and a corrections facility. *Journal of American Academy of Child and Adolescent Psychiatry, 29*(6), 909–913.

Cook, C. (1986). *The Youth Self-Report Hostility Scale.* Unpublished manuscript, Arizona State University, Program for Prevention Research, Tempe.

Costantino, G., Malgady, R., Casullo, M., & Castillo, A. (1991). Cross-cultural standardization of TEMAS in three Hispanic subcultures. *Hispanic Journal of Behavioral Sciences, 13*(1), 48–62.

Costello, E.J., Burns, B., Angold, A., & Leaf, P. (1993). How can epidemiology improve mental health services for children and adolescents? *Journal of American Academy of Child Psychiatry, 32*(6), 1106–1113.

Cross, T., Bazron, B., Dennis, K., & Isaacs, M. (1989). *Towards a culturally competent system of care: Vol. I: A monograph on effective services for minority children who are severely emotionally disturbed.* Washington, DC: Georgetown University Child Development Center, Child and Adolescent Service System Program, Technical Assistance Center.

Cuellar, I., Harris, L., & Jasso, R. (1980). An acculturation scale for Mexican-American and clinical populations. *Hispanic Journal of Behavioral Sciences, 2,* 199–217.

Cuffe, S., Waller, J., Cuccaro, M., Pumariega, A., & Garrison, C. (1995). Race and gender differences in the treatment of psychiatric disorders in young adolescents. *Journal of American Academy of Child and Adolescent Psychiatry, 34*(11), 1536–1543.

Dilworth-Anderson, P., Burton, L., & Turner, W. (1993). The importance of values in the study of culturally diverse families. *Family Relations, 42,* 238–242.

Eyman, R., Boroskin, A., & Hostetter, S. (1977). Use of alternative living plans for developmentally disabled children by minority parents. *Mental Retardation, 15*(1), 21–23.

Eysenck, H.J., & Eysenck, S.B.G. (1968). *Manual for the Eysenck Personality Inventory.* San Diego: Education and Industrial Testing Services.

Fabrega, H., Chul, W., Boster, J., & Mezzich, J. (1990). DSM-III as a systemic culture pattern: Studying intracultural variation among psychiatrists. *Journal of Psychiatric Research, 24*(2), 139–154.

Fabrega, H., Ulrich, R., & Mezzich, J. (1993). Do Caucasian and black adolescents differ at psychiatric intake? *Academy of Child and Adolescent Psychiatry, 32*(2), 407–413.

Finch, S., & Fanshel, D. (1985). Testing the equality of discharge patterns in foster care. *Social Work Research and Abstracts, 21*(3), 3–10.

Flaskerud, J.H., & Hu, L. (1992). Racial/ethnic identity and amount and type of psychiatric treatment. *American Journal of Psychiatry, 149*(3), 379–384.

Garrison, C., Addy, C., Jackson, K., McKeown, R., & Waller, J. (1991). The CES-D as a screen for depression and other psychiatric disorders in adolescents. *Journal of American Academy of Child and Adolescent Psychiatry, 30*(4), 636–641.

Garrison, C., Schoenbach, V., Schluchter, M., & Kaplan, B. (1989). Epidemiology of depressive symptoms in young adolescents. *Journal of American Academy of Child and Adolescent Psychiatry, 28,* 343–351.

Good, B., & Good, M. (1985). The cultural context of diagnosis and therapy: A view from medical anthropology. In M. Miranda (Ed.), *Mental health research in minority communities: Developing of cultural sensitive training programs* (pp. 1–27). Rockville, MD: National Institute of Mental Health.

Goodman, M. (1964). *Race awareness in young children* (Rev. ed.). New York: Collier.

Grossman, J., & Shigaki, I.S. (1994). Investigation of familial and school-based risk factors for Hispanic Head Start children. *American Journal of Orthopsychiatry, 64*(3), 456–467.

Gruber, M. (1980). Inequality in the social services. *Social Service Review, 54*(1), 59–75.

Guillermin, F., Bombardier, C., & Beaton, D. (1993). Cross-cultural adaptation of health-related quality of life measures: Literature review and proposed guidelines. *Journal of Clinical Epidemiology, 46,* 1417–1432.

Halfon, N., Berkowitz, G., & Klee, L. (1992). Mental health service utilization by children in foster care in California. *Pediatrics, 89*(6), 1238–1244.

Harter, S. (1985). *Manual for the Self-Perception Profile for Children.* Unpublished manuscript, University of Denver, Colorado.

Hawkins, J., & Salisbury, B.R. (1983). Delinquency prevention programs for minorities of color. *Social Work Research and Abstracts, 19*(4), 5–12.

Hoberman, H. (1992). Ethnic minority status and adolescent mental health services utilization. *Journal of Mental Health Administration, 19*(3), 246–267.

Holzer, C.E., Shea, B., Swanson, J., Leaf, P., Myers, J., George, L., Weissman, M., & Bednarski, M. (1986, Fall). The increased risk for specific psychiatric disorders among persons of low SES. *American Journal of Social Psychiatry, VI,* 259–271.

Jimenez, R. (1995, April 30–May 3). *Behavioral healthcare trends and the Hispanic workforce: Implications for service, quality, cost, and access.* Keynote address at the Strategic Planning Conference on Hispanic Behavioral Health Workforce Development, Denver.

Kaplan, S., & Busner, J. (1992). A note on racial bias in the admission of children and adolescents to state mental health facilities versus correctional facilities in New York. *American Journal of Psychiatry, 149*(6), 768–772.

Kilgus, M., Pumariega, A., & Cuffe, S. (1995). Influence of race on diagnosis in adolescent psychiatric inpatients. *Journal of American Academy of Child and Adolescent Psychiatry, 34*(1), 167–172.

Kinzie, J.D., Leung, P.K., Boehnlein, J., & Matsunaga, D. (1992). Psychiatric epidemiology of an Indian village. *Journal of Nervous and Mental Disorders, 180*(1), 33–39.

Knight, G., Virdin, L., Ocampo, K., & Roosa, M. (1994). An examination of the cross-ethnic equivalence of measures of negative life events and mental health among Hispanic and Anglo-American children. *American Journal of Community Psychology, 22*(6), 767–783.

Kovacs, M. (1980/1981). *Rating scales to assess depression in school-aged children. Acta Paedopsychiatrica, 46,* 437–457.

Leff, J. (1988). *Psychiatry around the globe: A transcultural view* (2nd ed., Parts I & II). London: Gaskell.

Lewis, D., Balla, D., & Shanok, S. (1979). Some evidence of race bias in the diagnosis and treatment of the juvenile offender. *American Journal of Orthopsychiatry, 49*, 53–61.

Lewis, D., Shanok, S., Cohen, R., Kligfeld, M., & Frisone, G. (1980). Race bias in the diagnosis and disposition of violent adolescents. *American Journal of Psychiatry, 137*, 1211–1216.

Lindsey, K., & Paul, G. (1989). Involuntary commitments to public mental institutions: Issues involving the overrepresentation of blacks and assessment of relevant functioning. *Psychological Bulletin, 106*(2), 171–183.

Longres, J., & Torrecilha, R. (1992). Race and the diagnosis: Placement and exit status of children and youth in a mental health and disability system. *Journal of Social Service Research, 15*(3-4), 43–63.

Malgady, R., & Rogler, L. (1993). Mental health status among Puerto Ricans, Mexican Americans, and non-Hispanic whites: The case of the misbegotten hypothesis. *American Journal of Community Psychology, 21*(3), 383–395.

Malgady, R., Rogler, L., & Costantino, G. (1987). Ethnocultural and linguistic bias in mental health evaluation of Hispanics. *American Psychologist, 42*(3), 228–234.

Mason, M., & Gibbs, J. (1992). Patterns of adolescent psychiatric hospitalization: Implications for social policy. *American Journal of Orthopsychiatry, 62*(3), 447–457.

McLeod, J., & Shanahan, M. (1993, June). Poverty, parenting, and children's mental health. *American Sociological Review, 58*, 351–366.

Mech, E. (1983). Out of home placement rates. *Social Services Review, 57*, 659–667.

Murray, H. (1943). *Thematic Apperception Test manual.* Cambridge, MA: Harvard University Press.

Neighbors, H.W. (1984). The distribution of psychiatric morbidity in Black Americans: A review and suggestions for research. *Community Mental Health Journal, 20*, 169–181.

Porrata, J. (1995). Scores on psychoticism of adolescent girls in Puerto Rico. *Psychological Reports, 76*, 808–810.

Portes, A.J., & Rumbaut, R. (1990). *Immigrant America.* Berkeley: University of California Press.

Pumariega, A.J. (1996). Culturally competent outcome evaluation in systems of care for children's mental health. *Journal of Child and Family Studies, 5*(4), 1–14.

Pumariega, A.J., Atkins, L., Hardin, S., Montgomery, L., Kowalski, T., & Culley, D. (1996). Psychopathology and symptomatology in incarcerated versus hospitalized youth. In C. Liberton, K. Kutash, & R.M. Friedman (Eds.), *The 8th Annual Research Conference Proceedings: A system of care for children's mental health expanding the research base* (pp. 217–222). Tampa, FL: University of South Florida, Florida Mental Health Institute, Research and Training Center for Children's Mental Health.

Pumariega, A.J., Holliday, B., & Holzer, C. (1995). *Conceptual paradigms in support of mental health research in immigrant and ethnic minority populations* (Research Institute Technical Reports series). Alexandria, VA: National Association of State Mental Health Program Directors.

Pumariega, A.J., Holzer, C.E., & Nguyen, H. (1993). Utilization of mental health service in a tri-ethnic sample. In A. Pumariega, C.E. Holzer, & H. Nguyen (Eds.), *Proceedings of the 3rd Annual Conference of the State Mental Health Agency Research* (pp. 214–222). Alexandria, VA: National Association of State Mental Health Directors Research Institute.

Pumariega, A.J., Holzer, C., & Swanson, J. (1991). Cross-ethnic comparison of youth self-report of behavioral symptomatology. *Proceedings of the Annual Meeting of the American Academy of Child and Adolescent Psychiatry, VII,* NR-119.

Pumariega, A.J., Johnson, N., & Cuffe, S. (1996). The influence of race and gender on depressive and substance abuse symptoms in high-risk adolescents. *Cultural Diversity and Mental Health, 2*(3), 1–9.

Pumariega, A.J., Johnson, N., & Sheridan, D. (1995). Emotional disturbance and substance abuse in youth placed in residential group homes. *Journal of Mental Health Administration, 22*(4), 426–432.

Pumariega, A.J., Swanson, J., Holzer, C., Linskey, A., & Quintero-Salinas, R. (1992). Cultural context and substance abuse in Hispanic adolescents. *Journal of Child and Family Studies, 1*(1), 75–92.

Radloff, L.S. (1977). The CES-D Scale: A self-report depression scale for research in the general population. *Applied Psychological Measurement, 1,* 385–401.

Reiger, D.A., Myers, J.K., Kramer, M., Robins, L.N., Blazer, D.G., Hough, R.L., Eaton, W.W., & Locke, B.Z. (1984). The NIMH epidemiologic catchment area program: Historical context, major objectives, and population characteristics. *Archives of General Psychiatry, 41,* 934–941.

Robbins, M.L. (1994). Native American perspective. In J.U. Gordon (Ed.), *Managing multiculturalism in substance abuse services* (pp. 148–176). Thousand Oaks, CA: Sage Publications.

Roberts, R., & Chen, Y. (1995). Depressive symptoms and suicidal ideation among Mexican origin and Anglo adolescents. *Journal of American Academy of Child and Adolescent Psychiatry, 34*(1), 81–90.

Roberts, R., & Sobhan, M. (1992). Symptoms of depression in adolescence: A comparison of Anglo, African, and Hispanic Americans. *Journal of Youth and Adolescence, 21*(6), 639–651.

Rogler, L. (1989). The meaning of culturally sensitive research in mental health. *American Journal of Psychiatry, 146,* 296–303.

Rogler, L. (1996, May). Framing research on culture in psychiatric diagnosis: The case of the DSM-IV. *Psychiatry, 59,* 145–155.

Rogler, L., Cortes, D., & Malgady, R. (1994). The mental health relevance of idioms of distress: Anger and perceptions of injustice among New York City Puerto Ricans. *Journal of Nervous and Mental Diseases, 182,* 327–330.

Rosenthal, D. (1987). Ethnic identity development in adolescents. In J.S. Phinney & M.J. Rotheram (Eds.), *Children's ethnic socialization: Pluralism and development* (pp. 156–179). Thousand Oaks, CA: Sage Publications.

Rubio-Stipec, M., Bird, H., Canino, G., & Gould, M. (1990). The internal consistency and concurrent validity of a Spanish translation of the Child Behavior Checklist. *Journal of Abnormal Child Psychology, 18*(4), 393–406.

Sack, W., Clarke, G., Him, C., Dickson, D., Goff, B., Lanham, K., & Kinzie, D. (1993). A 6-year follow-up study of Cambodian refugee adolescents traumatized as children. *Journal of American Academy of Child and Adolescent Psychiatry, 32*(2), 431–437.

Scherer, D., Brondino, M., Henggeler, S., Melton, G., & Hanley, J. (1994). Multisystemic family preservation therapy: Preliminary findings from a study of rural and minority serious adolescent offenders. *Journal of Emotional and Behavioral Disorders, 2*(4), 198–206.

Seaberg, J., & Tolley, E. (1986). Predictors of the length of stay in foster care. *Social Work Research and Abstracts, 22*(3), 11–17.

Shaffer, D., Schwab-Stone, M., Fisher, P., Cohen, P., Piacenti, J., Davies, M., Conners, K., & Regier, D. (1993). The Diagnostic Interview Schedule for Children–Revised Version (DISC–R): I. Preparation, field testing, interrater reliability, and acceptability. *Journal of American Academy of Child and Adolescent Psychiatry, 32*(3), 643–650.

Shrout, P., Canino, G., Bird, H., Rubio-Stipec, M., Bravo, M., & Burnam, M. (1992). Mental health status among Puerto Ricans, Mexican-Americans, and non-Hispanic whites. *American Journal of Community Psychology, 20*(6), 729–752.

Shyne, A. (1980). Who are the children? A national overview. *Social Work Research and Abstracts, 16*(1), 26–33.

Shyne, A., & Schroeder, A. (1978). National Study of Social Services to Children and their Families. Department of Health, Education, and Welfare, Office of Human Development Services Administration on Children. *Youth, and Families, Children's Bureau, National Center for Child Advocacy, 6,* 26.

Srole, L., Langner, T.S., Michael, S.T., Opler, M.D., & Rennie, T.C. (1962). *Mental health in the metropolis: The Mid-Manhattan Study* (Vol. 1). New York: McGraw-Hill.

Swanson, J., Linskey, A., Quintero-Salinas, R., Pumariega, A., & Holzer, C. (1992). A binational school survey of depressive symptoms, drug use, and suicidal ideation. *Journal of American Academy of Child and Adolescent Psychiatry, 31*(4), 669–678.

Takeuchi, D., Roberts, R., & Suzuki, S. (1994). Depressive symptoms among Japanese and American adolescents. *Psychiatry Research, 53,* 259–274.

Thornton, S., & Garret, K. (1995). Ethnography as a bridge to multicultural practice. *Journal of Social Work Education, 31*(1), 67–74.

Trautman, P., Rotherram-Borus, M., Dopkins, S., & Lewin, N. (1991). Psychiatric diagnoses in minority female adolescent suicide attempters. *Journal of American Academy of Child and Adolescent Psychiatry, 30*(4), 617–622.

U.S. Bureau of the Census. (1986). *Statistical abstract of the United States 1987* (107th ed.). Washington, DC: U.S. Department of Commerce.

Vega, W. (1992). Theoretical and pragmatic implications of cultural diversity for community research. *American Journal of Community Psychology, 20*(3), 375–391.

Vega, W., Gil, A., Warheit, G., Apospori, E., & Zimmerman, R. (1993). The relationship of drug use to suicide ideation and attempts among African-American, Hispanic, and white non-Hispanic male adolescents. *Suicide and Life-Threatening Behavior, 23*(2), 110–119.

Vega, W., & Rumbaut, R. (1991). Ethnic minorities and mental health. *Annual Review of Sociology, 17,* 351–383.

Westendorp, F., Brink, K., Roberson, M., & Ortiz, I. (1986). Variables which differentiate placement of adolescents into juvenile justice or mental health systems. *Adolescence, 21,* 23–35.

Wierson, M., & Forehand, R. (1995). Predicting recidivism in juvenile delinquents: The role of mental health diagnoses and the qualification of conclusions by race. *Behavior Research Therapy, 33*(1), 63–67.

Williams, D., Takeuchi, D., & Adair, R. (1992, September). Socioeconomic status and psychiatric disorder among blacks and whites. *Social Forces, 71,* 179–194.

Windle, C., Jacobs, J.H., & Sherman, P.S. (1986). *Mental health program performance measurement.* Rockville, MD: National Institute of Mental Health, ADAMHA, Division of Biometry and Applied Science.

Wrobel, N., & Lachar, D. (1995). Racial differences in adolescent self-report: A comparative validity study using homogeneous MMPI content measures. *Psychological Assessment, 7*(2), 140–147.

Yates, A. (1987). Current status and future directions of research on the American Indian Child. *American Journal of Psychiatry, 144*(9), 1135–1142.

Zahner, G., Pawelkiewicz, W., DeFrancesco, J., & Adnopoz, J. (1992). Children's mental health service needs and utilization patterns in an urban community: An epidemiological assessment. *Journal of American Academy of Child and Adolescent Psychiatry, 31*(5), 951–960.

Conceptual, Methodological, and Statistical Issues in Culturally Competent Research

Ana Mari Cauce,
Nora Coronado, and Jennifer Watson

The rapid demographic shifts that have taken place in the United States present opportunities and challenges both to mental health service providers and to researchers. The opportunities lie in the possibility of creating a more comprehensive knowledge base that can better inform mental health policies. The challenges lie in the need to revamp present methods of inquiry to better reflect the increasingly multicultural nature of American society. To what degree do current research models apply to diverse ethnocultural groups? How can *ethnicity* be defined in a more meaningful manner? When should preexisting instruments be used in research, and when should such measures be adapted or replaced by newly constructed ones? How should results be interpreted to best reflect the lives of the individuals whom researchers have studied? What types of research strategies come closest to reflecting the needs of those communities that have historically lacked social and economic capital and access to political power?

These questions are ones that researchers striving for cultural competence must ask themselves and that this chapter addresses. In doing so, it is important to keep in mind that how one designs and conducts research is at once a scientific and a sociopolitical process. Historically, scientific and sociopolitical research processes have not been benign in

---

The term *ethnocultural group* is used in this chapter to denote the fact that, in the United States, culture is viewed as largely embedded within ethnic groups. That is, for example, the term *Latinos* is typically used to denote both a cultural group and an ethnic group. However, because at times the term *ethnocultural group* becomes cumbersome, it is used interchangeably herein with *ethnic group*. The primary ethnocultural groups referred to in this chapter are African Americans, Latinos, Asian Americans, and Native Americans.

their consequences for people of color. Nowhere is this more obvious than in an examination of the conceptual models that have traditionally been used to examine cultural diversity in mental health research.

CONCEPTUAL ISSUES IN ETHNIC MINORITY RESEARCH

Research expressly designed to address questions of cultural diversity was carried out throughout the 20th century. The debates about immigration policy in the early 1900s were a catalyst for a surge of research activity addressing the intelligence of diverse European immigrant groups as well as African Americans and Mexican Americans (Cauce & Jacobson, 1981; Kamin, 1974).

In the earliest work (cf. Kamin, 1974), issues concerning ethnic minorities were typically conceptualized from the perspective of cultural deviance. The cultural deviance model views ethnic minorities from the perspective of traditional White cultural patterns and lifestyles. In the cultural deviance model of ethnographic research, any difference or deviation from the generic White mold is viewed as a culturally deviant and inferior adaptation. This view of inferiority or deviance is in turn generally attributed to cultural disadvantage or deprivation. For example, in Frazier's (1939/1966) analysis of African American families, the apparent absence of male involvement in family life was attributed to the culturally corrosive remnants of slavery, which Frazier believed led to these families' fragmentation. In a more recent, infamous example, Moynihan (1965) placed the blame for differences between African American and White families on a tangle of pathology spawned by an African American culture of poverty.

In the late 1950s and early 1960s, during the early stages of the Civil Rights movement, and afterward, ethnic minorities began to view their unique features in an increasingly positive light. The ubiquitous phrase "Black is beautiful" captured African Americans' awakening pride in self and culture of that period. In light of the more positive evaluation of minority cultures developing during the Civil Rights era, the cultural deviance model began to give way to the cultural equivalence model. At the heart of the cultural equivalence model is the acknowledgment by researchers and social critics that the superior socioeconomic status of Whites accorded them many of the advantages that the cultural deviance research perspective attributed to culture. From the cultural equivalence perspective, for example, the relative absence of husbands and fathers in African American family life would be interpreted largely in economic terms. The profound economic changes and dislocations that have occurred since the 1950s, which left a relatively high proportion of African American men unemployed or employed at wages that were too low to support their families (Wyche, 1993), would be viewed as the key causal agent in the so-called disintegration of the African American family. Although no one author has been as identified with the cultural equivalence perspective as Moynihan was identified with the cultural deviance perspective, the cultural equivalence perspective has infused the work of many researchers and theorists in the 1990s. For example, it is at the center of McLoyd's (1990) highly influential review on the effects of poverty on ethnic minority families, one of the most widely cited social science publications in the 1990s.

There are many data to support an economic interpretation of African American–White, Native American–White, or Latino–White cultural differences. Most noteworthy is that most of these differences decrease or entirely disappear once socioeconomic differences are controlled for, whether experimentally or statistically. The cultural equivalence model is attractive to reform-minded researchers because it moves the valence of causation for majority–minority differences from a source within the cultures themselves to one outside the cultures. Thus, greater equity among ethnocultural groups can be achieved, at least in theory, without substantially altering those aspects that make ethnic cultures unique.

Although researchers who use the cultural equivalence model take a more benign and progressive stance toward ethnic minority cultures than those who use the cultural deviance model, some researchers (e.g., Dickerson, 1995) believe that the cultural equivalence model implicitly accepts the notion that White cultural styles are superior to those of African Americans (or other people of color). These researchers have argued that the cultural equivalence model suggests that ethnic minorities would emulate or assimilate to White norms if it were not for external barriers. For example, a cultural equivalence model assumes that African American women would live in nuclear family units and marry in numbers parallel to White women if there were an equivalent pool of financially secure, marriageable men available.

In contrast to both the cultural deviance and cultural equivalence models, researchers who use the cultural variance model are most apt to interpret the differences between African Americans and Whites in terms of African American cultural resilience in the face of White oppression. Their resilience is most often attributed to the remaining influence of indigenous African cultures on African American modes of adaptation and survival. From the cultural variance perspective, differences in African American and White marriage rates are interpreted in light of the fact that African American families are more matriarch focused and based on values rooted in West African traditions, with a greater emphasis on consanguineous relationships as opposed to marriage-based ones (Dickerson, 1995; Sudarkasa, 1981, 1988).

Thus, the cultural variance perspective shares with the cultural deviance model an emphasis on culturally rooted, internal explanations for differences between African American and White cultures. Unlike the cultural deviance model and more similar to the cultural equivalence model, however, researchers who adopt the cultural variance perspective view cultural differences as adaptations to largely external forces. These external forces are viewed as being oppressive in both an economic and a political sense (e.g., the dominance of Eurocentrism). In contrast to both models, the unique adaptations that African Americans make in the face of such forces are generally viewed as strengths stemming in part from a rich and complex West African heritage. Proponents of an Afrocentric perspective are most closely identified with the cultural variance model (Asante, 1987, 1988; Asante & Asante, 1990). There is no direct equivalent of Afrocentrism among other ethnic minority groups. However, when the parenting styles of East Asians are described as *chiao shun,* or training, and are linked to the Confucian tradition (Chao, 1994) or when the self-sacrificing approach to motherhood of Latinas, known as *marianismo,* is viewed as a culturally unique attempt to mimic the Virgin Mary (Ginorio, Guittierrez, Cauce, & Acosta, 1996), the cultural variance perspective of the researcher is implied.

When conducting research that compares ethnic minorities with Whites, differences will surely be found. As noted elsewhere in this book, there are differences between ethnic minorities and Whites in rates of mental illness, help seeking for mental health–related problems, and use of inpatient and outpatient mental health or related services. However, it is inappropriate to simplistically equate such differences with cultural inferiority or deviance or with impairments.

The different, only partially overlapping, socioecological niches that different ethnic groups occupy in the United States require different adaptations. Referring to the higher rates of substance abuse–related problems and other delinquent behaviors in some ethnic minority groups, Rhodes and Jason noted that researchers should be careful not to conclude that these necessarily reflect "a deficit in the person rather than one possible response that any healthy, adequately functioning individual might have to the disordered or developmentally hazardous environmental conditions they confront" (1990, p. 396, cited in Collins, 1995, pp. 33–34). The same caution applies when attributing the causes of impairments to the individuals' cultures.

The frameworks or models used to interpret cultural differences are enormously important because they can greatly influence how researchers view interventions and policies. For example, a policy that one might develop to reintegrate African American men into family life would differ depending on whether the policy maker believed that their absence from family life resulted from economic forces, was inherent in African Americans' culture, or was a by-product of a culture of poverty that had been internalized. Similarly, the types of programs that policy makers would develop to address substance abuse among rural, southwestern Latino youth would differ vastly depending on whether they believed that such substance abuse was caused by a fundamental flaw in Latino culture; the risky environments in which many Latino youth grow up; or Latino independence and pride in the face of Whites' destruction of their traditional, agriculturally based lifestyles. How one conceptualizes research is more than just of theoretical interest; it has an enormous influence on how researchers think about solutions to social problems.

It is important to be aware of the underlying assumptions that guide researchers' explanations of cultural differences. However, no one particular model of ethnographic research for interpreting cultural differences is endorsed in this chapter. Both the cultural equivalence and cultural variance models can be helpful in understanding the unique adaptations that people of color have forged in the face of economic and social adversity. Such adversity represents a potential source of challenge and risk for people of color. When those challenges or risks are overcome, people of color become stronger. When those challenges cannot be overcome, people of color often experience self-doubt and vulnerability. These strengths or vulnerabilities and how they lead to and/or exacerbate mental health problems can be identified, understood, and studied at the interface between individuals and their cultures rather than at the macro level of an entire cultural or ethnic group. Studying people of color is most readily done when research strategies are used that eschew simplistic, minority group–dominant group cultural comparisons. In fact, a problem that is equally serious with regard to the use of inappropriate models for interpreting ethnic groups' differences is researchers' overreliance on the ethnocultural group comparative research design.

What Is Wrong with Comparative Research Designs

In the mid-1960s, the noted methodologist Campbell (1976), who few would describe as a proponent of superficial political correctness, noted that an overreliance on designs featuring cultural group comparisons would lead to ethnic stereotyping. Landrine did not mince words when she stated that "reporting ethnic differences without theoretical explanation belittles culture and simultaneously exploits it as a commodity for publication purposes and career advancement in the zeitgeist of multiculturalism" (1995, p. 1).

The stated goal of most researchers when they conduct ethnic group comparisons is to identify and understand differences or similarities across groups. All too often in these comparisons, however, ethnic group membership is used simply as a marker for a variety of conditions such as socioeconomic status, education, and language. Sometimes it also stands in for more complex constructs and processes such as discrimination and culture itself (Fullilove & Fullilove, 1995; Wilkinson & King, 1987).

The worst ethnic group comparison research is also the weakest form of social science research: data collection and analyses without a priori hypotheses and the interpretation of study results without theory-driven explanatory models (see subsequent section "Data Analysis in Services Research" for further discussion). Because human services research, particularly that which includes understudied ethnocultural samples, can have important social, political, and policy implications, it is crucial that it be based on the best that science has to offer, not the worst.

In the 1990s, some researchers (see, e.g., Betancourt & Lopez, 1993) have argued that ethnic group comparisons should not be done at all unless measures of culture and ethnicity are included in the research and unless an explicit theoretical framework for understanding the results of such comparisons is presented. Their argument is based in large part on the idea that when ethnocultural differences are found, researchers cannot always be sure what those differences mean. Neither can researchers tell whether the results of such research reflect cultural bias in assessment measures, selection of study participants, and analysis and/or interpretation of the results. In short, these researchers suggested that, in many and possibly most cases, cross-ethnicity group comparisons are neither valid nor meaningful. Although there is unquestionably much truth in this suggestion, calls for a ban on ethnic group comparisons are premature and akin to "throwing out the baby with the bath water." It is ironic that such calls come precisely at a time when researchers funded by the National Institute of Mental Health are increasingly pressured to conduct such analyses.

Can cross-ethnicity comparisons be meaningful and valid? Should they be conducted? The answer to both questions is a qualified and circumscribed "yes." The identification of ethnic group differences through comparative research designs can offer researchers important clues about areas that deserve more careful study using other strategies. This identification of ethnic group differences may be the case even when there is no clear reason to expect differences or when only cursory information about ethnicity is collected. For example, epidemiology is a field often criticized for its atheoretical approach, yet there is little doubt that its strict empiricism is behind some of the most influential theoretical advances in developmental psychopathology.

In children's mental health services and evaluation research, it is important, when feasible, to examine whether mental health programs or interventions can adequately serve ethnic minority group members. Knowing all that can be known about when and under what conditions children's mental health services are effective or unsuccessful for a culturally diverse clientele is the key to developing better community mental health programs. Research examining differential rates of mental health problems across ethnic groups may also be helpful to mental health policy makers developing plans to better serve their constituencies in the 21st century. Thus, under circumscribed conditions and as part of programmatic research, comparative research can play a positive role vis-à-vis ethnic minorities.

The problem with culturally competent research is not with cross-ethnicity comparative designs per se, but with its almost exclusive dependence on cross-ethnicity comparative designs as the dominant paradigm for the study of ethnic minorities. Speculative conclusions are often based on such research designs. Findings with regard to ethnic groups' differences that are based on such research designs are often not followed up with more focused and more culturally sensitive designs that would help researchers understand what such differences mean. The finding that Latino youth, for example, have higher high school dropout rates than White youth should launch a research program, not conclude it.

ASSESSMENT AND MEASUREMENT ISSUES

Three central questions face almost any mental health researcher in designing a culturally competent research program, regardless of its specific content area:

1. How should *ethnicity* be defined?
2. How should researchers select or construct measures?
3. Do the same measurement instruments have the same meanings in various ethnic groups?

Each of these questions is addressed in turn in the subsections that follow.

Assessment of Ethnicity in Mental Health Services

In most research, ethnicity is measured via individuals' self-identification of ethnic group membership. Typically, when face-to-face interviews are conducted, individuals' self-identification of ethnic group membership is accomplished by asking individuals to which racial and/or ethnic group they belong. When questionnaires are used, individuals are instead asked to check the box or boxes representing their racial and/or ethnic group.

When this information is gathered in a way that parallels the U.S. Bureau of the Census data, five broad ethnic and racial groups are derived: African American, Asian/Pacific Islander, Hispanic, Native American, and Non-Hispanic White. Thirteen more narrow categories can also be derived: Asian Indian, Chinese, Cuban, Hawaiian, Japanese, Korean, Mexican, Non-Hispanic African American, Non-Hispanic White, Pilipino, Puerto Rican, Vietnamese, and Other. Researchers working in different regions of the United States typically deviate somewhat from this schema. For example, in New York, it would make much more sense to include Dominican as a separate category; in Miami, a researcher would have Haitian and Jamaican categories; and in Seattle, specific categories for Cambodians, Laotians, and Pilipinos would be appropriate. Researchers should also seriously consider letting individuals identify with more than one category, thus allowing for classification into mixed-ethnicity groups.

Regardless of which specific schema is used, however, the resulting categories are crude approximations of ethnicity, which is, after all, a social construct. Knowing with which specific group an individual identifies at best hints at the cultural practices and social norms to which he or she adheres. It is not appropriate to base research or social policy on hints. If researchers want to more fully understand the roles of ethnicity and culture in shaping individuals' mental health care needs, choices, and desires or abilities to participate in interventions and profit from those interventions, they need to assess ethnocultural constructs in a manner that more directly provides them with the information that they need.

Entwistle and Astone (1994) suggested a good first step toward establishing better ethnocultural constructs in their guidelines for measuring youth's race/ethnicity and socioeconomic status. Among the core set of ethnicity measures that they set forth, Entwistle and Astone suggested that researchers collect data such as whether children's parents were born in the United States and at what age they came to the United States. If one is working with adults, one should obtain analogous information by asking them questions about their parents and about themselves. This extra bit of information allows one to determine the individual's generational status for individuals whose families are relatively recent immigrants to the United States. Such questions also allow one to gauge whether English is the individual's primary language and whether the individual learned English early in life. The individual's answers to these questions provide important information about the degree of caution that may be necessary in interpreting information gathered by using English-language questionnaires or experimental instructions.

Another step toward establishing better ethnocultural constructs is to measure individuals' ethnic identities and/or acculturation. Such measures should routinely be included in studies in which ethnicity and culture are a central focus or are likely to be called on in the planned interpretation of results. (A full discussion of these multidimensional constructs and the measures developed to gauge them is beyond the scope of this chapter; see Phinney, 1990, for an excellent review.) Such measures generally assess the degree to which individuals participate in prototypical cultural events or activities (e.g., belongs to an African American church, celebrates Cinco de Mayo), affiliate with others of the same ethnicity, and have knowledge of or take pride in their ethnic groups' histories.

The comprehensive assessment of ethnicity can prove invaluable in understanding the role of ethnicity in ethnic groups' differences. For example, assume that a study finds that, given equivalent levels of family discord, Whites are more apt than Puerto Ricans to seek out mental health services for their families. If Puerto Rican cultural norms about family privacy are the reason for lower levels of help seeking among Puerto Ricans, then one would assume that those Puerto Ricans with stronger ethnic affiliations and identities would be less apt to seek out mental health services than Puerto Ricans with lower levels of ethnic identity. However, if there were no relation between ethnic identity or acculturation and utilization of mental health services within the Puerto Rican group, the explanation for the White–Puerto Rican difference is apt to lie in factors other than ethnicity and culture. Instead, socioeconomic differences between Whites and Puerto Ricans might be responsible for the difference, or the community's mental health centers might be located in areas that are less accessible for Puerto Ricans than for Whites.

Although not directly related to the assessment of ethnicity, in studies in which ethnicity or culture is a central factor, it also makes a great deal of sense to assess variables that are apt to be related to the phenomenon of interest and that are typically confounded with ethnicity. Socioeconomic status most readily comes to mind as one such variable. Given the strong association between socioeconomic status and ethnicity in the United States, it is critical that such effects be examined before any ethnic differences found are attributed to ethnicity. If one were to find that boys in private schools performed better on an achievement test than girls in public schools, it would be unlikely that researchers would blithely attribute that difference to gender. Neither should researchers attribute ethnic groups' differences to their ethnicities when the groups examined vary substantially by socioeconomic status.

Family structure and neighborhood factors such as crime rates are other variables that are often confounded with ethnicity in the United States. For example, crack cocaine smoking was found to be more prevalent among African Americans and Hispanic Americans than among Whites (Lillie-Blanton, Anthony, & Schuster, 1993). However, when a series of neighborhood factors were examined, these differences disappeared. The researchers in that study concluded that social conditions rather than ethnicity had accounted for the ethnic group differences that they had found. Indeed, precisely because it is so difficult to account for the host of factors associated with ethnicity in the United States, within-ethnic-group designs are often recommended by researchers who are concerned with cultural competence (Betancourt & Lopez, 1993; Cauce & Gonzales, 1993; Hughes, Seidman, & Williams, 1993).

Cultural Equivalence of Measurements

A crucial consideration in conducting research with ethnic minority and multiethnic samples is the design and selection of measures and the question of measurement equivalence within and across groups. *Measurement equivalence* refers to the broad question of whether the same assessment tools measure the same underlying constructs across ethnic and cultural groups. Interpretation of any observed ethnic differences will be ambiguous as long as the question of measurement equivalence remains unanswered. A lack of measurement equivalence jeopardizes the validity of interpretations made about the data (Knight, Tein, Shell, & Roosa, 1992).

Cultural equivalence specifically refers to the extent to which measures have the same internal structure and hold similar meanings within and across cultural groups (Helms, 1992). Researchers have identified four kinds of cultural equivalence:

1. Functional
2. Conceptual
3. Linguistic
4. Psychometric or scalar (Lonner, 1986; cf. Helms, 1992)

Functional equivalence exists when scores derived from an assessment device have "similar precursors, consequents, and correlates across groups" (Knight, Virdin, Ocampo, & Roosa, 1994, p. 769). Evidence of the functional equivalence of a measure would exist, for example, if Mexican Americans, African Americans, and Whites were found to endorse items on a depression scale following a bereavement experience; if higher measures on the scale were associated with lower energy levels in all groups; and if individuals in all three groups who scored at the upper end of the scale responded in a similar fashion to antidepressant medication.

Conceptual equivalence refers to the contexts of test items or of experimental tasks. When the context of items or tasks is defined similarly across groups and is equally familiar across groups, conceptual equivalence exists. For example, interaction tasks that ask families to plan a vacation together may be biased against ethnocultural groups that are of lower socioeconomic status and hence are less likely to have experience in planning vacations.

Linguistic equivalence exists when the language in which items on an assessment device are written are understood in the same way across ethnocultural groups. Hughes et al. (1993) noted that, in a study that asked White and Japanese American individuals about either depression or *yuutsu*, the latter being the closest Japanese equivalent of *depression*, the Japanese individuals were more apt to respond with external referents such as *storm* or *dark*, whereas Whites responded with internal referents such as *sad* or *lonely*, suggesting that *depression* and *yuutsu* are not linguistically equivalent (Tanaka-Matsumi & Marsella, 1976). This finding also raised questions about the conceptual equivalence of depression.

In cases in which instruments are being translated into a new language, back translating is the technique most commonly used to establish linguistic equivalence. If one were interested in adapting an English language scale to Tagalog, for example, after the initial English to Tagalog translation, a different person would be asked to translate the Tagalog version back to English. This translation would then be checked against the original English version. Although translation and back translation are standard for establishing linguistic equivalence, they do not necessarily ensure the elimination of all sources of measurement nonequivalence (Candell & Huhn, 1986).

Also worth noting is that linguistic equivalence is important to ascertain even when individuals speak the same language. Different colloquial uses of terms can affect the linguistic equivalence of measures. In order to understand and respond appropriately to the communications of individuals being studied in an assessment of drug abuse among homeless adolescents, Cauce and colleagues (1994) had to consult with individuals who had knowledge of drug-related vernacular used by individuals in that subculture. This consultation was required on a regular basis because such "street language" is fluid and everchanging.

Psychometric or *scalar equivalence* examines whether an assessment device measures the same construct at the same levels (Lonner, 1986).

Scalar equivalence more specifically means that scores on a particular measure of a construct reflect the same level (e.g., magnitude, degree, intensity) of the construct in each ethnocultural group studied (Knight et al., 1994).

Knight and colleagues (1994) illustrated how functional and scalar equivalence can be examined. In their study, the two cultural groups examined were primarily Mexican Americans who spoke English and Whites. The constructs examined were depression, behavior disorders, and self-worth. Measures of each of these elements had been administered to children ages 9–13 years and their mothers as part of larger studies. Two different samples of Mexican Americans and Whites were examined.

In order to establish measurement equivalence, Knight and colleagues first examined the intercorrelations among the various constructs and whether they differed by ethnocultural grouping; they examined the correlation between depression and conduct disorder among Mexican Americans and Whites. Second, the relationship of negative life events, often considered an antecedent or correlate of psychological distress, with each construct was examined. Again, differences in these relationships across ethnocultural groups were assessed after controlling for socioeconomic status. Results generally supported cross-ethnicity equivalence for the measures of depression and behavior disorder. The intercorrelations between the indices of depression and behavior disorder were quite similar for Mexican Americans and Whites. Furthermore, regression analysis assessments of the relationships of negative life events to depression and behavior disorder also supported an interpretation of cross-ethnicity equivalence; both the regression slopes and the intercepts were similar across groups.

In contrast, Knight and colleagues found that the cross-ethnicity equivalence of the self-worth measure was questionable. There was no significant relationship between individuals' life events and their self-worth among the Mexican American children, and the relationship between conduct disorder and self-worth was different for the Mexican American children when compared with either White children or Mexican American children in another sample. Findings such as these are the most difficult to interpret because they leave researchers uncertain about whether such differences are a result of the nonequivalence of measures or the nonequivalence of the underlying psychological processes, whether in the perception, interpretation, or processing of information. In Knight and colleagues' study, nonequivalence in socioeconomic status between Whites and Mexican Americans may have also been an issue because measures of socioeconomic status were not obtained for children in the second sample.

The careful and methodical work done in studies such as that of Knight and colleagues (e.g., Knight et al., 1992; Knight et al., 1994) clearly demonstrate how researchers can ascertain the cultural equivalence of key measures used in children's mental health services. Unfortunately, this type of laborious and unglamorous work is rare. A true test of the maturity of the children's mental health field—and its researchers—may be whether its researchers have the patience to carry out this type of tedious but important work. If researchers do not have confidence in the cultural equivalence of the basic taxonomies and measures that they use in their research, they cannot have confidence in the interpretations of ethnic group differences that they ultimately find.

Interviewers and Raters

Thus far, the discussion in this chapter about cultural equivalence has involved self-report measures or questionnaires. An additional potential source of nonequivalence is introduced when measures are administered, rated, or coded by interviewers or assessors. Survey researchers have conducted numerous studies to assess whether participants give different responses to interviewers of different ethnicities. (For a more complete discussion of such studies, see Cauce, Ryan, & Grove, in press.) When asked race-related questions, African Americans report more negative attitudes toward Whites when the interviewer is African American than when the interviewer is White, and vice versa when Whites are asked about their attitudes toward African Americans. When issues unrelated to race are examined, however, no consistent pattern has been found with regard to the interviewer's ethnicity. Studies specifically addressing this issue in terms of relevant mental health constructs are notably absent.

Another area in which there is a conspicuous absence of research is on the effects of coder or rater ethnicity. Although self-report is the only possible way of assessing many internal thoughts or feelings, it is a methodology fraught with problems, such as respondents' desires to present themselves in a favorable or socially desirable light. For that reason, increasing emphasis has been placed on obtaining information from multiple respondents. In the 1990s, the multiple informant strategy has become the standard in family research, including research that examines the role of family processes as they affect the mental health and well-being of children. Typically, when children or adolescents are studied, information is obtained from one parent or both parents, from the children or adolescents themselves, and from a teacher. In addition, ratings from an outside, objective observer or rater are often used.

At times, the observer or rater may watch children's behavior *in vivo*. For example, an observer may watch the child interacting with other children at a playground. Often, however, the observer watches the child interacting with another person, typically the child's parent, on a videotape. The videotape generally involves the child engaging in a standard task in which all of the other children or families in the study have participated. The use of videotaping methodology allows for greater control of the assessment environment and of the environment demands than does live observation. It also offers the convenience of conducting the actual ratings in the comfort of a laboratory or at home and the advantage of being able to easily have multiple raters assess the same interaction.

In the late 1990s, however, the objectivity of ratings obtained by raters' observing videotapes has been questioned. In a study of inter-observer agreement in the assessment of parental behavior and parent–adolescent conflict, systematic ethnicity-based differences were found in the ways in which videotaped interactions of African American mothers and daughters were rated by independent observers (Gonzales, Cauce, & Mason, 1996). African American observers rated mothers as less controlling and rated the mother–daughter interactions as marked by less conflict than did non–African American, or out group, observers. Furthermore, the ratings of the African American (e.g., in group) observers were more consistent with the perceptions of the mothers and daughters who participated in the interaction.

Such findings suggest that researchers need to address the issue of potential observer effects or biases with regard to ratings that are made by supposedly independent and objective observers. The potential problem of ethnicity-based variance of independent observers may be further magnified when different ethnocultural groups are examined in the same study. For example, assume that the study described in the previous paragraph had included a White sample. If the interactions between White mothers and their daughters had been rated as having less conflict than those between African American mothers and their daughters who were being rated by White observers, researchers would not know whether this result was due to ethnic differences in the interactions themselves or to ethnicity-based differences in how the observers perceived the interactions. The work that is being conducted to examine the cross-ethnicity equivalence of self-report and/or parent report measures of families' functioning and mental health needs is just beginning when measures are based on independent observers' reports.

DATA ANALYSIS IN SERVICES RESEARCH

Data analysis should flow naturally from a study's conceptualization and design. There is no specific analytic technique or set of techniques inherently inappropriate for the analysis of ethnic group differences or the effects of ethnicity on psychological outcomes of interest. Neither are there specific techniques that are inherently more appropriate than others. A determination of the most appropriate analytic technique or set of techniques depends on the theoretical concerns that drive the particular study and the particular questions being asked in the study.

Not too long ago, unless a study explicitly focused on ethnicity, it was almost always conducted with a primarily White sample. If a researcher in Seattle, for example, was interested in whether a specific treatment decreased school behavior problems among children, the researcher would not have thought twice about conducting the study with a convenience sample, typically composed entirely or almost entirely of Whites. As the United States has become more ethnically diverse, homogeneous White samples have become less convenient. In almost all urban areas and in many suburban areas as well, ethnically heterogeneous samples are far more common when nonrestrictive sampling strategies are employed. In addition, the external validity of studies with exclusively White middle-class samples has been called into question. Because of the last issue, grant and journal editors have increasingly begun to demand the examination of ethnically diverse samples as a condition of grant awards and book or article publications.

Thus, as previously noted, in mental health services research and in psychological research more generally, ethnic group comparisons are often conducted for pragmatic rather than theoretical reasons. For example, the previous example of the Seattle researcher who wanted to know whether her program would decrease behavior problems among children would in all likelihood also want to examine whether it worked as effectively for African Americans or Asian Americans as it did for Whites. Those questions might be answered by using analysis of variance (ANOVA) techniques to test whether the groups differed at the outcome on the variable of interest, which in this example is school behavior problems. A repeated measures ANOVA might be used to test whether there were ethnic group differences in the changes in students' behavior problems from baseline to outcome. If no differences were detected, the researcher might well conclude that the program had worked as well for Whites as it had for African Americans and Asian Americans. Everyone would be happily assured that there was no need to worry further about issues related to the cultural competence of the intervention. Forgotten amid all of the congratulations, however, would be two major problems, which are described in the next two paragraphs.

First, as students learn in first-year statistics classes, the null hypothesis can be tested but cannot be proved. In the scenario just described, the between-groups comparisons were conducted with no explicit hypothesis in mind regarding ethnicity. There was no reason to posit that the treatment would work better for Whites than it would for

African Americans or for Asian Americans. In studies of this sort, the most common expectation is that an intervention will work equally well for both groups. All researchers should know that it is bad science to set up a study to test the null hypothesis, yet analyses such as the one described in this section are being carried out in many—perhaps most—of the major intervention outcome studies in the United States. Indeed, many naïvely believe that they will lose their funding if they do not conduct such analyses.

Second, most studies do not have a large enough sample size to allow one to adequately detect ethnic group differences, even in studies in which ethnic group differences do exist. Sample sizes that are large enough to detect small to moderate ethnic group differences—typically about 60 participants per ethnicity, assuming no gender differences—are uncommon in clinical intervention studies. Indeed, in most studies of this nature, ethnic group differences would have to be quite large to be detected. In an effort to circumvent this problem, such researchers place various ethnic minority group members into one non-White group. Rather than fix the problem, however, this practice may compound it.

Not all ethnic minority groups differ from Whites in the same manner, if at all. For example, the academic achievement levels of Asian Americans are generally higher than those of Whites, whereas those of Latinos are lower. Averaging Asian American and Latino achievement test scores before comparing them with those of Whites would mask this fact. There is absolutely no defensible reason for creating these mixed ethnicity groupings unless the purpose is solely and explicitly to examine the effects of racial or ethnic discrimination. Even in that case, whereas most people of color face some similar discriminatory experiences, the nature of the discrimination against and stereotyping of people of color varies considerably between ethnic groups.

As stated previously, it is not necessarily wrong to examine ethnic group differences, even if it is done solely for pragmatic purposes. However, it is important to think through what those purposes are so that research designs and analyses can appropriately reflect them. In the example presented in this chapter and in most other intervention studies like it, the purpose behind the group comparison does not reflect an interest in ethnic differences per se. The purpose of focusing on ethnicity is to determine whether the intervention works across the various ethnic groups studied. Thus, the key question of interest is, Does the intervention work with Whites, Asian Americans, and African Americans? Once this question is viewed as the primary study question, it is quite clear from the outset, during the sample recruitment phase, that it is crucial to ensure that there are enough individuals of each ethnicity to ensure sufficient power for the full set of analyses. If that is not feasible, perhaps a sample comprising only one or two ethnicities should be studied. If more than one ethnic group is retained in the sample on a more exploratory basis, a comparison of effect sizes obtained for each group can be undertaken to better gauge whether effectiveness varied across ethnic groups. However, in all likelihood, the comparison of effect sizes is of only secondary interest.

Separate analyses by ethnic groups would not be necessary to answer whether the intervention had worked in the previous example of the Seattle researcher. In that study, it would be necessary to ensure only that the sample had approximated the proportionate population distribution by ethnicity in Seattle. Often researchers simply check the ethnic distribution in their samples against city or area demographics to ensure that their selection techniques are culturally competent. Unfortunately, although this type of sample selection is the standard sometimes used for grant review purposes, researchers are seldom interested in developing culturally competent, city-specific interventions.

Thus, the problem is not with the statistical techniques used to conduct ethnic group comparisons; ANOVAs, repeated measures ANOVAs, and regression analysis techniques are acceptable ways of comparing results across ethnic groups. The problem is that mental health services or intervention researchers often attempt to assess ethnic group differences post hoc rather than selecting a sample and design that would naturally lend themselves to addressing the question in which researchers are really interested: Does the intervention work with members of each ethnic group that is involved in the study?

Another problem stemming from researchers' failure to clearly conceptualize their research questions is that the conclusions that can be drawn from comparative group designs are overstated. Researchers often conclude that ethnic group differences that they have found are due to ethnicity and/or to culture. As alluded to previously, however, given the overwhelmingly divergent socioecological niches that each ethnic group in the United States inhabits, a host of variables other than ethnicity and culture may be responsible for ethnic group differences. For example, at the ethnic group level, African Americans differ from Whites in myriad ways, including socioeconomic status, family structure and size, neighborhood safety and resources, quality of schooling, experiences of prejudice and discrimination, and attitudes toward mental health help seeking. Any of these factors alone or in combination with each other may better explain ethnic group differences found in psychiatric status or psychological functioning than ethnicity or culture.

Indeed, researchers who are interested in the roles of ethnicity and culture should seriously consider using research designs that allow for more interesting and more complex interpretations than comparative designs. Steinberg and Fletcher (in press), writing about data analytic strategies used in conducting research on ethnic minority youth, noted that it is essential for an individual investigator, before launching into a series of analyses, to ask why ethnicity has been included in a research study and how it might affect the hypotheses to be examined. One often overlooked strategy that Steinberg and Fletcher recommended to researchers who are interested in determining whether ethnic group differences are attributable to ethnicity is the examination of ethnicity as a moderating variable. Using this approach, the emphasis is on examining whether the relationship between a predictor variable or a set of predictor variables and outcome variables is different across ethnic groups (e.g., focusing on differences in regression slopes rather than intercepts). This strategy can better illuminate developmental processes than comparative designs.

Hughes and colleagues (1993) recommended increased use of idiographic methods of data analysis, which can provide richer and more meaningful descriptions of behavior in context. They specifically pointed to the cluster analytic techniques that Rapkin and Luke (1993) used to describe similarities and differences in character profiles of Korean American and Chinese American adolescents. As previously discussed in the section on comparative research designs, within-ethnicity research designs can help researchers understand how culture and ethnic group affiliation affect individuals' behavior when acculturation and ethnic identity are assessed.

CULTURALLY COMPETENT
INTERPRETATIONS OF RESEARCH RESULTS

Sometimes researchers need to move beyond quantitative techniques to really understand how interventions may operate differently within different ethnic groups. Indeed, quantitative methods can obscure as often as they clarify the meanings that superficially similar behaviors may have in different sociocultural contexts. Landrine (1995) described an example of how this disparity can occur. She noted that young, unmarried, heterosexual Latinas are more apt than heterosexual women of other ethnic groups to engage in risky sexual behavior, including unprotected anal intercourse. Some researchers have interpreted this information to suggest that young, unmarried, heterosexual Latinas are less informed than women of other ethnic groups about how the human immunodeficiency virus, which causes acquired immunodeficiency syndrome (AIDS), is transmitted. Hence, the development of culturally tailored AIDS education programs has been viewed as the solution to the problem. Although on the surface such an interpretation and solution appear to be straightforward, a contextual analysis reveals something altogether different. Based on conversations with the young Latinas who engaged in such behavior, Arguello (1993), a former gang member, and her colleagues at the Center for the Study of Latino Health in Los Angeles concluded that, for these young women, engaging in anal intercourse was a premeditated strategy used to meet their boyfriends' demands for sexual intercourse while simultaneously meeting their boyfriends' demands for a wife who was a virgin. In Arguello's sample, the possibility of Latinas' rendering themselves unmarriagable by losing their virginity outweighed their risk of contracting AIDS. Based on that information, the intervention that Arguello developed focused not on AIDS education workshops but instead on feminist workshops focusing on virginity as a form of social control, virginity as oppression, and Latinas' control of their own bodies. Arguello's approach was different from one that would be used in developing an intervention for White gay men who were found to engage in superficially similar behavior. The empirical finding that heterosexual Latinas engaged in unprotected anal sex more often than women of other ethnic groups was the impetus for Arguello's work. It was Arguello's conversations with Latinas, however, that led her to better understand their behavior and thus to develop a culturally competent intervention.

Focus groups can be used to mimic Arguello's strategy. (Ethnographic studies can also be used, but discussion of these is beyond the scope of this chapter.) Focus groups, alone or in conjunction with more traditional approaches, can be a valuable information-gathering method to use when conducting research with people of color. Focus groups can be used throughout the research process as a means of culturally anchoring the research (Hughes & DuMont, 1993). Focus group members can help researchers answer questions about the language that a community uses to talk about psychological constructs of interest to the researcher and how to interpret the answers that community members give. Focus groups can play a key role in making research a more collaborative process. For example, focus group discussions can be conducted repeatedly over time to continually assess whether community members view the research process as legitimate (Knodel, 1993). When members of the community are involved in the research process, their stake in the research is ensured (Hughes & DuMont, 1993; Krueger, 1994). When developing interventions is the goal of research, use of focus group discussions can increase the likelihood that the target community will ultimately adopt the intervention strategy that is developed.

A focus group can empower its members by teaching them new skills and making them feel that they have made a contribution to the research process and ultimately to their community. Focus groups that involve community members benefit the research process by producing an outcome that the community deems worthwhile and trustworthy and also may lead to recommendations by community members that are both practical and useful (Krueger, 1994). Researchers have less of a tendency to misinterpret data when community members are involved in the research process. The benefits of this collaborative, iterative process are especially pronounced for communities of color, which have often viewed traditional research and mental health services as vehicles of oppression rather than as sources of empowerment.

CONCLUSIONS

It is imperative that researchers conduct research on mental health services with people of color. In doing so, however, care and caution are advisable. Researchers usually conduct mental health services research with an eye toward influencing public policies. Such policies may prove to be beneficial for one ethnic group while being detrimental for another. The majority of researchers, whether they are members of the majority or a minority ethnic group, have been trained by an education system that is based on a White world view. Researchers' favored frameworks, constructs, and methodologies reflect their training in that system. It is hard for researchers to move beyond the bias inherent in their education and training background. Unless they do, however, they are apt to continue to conduct research that supports practices that are alien to and alienating of communities of color. For example, children of color have relatively low rates of use of mental health services, given their high rates of need (Srebnik, Cauce, & Baydar, 1996). New modes of participatory research, ethnographic studies, and culturally anchored focus groups can augment researchers' traditional approaches in helping them develop ways to address such disparities. In developing such research approaches, researchers would be wise to keep the following simple guidelines in mind:

1. Explicitly examine the theoretical framework that undergirds the research and its interpretation. Make sure that the research design reflects the theory or framework that informs the research. For example, if, in a study with multiple minority groups, all of the ethnic minority groups were compared with the dominant White group but not with each other (see, e.g., Dornbusch, Ritter, Leiderman,

Roberts, & Fraleigh, 1987), the implication is that the majority group sets the norm; hence, the research would reflect the cultural deviance perspective.

2. If the researcher's interest is in ethnicity, the researcher must define and measure ethnicity in a meaningful manner. To the degree possible, the researcher should also define and measure key constructs such as socioeconomic status that are known to covary by ethnicity. The researcher does not need to define ethnicity in a fine-grained manner if the goal of the research is simply to determine whether an intervention will be successful with a specific ethnic group or even if the research goal is to compare whether a particular intervention will work better with one group than with another. If ethnic group differences are found, however, researchers cannot comfortably attribute them to ethnicity if ethnicity is measured only by group membership.

3. Choose measures that are appropriate for all of the ethnic groups in the study and/or check those measures that are used for their equivalence across groups. When researchers use measures that do not have a history of extensive use with members of the ethnic groups studied in their samples, they must check the reliability and validity of their measures within the ethnic groups represented in their study's sample population. If the measures have been translated, make sure that they are back-translated and then examine the final product to ensure that colloquial expressions and other aspects of the translation are accurate and understandable to the sample population. For example, having someone of Cuban background check a Spanish translation that is to be used with Chicanos is not sufficient.

4. Make sure that analyses reflect study questions, and make sure that the study sample allows for sufficient power to obtain reliable answers. All too often, researchers conduct ethnic group comparative analyses as a matter of course, even if a comparison across ethnic groups is not needed to answer the study's questions. If a researcher is really interested in whether Latinos or African Americans profited from an intervention program as much as Whites did, the researcher should conduct the comparative analysis needed to answer that question. If the researcher's interest is in whether the intervention worked for Latinos and/or African Americans, however, a within-ethnicity research analysis design is more appropriate. In either case, the researcher must make sure that the research sample populations of each ethnicity are large enough to detect small to moderate effect sizes.

5. Researchers must interpret their study results in such a way as to reflect the lives of the people studied. Chances are that White or ethnic minority researchers can draw upon their own experiences or those of their close friends to help them understand findings obtained with White middle-class samples. The less day-to-day experience that such researchers have had or presently have with the ethnic minority populations they study, the less apt they will be to appropriately contextualize their research findings. Focus groups or ethnographic studies can be of invaluable help in the process of contextualizing research. When researchers are not sure how to interpret their findings, they must seek out the expertise of people of similar ethnicities to those in their study's sample populations and listen to what they have to say.

Researchers must strive toward conducting culturally competent research. There is no "gold" standard by which to measure culturally competent research. It cannot be ensured by the researcher's doing X or Y, and it is unlikely that a researcher will achieve it by conducting a particular type of study. The researcher must consider research programmatically, with each study building toward a new one and each one improving a little on the methodology and sensitivity of the previous one. By thinking about the issues raised and attempting to follow the guidelines contained in this chapter, researchers will be on the right track. If, in the first decade of the 21st century, researchers can look back at the best of the research conducted in the late 1990s and understand just how far away from culturally competent it was, it means that progress has been made toward culturally competent research. It is enough to be part of that progress.

REFERENCES

Arguello, M. (1993, February). *Developing outreach programs for AIDS prevention with Latino youth.* Paper presented at the Institute for Health Promotion and Disease Prevention Research, University of Southern California Medical School, Los Angeles.

Asante, M.K. (1987). *The Afrocentric idea.* Philadelphia: Temple University Press.

Asante, M.K. (1988). *Aftocentricity.* Trenton, NJ: Africa World Press.

Asante, M.K., & Asante, K.W. (Eds.). (1990). *African culture: The rhythms of unity.* Trenton, NJ: Africa World Press.

Betancourt, H., & Lopez, S.R. (1993). The study of culture, ethnicity, and race in American psychology. *American Psychologist, 48*(6), 629–637.

Campbell, D.T. (1976). Stereotypes and the perception of group differences. *American Psychologist, 22,* 817–829.

Candell, G.L., & Huhn, C.L. (1986). Cross-language and cross-cultural comparisons in scale translations: Independent sources of information about item nonequivalence. *Journal of Cross-Cultural Psychology, 17,* 417–440.

Cauce, A.M., & Gonzales, N. (1993). Slouching toward culturally competent research: Adolescents and families of color in context. *Focus: Notes from the Society for The Psychological Study of Ethnic Minority Issues, 7*(2), 8–9.

Cauce, A.M., & Jacobson, L.I. (1981). Implicit and incorrect assumptions concerning the assessment of the Latino in the United States. *American Journal of Community Psychology, 8,* 571–586.

Cauce, A.M., Morgan, C.J., Wagner, V., Moore, E., Wurzbacher, K., Weeden, K., Tomlin, S., & Blanchard, T. (1994). Effectiveness of case management for homeless adolescents: Results for the three month follow-up. *Journal of Emotional and Behavioral Development, 2,* 219–227.

Cauce, A.M., Ryan, K., & Grove, K. (in press). Children and adolescents of color where are you? Methodological challenges to the selection, recruitment, and retention of adolescents of color in developmental research. In V. McLoyd & L. Steinberg (Eds.), *Research with ethnic minority adolescents: Methodological issues and challenges.* Thousand Oaks, CA: Sage Publications.

Chao, R. (1994). Beyond parental control and authoritarian parenting style: Understanding Chinese parenting through the cultural notion of training. *Child Development, 65,* 1111–1120.

Collins, L.R. (1995). Issues of ethnicity in research on the prevention of substance abuse. In G.J. Botvin, S.P. Schinke, & M.A. Orlandi (Eds.), *Drug abuse prevention with multiethnic youth* (pp. 28–45). Thousand Oaks, CA: Sage Publications.

Dickerson, B.J. (1995). Centering studies of African American single mothers and their families. In B.J. Dickerson (Ed.), *African American single mothers: Understanding their lives and families* (pp. 43–56). Thousand Oaks, CA: Sage Publications.

Dornbusch, S.M., Ritter, P.L., Leiderman, P.H., Roberts, D.F., & Fraleigh, M.J. (1987). The relation of parenting style to adolescent school performance. *Child Development, 58,* 1244–1257.

Entwistle, D.R., & Astone, N.M. (1994). Some practical guidelines for measuring youth's race/ethnicity and socioeconomic status. *Child Development, 65,* 1521–1540.

Frazier, E.F. (1966). *The Negro family in the United States.* Chicago: University of Chicago Press. (Original work published 1939)

Fullilove, R.E., & Fullilove, M.T. (1995). Conducting research in ethnic minority communities: Considerations and challenges. In G. Botvin, S. Schinke, & M. Orlandi (Eds.), *Drug abuse prevention with multiethnic youth* (pp. 46–56). Thousand Oaks, CA: Sage Publications.

Ginorio, A., Guittierrez, L., Cauce, A.M., & Acosta, M. (1996). The psychology of Latinas. In C. Travis (Ed.), *Feminist perspectives on the psychology of women* (pp. 72–81). Washington, DC: American Psychological Association.

Gonzales, N., Cauce, A.M., & Mason, C.A. (1996). Interobserver agreement in the assessment of parental behavior and parent–adolescent conflict: African American mothers, daughters, and independent observers. *Child Development, 67,* 1483–1498.

Helms, J.E. (1992). Why is there no study of cultural equivalence in standardized cognitive ability testing? *American Psychologist, 47,* 1083–1101.

Hughes, D., & DuMont, K. (1993). Using focus groups to facilitate culturally anchored research. *American Journal of Community Psychology, 21,* 727–746.

Hughes, D., Seidman, E., & Williams, N. (1993). Cultural phenomena and the research enterprise: Toward a culturally anchored methodology. *American Journal of Community Psychology, 21,* 687–703.

Kamin, L. (1974). *The science and politics of IQ.* Mahwah, NJ: Lawrence Erlbaum Associates.

Knight, G.P., Tein, J.Y., Shell, R., & Roosa, M. (1992). The cross-ethnic equivalence of parenting and family interaction measures among Hispanic and Anglo American families. *Child Development, 63,* 1392–1403.

Knight, G.P., Virdin, L.M., Ocampo, K.A., & Roosa, M. (1994). An examination of the cross-ethnic equivalence of measures of negative life events and mental health among Hispanic and Anglo-American children. *American Journal of Community Psychology, 22*(6), 767–783.

Knodel, J. (1993). The design and analysis of focus group studies: A practical approach. In D.L. Morgan (Ed.), *Successful focus groups: Advancing the state of the art* (pp. 35–50). Thousand Oaks, CA: Sage Publications.

Krueger, R. (1994). *Focus groups: A practical guide for applied research.* Thousand Oaks, CA: Sage Publications.

Landrine, H. (1995). Introduction: Cultural diversity, contextualism, and feminist psychology. In H. Landrine (Ed.), *Bringing cultural diversity to feminist psychology: Theory, research, and practice* (pp. 1–19). Washington, DC: American Psychological Association.

Lillie-Blanton, M., Anthony, J.C., & Schuster, C.R. (1993). Probing the meaning of racial/ethnic group comparisons in crack cocaine smoking. *Journal of the American Medical Association, 269,* 993–997.

Lonner, W.J. (1986). *Field methods in cross-cultural research.* Thousand Oaks, CA: Sage Publications.

McLoyd, V.C. (1990). The impact of economic hardship on black families and children: Psychological distress, parenting, and socioemotional development. *Child Development, 61,* 311–346.

Moynihan, D.P. (1965). *The Negro family: A case for national action.* Washington, DC: U.S. Department of Labor, Office of Policy Planning and Research.

Phinney, J.S. (1990). Ethnic identity in adolescents and adults: Review of research. *American Psychologist, 108,* 499–514.

Rapkin, B.D., & Luke, D.A. (1993). Cluster analysis in community research: Epistemology and practice. *American Journal of Community Psychology, 21,* 247–277.

Rhodes, J.E., & Jason, L.A. (1990). A social stress model of substance abuse. *Journal of Consulting and Clinical Psychology, 58,* 395–401.

Srebnik, D., Cauce, A.M., & Baydar, N. (1996). Help-seeking pathways for children and adolescents. *Journal of Emotional and Behavioral Disorders, 4*(4), 210–220.

Steinberg, L., & Fletcher, A.C. (in press). Data analytic strategies in research on ethnic minority youth. In V. McLoyd & L. Steinberg (Eds.), *Research on minority adolescents: Conceptual, theoretical, and methodological issues.* Mahwah, NJ: Lawrence Erlbaum Associates.

Sudarkasa, N. (1981). Interpreting the African heritage in Afro-American family organization. In H.P. McAdoo (Ed.), *Black families* (pp. 37–53). Thousand Oaks, CA: Sage Publications.

Sudarkasa, N. (1988). Reassessing the Black family: Dispelling the myths, reaffirming the values. *Sisters, 22–23,* 38–39.

Tanaka-Matsumi, J., & Marsella, A.J. (1976). Cross-cultural variations in the phenomenological experience of depression: Word association. *Journal of Cross-Cultural Psychology, 7,* 379–396.

Wilkinson, D.Y., & King, G. (1987). Conceptual and methodological issues in the use of race as a variable: Policy implications. *Milbank Quarterly, 65,* 56–71.

Wyche, K.F. (1993). Psychology and African American women: Findings from applied research. *Applied and Preventive Psychology, 2,* 115–121.

Culturally Competent Methods Based on Evaluation and Research

How to Use Research Results in Systems of Care

Amando Cablas

Cultural competence does not occur in isolation. Its development and implementation require the support of all sectors of systems of care. In order to begin culturally competent research and evaluation activities, the groundwork for cultural competence must be either in the development process or already established. The goal of this chapter is to provide a conceptual framework and a model for implementation of culturally competent research and evaluation in a system of care. (For further discussion of cultural competence in systems of care, see Cross, Bazron, Dennis, & Isaacs, 1989.) The model presented is based on the work (Cablas & Mata, 1994; Cablas & Mesa, 1994; Cablas & Moore-Guerra, 1994; Meinhardt & Vega, 1987) of the Santa Clara Valley Health and Hospital System, Department of Mental Health, Mental Health Services Research Division, located in San Jose, California. The discussion covers the critical linkages and strategies that can be employed and the types of research and evaluation projects that can be conducted. The final part of this chapter provides two applied examples for measuring the mental health needs of ethnic minority communities and the development of an intervention outcome measure.

THE INTERFACE BETWEEN POLICY AND RESEARCH

The clear delineation of the importance of research to administrators, fiscal individuals, policy makers, and elected officials is critical to the implementation of evaluation and research in systems of care. These influential decision makers need to believe in the value of research aimed at the development of cultural competence. Without a commitment from these officials in a public system of care, research and evaluation do not flourish. The commitment of financial resources by these officials does not mean that everyone within a system of care believes that evaluation and research are useful; however, these key individuals must understand the importance of research and its purpose in an applied setting. Convincing them of its value is a continuous education process that occurs at all levels within children's mental health organizations.

THE ROLES OF POLITICS AND SCIENCE

Culturally competent evaluation and research require not only scientific knowledge but also political savvy. Politics is the unspoken side of research and evaluation that has cultural competence in systems of care as a goal. Scientific epistemology is based on objective, dispassionate methods that rely on certain rules and procedures. The politics of mental health research is not often taught in graduate school.The ability to complete a study or research project is based on the political clout of the researcher. Culturally competent research requires good science and good politics.

To create a system that supports culturally competent activities requires internal and external political strategies. The internal strategy focuses on the enlistment and the maintenance of continued cooperation of the system of care with research and evaluation projects. It is the implicit and explicit collaboration and cooperation of executive management, program managers, and service providers. Executive management and program managers are the decision makers regarding the commitment of resources in terms of time, staffing, and project funding. The external portion of the political strategy involves the support of the ethnic minority communities for culturally competent research. More often than not, ethnic minority communities have been exploited by researchers who failed to share their findings and/or used impairment models as a means by which to explain phenomena or did not sufficiently understand the culture and therefore made erroneous conclusions (Ryan, 1980). Consequently, many ethnic minority communities are unwilling to permit research and evaluation to occur without their knowledge of, input into, and control of the research and evaluation processes. Thus, key individuals or informants who are in good standing within the various ethnic minority communities must be identified and collaborated with to ensure that the research and evaluation projects do not exploit the community under study, pathologize the perception of outsiders regarding the community, or propagate stereotypes and impairment models. It is important that some of these informants be consumers and family members. The collaboration of these vital stakeholders in the system of care is an integral part of the research and evaluation process.

COMMUNICATION AND SUPPORT

The best way to ensure the support of evaluation and research is to establish mutually beneficial relationships with ethnic community leaders and express the goals, objectives, and findings of the research in simple, understandable language. Researchers' and evaluators' professional language is replete with technical jargon, and they often do not communicate clearly with other professionals. Presentation of findings to key individuals without use of technical jargon helps these key individuals understand why it is important that they continue to support research. Although it is important that nonresearchers understand evaluation and research terminology and techniques and although it is important to design the most scientifically rigorous studies possible, the majority of individuals who benefit from research results are generally not as intellectually sophisticated as key decision makers. Consequently, support of those who need the information may be lost if research results presented are criticized as being "too academic" or "not practical." Thus, researchers need to develop the ability to express their findings at two levels and switch easily from one to the other.

One type of language researchers need to use is professional language, which is necessary for project design and for communications with colleagues and external funding sources. The other type of language researchers need to use is that of policy makers, administrators, and program managers. The researcher may actively educate those working in systems of care regarding sophisticated methodology while speaking about program and policy issues. The researchers' goals in using this type of communication is to become embedded in the system of care and to be sought out by management to provide critical and timely information. This is a long-term process that requires strategic planning. For example, in Santa Clara County, services research has existed since 1980. Since the division's founding in 1987, managers, elected officials, and policy makers have been educated and many, though not all, actively support the division's work. Although the division relies heavily on external funding and is often the last priority for local funding, without the education process that occurred at the system of care level, the division would already have been terminated.

TARGETED EVALUATIONS AND RESEARCH PROGRAMS

Evaluation and research projects require a systemic or programmatic focus to gain acceptance. The goal of such efforts is to obtain practical information that can be applied to real problems rather than theory development or explanatory information that does not lead to solutions.

One method by which to foster collaboration is to meet with service providers and system of care administrators to find out what type of information that they need to make policy and program decisions. Collaborative discussions with these professionals can take many forms, such as focus groups, facilitated discussions, or retreats. In Santa Clara County, discussions between researchers and service providers have led to a variety of studies that span the range from purely local interest to studies that contribute to the national discussion on mental health services (Cablas & Mata, 1994; Cablas & Mesa, 1994; Cablas & Moore-Guerra, 1994; Jerrell, 1995; Meinhardt, Tom, Tse, & Yu, 1985–1986).

Evaluation and Research Must Have Systemwide Impact

Whether the goal is to assess intervention outcomes, program performance, or the needs of the community for services, the results of research have to be pertinent to the system of care. Projects that do not answer the questions posed by management or by ethnic communities that the system of care serves or that do not affect the policy and financing of the system of care will not be supported. Essentially, projects need to address systemic issues. For example, managed care requires clear and measurable outcomes with regard to client satisfaction, intervention outcomes, and costs. Without these essential elements included or targeted specifically in an evaluation or in applied research, system of care management will find it difficult to support the project.

Research and Evaluation Consultants

In many local mental health services agencies, access to sophisticated resources such as consultants' services and complex research analysis is limited. To develop an evaluation and research unit within a system of care, access to these resources becomes necessary. These resources are usually available only through colleges and universities. Thus, linkages to local academic communities should be sought out and developed. Researchers can be contracted to design and consult with local governments regarding the implementation of evaluation projects. Furthermore, such affiliations are useful in developing proposals for funding the use of these resources and in developing a fully functioning evaluation and research division within the system of care. Santa Clara County, California, has built its research division on these types of affiliations and grant funding. Its affiliations have included the University of California campuses at Berkeley and San Francisco, Stanford University, and the Western Consortium for Public Health.

In brief, the ability of a system of care to put culturally competent evaluation and research to immediate use requires that it develop a strategic plan that incorporates good science, effective internal and external politics, the ability to clearly communicate with all levels of the system of care, targeted evaluations of special significance to the system of care, access to sophisticated resources, and a driving commitment to excellence and cultural competence in service delivery. Not all of these components need to be in existence for a system of care to begin implementation of research and evaluation efforts; however, the most helpful components would be the commitment to good science and the internal and external political skills to support research and evaluation efforts.

Two examples of how research and evaluation have played important roles in the development of a culturally competent system of care are discussed in the following sections. The background of Santa Clara County is laid out, and two projects that have both policy and programmatic impact are described. The first example demonstrates how equity goals were developed and used, and the final example presents the development of a culturally competent functional assessment scale that can be used to measure intervention outcomes.

SANTA CLARA COUNTY

The Santa Clara County, California, population of 1.6 million people (Santa Clara Valley Health and Hospital System, 1995) is largely concentrated in the San Jose area and represents an ethnically diverse mixture of Hispanic, Asian American, African American, and Native American cultures. The Department of Mental Health of the Santa Clara Valley Health and Hospital System serves about 19,000 clients (unduplicated) per year, of which 5,000 are age 17 years or younger (Mental Health Department, 1996). The department offers a range of services from acute inpatient, subacute residential, and intensive day intervention to outpatient case management. Cultural competence has been evolving within the Department of Mental Health since 1975, and the department is nationally recognized for its contributions to the development of cultural competence (Isaacs & Benjamin, 1991).

Equity Goals

In population studies, parity figures are used to compare population demographics of a given organization or population serviced with U.S. Census data. They are commonly used in affirmative action plans as a measure of employers' compliance with the law and of the incorporation of protected classes into federally defined employment categories.

However, mental health needs assessment studies (Meinhardt, 1988; Meinhardt & Vega, 1987) found that parity underrepresented measured need in specific racial and ethnic groups. Hence the move to establish equity in systems of care developed. Equity and equity goals established the baseline for population service requirements for mental health.

Equity goals were incorporated into the policies of the Santa Clara County Mental Health Department in 1983. These goal-based policies were driven by the results of local research activities that measured the mental health needs of specific ethnic populations (Meinhardt & Vega, 1987). These goals differed from parity, which was merely a percentile representation within the population. Parity does not take into account measured needs and consequently is an inadequate means of judging the services that the department provides to ethnic populations. Equity goals are compared with treated populations for any given fiscal year. Table 1 (Meinhardt, 1992) illustrates the difference between parity and equity. Equity and parity clearly demonstrate the need for targeted programs, services, and policies to address the measured need for mental health services among ethnic minorities.

When analyzing equity goal data, it is important to remember that mental health systems of care are dynamic in nature. Factors that may affect services in one year may not occur in the next, or a different set of issues may arise that result in implementation of policies that may not have any impact for 3 years. Thus, interpretation of efforts to achieve equity in service provision is subject to myriad factors that affect use of services by ethnic minority communities. The evaluator must understand the system of care and be familiar with the system of care's operations. An internal evaluator who is a part of the system of care's management team has ready access to administrators and staff who have thorough knowledge of the system. Staffing patterns can dramatically affect the number of ethnic minority clients served, and the evaluator should be aware of and have access to this information as well as take it into consideration in evaluating progress toward the system's equity goals and efforts to achieve cultural competence.

When serving large numbers of Latinos, bilingual Spanish-speaking service providers are necessary. Because Spanish-speaking therapists are sometimes difficult to find, a system of care may find it difficult to meet its equity goals regarding its Hispanic and Latino clients, particularly when such positions remain open for longer than 3 months. Other factors that can affect interpretations of ethnic population service data are budget issues (e.g., funding cuts, hiring freezes, layoffs), programmatic considerations (e.g., adequate outreach, lack of special programming for ethnic minorities, culturally competent staffing, method of service con-

Table 1. Equity goals and parity in Santa Clara Valley Health and Hospital System

Ethnicity	Equity goals (%)	Parity (%)
Caucasians	42.19	58.09
African Americans	6.27	3.51
Latinos/Hispanics	32.14	21.00
Asian Americans	17.76	14.84
Native Americans	3.08	.60

tracting employed, method of contract compliance monitoring), policy issues (e.g., enforcement of equity goals, implementation of sanctions for noncompliance with policy), and administrative issues (e.g., competing priorities, lack of commitment by executive management, data integrity). Ethnic population service usage data are useful for the background knowledge gained about underlying reasons for clients' use of services and about the various problems that can affect the collection and interpretation of these types of data. The preceding statement is not meant to impugn the integrity of such data; the quality of the information is assumed. Rather, it raises the issue of which factors produce the resulting data. For example, if a drop in a particular population's receiving needed services is due to the agency's staffing problems, then the data indicate that the agency's management needs to resolve that issue.

Table 2 presents a comparison of equity goals with actual clients served in Santa Clara County over the course of 5 years. What is most noticeable regarding equity goals is that Caucasians and African Americans were overusing services during the period studied. The issue was not whether services to these groups should be reduced but rather how to achieve equity among the other ethnic groups in the community. For example, many of the Caucasians in the sample were single males who lived in some type of supported housing (e.g., board and care homes, supervised independent living) and were emotionally fragile and at risk for needing higher levels of care because of a lack of an identifiable primary support system. Consequently, the types of programming and services available for this population were greater than they were for other ethnic groups. The African American clients in the sample were crisis-oriented users who often came into the system through their need for acute services. Their families were usually available and provided a strong support system that maintained the individual during the crisis.

Entry into the mental health system of care occurs when the individual experiences acute psychosis and the family support system can no longer manage the individual's behavior or when the family is physically exhausted by caring for the individual. The types of programs

Table 2. Ethnicities of clients served over a 5-year period as percentage of total client population

Ethnicity	FY92 (%)	FY93 (%)	FY94 (%)	FY95 (%)	FY96 (%)
Caucasians	50.23	49.20	51.90	50.40	49.10
African Americans	9.50	8.90	9.30	7.80	8.30
Latinos/Hispanics	21.27	24.80	25.10	24.30	25.60
Asian Americans	11.55	12.80	9.10	12.90	12.50
Native Americans	.60	.80	1.10	1.10	1.10

FY, fiscal year

required to work with just these two groups are fundamentally different in the types of service and the continuing supports provided. Among Asian Americans, the drop in clients served in the period studied (see Table 2) was directly attributable to a lack of culturally proficient service providers during 1993–1994. Staff vacancies and turnover were unusually high among Asian American staff during that period, which had a direct impact on the number of Asian American clients served. Growth in services for Latinos and Native Americans was due to efforts on behalf of the service providers and county administration to ensure that progress was made toward equity in providing services for those ethnic groups.

FUNCTIONAL ASSESSMENT OF CLIENTS

A practical example of how evaluation and research can augment a system and dynamically function with several community groups and divisions within a system of care occurred with the development of the Santa Clara County Functional Assessment Scale (SCCFAS) (Mental Health Services Research Division, 1996), a culturally inclusive functional assessment scale that was developed over the course of 3 years and is in its fourth revision. More than 60 clinicians, service coordinators, program managers, and administrative staff worked together to develop the SCCFAS. The Santa Clara County Mental Health Board requested that a task force be formed to address the issue of functionality and diagnosis. In August 1993, the Santa Clara County mental health director established the Severity Criteria Task Force. The task force was charged with the task of developing consistent and fair service access criteria to assess individual needs for mental health services. The criteria needed to be applicable to the diverse client population in Santa Clara County, California, and useful in a managed care environment. The department's ethnic population specialist was named the task force's project director. The research division was responsible for ensuring the scientific integrity of the scale. The SCCFAS was designed to measure functioning across all age and cultural groups. What follows is a brief history and discussion of the scale, the process by which it was created, and the results of the preliminary reliability and validity tests of it. The implications for use of the scale are discussed in the context of managed care and intervention outcomes.

In Santa Clara County, California, a heated discussion had been in progress for at least 5 years regarding the assessment of ethnic minorities and their diagnoses. It became clear during this discussion that diagnosis of ethnic minorities was not a useful service indicator. Service providers believed that although symptom assessment might provide a current perspective on ethnic minority clients' mental health, symptoms do not always equate with the need for intervention. For example, among those clients diagnosed as having schizophrenia, the diagnosis did not inform program managers or senior management in the system of care of the array of services that these clients would use. A person diagnosed with schizophrenia can function sufficiently so that he or she might require only a quarterly medication visit. Yet, not all individuals diagnosed with schizophrenia function at the same level, and some may require more intensive services and a different array of services (e.g., day intervention, medications, outpatient psychotherapy, vocational rehabilitation).

Thus, given the broad range of functioning within a diagnosis, it was difficult for service coordinators to manage programs and allocate resources based solely on diagnoses. Ethnicity and diagnosis had been the bases for many management reports and had been used during the budget process. Although the Global Assessment of Functioning (GAF) (American Psychiatric Association, 1994) is required for diagnostic purposes, that instrument did not meet the needs of the Santa Clara County Mental Health System because of its unidimensional score. Functioning was not a single dimension but instead consisted of several areas that could not be expressed in a single score.

The basic premise underlying the debate was that clients' needs for services were based on functionality and not on diagnoses. For clients' with mental illnesses that were severe and ongoing, a single diagnosis is not flexible enough to indicate the clients' real need for different services at various points in the course of their illnesses and of the clients' lives. The client's daily coping is the best indicator of the client's current need for intervention. However, prior to development of the SCCFAS, there had been no standardized instrument available that included the impact of culture and acculturation stress on the mental health of clients.

OVERVIEW OF THE
SANTA CLARA COUNTY FUNCTIONAL ASSESSMENT SCALE

Essentially, the SCCFAS helps systems of care determine the clients' needs for mental health services. Clients' intervention histories may skew service providers' judgments about the clients' present needs and give precedence to clients with ongoing problems at the expense of new clients who have no intervention history. Thus, the SCCFAS provides baseline coping information for all clients assessed. As a tool, it provides a conceptual framework that consists of 11 distinct dimensions. Each dimension is rated on a scale from 1 (lowest) to 5 (highest), with criteria defined for each level. These dimensions were developed with the input of the Severity Criteria Task Force. The 11 SCCFAS dimensions measured are

1. Self-care
2. Meaningful day activity
3. Moods, emotions, or thoughts
4. Social behavior
5. Substance abuse
6. Developmental or medical or physical disorder
7. Family or support system functioning
8. Cultural experience
9. Sociophysical environmental risk
10. Suicide risk
11. Homicide risk

The SCCFAS has three unique dimensions: cultural experience; sociophysical environmental risk; and moods, emotions, and thoughts subscales. In the cultural experience subscale, the main consideration is the impact of clients' cultural experiences on their mental health. The subscale relies on the cultural competence of the individual performing the assessment and requires a multitude of culture-specific skills to implement. The social or physical environmental risk dimension measures actual risks to physical health and well-being in the community in which the individual resides. This subscale was developed because clinicians wanted a measure by which to distinguish real threats to clients in their neighborhood of residence from symptoms of paranoia, especially among older adult clients. This subscale also requires that the clinician be aware of the areas and communities in which clients reside. Elements of danger include but are not limited to criminal activity, the presence of local authorities (e.g., police, sheriffs) who harass ethnic minorities because of their race, and substandard housing conditions. Finally, the moods, emotions, and thoughts subscale combines the affective and psychosis dimensions. Clinicians believed that, because of the comorbidity of these dimensions and the severity of mental illnesses experienced among clients served, one subscale could best describe this area of coping.

The SCCFAS facilitates the determination of clients' needs for mental health services and the planning of appropriate service responses to their needs. Matching interventions with clients' actual needs maximizes limited system of care resources. When the SCCFAS is used at intake, clients and clinicians can focus on clients' areas of greatest need for services and develop mutual intervention goals. The available array of services can then be used to help clients address the needs and goals identified in their intervention plans. Thus, both the clinician and client benefit from use of the SCCFAS with regard to effective intervention planning, and use of this instrument also helps to focus the system of care's service array and available resources so that clients receive the services that they need. When the SCCFAS is used again at discharge or at the next semiannual service plan update, the scale serves as an outcome measure. Areas in which the client was initially assessed as being impaired can be compared with the client's current rating. Thus, the clinician or service coordinator is able to judge the client's progress, determine whether the client's intervention plan is working, and make adjustments or design an appropriate intervention response.

It should be noted that the SCCFAS does not replace clinical judgment; it enhances it. The instrument does not represent a client perfectly—no instrument can. However, it provides sufficient information for clinical decision making. Ultimately, the decision of which intervention type to employ is a clinical judgment. As one patient advocate asked about the SCCFAS, "If we have a complaint about denied service, will the decision be based on this scale?" The answer to the question was an emphatic "no"; the clinician, not the instrument, is responsible for making that decision. The instrument may be used to justify the clinician's decision, but the responsibility for making the decision belongs to the clinician.

There are other benefits associated with the SCCFAS instrument. Because the instrument was designed and tested by clinicians, it was designed for rapid use. Once clinicians are trained to use the SCCFAS and have done so in practice, they can administer it in approximately 5 minutes or less. Furthermore, intrasystem communication has been augmented because clinicians can refer to the scale or its subscales to emphasize particular needs of particular clients.

INTERRATER RELIABILITY

The goal of the interrater reliability portion of the project was to establish that those who would be doing the rating of actual clients would use the SCCFAS instrument uniformly. The reliability of the SCCFAS was tested by comparing the scores that a group of clinicians and service coordinators obtained with the standard scores obtained from information contained in 20 vignettes. Vignettes involving adults, children, and adolescents were used. The results are presented in Tables 3 and 4 (Mental Health Services Research Division, 1996).

Given the size of the mental health system and the applied environment in the interreliability rating population used to test the SCCFAS, researchers decided that the minimum score required to meet their interrater reliability standard would be $r = .70$. The pattern of scores clearly demonstrated reliability generally above that minimum requirement. The only SCCFAS subscale that showed minor interrater reliability difficulties was the family or support system functioning subscale. The relatively weaker reliability of this dimension is not problematic when considered together with the overall reliability score for the SCCFAS. It can easily be addressed through additional training of service providers in its use. Table 3 presents scores according to two dimensions: individual functioning and social functioning. The elements included in each scale represent a sum of subscale scores that are correlated with the recommended subscale scores. The data in Table 3 show that the SCCFAS's reliability was well established.

PREDICTIVE VALIDITY

The purpose of the predictive validity part of the study was to answer the question "Does this scale predict service access or not?" This aspect of using the SCCFAS was tested on actual clients who used services and their subscale scores assigned by the clinicians and service coordinators who participated in the reliability study (Mental Health Services Research Division, 1996). The time frame for units of service was 3 months following the rating. A total of 522 clients were assessed using the SCCFAS. The results are presented in Table 4. Most of the significance levels were greater than .0001 but for the sake of simplicity were truncated to the tabled value. Only those scores that met or exceeded the minimum requirement were included in the tables. In response to the question of whether the SCCFAS predicts service access and service types, the answer is yes.

FUNCTIONAL ASSESSMENT
IN A MANAGED CARE ENVIRONMENT

As the mental health system of care prepares for service delivery in a managed care environment, the SCCFAS serves as a pivotal tool. Client intervention outcomes, assessment of performance of individual service

Table 3. Adults', children's, and total reliability scores

Subscale	Adults' reliability scores (n = 319)	Children's reliability scores (n = 263)	Total reliability score (N = 582)
Self-care	.82	.85	.84
Meaningful day activity	.83	.80	.82
Moods, emotions, or thoughts	.77	.71	.75
Social behavior	.88	.74	.84
Substance abuse	.89	.85	.88
Developmental or medical or physical disorder	.86	.79	.81
Family or support system functioning	.82	.65	.75
Cultural experience	.76	.83	.79
Sociophysical environmental risk	.92	.82	.88
Suicide risk	.88	.84	.88
Homicide risk	.85	.88	.84
Overall scale	.91	.85	.89

Note: Adults' and children's reliability scores were based on information contained in 40 vignettes, with 20 involving children and 20 involving adults.
All scores shown are statistically reliable ($p < .001$).

providers, services, and programs can be based on the consistent use of this instrument. For program managers and administrators, service contracts can be monitored and feedback to individual clinicians and programs can be useful in determining outcomes. Services programming that appears problematic or shows little or no progress with regard to improvement in clients' outcomes can be assessed and a different service array can be adopted to facilitate clients' progress. Completion of the SCCFAS by contract providers can be useful. Such a requirement can permit an agency to set baseline performance indicators and track contract performance. When combined with service utilization information, the SCCFAS can help establish performance criteria (e.g., 80% of clients who are initially assessed as reporting a 2 on the moods, emotions, and thoughts subscale show improvement within a 6-month period). Thus, deficiencies in service delivery can be addressed before problems in a program area become a crisis, and the assessment process can be used to determine whether the contract should be renewed. What maintains honesty within the system of care is that service utilization will be tracked. Utilization tracking informs management of which types of services clients have received. When combined with program summaries of both utilization data and clients' outcomes, the two should match. For example, if hospitalizations were reduced for a 30-day period following discharge, the functional assessment scores would show an increase in functioning on some critical scales. A failure to match the service utilization information with the functional rating would mean either that

Table 4. Santa Clara County Functional Assessment Scale's predictive validity when used with adults' and children's interventions

Factor measured	Multiple r	Significance
Adults' interventions (N = 248)		
Intervention units received	.30	.0001
Length of intervention	.33	.0001
24-hour care	.34	.0001
Medication	.34	.0001
Outpatient intervention	.31	.0001
Children's interventions (N = 274)		
Intervention units received	.47	.0001
Length of intervention	.43	.0001
Medication	.50	.0001
Day intervention	.54	.0001
Outpatient intervention	.33	.0001
Outpatient intervention without medication	.33	.0001
Broker	.29	.0001

staff needed retraining or that there were some other issues affecting clients' outcomes. Both areas would need to be investigated. As a managed care tool, the SCCFAS provides client intervention outcomes and program and service array evaluations and establishes performance outcomes for contract and service provider monitoring.

CONCLUSIONS

In order to maintain an evaluation and research unit in a system of care, considerable skills and knowledge are required beyond the ability to conduct research. Researchers' skills should include the ability to negotiate with and include consumers, families, managers, administrators, and elected officials. The information presented needs to target the various audiences without the complex language associated with research so that the unit remains valuable and is viewed as necessary. Evaluations within a system of care should be targeted and useful, and should be planned collaboratively. The goal is to maximize the use of the results so that the system of care is information driven and remains focused on the client. Evaluation and research are vital components of a culturally competent system of care. Without accurate and unbiased information on ethnic minorities regarding measured needs for services and intervention outcomes, the ability of a system of care to meet the demands of the cultural imperative are greatly limited (Stroul & Friedman, 1986).

REFERENCES

American Psychiatric Association. (1994). *Diagnostic and statistical manual of mental disorders* (4th ed.). Washington, DC: Author.

Cablas, A., & Mata, L. (1994, March). *The 1992 Mental Health Needs Assessment Survey of American Indians in Santa Clara County* (Ethnic Populations Task Force Rep. No. 3). San Jose, CA: Santa Clara County Mental Health Department, Mental Health Services Research Center.

Cablas, A., & Mesa, L. (1994). Mental health services: The case for Filipino Americans. *Journal of the American Association for Philippine Psychology, 1,* 75–87.

Cablas, A., & Moore-Guerra, L. (1994, April). *The 1993 Mental Health Needs Assessment Survey of African Americans in Santa Clara County* (Ethnic Populations Task Force Rep. No. 4). San Jose, CA: Santa Clara County Mental Health Department, Mental Health Services Research Center.

Cross, T.L., Bazron, B.M., Dennis, K.W., & Isaacs, M.R. (1989). *Towards a culturally competent system of care: Vol. I. A monograph on effective services for minority children who are severely emotionally disturbed.* Washington, DC: Georgetown University, Child and Adolescent Service System Program, Technical Assistance Center.

Isaacs, M.R., & Benjamin, M.P. (1991). *Towards a culturally competent system of care: Vol. II. Programs which utilize culturally competent principles.* Washington, DC: Georgetown University, Child Development Center, Child and Adolescent Service System Program, Technical Assistance Center, Center for Child Health and Mental Health Policy.

Jerrell, J.M. (1995). The effects of client–therapist match on service use and costs. *Administration and Policy in Mental Health, 23,* 119–126.

Meinhardt, K. (1988). *Mental health and disorder in Silicon Valley.* San Jose, CA: Santa Clara County Center for Mental Health Research.

Meinhardt, K. (1992, January). *Mental health services goals for ethnic populations in Santa Clara County* (1990 Census Rep. No. 2). Santa Clara, CA: Santa Clara County Mental Health Services Research Center.

Meinhardt, K., Tom, S., Tse, P., & Yu, C.Y. (1985–1986). Southeast Asian refugees in the "Silicon Valley": The Asian health assessment project. *Amerasia, 12*(2), 43–65.

Meinhardt, K., & Vega, W. (1987). A method for estimating underutilization of mental health services by ethnic groups. *Hospital and Community Psychiatry, 38,* 1186–1190.

Mental Health Department. (1996, March). *Mental health redesign concept paper.* Santa Clara, CA: Santa Clara Valley Health and Hospital System, Mental Health Department.

Mental Health Services Research Division. (1996, March). *Results of the reliability and validity of the Santa Clara County Functional Assessment Scale.* Santa Clara, CA: Santa Clara Valley Health and Hospital System, Mental Health Department.

Ryan, R.A. (1980). A community perspective for mental health research. *Social Casework: A Journal for Contemporary Social Work, 42,* 507–511.

Santa Clara County Mental Health Department. (1998). *Santa Clara County Functional Assessment Scale–Short Form* (Verson 4.0). Santa Clara, CA: Author.

Santa Clara Valley Health and Hospital System. (1995, June). *Through the ages: Health status of Santa Clara County.* Santa Clara, CA: Santa Clara County Public Health Department.

Stroul, B.A., & Friedman, R.M. (1986). *A system of care for children and youth with severe emotional disturbances* (Rev. ed.). Washington, DC: Georgetown University, Child and Adolescent Service System Program, Technical Assistance Center.

Appendix: The Santa Clara County Functional Assessment Scale: Short Form

Client name: _____

Client ID#: _____

Staff name: _____

Staff ID#: _____   Client age: _____

Date: _____ / _____ / _____

Time started: _____ : _____   Time completed: _____ : _____

Circle the number of the type of assessment performed:

1. Intake Assessment (open)
2. Follow-Up Assessment
3. Transfer Assessment
4. Discharge Assessment

If the client is being discharged, complete the following:

Discharge Codes (Check only one):
1. Mutual Agreement/Treatment Goals Reached
2. Mutual Agreement/Treatment Goals Partially Reached
3. Mutual Agreement/Treatment Goals Not Reached
4. Client Withdrew: AWOL, AMA, Treatment Partly Complete
5. Client Withdrew: AWOL, AMA, No Improvement
6. Client Died
7. Client Moved Out of Service Area
8. Client Discharged/Program Unilateral Decision
9. Client Incarcerated
10. Discharge/Administrative Reasons
11. Other: _____

From Santa Clara County Mental Health Department. (1998). *Santa Clara County Functional Assessment Scale–Short Form* (Version 4.0) Santa Clara, CA: Author. Copyright © 1998 by Santa Clara County Mental Health Department.

Scale Column Descriptions (Mark only one statement in each scale column that best describes your client. If this is a reassessment, mark the statement that best describes your client since the previous assessment.)

I. **Self-Care:** Client's apparent ability to secure basic personal care based on his or her own initiative within the maximum expected of someone of his or her developmental stage or medical condition or physical limitations. *Differential:* This scale refers to the client's initiative as opposed to the initiative of his or her support system, which is rated instead on the Family OR Support System Functioning scale.

II. **Meaningful Day Activity:** Client's apparent ability to connect regularly with some activity that is personally meaningful AND appropriate AND is not dangerous or damaging within the maximum expected of someone of his or her developmental stage or medical condition or physical limitations. *Differential:* This scale refers to the client's initiative as opposed to the impact or limitations imposed by his or her environment, which are rated instead on the Sociophysical Environmental Risk scale.

III. **Moods, Emotions, or Thoughts:** Apparent degree of interference with daily living because of the client's internal experience OR due to outward expression of emotional state OR due to thought disorganization or distrubance. *Differential:* This scale refers not to the client's subjective experience of distress but rather to the client's functioning; this scale does not refer to distress resulting from physical or medical or developmental limitations, which are rated instead on the Developmental or Medical or Physical Disability scale, nor does it refer to drug-induced states, which are rated instead on the Substance Abuse scale.

IV. **Social Behavior:** Client's apparent ability or difficulty with regard to moderating or controlling impulses, which are potentially dangerous, damaging, or socially isolating. *Differential:* This scale does not refer to knowledgeable and deliberate intent, which is rated instead on the Suicide Risk or Homicide Risk scales; this scale refers to behavior, not to mental functioning, which is rated instead on the Moods, Emotions, OR Thoughts scale.

V. **Substance Abuse:** Apparent voluntary use or misuse of substances in a way that is unhealthy, OR illegal, OR inappropriate, OR inherently dangerous. *Differential:* This scale does not refer to deliberate attempts to take one's life, which are rated instead on the Suicide Risk scale; nor does it refer to problems with impulse control, which are rated on the Social Behavior scale.

VI. **Developmental or Medical or Physical Disability:** Apparent degree to which the client's mental health is affected by limitations in daily living as a result of or caused by developmental disability, OR physical deterioration, OR physical disability, OR medical condition. *Differential:* This scale does not refer to the client's actual attempts to live meaningfully or to his behavior with or toward other people, which are rated instead on the Self-Care, Meaningful Day Activity, and Social Behavior scales.

VII. **Family or Support System Functioning:** Apparent degree to which the primary human support system (residential home, family, or friendship circle) surrounding or intended to be available to the client provides for or interferes with his or her safety OR emotional support OR access to basic needs. *Differential:* This scale does not refer to the client's choice or ability to take advantage of what is available, which is rated instead on either the Self-Care or Meaningful Day Activity scale, nor does it refer to the human or physical environment outside of his or her "home" (residential home, family, or friendship circle), which is rated instead on the Sociophysical Environmental Risk scale.

VIII. **Cultural Experience:** Client's apparent ability to connect with and draw emotional sustenance from his or her cultural surroundings. *Differential:* This scale does not refer to symptoms of mental illness that interfere with the ability to make this connection, such as paranoia, which are rated instead on the Moods, Emotions, OR Thoughts scale; nor does this scale refer to actual threats to the client made by people in his or her environment, which are rated instead on either the Sociophysical Environment or the Family OR Support System Functioning scale.

IX. **Sociophysical Environmental Risk:** Apparent degree of danger inherent in the client's non-"home" environment that results in the client becoming isolated, OR unable to fully participate in activities of daily living, OR that results in other symptoms of mental illness. *Differential:* This scale does not refer to the impact of the "home" environment, which is rated instead on the Family OR Support System Functioning scale; nor does it refer to symptoms of mental illness that interfere with the ability to make connections, such as agoraphobia or paranoia, which are rated instead on the Moods, Emotions, OR Thoughts scale.

X. **Suicide Risk:** Client's apparent level of intent to deliberately harm him- or herself. *Differential:* This scale does not refer to problems with self-mutilating or self-destructive impulse control, which are rated instead on the Social Behavior scale.

XI. **Homicide Risk:** Client's apparent level of intent to deliberately harm other people. *Differential:* This scale does not refer to problems with aggressive or destructive impulse control, which are rated instead on the Social Behavior scale.

COMMENTS: _____
_____
_____
_____
_____
_____
_____

The Santa Clara County Functional Assessment Subscales: Short Form

I Self-Care	II Meaningful Day Activity	III Moods, Emotions, OR Thoughts
1. Completely dependent for all basic needs	1. Unable to perform functional activity	1. Displays uncontrollable moods, emotions, OR thoughts
2. Constant supervision needed to manage basic needs	2. Functional activity with constant assistance	2. Displays mostly out-of-proportion moods, emotions, OR thoughts
3. Routine assistance needed to manage basic needs	3. Functional activity with moderate assistance	3. Has considerable difficulty with moods, emotions, OR thoughts
4. Moderately self-sufficient/adequate ability to manage basic needs	4. Functional activity with minimal assistance	4. Has some difficulty with moods, emotions, OR thoughts
5. Appropriate or independent management of basic needs	5. Independent functional activity	5. Positively manages moods, emotions, OR thoughts
99. Incomplete information OR scoring must be deferred	99. Incomplete information OR scoring must be deferred	99. Incomplete information OR scoring must be deferred

IV Social Behavior	V Substance Abuse	VI Developmental or Medical or Physical Disability
1. *Severely:* Bizarre/inappropriate OR assaultive OR destructive OR acting-out behavior (whether sudden onset OR current)	1. Hazardous use of substances with immediate threat to health	1. Severe personal emotional disruption causing or caused by loss of functions in two or more of following domains: Communication, learning, mobility, independent living
2. *Seriously:* Bizarre/inappropriate OR assaultive OR destructive OR acting-out behavior (whether recent OR occasional/intermittent).	2. Current, serious, uncontrolled substance abuse with dependence	2. Substantially limited; significant personal distress or emotional disruption caused by loss of function in one domain
3. *Moderately:* Bizarre/inappropriate behavior OR verbal threats of assaultive OR destructive OR acting-out behavior	3. Current, serious substance abuse without apparent dependence	3. Minimally limited with some personal concern or discomfort; performance partially affected in at least one domain of functioning
4. Has some minor difficulties in relationships with peers or family due to impulse control	4. Current substance misuse that is contraindicated by medical condition OR prescribed medication OR other risk	4. Has developmental or medical or physical disability, but with no functional limitations
5. Usually gets along well with peers and family and has no impulse control problems	5. Current legal substance use that is moderate and never out of control, or no current substance use	5. No developmental or medical or physical disability
99. Incomplete information OR scoring must be deferred	99. Incomplete information OR scoring must be deferred	99. Incomplete information OR scoring must be deferred

(continued)

VII Family OR Support System Functioning	VIII Cultural Experience	IX Sociophysical Environmental Risk
1. Markedly deteriorated primary support system to level that is immediately unhealthy or inherently unsafe	1. Unable to function in two or more domains (e.g., self, family, job/school, community) as a result of cultural experience	1. Extremely dangerous environment
2. Seriously deteriorated or no primary support system identified	2. Unable to function in one domain as a result of cultural experience	2. Clear and present danger in the environment
3. Unstable or inconsistent primary support system	3. Demonstrates some problems in one or more domains as a result of cultural experience	3. At least two aspects of environment may be dangerous and/or hostile
4. Usually stable and non-problematic primary support system	4. Moderately adjusted in all domains	4. Sociophysical environment is not entirely safe
5. Stable and nonproblematic primary support system	5. Well adjusted in all domains	5. Sociophysical environment is safe
99. Incomplete information OR scoring must be deferred	99. Incomplete information OR interviewer not sufficiently culturally competent to score OR scoring deferred	99. Incomplete information OR scoring must be deferred

X Suicide Risk	XI Homicide Risk
1. Immiment risk; requires external limits to control	1. Imminent risk; requires external limits to control
2. High-risk behaviors are present and will continue to occur but may still be controllable; active threats and gestures	2. High-risk behaviors are present and will continue to occur but may still be controllable; active threats or gestures
3. Some significant and current risk potential: plans, means, and ideation	3. Some significant and current risk potential: plans, means, and ideation
4. Some current evidence of risk potential; ideation but no plans	4. Some current evidence of risk potential; current ideation but no plans
5. No reason to suspect that this is a current issue	5. No reason to suspect that this is a current issue
99. Incomplete information OR scoring must be deferred	99. Incomplete information OR scoring must be deferred

Index

Page numbers followed by "f" or "t" indicate figures or tables, respectively.